# THE MONEY BOOK NOBODY GAVE YOU

# THE MONEY BOOK NOBODY GAVE YOU

A COMPLETE GUIDE TO MONEY, MIND, AND MEANING

RAVINDER BHALLA

**Copyright Page**

**The Money Book Nobody Gave You**

*A Complete Guide to Wealth, Mind, and Meaning*



This book is a work of nonfiction. The reflections, interpretations, and examples presented are intended for educational and informational purposes. While the author has taken care to ensure accuracy, readers should understand that financial, psychological, and philosophical matters are complex, context-dependent, and open to reasonable disagreement.

**Medical, Financial, and Legal Disclaimer**

The author is a licensed physician; however, this book is **not** intended as medical advice, mental health treatment, financial advice, investment advice, legal advice, or professional counseling of any kind. Nothing in this book should be construed as a substitute for consultation with qualified professionals regarding medical, psychological, financial, legal, or other personal matters.

Readers should not use this book as a basis for diagnosing or treating any medical or mental health condition, nor for making financial or investment decisions without seeking appropriate professional guidance. The author and publisher disclaim any liability for actions taken or not taken based on the contents of this book.

**General Disclaimer**

Any references to specific companies, products, financial instruments, or investment strategies are for illustrative purposes only and do not constitute endorsement or recommendation. Past performance does not guarantee future results. All investing involves risk, including the possible loss of principal.

**Philosophical Note**

This book does not promote any political ideology or economic doctrine. Its aim is to encourage understanding, reflection, and thoughtful engagement with money as both a practical tool and a human concern. Readers are encouraged to think critically and make decisions aligned with their own values and circumstances.

**Edition and Publication Information**

First Edition

Printed in the United States of America

ISBN: [978-1-971562-15-5 (ebook); 978-1-971562-13-1 (paperback);

978-1-971562-14-8 (hardback); 978-1-971562-16-2 (audiobook)]

Publisher: [Ravinder N Bhalla]

# ACKNOWLEDGMENTS

A book like this does not emerge from a single mind. It is the product of countless conversations, teachings, disagreements, and generosities accumulated over years.

My first debt is to the writers and thinkers whose work shaped my understanding: the economists who illuminated how money and markets function, the psychologists who revealed the hidden patterns in financial behavior, the philosophers who insisted on asking what any of it is for. Some are cited in these pages; others influenced me in ways too diffuse to trace. I have tried to synthesize their insights faithfully, and any errors in that synthesis are mine alone.

I am grateful to those who read early drafts and offered their honesty. Writing about money requires navigating between oversimplification and inaccessibility, between false certainty and paralyzing nuance. Their feedback helped me find the path. Where I have succeeded in being clear without being shallow, they deserve much of the credit.

To my family, who shaped my earliest understanding of money—its presence and absence, its possibilities and limitations, its capacity to comfort and to wound. Our conversations about finances were not always easy, but they were formative. Much of what I have tried to articulate in these pages began as an attempt to understand what I absorbed, without examination, as a child.

To the friends and colleagues who shared their own financial struggles and triumphs with candor. Their stories reminded me that behind every balance sheet is a human life, with all its complexity and contradiction. This book is richer for their willingness to be vulnerable.

To my editors, who believed this book was worth writing and pushed me to write it better. The patience required to guide a manuscript of this scope is considerable, and I did not make their job easy.

To you, the reader, for your time and attention. A book is nothing until it is read—marks on paper or pixels on a screen, inert until someone engages with them. Whatever value exists here is realized only in that encounter. I do not take your attention for granted.

And finally, to everyone who will never read this book but who needed it most. The single mother working two jobs who cannot find the hours. The young person drowning in debt who cannot afford the cover price. The elderly person who has already made the mistakes these pages might have prevented. This book cannot reach everyone, and that failure haunts me. My hope is that those who do read it will share what they learn, extending its reach beyond what I alone could achieve.

If this book helps you make better decisions, understand yourself more clearly, or live with greater financial peace, that is enough. If it helps you help someone else do the same, that is more than I dared hope for.

# CONTENTS

# READER'S NOTE

This book is written primarily for readers in the United States. The principles apply broadly, but specific references to tax-advantaged accounts, regulations, and financial products reflect the American context. Readers elsewhere will need to translate certain details to their own systems.

I have tried to make this book timeless, focusing on principles over products, on frameworks over tactics. But financial rules change, and any specific numbers or limits mentioned may be outdated by the time you read this. Verify current figures before acting on them.

Nothing in this book constitutes personalized financial, tax, or legal advice. Your situation is yours, and complex matters may require professional guidance. This book aims to make you a more informed participant in those conversations, not to replace them.

Finally: I have no financial relationship with any product, fund, or institution mentioned in these pages. My only interest is in being genuinely useful to you.

# PREFACE

I have spent my career observing human beings in their most vulnerable moments. As a physician, I have sat with patients through illness, recovery, fear, and hope. What I did not expect was how often money would appear in the examination room, not as the presenting complaint but as the silent weight pressing down on everything else.

A mother delays necessary treatment because she cannot afford the copay. A father's chest pain turns out to be anxiety rooted in mounting debt. A young professional ignores warning signs because taking time off work feels financially impossible. Over the years, I came to see that health and wealth are not separate domains. They are intertwined in ways that our fragmented approach to education and expertise fails to acknowledge.

But it was not only patients who struggled. I watched colleagues, brilliant men and women who had navigated the grueling path through medical training, make elementary financial mistakes. Doctors earning substantial incomes yet living paycheck to paycheck. Surgeons who could perform procedures of exquisite complexity but had never learned the basics of saving and investing. Specialists who understood the human body in extraordinary detail but approached their finances with confusion, avoidance, or magical thinking.

The pattern repeated itself enough times that I stopped seeing it as individual failure. Something was missing from how we educate people, even highly educated people. We teach calculus and organic chemistry, anatomy and pharmacology, but we leave people to figure out money on their own, as if financial competence were either obvious or unimportant. It is neither.

This is the book nobody gave us.

I also observed something more troubling. Emotional problems and money problems feed each other in a vicious cycle. A marriage strained by financial stress becomes a marriage where productive financial conversation becomes impossible. Anxiety about money leads to avoidance, and avoidance makes the underlying problems worse. Depression drains the energy needed to address financial chaos, and financial chaos deepens depression. I saw relationships destroyed not by the amount of money involved but by what money had come to represent: power, control, resentment, fear, love withheld or demanded.

Money, I came to understand, is never just money. It is a surface on which we project our deepest hopes and terrors. And until we address the emotional and psychological dimensions, no amount of practical advice will be sufficient.

My own financial journey began without grand strategy. In 2000, I started ordering books from a relatively new company called Amazon. I was impressed immediately by the service, the selection, the evident intelligence behind the business model. In 2001, following what I later learned was essentially Peter Lynch's advice to invest in what you know and understand, I bought shares in the company. It was not a calculated decision based on spreadsheet analysis. It was intuition grounded in direct experience as a customer.

I made similar decisions with other companies over the years.

Microsoft, Google, Apple. Each time, the logic was the same: I used these products, I understood why they were valuable, and I believed they would continue to matter. I also invested in mutual funds, which I liked for a different reason entirely. They allowed me to invest automatically every month. Dividends and capital gains were reinvested without requiring my attention or decision. Compounding happened in the background, doing its patient work while I focused on patients and family.

For years, I rarely looked at my investments. I was too busy. The demands of professional life, the responsibilities of parenthood, the ordinary chaos of human existence left little time for monitoring portfolio performance. In retrospect, this benign neglect was one of the best financial decisions I ever made, though I did not recognize it as a decision at the time.

Then came the pandemic.

Like so many others, I found myself in an unfamiliar state: looming stress combined with unexpected free time. The usual structures of life had dissolved. Work continued but differently. Social life contracted. And into that space rushed a new obsession.

I began reading about the markets in a way I never had before. Not the patient, long-term perspective that had guided my earlier investing, but the frenetic world of trading. I devoured books about technical analysis and market indicators. I studied options and futures, instruments I had previously ignored as too complex or too risky. One of my colleagues introduced me to a WhatsApp group dedicated to investment discussions. The group was collectively investing in pre-IPO companies like Robinhood and others, pooling resources to access opportunities normally reserved for institutional investors. I observed but did not participate.

Instead, I traded options and futures on my own. It was exciting in a way that long-term investing had never been. The leverage magnified everything. Gains came fast and felt euphoric. Losses came faster and felt devastating. I experienced in compressed form what many traders discover: the emotional intensity of short-term speculation is asymmetric. The highs are high, but the lows are lower still. The cumulative psychological toll exceeds what the numbers on a screen might suggest.

Eventually, I stopped. Not because I had lost catastrophically, but because I recognized that this approach did not match my personality. I am not built for the emotional volatility of active trading. I do not enjoy the constant vigilance it requires. And when the pandemic receded and life returned to something resembling normality, the strange interlude of day trading began to feel like what it was: a flight into fantasy, stimulated by unprecedented circumstances, ultimately disconnected from who I am and what I actually value.

I returned to my earlier approach, humbled and educated.

That experience crystallized something that had been forming for years. I wanted to understand money more deeply, not just the mechanics but the meaning. What is money, really? Why does it hold such power over human beings? What makes some people wise with money and others foolish? Why do intelligent people make predictable mistakes? What is the relationship between financial success and human flourishing?

These questions led me to thinkers I had not expected to consult on financial matters. Ludwig von Mises, the Austrian economist, helped me understand markets as information systems and money as a tool for coordinating human action across time. Daniel Kahneman, the psychologist, revealed the systematic biases that distort our financial decisions and showed me why even awareness of these biases does not make us immune to them. Friedrich Nietzsche, the philosopher, illuminated the psychological dangers of resentment and the importance of creating meaning rather than waiting to receive it.

From Mises I learned to respect markets without worshiping them. From Kahneman I learned to distrust my instincts without becoming paralyzed. From Nietzsche I learned that the most dangerous financial mistake is not losing money but losing yourself, allowing frustration and comparison to curdle into bitterness that poisons everything it touches.

These three thinkers come from different centuries, different disciplines, different intellectual traditions. They would not agree with each other on many things. But brought together, they offer something valuable: a framework for understanding money that honors both its practical importance and its deeper human dimensions.

There is another dimension I cannot ignore, one that extends beyond personal finance into the fate of societies. The widening wealth gap troubles me deeply, and I believe it would trouble all three of my intellectual guides, though each would diagnose it differently.

Mises understood that markets function well only when they operate within a framework of genuine competition and widely distributed opportunity. He warned against concentrations of power, whether governmental or private, that distort the price signals on which healthy markets depend. A society where wealth accumulates in ever fewer hands is not a free market flourishing but a market failing, its information systems corrupted, its dynamism calcifying into oligarchy.

Kahneman's research reveals how cognitive biases compound across generations. Those born into scarcity make decisions under psychological pressures that those born into abundance never experience. Stress narrows thinking. Poverty taxes mental bandwidth. The playing field is not level not because some people are smarter or more disciplined but because the very conditions of deprivation impair the cognitive resources needed to escape it. Extreme inequality is not merely unfair in some abstract sense; it systematically degrades human potential on a massive scale.

Nietzsche, for all his aristocratic posturing, understood that a society organized solely around the accumulation of wealth produces not greatness but a peculiar kind of smallness. When money becomes the only measure of value, the rich become complacent and the poor become resentful, and both conditions poison the soul. The ressentiment he diagnosed does not emerge from poverty alone but from the lived experience of a rigged game, the sense that effort and merit matter less than the accident of birth. A society that generates such widespread bitterness is corroding itself from within.

I write this book primarily as a practical guide for individuals navigating their own financial lives. But I would be dishonest if I pretended that personal finance exists in a vacuum. The choices we make about money, how we earn it, invest it, spend it, and think about it, ripple outward into the social fabric. And the social fabric, in turn, shapes the conditions within which we make those choices. Extreme inequality is not just a political issue to be debated by economists and legislators. It is a human issue that affects health, happiness, social trust, and the very possibility of shared meaning.

I do not pretend to have policy solutions. That is not what this book offers. But I believe that anyone seeking true financial wisdom must grapple with the tension between individual flourishing and collective wellbeing. Wealth built on a crumbling society is not security but illusion. And a society that abandons the principle that hard work and talent should matter is a society that betrays its own future.

This book is my attempt to synthesize what I have learned from patients, colleagues, personal experience, and these intellectual guides into something useful for ordinary people trying to navigate their financial lives.

I am not a financial advisor. I am not an economist. I am a physician who has spent decades observing how money affects human health and happiness, and a person who has made both wise decisions and foolish ones with his own resources. I write not as an expert dispensing wisdom from above but as a fellow traveler sharing what the journey has taught me.

This book aims to bring different aspects of money and wealth together in one place. The basics and the complicated. The practical and the philosophical. The spreadsheet and the soul. Too many financial books treat money as a purely technical subject, ignoring the emotional and psychological forces that actually drive behavior. Too many psychology books ignore money's material reality. Too many philosophy books disdain practical application. I have tried to weave all three together because I believe a truly useful guide to money must address all three.

My deepest hope is that this book makes money less mysterious without making it less meaningful. I want readers to understand how the economic machine works, how their own minds work, how to save and invest wisely, how to spend in ways that actually produce satisfaction, and how to maintain their humanity across the inevitable ups and downs of financial life.

Money is a tool. It can purchase comfort, security, opportunity, and the time to pursue what matters most. But it cannot purchase meaning. That we must create for ourselves. And if we are not careful, the pursuit of money can become a substitute for the pursuit of meaning, a displacement that leaves us wealthy in dollars and impoverished in everything that actually matters.

I have seen this happen. I have felt its pull myself. And I have come to believe that financial wisdom is not just about maximizing returns. It is about remembering what money is for and refusing to let the means become the end.

This is the book nobody gave you. I hope it serves you well.

# INTRODUCTION

Nobody gave you a book about money. Not really.

Perhaps you received advice—fragments passed down from parents who were themselves figuring it out, tips from friends in circumstances different from yours, slogans from financial institutions with their own interests at stake. Perhaps you absorbed lessons from the culture: that money is the measure of success, or that wanting money is shameful, or that the whole subject is too complicated for ordinary people and should be left to experts. Perhaps you learned by trial and error, by mistakes that cost you, by luck good or bad.

But a complete guide—one that addresses not only the mechanics of earning, saving, and investing but also the psychology that shapes your behavior, the values that should inform your choices, the way financial life unfolds across decades, and the larger economic context within which your individual decisions occur? That book, most likely, nobody gave you.

This is that book.

The title makes a claim that requires defense. Why "complete"? No book can address every financial situation, every contingency, every reader's particular circumstances. What I mean by complete is something different: this book addresses money as a whole phenomenon in a human life, not just as a technical problem to be optimized.

Most financial guidance focuses narrowly. Books on investing tell you about asset allocation and compound interest but not about the psychology that will cause you to abandon your strategy at the worst possible moment. Books on budgeting tell you how to track expenses but not how to think about what spending is actually worth doing. Books on retirement tell you how to calculate whether you have enough but not how to find meaning when the structure of work falls away. And almost no books address the moral dimensions of money—what you owe to others, how to think about inequality, what wealth means in a society where it is so unevenly distributed.

This book attempts to hold all of these dimensions together. It covers the practical matters: earning and spending, saving and investing, taxes and legacy planning. But it embeds that practical guidance within a larger framework that addresses mind—the psychology of financial behavior—and meaning—the values and purposes that money should serve.

The structure reflects this ambition.

**Part I, Foundations**, establishes what money actually is and how it works. These are questions that seem so basic most books skip them, assuming you already understand. But understanding the nature of money and the workings of the economic machine provides the groundwork for everything that follows. Without this foundation, practical advice floats untethered, rules without reasons.

**Part II, The Inner Game**, turns inward. Your relationship with money was shaped long before you read any financial advice—by your family, your early experiences, the beliefs you absorbed without examination. The psychology of money is not a peripheral topic; it is often the determining factor in financial outcomes. Smart people make foolish decisions. Disciplined people lose control.

Anxious people avoid choices that would help them. Understanding these patterns in yourself is prerequisite to changing them. And beyond psychology lies the question of meaning: What is money for? What kind of life are you trying to build?

**Part III, Building the Foundation**, addresses the fundamental practices of financial life: earning, spending, and saving. These topics may seem simple, but there is an art to each. Earning is not just about working harder but about creating and capturing value. Spending is not just about restraint but about alignment between your expenditures and your values. Saving is not just about willpower but about systems and habits. Mastering these basics matters more than any sophisticated investment strategy.

**Part IV, Investing**, is the largest section because investing is both consequential and complex. It begins with philosophy—what is investing, really, and how should we think about it? It surveys the investment universe: the range of assets available to you. It makes the case for simplicity, because in investing, complexity is often the enemy of results. It teaches you to read the numbers, to understand what you own. It addresses derivatives—not because everyone needs to use them, but because understanding them illuminates the broader system. It confronts the investor's worst enemy, which is usually the investor themselves. And it guides you through building a portfolio and understanding the accounts and tax rules that shape your options.

**Part V, Spending Wisely**, returns to spending at a deeper level. The hedonic treadmill explains why more consumption often fails to deliver lasting satisfaction. Some spending compounds in value over time; other spending depreciates the moment it occurs. And generosity—giving money away—turns out to have returns that spreadsheets cannot capture. These chapters explore what makes spending worthwhile.

**Part VI, Money Across Life**, traces how financial priorities and challenges shift as you age: the particular concerns of starting out, the complexities of the middle years, the transition of approaching retirement, and the final questions of legacy and letting go. Financial life is not static; it unfolds through phases, and each phase requires different thinking.

**Part VII, The Larger Context**, steps back to consider the systems within which individual financial lives occur. Inequality and personal responsibility. Capitalism, markets, and the system we live in. And a final synthesis that brings together wealth, mind, and meaning. Your financial life does not occur in a vacuum; understanding the context helps you understand your place within it.

Several convictions run through this book.

The first is that personal finance is not merely personal. Your financial life occurs within economic systems, social structures, and historical circumstances that shape what is possible. Pretending otherwise—writing as if outcomes are purely the result of individual choices—is not honest. This book takes individual agency seriously while acknowledging the context that constrains and enables it.

The second conviction is that psychology matters as much as mathematics. The arithmetic of compound interest is simple; a child can understand it. What is not simple is behaving in accordance with that arithmetic over decades, through market crashes and booms, through the temptations of consumption and the anxieties of uncertainty. Your inherited beliefs about money, the emotions it triggers, the patterns you learned in childhood—these shape your financial behavior more than any formula. A useful book must address not only what to do but how to actually do it, given the minds we have.

The third conviction is that meaning matters. Money is instrumental—valuable for what it enables, not in itself. But what should it enable? Security, certainly. Freedom, within limits. The ability to care for those we love. The capacity to contribute to purposes beyond ourselves. But also: experiences that constitute a good life, relationships that matter, time for what we value. A purely technical approach to finance misses these questions entirely. This book does not.

The fourth conviction is that enough is a real concept. The dominant cultural message is that more is always better, that financial life is a game won by accumulating the highest score. This book takes a different view. There is a level of security that is sufficient—and beyond it, more money may or may not contribute to a good life. Helping you determine what enough means for you, and orienting your financial decisions around that concept rather than indefinite accumulation, is one aim of this book.

The fifth conviction is that honesty about uncertainty is essential. We do not know what markets will do, what the economy will do, what our own health and needs will become. Financial planning is planning under uncertainty, and any approach that offers false confidence misleads. The best we can do is make decisions robust across a range of possible futures. This book will not tell you what will happen; it will help you prepare for what might.

A word about what this book is not.

It is not a promise of wealth. If you are looking for secrets that will make you rich quickly and easily, you will not find them here. Building financial security is mostly a matter of earning, saving, investing, and waiting—activities that require discipline over cleverness. There are no shortcuts, only trade-offs.

It is not personalized advice. Your situation has specificities no book can address. You may need professional guidance for complex matters—and this book will help you know when and what kind. But it aims to make you a better decision-maker, not to make your decisions for you.

It is not a guarantee that everything will work out. Illness, job loss, economic crisis, plain bad luck—these are real, and prudent planning reduces but does not eliminate their impact. What this book offers is better odds and reduced severity of bad outcomes. That is worth pursuing, even without guarantees.

The title says "nobody gave you" this book. That framing is deliberate.

Financial knowledge is unequally distributed. Some people grow up in families where money is discussed openly, where sound practices are modeled, where the concepts are absorbed naturally. Others grow up where money is a source of shame or conflict or silence, where no one knows how to navigate the system, where mistakes compound across generations. Some people have access to good advice—fiduciary advisors, knowledgeable mentors, quality education. Others encounter only salespeople disguised as advisors, predatory products, information designed to confuse.

This inequality is unjust, and addressing it fully requires systemic changes beyond any book's scope. But a book can do something: make the knowledge available, clearly and honestly, to anyone who reads it. It cannot give you advantages some people are born with, but it can give you access to what those people know.

That is the spirit in which this is offered. Nobody gave it to you, perhaps. But you have it now.

How should you read this book?

From the beginning. Even if you consider yourself financially sophisticated, the early chapters establish concepts and frameworks that later chapters build upon. The book is designed as a progression, each part preparing you for the next.

Actively. This is not a book to skim but to engage with—to underline, to argue with, to apply. The chapters on psychology will be useful only if you examine your own patterns honestly. The chapters on values will be useful only if you think seriously about your own.

Repeatedly. Your circumstances will change. What matters in your twenties differs from what matters in your fifties. Return to relevant sections as your life unfolds. The book is designed to remain useful across decades.

With patience. Financial security is built over years, not weeks. The knowledge here compounds like a good investment—the earlier you acquire it, the more it benefits you over time. But the benefits accrue gradually. Resist the urge to rush.

One more thing.

This book is comprehensive, but it is not the final word. Knowledge evolves; circumstances change; reasonable people disagree. I have tried to be honest about uncertainty, to acknowledge where the evidence is contested, to present my views as views rather than as revealed truth.

What I offer is my best thinking, informed by research and experience and reflection, on questions that matter. It is offered in a spirit of genuine helpfulness, with no product to sell and no agenda beyond your flourishing.

Take what is useful. Question what seems wrong. Apply what fits your circumstances. And pass on what you learn, so that the next generation receives what you did not—the book nobody gave them, until someone did.

Let us begin.

# PART 1
# FOUNDATIONS

*Understanding what money is and how it works*

# ONE
# WHAT IS MONEY, AND WHY NOBODY TAUGHT YOU

There is a question so basic that most people never think to ask it. We spend money, earn money, save money, worry about money, argue about money, dream about money. We organize much of our lives around its acquisition and management. And yet if someone stopped us on the street and asked, "What is money, actually?"—most of us would struggle to answer.

We might say money is currency, those paper bills and metal coins we carry in our wallets. But most money today exists as numbers on screens, transferred electronically, never taking physical form. We might say money is what we use to buy things. But that only pushes the question back: why does everyone agree to accept these particular pieces of paper or digital entries in exchange for real goods and services? We might say money is wealth. But is it? A pile of cash buried in a backyard, unknown and unused, does not feel like wealth in any meaningful sense.

The difficulty of answering this simple question reveals something important. Money is so woven into the fabric of daily life that we have stopped seeing it clearly. It has become like water to a fish—

the invisible medium through which everything else moves. And this invisibility is precisely the problem. When we do not understand what money is, we cannot think clearly about how to earn it, save it, spend it, or invest it. We become vulnerable to manipulation, confusion, and our own unexamined assumptions.

This chapter attempts to make the invisible visible.

**The Long Road from Barter**

To understand money, we must begin before money existed. Imagine a world without it. You are a farmer who grows wheat. Your neighbor raises chickens. Another makes pottery. A fourth builds furniture. Each of you produces something valuable, and each needs things the others produce. How do you exchange?

The obvious answer is barter—trading your wheat directly for eggs, eggs for pottery, pottery for furniture. This system works, but only barely.

The problem is what economists call the "double coincidence of wants." For a trade to happen, you must find someone who has what you want and simultaneously wants what you have. If the furniture maker wants eggs rather than wheat, you are stuck. You must first find someone willing to trade eggs for wheat, then return to the furniture maker. In a complex economy, these chains become impossibly cumbersome.

Barter also struggles with divisibility. You cannot easily trade a portion of a cow for a single meal. And it struggles with storage—wheat rots, eggs spoil, furniture takes up space. How do you save your surplus if everything you produce decays?

These limitations meant pure barter economies remained small and primitive. For civilization to advance, something else was needed.

**The Emergence of Money**

The solution emerged organically. In various societies, people began converging on certain goods that could serve as intermediaries. Instead of trading wheat directly for furniture, you would trade wheat for this intermediate good, then trade it for furniture. This good became money.

Not just anything could serve this function. Successful monies shared key characteristics: they were durable, divisible, portable, recognizable, and relatively scarce. Different societies settled on different solutions—cattle (giving us "pecuniary" from the Latin pecus), salt (giving us "salary"), shells, beads, tea bricks, tobacco.

Over time, precious metals emerged as the dominant form. Gold and silver possessed all the necessary characteristics in abundance. They did not corrode. They could be divided or melted. They were dense enough to carry substantial value in a small package. Their distinctive appearance made verification easy. And their scarcity kept values stable.

This was not a decision made by kings or committees. It was emergent, arising from millions of individual choices. Gold was valued for ornamentation before it became money. Its monetary function grew out of that prior value.

**The Three Functions of Money**

Economists describe money as serving three distinct functions.

First, money is a medium of exchange. It eliminates the need for double coincidence of wants. When you accept money for your labor, you accept it because you know others will accept it when you wish to buy something. Money is a universally honored claim on future goods and services.

Second, money is a unit of account. It provides a common measuring stick for value. Without money, comparing the value of different goods becomes extraordinarily difficult. How many eggs equal one chair? Money simplifies this by expressing all values in a single unit, making economic calculation possible.

Third, money is a store of value. It allows you to save purchasing power for future use. If you produce more than you consume today, you can hold the surplus as money and spend it years from now. This function is essential for planning, security, and capital accumulation.

These functions are related but distinct. A currency experiencing rapid inflation may still work as a medium of exchange but fails as a store of value. Real estate may store value well but works poorly as a medium of exchange. Understanding these distinctions helps you think more clearly about what money is doing in your own life.

**From Gold to Paper to Digits**

The story of money did not end with precious metals. Over centuries, money became ever more abstract.

First came representative money. Carrying gold was inconvenient and dangerous, so people deposited metals with goldsmiths who issued paper receipts. These receipts could be traded in place of the metal itself. This practice gave rise to modern banking and paper currency. Governments began issuing notes, initially promising to redeem them for gold on demand.

Then came the final abstraction. In 1971, the United States severed the last link between the dollar and gold. Money became purely fiat—valuable simply because the government declares it legal tender. There is no gold backing your bank account. The value rests entirely on collective belief and government enforcement.

This troubles many people, and not without reason. Fiat money places enormous power in government hands. History is littered with examples of abuse—the hyperinflations of Weimar Germany, Zimbabwe, Venezuela. Fiat money is only as trustworthy as the institutions managing it.

Yet fiat money is what we have. Your salary, savings, and debts are all denominated in it. Whether you approve or not, you must learn to operate within this system.

Today, money has become even more abstract. Most exists only as electronic database entries. When you receive your paycheck through direct deposit, no physical currency changes hands. The money is real in its effects but has no physical existence whatsoever.

This progression from cattle to gold to paper to digits represents one of humanity's great collective achievements—a technology for coordinating action across vast distances and time horizons. But it also represents a collective vulnerability. A system depending entirely on trust can fail if that trust erodes.

**The Experiment in Trustless Money**

The story of money does not end with fiat currency. In 2008, as the global financial system teetered on collapse and central banks created trillions of dollars to rescue failing institutions, an anonymous programmer using the pseudonym Satoshi Nakamoto published a nine-page paper proposing something radical: money that required no central authority, no trusted institution, no government backing. Bitcoin, as this new form of money came to be called, offered a fixed supply of twenty-one million coins—ever—secured not by armies or laws but by mathematics. Specifically, by cryptography, the science of encoding information so that it can be verified by anyone but altered by no one.

The timing was not coincidental. People had just watched banks that were supposed to be prudent make catastrophic bets. They watched regulators who were supposed to protect the public fail spectacularly. They watched governments respond by creating money on a scale previously unimaginable, diluting the savings of ordinary people to rescue institutions whose recklessness had caused the crisis. Bitcoin emerged as an answer to a question millions were suddenly asking: Is there a form of money that does not require trusting institutions that have just proven themselves unworthy of trust?

Whether Bitcoin and the thousands of cryptocurrencies that followed represent the next chapter in money's evolution or a speculative dead end remains genuinely uncertain. What is certain is that they emerged from the same human needs that drove every monetary innovation before them: the desire for a medium of exchange that holds value across time and space, that cannot be debased by those in power, and that strangers can trust without trusting each other. We will return to cryptocurrency in a later chapter, examining what it actually is, how the underlying technology works, and how to think about it as an investment. For now, simply note that the story of money continues to be written, and you are living through a chapter whose ending no one yet knows.

**Money as Information**

Ludwig von Mises offered a transformative insight: money is fundamentally a system of information.

Consider the price of bread—say, three dollars. That single number contains enormous embedded information. It reflects wheat costs, weather patterns, farming techniques, fuel prices, labor costs, milling, baking, packaging, transportation, rent, wages, consumer demand, and countless other factors.

No single person could know all this. No committee could gather it. Yet prices aggregate this dispersed information from millions of people and compress it into signals guiding production and consumption. When bread prices rise, bakers produce more and consumers economize. No one issues orders. Each person responds to prices, and coordination emerges on a scale conscious planning could never achieve.

This is why socialist economies failed. Without genuine market prices, planners had no way to know what to produce, in what quantities, using which methods. They were flying blind.

Understanding money as information changes how you think about financial decisions. When you spend, you signal that something is valued. When you save, you make resources available for investment elsewhere. When you invest, you direct capital toward enterprises you believe will create value. Every financial decision participates in this vast coordination system.

**Why Nobody Taught You This**

If money is so important, why did nobody teach you how it works? Why do intelligent people graduate without understanding compound interest or the difference between stocks and bonds?

The answer involves several factors.

First, history. For most of human existence, financial education was unnecessary for most people. The modern financial system, with its complexity and demands on individual decision-making, is remarkably new. Universal bank access is barely a century old. The shift from pensions to individual retirement responsibility happened within recent decades. Educational institutions have not caught up.

Second, discomfort. Money is tangled with emotion, status, and morality in ways making it difficult to discuss. Parents who teach children about nutrition and safety often fall silent about money, feeling their own situation is shameful or lacking confidence in their knowledge.

Third, mixed incentives. Many financial institutions profit from consumer confusion. The credit card company benefits when you do not understand compound interest. The actively managed fund benefits when you do not know index funds typically outperform. Powerful interests have little motivation to fund comprehensive financial education.

Fourth, political sensitivity. Unlike many subjects, personal finance is not neutral. Teaching that compound interest favors savers implies values about discipline and delayed gratification. In an educational environment anxious about imposing values, financial literacy becomes a minefield.

The result: a society where most people handle money daily but few understand it, where intelligent adults make elementary mistakes, and where financial stress contributes to illness, divorce, and despair.

**The Cost of Ignorance**

The consequences of this educational failure manifest in individual lives constantly.

Consider debt. The average American household carries substantial credit card debt at rates exceeding twenty percent annually. At that rate, debt doubles in less than four years. People who would never agree to such terms if they understood them sign up without a second thought.

Consider retirement. Studies show most people have saved far too little. They underestimate inflation, overestimate Social Security benefits, fail to take advantage of employer matching, and invest too conservatively when young or too aggressively when old.

Consider investing. During every bubble, people pile into assets they do not understand because prices have been rising. They buy at the top, panic and sell at the bottom, then sit in cash while recovery happens without them—the precise opposite of successful investing.

Consider fees. An investment charging two percent annually instead of two-tenths of a percent may seem nearly identical. But over forty years, that difference compounds into losing a third or more of potential wealth.

These are not failures of intelligence. Brilliant physicians and accomplished researchers fall into every one of these traps. They failed because nobody taught them, and because money's emotional complexity made it easy to avoid thinking clearly.

**Your Money Story**

Before proceeding further, consider something personal. Each of us carries a money story—beliefs, assumptions, and emotional reactions shaping how we relate to money. This story was written early, often before we could think critically, and continues influencing us in ways we may not recognize.

Daniel Kahneman's research illuminates this. Our brains operate with two systems: a fast, intuitive system making snap judgments based on emotion, and a slow, deliberate system that analyzes but requires effort. With money, the fast system usually dominates.

Consider where your money story came from. Did your family talk openly about money, or was it a source of tension? Did you grow up with scarcity or abundance? Were you taught money is evil, or that it measures success? Did your parents model careful planning or impulsive spending? Were there financial crises shaping your sense of security?

These early experiences created patterns persisting into adulthood. Someone who grew up in poverty may hoard anxiously or spend recklessly. Someone raised wealthy may feel entitled to an unaffordable lifestyle or feel guilty in ways preventing effective management.

Recognizing your money story is the first step toward changing it. You cannot think clearly about financial decisions while unconscious beliefs pull you in directions you do not understand.

**What This Book Offers**

This chapter has covered substantial ground—from prehistoric barter to digital abstractions, from the information function of prices to the emotional inheritance shaping financial behavior.

The chapters that follow will build on this foundation. We will examine how to earn money in ways aligning with your values. We will explore saving and spending as tools for designing a life reflecting your true priorities. We will learn about investing, from basic principles to advanced strategies. We will confront money psychology more deeply, learning to recognize biases that lead us astray. We will consider what money can and cannot buy.

Throughout, I will draw on my experience as a physician and investor, on insights from Mises, Kahneman, Nietzsche, and other thinkers, and on stories of patients and colleagues who taught me what money does to human beings. My goal is not to make you rich—though I hope this helps you build wealth if that is what you seek. My goal is to make money less mysterious and more meaningful.

This is the education nobody gave you. But it is not too late.

**Summary: Key Takeaways from Chapter One**

Money is a technology, not a thing. It evolved from barter through commodity money to gold to paper to purely digital forms. Understanding this evolution reveals that money's value rests on collective trust and shared belief—not on any inherent physical property.

Money serves three distinct functions. It acts as a medium of exchange (eliminating barter's inefficiencies), a unit of account (providing a common measure of value), and a store of value (allowing you to save purchasing power for the future). Different forms of money perform these functions with varying success.

Money is information. Prices aggregate knowledge from millions of people into signals that coordinate economic activity. Every financial decision you make—spending, saving, investing—participates in this vast information system.

Your financial education was neglected by design and by default. Historical lag, emotional discomfort, institutional inertia, and misaligned incentives have left most people unprepared for the financial decisions modern life demands. Recognizing this gap—and your own inherited money story—is the essential first step toward financial clarity.

# TWO
# THE ECONOMIC MACHINE

Money does not exist in isolation. It flows through a vast, interconnected system we call the economy—a word so familiar we rarely pause to consider what it actually describes. The economy is not a thing you can point to or touch. It is a pattern of relationships, a web of exchanges, a collective improvisation performed by billions of participants who mostly do not know each other yet depend on each other in ways both profound and invisible.

Understanding this larger system matters for personal finance in ways that are not immediately obvious. You cannot navigate a river well without understanding currents. You cannot sail effectively without understanding wind and tide. Similarly, you cannot make sound financial decisions across a lifetime without grasping the economic forces shaping the environment in which those decisions play out. Interest rates rise and fall. Jobs appear and disappear. Prices shift. Opportunities emerge and close. These are not random events but outcomes of a system that, while complex, operates according to patterns that can be understood.

This chapter offers a functional map of the economic machine—

sufficient to orient you within the larger system and make sense of the economic conditions affecting your financial life.

**What Is an Economy?**

An economy is the sum total of all production, distribution, and consumption of goods and services within a defined area. But this definition misses the essential character. An economy is better understood as a system of coordination, a way of solving a problem that would otherwise be unsolvable.

The problem is this: human beings have diverse needs and desires, and resources to satisfy them are limited and unevenly distributed. One person grows food but needs shelter. Another builds houses but needs food. A third heals the sick but needs both. How do these people find each other? How do they determine relative value? How do they coordinate so that what each produces is what others want, in the quantities and timing they need?

In small communities, coordination happens through direct personal relationships. But as societies grow larger, this becomes impossible. No one can know more than a tiny fraction of the people whose activities affect their life. No central authority can gather and process the information needed to direct millions of decisions.

Markets emerge as the solution. A market is any arrangement bringing buyers and sellers together—physical or virtual. What matters is that markets allow people who do not know each other to exchange goods, services, and money in mutually beneficial ways.

The magic of markets lies in what they accomplish without direction. No one decides how many apples should be grown or how many accountants trained. These outcomes emerge from millions of individual decisions. The coffee you drink involves coordinated efforts of farmers in Colombia, shipping companies, roasters, distributors, and retailers across continents. No one planned this. It happened through markets.

**The Price Mechanism**

The key to market coordination is the price mechanism. Prices are signals carrying information about scarcity and demand. When a product is scarce relative to demand, its price rises, signaling: produce more, consume less, find substitutes. When abundant, prices fall, signaling the opposite.

Consider what happens when frost destroys much of the Florida orange crop. Supply decreases while demand remains constant, creating shortage at the old price. The price rises. This does several things simultaneously: it discourages some consumption as people switch to alternatives, encourages production as farmers elsewhere see profit opportunities, and allocates scarce oranges to those who value them most.

No committee decided any of this. The price mechanism handled it automatically, processing information no committee could gather and responding faster than any bureaucracy could manage.

This is what Friedrich Hayek called the "knowledge problem." The knowledge needed to coordinate economic activity is dispersed across millions of minds. No central authority can possess it all. But prices aggregate this dispersed knowledge into signals everyone can use. The price of oil reflects combined knowledge of geologists, engineers, consumers, and speculators—none of whom need share their knowledge explicitly. Their buying and selling actions reveal it.

The price mechanism is not perfect. Prices can be distorted by market power, externalities, information asymmetries, and manipulation. But understanding prices as signals that coordinate activity and allocate resources is essential to understanding how economies work.

**Supply and Demand**

The forces determining prices are supply and demand.

Demand refers to how much of something people want to buy at various prices. Generally, as price falls, people want more; as it rises, they want less. This is the law of demand. When airline tickets are cheap, more people fly. When expensive, fewer do.

Supply refers to how much producers are willing to sell at various prices. As price rises, producers want to sell more because profits increase. As price falls, production becomes less profitable and supply decreases.

The market price is determined where supply and demand intersect—the price at which quantity buyers want equals quantity sellers want. This equilibrium price means no shortage and no surplus. When conditions change, equilibrium shifts. The graduate entering a booming job market faces different conditions than one entering a recession.

The labor market operates by these same principles. Workers supply labor, employers demand it. Wages equilibrate supply and demand. When certain skills are scarce and highly demanded, wages rise. When workers are abundant and jobs scarce, wages stagnate. Understanding this helps you make better career decisions—positioning yourself where demand is high and supply is limited.

**The Circular Flow**

Money flows through the economy in a circular pattern connecting different participants.

The simplest version involves households and businesses. Households own factors of production—labor, land, capital—and sell these to businesses. Businesses use them to produce goods and services sold to households. Money flows opposite to real resources: businesses pay wages, rent, and interest to households; households pay businesses for products.

This creates a circular flow. Household income becomes business revenue when households buy products. Business costs become household income when businesses pay for labor.

This model expands to include government (collecting taxes, purchasing goods, making transfer payments), financial institutions (collecting savings, making loans), and foreign participants (buying exports, selling imports).

The key insight: spending and income are two sides of the same coin. One person's spending is another's income. When consumers stop spending, businesses lose revenue and lay off workers. Those workers have less income and spend less, causing more revenue loss. This is how recessions propagate. Conversely, when spending increases, incomes rise, enabling further spending. This is how expansions build on themselves.

**Credit: The Amplifier**

If the circular flow were the whole story, economies would grow only as fast as real resources expand—steadily and slowly. But real economies grow faster and also experience dramatic contractions. The reason is credit.

Credit is the ability to spend money you do not currently have, in exchange for a promise to repay later. When a bank lends you money for a house, you can spend now rather than waiting until you have saved the full price. This borrowed spending adds to total demand. The seller receives money that would not otherwise exist and can spend it on other things.

Credit amplifies economic activity. In the short run, it allows spending to exceed income. But credit is not free money—it is spending borrowed from the future. The borrower must eventually repay, and during repayment, spending will be less than income. What credit gives today, it takes back tomorrow.

This creates cycles. During expansion, credit is easy. Lenders are confident, borrowers see opportunities. Spending exceeds income, generating growth that validates further lending. Asset prices rise, making borrowers feel wealthier. The cycle feeds on itself.

Eventually, debt levels become unsustainable. Some borrowers default. Lenders become cautious and restrict credit. Borrowers must spend less than income to repay debts. The virtuous cycle becomes vicious: falling spending leads to falling incomes, more defaults, tighter credit, and further spending declines.

This is what Ray Dalio calls the "debt cycle." Economies move in waves driven by credit expansion and contraction. Understanding this explains why recessions often follow apparent prosperity—the prosperity was partly borrowed.

**Interest Rates: The Price of Money**

If credit is the amplifier, interest rates are the dial controlling it.

An interest rate is the price of borrowing—what you pay for spending now rather than later.

When rates are low, borrowing is cheap. More projects justify borrowing costs. More families can afford homes. Low rates stimulate borrowing, spending, and economic activity.

When rates are high, borrowing is expensive. Fewer projects make sense. Fewer families can afford purchases. High rates dampen activity.

Central banks—the Federal Reserve in the United States, the European Central Bank in Europe—use control over certain interest rates to influence economic conditions. When the economy is weak, they lower rates to encourage borrowing. When overheating, they raise rates to cool things down.

This is monetary policy. The central bank does not directly control business investment or consumer spending, but by making borrowing cheaper or more expensive, it influences millions of individual decisions that determine overall economic activity.

Interest rates affect your finances in multiple ways: what you pay to borrow for mortgages, car loans, and credit cards; what you earn on savings; and asset prices for stocks and real estate, which tend to rise when rates fall and fall when rates rise.

**Inflation: When Money Changes Value**

The purchasing power of money is not constant. Over time, the same amount typically buys less. This erosion is called inflation.

Moderate inflation is normal and even considered desirable by many economists. A little inflation encourages spending and investment: if money will be worth less tomorrow, there is incentive to put it to use today. Central banks typically target around two percent annually.

Higher inflation becomes problematic. When prices rise rapidly and unpredictably, planning becomes difficult. Contracts are harder to write. Savings lose value. People spend energy protecting themselves from inflation rather than producing.

Inflation is caused by too much money chasing too few goods.

This can happen when central banks create too much money, governments run large deficits financed by money creation, or supply shocks reduce goods while demand remains constant.

For personal finance, inflation is a silent tax on savings. Money sitting in a low-interest account loses real value every year. One hundred dollars in 1990 would need to be about two hundred forty dollars in 2024 to have the same purchasing power. Failing to account for inflation leads to underestimating how much you need for goals like retirement.

Investments that outpace inflation—stocks, real estate, inflation-protected bonds—protect against this erosion. Understanding inflation is essential to understanding why investing, rather than simply saving, is necessary for long-term financial security.

**Business Cycles: Expansion and Contraction**

Economies do not grow steadily. They expand and contract in a pattern called the business cycle.

The cycle has four phases. During expansion, economic activity increases—output rises, employment grows, incomes increase, confidence is high, credit flows. This can last years, and during it, prosperity often feels permanent.

The peak is when expansion ends. Activity is highest, but factors causing contraction are already in place—often excessive debt, overinvestment, or inflation prompting rate increases.

During contraction, activity declines. Businesses cut back and lay off workers. Unemployment rises. Confidence erodes. Credit tightens. A significant, prolonged contraction is called a recession.

The trough is the bottom, when activity is lowest. From here, recovery begins.

These cycles are irregular in length and severity. Some expansions last a decade. Some recessions are brief. Others, like the Great Depression or 2008 financial crisis, are severe and long-lasting. Warning signs often appear before peaks: excessive optimism, high debt levels, asset prices disconnected from reality.

For personal finance, cycles matter enormously. Job security, wages, and investment returns all vary across the cycle. This does not mean you should try to time cycles—that is notoriously difficult. But it does mean building financial resilience that can withstand downturns: emergency savings, diversified investments, valuable skills, and sustainable debt levels.

**The Major Players**

Several institutional players shape the economic environment.

Central banks control money supply and set key interest rates. Their decisions ripple through the entire economy, affecting borrowing costs, asset prices, and activity levels. They also serve as lenders of last resort during crises.

Commercial banks are the primary credit creators. When a bank makes a loan, it creates new money by crediting the borrower's account. This makes banks central to economic activity but also potential sources of instability if too many loans go bad.

Governments collect taxes, spend money, establish regulations, and set fiscal policy—decisions about taxing and spending that can stimulate or restrain activity.

Corporations produce most goods and services. Their decisions about investment, hiring, and production drive much of the business cycle.

Households are the ultimate consumers and suppliers of labor. When households feel confident and spend freely, the economy grows. When anxious, it contracts.

Foreign participants add complexity through trade and capital flows. International connections transmit both prosperity and shocks.

These players interact in complex ways. The central bank raises rates; banks tighten credit; corporations reduce investment; workers are laid off; households cut spending; tax revenues fall. Each action triggers responses, and combined effects often differ from any single player's intentions.

**Markets Are Not Perfect**

Markets do not always produce good outcomes. Understanding market failures is as important as understanding how markets work.

Externalities occur when activity affects non-participants. Pollution imposes costs on neighbors who receive no compensation. Without intervention, markets produce too much of activities with negative externalities and too little of those with positive ones.

Market power distorts outcomes when large players can influence prices. Monopolists restrict supply and raise prices. Market power can also suppress wages when few employers dominate a labor market.

Information asymmetries arise when one party knows more than another. The used car seller knows its history; the buyer does not. These asymmetries can cause markets to function poorly.

Public goods benefit everyone and cannot easily be restricted to paying customers. National defense and basic research are examples. Private markets underprovide them because providers cannot capture full value.

Bubbles occur when asset prices rise far above justified levels. Participants buy not because they believe assets are worth the price but because they expect someone else to pay more later. When bubbles collapse, damage can be severe.

These failures do not mean markets should be abandoned—no alternative has proven better at coordinating complex activity—but they require regulation and supplementation to function well.

**Where You Fit In**

You are embedded in this economic machine, and its operations affect you daily.

You sell your labor in a market. Your wage reflects supply and demand for your skills. Understanding this can guide career decisions: developing skills in high demand and limited supply.

You buy goods and services in markets. Prices you pay reflect the forces described here.

You borrow and lend. Your mortgage rate reflects broader interest rates and central bank policy. When you borrow, you pull spending from the future. When you save, you push it back.

You are affected by business cycles. Job security, wage growth, and investment values all vary across the cycle. Building resilience against downturns requires understanding this cyclical nature.

You are affected by inflation. Money saved today must be invested to preserve purchasing power over time.

You interact with all major players—paying taxes, depositing money in banks, working for and buying from corporations, connecting to capital markets through investments.

Understanding the economic machine does not give you control over it. You are a small participant in a vast system. But understanding helps you navigate more skillfully—making better decisions about where to work, how much to save, how to invest, when to take risks and when to be cautious.

**The Limits of Understanding**

A note of humility is warranted. The economy is a complex adaptive system whose components respond to conditions and to each other in ways making prediction extremely difficult. Economists disagree about fundamental questions. Forecasters are regularly wrong. The 2008 financial crisis surprised most experts. Pandemic economic effects defied many predictions.

The frameworks in this chapter are useful approximations, not exact descriptions. They help organize thinking and provide vocabulary for discussion. But they are simplifications of a reality far more complex and unpredictable than any model can capture.

This does not mean understanding is useless. A map that simplifies terrain is still far better than no map. But the appropriate attitude is informed humility: using frameworks while remaining aware of limits, making decisions based on probabilities rather than certainties, and building resilience against the unexpected.

## SUMMARY: **Key Takeaways from Chapter Two**

**The economy is a coordination system, and prices are its language.** Markets solve the otherwise impossible problem of coordinating billions of people's needs and activities. Prices aggregate dispersed knowledge into signals that guide production and consumption without any central direction.

**Credit amplifies everything—growth and contraction alike.** Borrowing allows spending to exceed income temporarily, accelerating economic activity. But credit borrowed today must be repaid tomorrow, creating the cycles of expansion and recession that characterize all modern economies.

**Interest rates and inflation directly shape your financial life.** Interest rates determine the cost of borrowing and the return on saving. Inflation erodes purchasing power over time, making investing—not just saving—essential for long-term financial security.

**You are a participant in this system, not a bystander.** Your wages reflect labor market supply and demand. Your savings and debts respond to interest rates. Your financial security depends on understanding business cycles and building resilience to withstand their inevitable downturns.

# PART 2
# THE INNER GAME

*Psychology, emotion, and inherited beliefs about money*

# THREE
# THE PSYCHOLOGY OF MONEY

We like to think of financial decisions as rational calculations. Income minus expenses equals savings. Risk and return are balanced according to time horizon. But if you have ever watched yourself make a financial decision—really watched—you know that something else is happening beneath the spreadsheet.

You feel anxiety when markets drop, even though you know volatility is normal. You experience pleasure when a stock rises, though the gain is only on paper. You avoid looking at your credit card statement after a spending binge. You know you should start investing, but somehow the years slip by without action.

These are not character flaws. They are the predictable operations of a human mind that evolved for a world very different from the one in which we now make financial decisions.

## The Brain We Inherited

The human brain was shaped by hundreds of thousands of years of evolution in environments that bear little resemblance to modern financial life. Our ancestors faced immediate, tangible threats—predators, enemies, scarcity. The brain evolved to respond quickly and emotionally to these threats, prioritizing survival over careful deliberation. This makes sense when a lion might be lurking in the grass. It makes less sense when evaluating a thirty-year investment strategy.

Psychologist Daniel Kahneman describes this as System 1 and System 2 thinking. System 1 is fast, automatic, and emotional—it operates below conscious awareness, generating impressions that feel like direct perceptions of reality. System 2 is slow, deliberate, and effortful—it handles complex calculations but tires easily and is often bypassed.

Financial decisions frequently trigger System 1 responses that feel like reasoned conclusions but are actually intuitive reactions. The stock that "feels" like a good investment. The purchase that seems like a bargain. These feelings arise instantly, while genuine analysis rarely gets done.

Recognizing when System 1 is driving allows you to pause and engage more deliberate processing before acting.

**The Biases That Distort**

Cognitive biases are not random errors but predictable tendencies built into how minds work. Several are particularly relevant to financial decisions.

Loss aversion may be the most powerful. Losses hurt roughly twice as much as equivalent gains feel good. This asymmetry made sense in ancestral environments where losses could mean death. But in financial contexts, it leads to irrational behavior—holding losing investments too long, selling winners too quickly, avoiding appropriate risks because the possibility of loss looms larger than potential gain.

Anchoring is the tendency to rely too heavily on the first piece of information encountered. If a stock previously traded at one hundred dollars, that number influences whether fifty dollars feels cheap or one hundred fifty feels expensive—regardless of actual worth.

The availability heuristic leads people to overweight information that comes easily to mind. Recent events feel more probable than they are. The investor who just heard about a friend's stock market success overestimates the likelihood of similar results.

Confirmation bias drives us to seek and interpret information in ways that confirm existing beliefs. The investor convinced a stock is promising notices every positive indicator while discounting negative ones.

Overconfidence is endemic among investors. Most people believe their investment acumen is superior to the typical investor. This leads to excessive trading, inadequate diversification, and the belief that one can time markets that professionals struggle to beat.

Present bias describes the tendency to overvalue immediate rewards. The pleasure of spending now feels vivid, while retirement decades away feels abstract. This explains why people consistently fail to save as much as they know they should.

The endowment effect causes people to overvalue things they already own. The stock you hold seems more promising than one you might purchase with the same money, creating inertia that prevents beneficial changes.

Herding is the tendency to follow the crowd. When everyone is buying, buying feels safe. But herding creates bubbles and crashes—prices rise as enthusiasm feeds on itself, then collapse when sentiment reverses.

### The Emotional Undercurrents

Beneath cognitive biases run deeper emotional currents. Money connects to survival, status, security, freedom, and self-worth. These connections generate responses that pure cognitive analysis misses.

Fear is the most primal—fear of not having enough, of losing what you have, of being seen as unsuccessful. Fear triggers fight-or-flight responses that in financial contexts often mean selling at exactly the wrong time or avoiding investing altogether.

Greed drives people to take excessive risks, chase returns, and believe in schemes too good to be true. It feels different from fear—energizing rather than paralyzing—but is equally capable of producing poor decisions.

Envy poisons financial satisfaction. No matter how much you have, someone has more. Social comparison drives spending beyond means and creates a constant sense of inadequacy that no amount of money cures.

Shame lurks around financial failure—the debt that feels like moral failing, the investment loss that feels like stupidity. Shame makes it difficult to acknowledge problems, seek help, or make necessary changes.

Pride attaches to financial success, sometimes taking credit for outcomes that involved significant luck, creating overconfidence that leads to future mistakes.

These emotions interact and reinforce each other, creating patterns that shape behavior over decades. Understanding your own emotional relationship with money is essential work that no spreadsheet can replace.

**Money Stories**

Before you ever made a conscious financial decision, you absorbed beliefs about money from your environment. These operate as unconscious scripts, shaping behavior without ever being examined.

What did your family model about money? Did your parents discuss finances openly or treat them as secret? Was money a source of constant stress or barely mentioned? Were you taught to save or to enjoy life while you can?

Someone raised in scarcity may feel compulsive about saving, unable to enjoy spending even when they can easily afford it. Someone raised in abundance may struggle with limits. Someone whose parents fought about money may avoid financial discussions in their own relationships.

Money stories also come from culture—the American dream of upward mobility, the equation of success with wealth. These narratives interact with personal experience to create a complex internal landscape.

The power of money stories lies in their invisibility. They feel like reality rather than interpretation. Making them visible is the first step toward freedom. What do you believe about money? Where did these beliefs come from? Do they serve you now?

**The Emotional Investor**

Markets are cyclical. They rise to heights that seem irrational in retrospect, then fall to depths that seem equally irrational. These cycles follow predictable emotional patterns.

Near market peaks, optimism dominates. Prices have risen long enough that gains feel normal. Risk seems to have disappeared. New investors enter, drawn by stories of easy profits. The emotional signature is confidence, perhaps euphoria.

Then something shifts. Prices fall. Optimism gives way to anxiety, then fear, then panic. At the bottom, despair—the belief that things will never recover, that selling is the only sensible response.

These emotional states are precisely wrong. The time to be cautious is near the peak, when confidence is highest. The time to be bold is near the bottom, when despair is deepest. But emotions push in the opposite direction, urging buying when prices are high and selling when they are low.

Knowing this intellectually does not make the emotions disappear. The challenge is not to feel differently but to act wisely despite the feelings.

**Strategies for Managing Bias**

Given that biases and emotions will inevitably affect decisions, what can be done?

Awareness itself is protective. Simply knowing about loss aversion and herding makes you slightly less susceptible. When you notice yourself refusing to sell a losing investment, you can ask whether loss aversion is operating.

Rules and automation reduce the role of judgment. Automating retirement contributions means you do not need to decide each month whether to save. Rules like "I rebalance once per year regardless of market conditions" remove the temptation to react emotionally.

Delay creates space for deliberation. Building delays into decisions—sleeping on major purchases, waiting twenty-four hours before trading—gives the slower part of your mind time to engage.

Checklists ensure important considerations are not overlooked. Before investing, a checklist might include questions like: Have I considered the opposite case? What would have to be true for this to be a mistake?

Writing forces clarity. A financial journal recording decisions and reasons creates data for learning from mistakes and exposes patterns of emotional decision-making.

Accountability through others provides external perspective. A trusted friend or advisor who knows your goals can check biased decision-making.

Meditation strengthens the capacity to observe emotions without being controlled by them. The investor who can notice fear arising without immediately acting on it has a significant advantage.

**The Stories We Tell**

Beyond individual decisions, there is the overarching narrative of your financial life.

Some people tell stories of victimhood—things happen to them, the economy is rigged, success belongs to others. This narrative creates passivity.

Others tell stories of inevitable success—setbacks are temporary, the big break is coming. This can justify magical thinking and poor planning.

Still others tell stories of moral judgment—money is dirty, wealthy people are suspect. This provides comfort for not having more but forecloses possibilities.

The most useful narratives balance agency with realism. They acknowledge what you can control and what you cannot. They recognize luck without denying effort. They treat money as a tool without worshipping or despising it.

What story do you tell about your financial life? Is it one that motivates wise action? Stories can be revised.

**When Professional Help Is Needed**

For some people, difficulties around money go beyond normal bias—compulsive spending despite severe consequences, debilitating anxiety, pathological gambling, hoarding from trauma. These require therapists or counselors who specialize in the intersection of psychology and money.

The stigma around financial mental health prevents people from getting help that could dramatically improve their lives. If you recognize yourself in these descriptions, know that help exists and seeking it is a sign of strength.

**Toward Integration**

This chapter has treated psychology as something to be managed, biases as errors to be corrected. This is partly accurate—many psychological tendencies do lead to poor outcomes.

But the goal is not to become a calculating machine devoid of emotion. Emotions provide information. Fear may signal genuine danger. Enthusiasm may signal genuine opportunity.

The goal is integration—the capacity to feel emotions fully while also engaging deliberate reasoning, to carry money stories consciously rather than unconsciously. You feel the fear and make the thoughtful decision anyway. You notice the anchoring and seek additional reference points. You recognize the family script and choose which parts to honor.

The psychology of money is not a problem to be solved but a dimension of life to be navigated. What matters is understanding these forces well enough to make decisions you can stand behind and build a relationship with money that supports the life you are trying to create.

## SUMMARY: **Key Takeaways from Chapter Three**

**The Evolved Brain:** Your brain was shaped for ancestral environments with immediate physical threats, not modern financial decisions. System 1 (fast, emotional, automatic) often overrides System 2 (slow, deliberate, effortful), producing intuitive reactions that feel like reasoned conclusions.

**Core Cognitive Biases:** Loss aversion makes losses hurt twice as much as equivalent gains feel good, leading to holding losers and selling winners. Anchoring causes over-reliance on initial reference points. The availability heuristic overweights recent or vivid information. Confirmation bias filters evidence to support existing beliefs. Overconfidence leads to excessive trading and inadequate diversification. Present bias makes immediate rewards feel disproportionately valuable. The endowment effect creates inertia. Herding produces bubbles and crashes.

**Emotional Undercurrents:** Fear triggers panic selling. Greed drives excessive risk-taking. Envy creates perpetual dissatisfaction. Shame prevents acknowledging problems. Pride misattributes luck to skill.

**Money Stories:** Unconscious beliefs about money, absorbed from family and culture, operate as invisible scripts shaping behavior. Making them visible allows conscious choice about which to keep.

**The Emotional Market Cycle:** Optimism peaks when caution is needed; despair bottoms when boldness would pay. Emotions push investors to buy high and sell low.

**Protective Strategies:** Awareness reduces susceptibility. Automation removes ongoing judgment. Delay engages deliberate thinking. Checklists prevent oversights. Writing forces clarity. Accountability provides external perspective. Mindfulness practice separates emotion from action.

**Integration Over Suppression:** The goal is not eliminating emotion but feeling fully while reasoning carefully—understanding psychological forces well enough to make decisions you can stand behind.

# FOUR
# MONEY AND MEANING

There comes a moment in many lives when the pursuit of money reveals its own emptiness. The promotion arrives, the salary increases, the account balance grows—and yet something essential remains unsatisfied. The achievement that was supposed to bring fulfillment brings instead a fleeting pleasure followed by a recalibrated desire for more. The finish line, once crossed, reveals another finish line beyond it, stretching toward a horizon that never arrives.

Marcus Chen had done everything right. Valedictorian in suburban Ohio, economics degree from a prestigious university, then an offer from a top investment bank. By thirty-two, he was a vice president earning seven figures. His parents, immigrants who had worked sixteen-hour days running a dry cleaning business, wept with pride.

His apartment overlooked Central Park. His suits were bespoke. His bonus alone exceeded what his parents had earned in a decade. By every external measure, he had arrived.

Yet Marcus found himself, on a Sunday evening in late autumn, sitting in his immaculate living room feeling something he could not name. Not depression exactly—he was too driven for that. Not regret —he had made no obvious mistakes. It was more like a question that had no answer, a hunger that had no food. He had spent a decade climbing, and now that he had reached the height he had imagined as a young man, he discovered that the view was not what he had expected.

He poured himself an expensive whiskey he did not particularly want and wondered when, exactly, he had stopped asking questions that mattered.

THIS EXPERIENCE IS SO common it has become almost cliché: the successful professional wondering "Is this all there is?", the wealthy retiree discovering that money cannot purchase meaning. Yet its frequency does not diminish its importance. It points to something fundamental about the relationship between money and the deeper currents of human life.

The previous chapters examined money from the outside in: what money is, how it flows through economies, how psychology shapes our relationship with it. This chapter reverses direction, examining money from the inside out. What role does money play in the search for meaning? How does the pursuit of wealth interact with the pursuit of a life worth living?

These questions might seem out of place in a book about personal finance. Most financial advice concerns itself with quantities—how much to save, where to invest. It treats money as a purely technical matter. But this approach, however necessary, is insufficient. Money is embedded in the deepest questions of existence: What is a good life? What truly matters? How should I spend my brief time on earth?

**The Meaning Crisis**

We live in an age of unprecedented material abundance and widespread spiritual poverty. More people have more wealth than at any point in history. Global poverty has declined dramatically. Lifespans have lengthened. By any material measure, we are extraordinarily fortunate.

Yet surveys consistently reveal high levels of anxiety, depression, and loneliness. These afflictions have been climbing in developed nations, particularly among younger generations who have known nothing but abundance. Wealth, it seems, has not purchased wellbeing.

This is what some thinkers have called the "meaning crisis"—a widespread difficulty in finding purpose and significance in modern life. Traditional sources of meaning—religion, community, inherited tradition—have weakened for many people. What has replaced them, often, is consumption. We shop to fill the void. We pursue money as a proxy for meaning we cannot find elsewhere.

Ludwig von Mises understood that value is radically subjective—no external observer can determine what something is worth to another person. If value is subjective, then no one can tell you what your life should mean. This is your responsibility alone.

But Mises also understood that humans act purposefully, always directing behavior toward goals they believe will improve their situation. Every choice reveals a preference. Every action expresses a value. The question is not whether you have values but whether your values are truly your own or merely absorbed from your environment.

This is where Nietzsche's challenge becomes urgent. He distinguished between those who create their own values and those who merely inherit them. Money, in modern life, often functions as a substitute for genuine valuation. Rather than asking "What do I truly want?", we ask "What pays well? What will others admire?" We outsource our valuation to the market, to social expectations, to whatever is conventional.

. . .

ELENA VASQUEZ HAD BEEN a promising cellist. At seventeen, she performed at Carnegie Hall. Her teachers spoke of a possible career. Music was not just what she did; it was who she was.

Her father encouraged her to "have something to fall back on." She double-majored in music and finance. After graduation, she faced a choice: audition for orchestras, accepting years of uncertainty and modest pay, or take an analyst position that would pay more in her first year than her music teachers earned in three.

She told herself she would do consulting for a few years, save money, then return to music.

That was eleven years ago. Her cello sits in a closet. She has not opened it in four years. Sometimes she dreams of playing and wakes with her fingers curved as if around an absent neck. She is a senior manager now, respected, well-compensated.

She tells herself she made the right choice. She tells herself this often.

THE SUBSTITUTION of money for meaning does not work. It cannot work, because money and meaning operate in different registers. Money is quantitative, fungible, external. Meaning is qualitative, particular, internal. The attempt to purchase meaning with money is a category error.

**What Money Can and Cannot Buy**

Money can purchase comfort—shelter, sufficient food, relief from physical suffering. It can purchase security—protection against catastrophes. It can purchase time—freedom from labor. It can purchase options—the capacity to travel, learn, change direction. These are not trivial benefits. Anyone who has experienced genuine poverty knows that lack of money brings real suffering.

But there is much money cannot buy. It cannot buy love—though it can attract those who love money rather than you. It cannot buy friendship—though it can attract those who want access to what you have. It cannot buy respect—though it can buy deference and flattery, which are not the same. It cannot buy meaning—though it can buy distraction from its absence.

Daniel Kahneman's research illuminates this territory. His study with Angus Deaton found that emotional wellbeing—the quality of everyday experience—rises with income but plateaus at around $75,000 per year (roughly $90,000-100,000 today). Beyond this threshold, more money does not reliably produce more day-to-day happiness.

What does continue to rise with income is "life evaluation"—the sense, when you step back and assess, that your life is going well. This is the satisfaction you feel when comparing yourself to others or to expectations. It is the domain of the "remembering self," which constructs narratives about life rather than experiencing it directly.

The experiencing self—the one who actually lives each moment—does not benefit much from income beyond sufficiency. Understanding which self you are serving when you pursue additional income is essential for making choices you will not regret.

**The Colonization of the Soul**

A peculiar danger of money is its tendency to colonize areas of life where it does not belong. Money is useful as a tool, but it has a way of becoming a master. It starts as a means and becomes an end.

This colonization happens gradually, almost imperceptibly. A young person takes a job they find unfulfilling because it pays well, intending to pursue their real interests later. But lifestyle inflates to match salary. Obligations accumulate. The temporary compromise becomes permanent.

A family moves to a larger house, reasoning the children will benefit. But the mortgage requires both parents to work longer hours. Time with children shrinks. The house is spacious but the life within it is cramped.

A friendship cools because one person has advanced economically and the other has not. The inequality creates awkwardness. The relationship is sacrificed on the altar of difference.

These are examples of economic logic colonizing the soul. Areas of life that should be governed by love, loyalty, or moral commitment become governed by financial calculation. Everything gets weighed on the same scale, reduced to the same denominator of money.

The problem is not that money is bad. The problem is that when money becomes the measure of all things, things that cannot be measured by money get neglected or destroyed. How do you measure the value of a marriage? The worth of an afternoon with your child? The significance of work that helps others but pays poorly? These things matter—indeed, they may matter most—but they cannot be captured in a balance sheet.

### The Hedonic Treadmill

Part of what drives the relentless pursuit of more is hedonic adaptation. We adjust to our circumstances. What once seemed luxurious becomes normal. What once delighted becomes expected. What once was enough becomes insufficient.

A person receives a significant raise and experiences genuine pleasure. But within months, the new income becomes baseline. The hedonic boost fades, and they find themselves wanting more—the next raise, the next promotion, the next level of consumption.

Kahneman calls this the difference between experienced utility (how you feel moment to moment) and decision utility (what you choose to pursue). We pursue things we believe will make us happy, but our predictions are systematically biased. We overestimate the duration and intensity of pleasure that achievements will bring. We underestimate our capacity to adapt.

We are not pursuing a fixed target that, once reached, will satisfy us. We are pursuing a moving target that recedes as we approach it. The goalposts shift. The destination is always just ahead, never here.

What does satisfy, research suggests, are things that resist adaptation: meaningful relationships, engaging work, ongoing growth, contribution to something beyond oneself. These sources of well-being do not wear out the way material pleasures do. They deepen rather than fade.

### The Inner Economy

Just as there is an external economy of production and exchange, there is an inner economy of the soul. This inner economy involves different currencies: attention, energy, care, commitment. It has its own scarcities and abundances, its own investments and returns.

The concept helps illuminate how pursuing external wealth can impoverish us internally. Every hour spent earning money is an hour not spent elsewhere. Every unit of attention devoted to financial advancement is unavailable for other concerns.

This is not merely about time allocation. It is about what we cultivate within ourselves. The person who spends years developing skills of financial acquisition may underdevelop skills of friendship, parenting, or creative expression. The inner capacities we neglect atrophy.

Nietzsche spoke of becoming who you are—a paradoxical phrase suggesting we must create ourselves through choices and actions. The choices we make about money are choices about who we become. The person who chooses work they hate for money they do not need is becoming someone they might not wish to be.

**What Markets Value**

There is a profound difference between what markets value and what is valuable. Markets value scarcity plus demand. A thing commands a high price if it is rare and wanted. This is true whether the thing is life-saving medicine or a speculative asset with no intrinsic worth. Markets do not assess merit or moral worth. They assess willingness and ability to pay.

This means market prices often diverge wildly from genuine value. Caregiving—raising children, tending the sick, accompanying the dying—is essential to human flourishing but commands low wages or none. Financial speculation may be socially useless but commands enormous rewards. The teacher who shapes young minds earns a fraction of what the hedge fund manager earns.

None of this reflects moral judgment about relative worth. It reflects only the impersonal operation of supply and demand. Markets are not designed to reward virtue or importance.

The danger comes when we internalize market valuations as

measures of genuine worth—believing that high pay indicates high worth and low pay indicates low worth. This is to surrender your capacity for independent valuation to an impersonal mechanism that was never designed to measure what matters.

Recognizing this distinction creates space for choices markets would not validate. You can choose work that matters over work that pays. You can resist pressure to maximize income and instead optimize for meaning.

**Enough**

One of the most important concepts for a healthy relationship with money is "enough"—the point at which more ceases to add meaningfully to life, where additional wealth brings costs that exceed benefits.

This concept is surprisingly difficult to internalize. Our culture provides endless stimulation toward wanting more but little guidance toward recognizing sufficiency. Advertising exists to create dissatisfaction. Social comparison exposes us constantly to those who have more. Everything conspires against the sense that what we have is enough.

Kahneman's research on reference points is illuminating. We evaluate outcomes not in absolute terms but relative to some reference—usually our current state or the situation of others. The same objective wealth can feel like abundance or scarcity depending on the reference point.

This is why keeping up with the Joneses is such a trap. The Joneses are themselves trying to keep up with someone else. The entire chain is running without ever arriving. The only escape is to choose your own reference points deliberately.

MARGARET CHEN—MARCUS'S mother—had spent forty years running a dry cleaning business with her husband. They had arrived in Ohio with three hundred dollars and willingness to work harder than anyone else. The business never made them rich, but it put their son through school, gave them a modest house now paid off, provided stability and dignity.

When Marcus suggested they sell and retire to Florida, Margaret laughed. "What would I do there? Play bridge with strangers? Wait to die in comfort?"

She still went to the shop every day. She knew customers by name, knew their children and grandchildren, knew who was sick and who had just gotten married. The shop was not just a business; it was a node in a web of relationships, a place where she mattered to people who mattered to her.

She had enough. She had always had enough. The trick was knowing it.

DEVELOPING a personal sense of enough requires swimming against powerful cultural currents. It requires asking: How much do I actually need? What would be sufficient for a good life? At what point does pursuing more begin to undermine what I already have?

The practice of gratitude can help. Attending to what we have, rather than what we lack, shifts orientation from scarcity to abundance. It is not about pretending challenges do not exist but recognizing that the present moment may already contain conditions for a good life—if we can perceive them clearly.

**Work and Meaning**

Nowhere is the intersection of money and meaning more fraught than in work. For most people, work is the primary means of earning money and also a primary source of identity, purpose, and connection. These dimensions can align beautifully or conflict painfully.

When they align, work becomes a source of both financial security and existential satisfaction. Time spent at work is not time stolen from life but time well-lived.

When they conflict, difficult choices arise. The meaningful work may pay poorly. The well-paid work may feel empty. The person must choose between security and fulfillment—or find compromises.

What can be said generally is that the choice deserves conscious attention. Many people drift into careers for financial reasons and never revisit the choice, even when circumstances change. They remain in meaningless work long after financial necessity has passed, bound by habit or fear.

It can also be said that meaning often can be found within work that initially seems merely instrumental. The job taken for the paycheck can become engaging through mastery, through relationships, through finding ways to contribute that matter. Meaning is not only found but created. The stance we bring to work shapes the meaning we derive from it.

**Money and Relationships**

Money affects relationships in ways often unacknowledged. Financial stress is consistently cited as a leading cause of marital conflict. Disagreements about spending and saving reflect deeper differences in values. Imbalances in earning power create difficult dynamics. Secrets about money erode trust.

RACHEL AND MICHAEL TORRES had been married for twelve years, and the money fights had been constant for eleven of them. He thought she spent too freely; she thought he was needlessly anxious.

It was a therapist who helped them see what was underneath. Michael had grown up watching his parents lose their home in a recession. The fear lived in his body. When Rachel bought something unplanned, it was not the money that upset him; it was the terror of loss that her purchase awakened.

Rachel had grown up financially stable but emotionally deprived. Her parents deferred pleasure indefinitely, died with full bank accounts and empty lives. When Michael refused to spend on vacation, it was not the missed trip that upset her; it was fear they would become her parents.

Once they understood this, the fights changed. They were no longer about money. They were about fear, and fear could be discussed with compassion. They learned to say "I'm scared" instead of "You're wrong."

HEALTHY FINANCIAL RELATIONSHIPS require communication beyond numbers. Partners need to understand not just what each other wants to do with money but why. The motivations, explored with curiosity and compassion, can be understood and honored even when they create tension.

**Generosity as Practice**

One of the most reliable ways to develop a healthy relationship with money is through generosity. Giving money away—to people in need, to causes you believe in—counteracts acquisitive tendencies. It loosens the grip of attachment. It shifts orientation from accumulation to contribution.

This is not primarily about impact, though impact matters. It is about what giving does to the giver. The act of releasing money exercises different inner muscles than acquiring it. It affirms, in practice, that there are things more important than maximizing wealth. It creates the experience of sufficiency: if I can give this away, I must have enough.

Research supports what spiritual traditions have long taught: generosity is associated with wellbeing. People who give report greater happiness than those who do not, even controlling for income. Spending on others activates different psychological processes than spending on oneself—creating connection rather than isolation, meaning rather than mere pleasure.

The practice need not be dramatic. Regular giving of modest amounts, sustained over time, can shape character as effectively as occasional large gifts.

**Integrating Money and Meaning**

The goal of this chapter is not to denigrate money or suggest financial concerns are unimportant. Money matters. Financial security provides a foundation for flourishing. The practical skills of earning, saving, and investing are worth developing.

The goal is to situate money within a larger understanding of what makes life meaningful. Money is a tool—important and powerful, but a tool nonetheless. Tools are judged by usefulness in serving purposes beyond themselves.

Integrating money and meaning involves several ongoing practices. Clarity about values comes first: What actually matters to you? What would you regret not doing, not becoming? Money should serve these values, not replace them.

Awareness of tradeoffs matters equally. Every choice about money is a choice about how to live. The job that pays more requires something in exchange. Understanding these tradeoffs allows for deliberate choices rather than drift.

Regular recalibration is necessary because circumstances change. What made sense at one stage of life may not make sense at another.

Cultivation of non-monetary sources of meaning protects against colonization of the soul. Relationships, creative pursuits, service to others—these sources of meaning do not depend on wealth and often are more reliable in providing lasting satisfaction.

Development of a sense of enough liberates from the endless treadmill. Knowing when sufficient has been reached creates freedom. This is not about limiting ambition but directing it toward what matters.

**The Examined Financial Life**

Socrates declared that the unexamined life is not worth living. The same might be said of the unexamined financial life. Money is too central to modern existence to be handled on autopilot.

This chapter has explored questions that examination might involve. What is money for? What can it buy and what can it not? How does its pursuit affect my inner life? Am I using money, or is money using me? Have I found my sense of enough? Is my work aligned with my values?

These questions have no final answers. They must be asked

repeatedly across a lifetime. But asking them creates the possibility of a financial life integrated with meaning rather than severed from it.

MARCUS CHEN LEFT New York three years after that Sunday evening in his apartment. He did not leave finance entirely—he had skills and obligations. But he moved to a smaller city, took a position that paid less but demanded less, began teaching financial literacy at a community center on weekends.

His income was a third of what it had been. His apartment was smaller. His suits no longer came from tailors. And yet something had shifted. He felt, for the first time in years, that his life was his own.

His mother, watching her son at Thanksgiving, saw something in his eyes that had been missing for years. He was present. He was there.

"You seem different," she said.

"I am different," he said. "I'm finally asking the right questions."

THE CHAPTERS that follow will turn to practical matters: how to earn, save, spend, invest, and protect wealth. These technical skills are necessary for financial competence. But they are not sufficient for financial wisdom. Wisdom requires the larger perspective this chapter has attempted to provide—an understanding of money's proper place in a life oriented toward what truly matters.

Money is a powerful servant and a terrible master. The choice of which role it plays is, ultimately, yours.

## SUMMARY: **Key Takeaways from Chapter Four**

**The Meaning Crisis:** Material abundance has not produced spiritual wellbeing. Traditional sources of meaning have weakened, and consumption often substitutes for genuine purpose. Money becomes a proxy for meaning we cannot find elsewhere—a substitution that cannot work because money and meaning operate in different registers.

**What Money Can and Cannot Buy:** Money purchases comfort, security, time, and options—genuine goods that matter. But it cannot buy love, friendship, respect, or meaning. Research shows emotional wellbeing plateaus around $90,000-100,000 in today's dollars; beyond this, more money does not reliably produce more day-to-day happiness.

**The Colonization of the Soul:** Money has a tendency to become master rather than tool, expanding from one consideration among many to the only consideration that counts. Temporary compromises become permanent. Economic logic invades domains that should be governed by love, loyalty, or moral commitment.

**The Hedonic Treadmill:** We adapt to our circumstances. Raises and acquisitions produce temporary pleasure that fades as the new level becomes baseline. We chase a moving target that recedes as we approach it. What resists adaptation—relationships, engaging work, contribution—provides more lasting satisfaction.

**The Inner Economy:** Every hour spent earning money is an hour not spent elsewhere. The skills and dispositions we cultivate through our work shape who we become. Financial choices are choices about character.

**Markets and Value:** Market prices reflect willingness to pay, not moral worth or genuine importance. Internalizing market valuations as measures of human worth surrenders your capacity for independent valuation.

**Enough:** Developing a personal sense of sufficiency is essential but difficult in a culture that stimulates endless wanting. Choosing your own reference points deliberately, rather than absorbing them from your environment, is the only escape from the endless race.

**Work, Relationships, and Generosity:** Meaning can be found or created within work. Money conflicts in relationships often reflect deeper fears and values that deserve compassionate exploration. Generosity counteracts acquisitive tendencies and creates experiences of abundance.

**Integration:** Money should serve your values, not replace them. Regular examination of whether your financial life aligns with what matters allows for adjustment when they have drifted apart. The goal is a financial life integrated with meaning—using money as a powerful servant rather than allowing it to become a terrible master.

# PART 3

# BUILDING THE FOUNDATION

*Earning, saving, and managing cash flow*

# FIVE
# THE ART OF EARNING

All wealth begins with production. Before money can be saved, invested, or spent, it must first be earned. And earning, in a market economy, means providing value that others are willing to pay for. This simple truth—that income flows to those who serve the needs and wants of others—is the foundation upon which all personal finance rests.

Yet earning is not merely a technical matter of matching skills to markets. It is deeply intertwined with questions of identity, purpose, and meaning. How we earn affects who we become. The work we choose shapes our days, our relationships, our sense of self. Earning is where economic life and inner life intersect most directly, where the abstract logic of markets meets the concrete reality of human experience.

This chapter examines earning from multiple angles: the economic principles that determine income, the practical strategies for increasing it, the psychological dimensions that affect our relationship with work, and the ethical considerations that arise when we must choose how to make our living.

**The Economics of Earning**

In a market economy, income is not distributed according to need, merit, or moral worth. It is determined by supply and demand—by what buyers are willing to pay and how many sellers are offering similar services. This is neither just nor unjust in any cosmic sense; it is simply how markets function.

Ludwig von Mises understood this with particular clarity. In his analysis, the market is a process of social cooperation in which individuals, pursuing their own ends, generate prices that coordinate their activities. Wages, like all prices, emerge from this process. They reflect the subjective valuations of all market participants—employers assessing the value workers can add, workers assessing the value of their time and effort, both operating within constraints of knowledge, uncertainty, and competing opportunities.

This means that your income depends not on how hard you work, how much you need the money, or how virtuous you are, but on how much value you provide to others who can pay for it. A teacher may work as hard as a hedge fund manager and contribute more to society by many measures, but the hedge fund manager earns more because financial markets value and can pay for their services at higher rates.

Understanding this is liberating in a way. It removes the moralistic baggage that often accompanies discussions of income. High earners are not necessarily better people; they are providing services that markets happen to value highly. Low earners are not necessarily failing; they may be providing services that markets undervalue or that serve populations without resources to pay. The market's valuation is information, not judgment.

This understanding also clarifies what is required to earn more. Since income depends on value provided to paying customers, increasing income requires some combination of four paths.

The first path—providing more value—involves becoming better at what you do. Skill development, knowledge acquisition, and improved execution all increase the value you can offer. A more skilled programmer writes better code. A more knowledgeable consultant gives better advice. Enhanced capability translates to enhanced value, which can translate to enhanced income.

The second path—reaching more people—involves scale. The author who sells a million books earns more than one who sells a thousand, even if the quality is identical. Technology has dramatically expanded opportunities for scale, allowing individuals to reach global markets in ways previously available only to large organizations.

The third path—serving those who can pay more—involves moving toward markets with greater resources. The corporate lawyer earns more than the public defender not because corporate law is more difficult but because corporate clients have more money. This is not a moral judgment; it is a market reality.

The fourth path—providing value that others cannot—involves differentiation. When you offer something rare, you face less competition and can command higher prices. This might come from unique skills, specialized knowledge, or unusual combinations of capabilities. The goal is not necessarily to be the best but to be sufficiently different that direct comparison becomes difficult.

These paths are not mutually exclusive. The highest earners often combine several: exceptional skill, broad reach, wealthy clientele, and distinctive positioning.

**Human Capital**

Economists speak of "human capital" to describe the skills, knowledge, and capabilities that enable earning. Like financial capital, human capital can be accumulated, invested, and deployed to generate returns. Unlike financial capital, it cannot be separated from the person who possesses it.

The concept illuminates several important truths. First, earning capacity is an asset—often the most valuable asset a person possesses. A young professional with strong skills and decades of working years ahead may have human capital worth millions in present value, even if their bank account contains only thousands. This asset deserves the same careful attention we give to financial assets.

Second, human capital requires investment. Skills do not develop automatically; they require time, effort, and often money. Education, training, practice, mentorship—these are investments in human capital, exchanging present resources for future earning capacity.

Third, human capital depreciates if not maintained. Skills become obsolete. Knowledge becomes outdated. Industries transform. The professional who stops learning eventually finds their capabilities less valuable in a changing market.

Fourth, human capital is risky in ways financial capital is not. An injury or illness can destroy earning capacity in an instant. A technological shift can render entire skill sets obsolete. Diversification of human capital—developing multiple marketable skills, maintaining professional networks, staying adaptable—provides some protection against these risks.

Mises would remind us that the value of human capital, like all value, is subjective and forward-looking. It depends on what others will be willing to pay in the future for the services that capital enables. The skills that command high wages today may be automated tomorrow. Investing in human capital requires not just current assessment but prediction about future market conditions.

This uncertainty counsels humility about career planning. The person who optimizes narrowly for current market conditions may find themselves stranded when conditions change. Some investment in breadth and adaptability—even at the cost of specialized expertise—provides insurance against unpredictable shifts.

JAMES OKONKWO HAD SPENT fifteen years becoming one of the best print journalists in Chicago. He had won awards, broken important stories, built a reputation that opened doors. His human capital was substantial—but it was concentrated in an industry that was collapsing.

By forty-two, he had been laid off twice. The second time, he sat in his apartment cycling between panic and despair. Everything he knew how to do well was becoming worthless. The market did not care about his awards. It cared about what people would pay for, and fewer people were paying for what he produced.

A friend suggested he learn to make videos—short documentaries for online platforms. James resisted. He was a writer, not a filmmaker. The suggestion felt like an insult to his craft. But eventually, desperation overcame pride. He bought a cheap camera. He watched tutorials. He made terrible videos and then less terrible ones.

Three years later, his documentary series on urban farming had been viewed twelve million times. He was earning more than he ever had in newspapers, with more creative freedom. The skills he had developed as a journalist—finding stories, earning trust, explaining complexity—transferred more readily than he had expected.

"I thought I was a newspaper reporter," he told a journalism class years later. "But that was just one expression of something deeper. I'm a storyteller. The medium was never the point."

## CAREER AS INVESTMENT

Viewing career decisions as investments clarifies choices that might otherwise seem confusing. Like financial investments, career choices involve tradeoffs between risk and return, between present sacrifice and future gain.

The decision to pursue additional education is an investment decision. It requires calculating costs (tuition, foregone earnings, time) against expected benefits (higher future earnings, better opportunities, intrinsic satisfaction). Research on returns to education shows generally positive but highly variable results. The return depends on field of study, institution, individual capabilities, and labor market conditions. Some graduate degrees pay for themselves many times over; others represent financial losses never recovered.

The decision to change jobs or industries is also an investment decision, involving assessment of current trajectory against alternatives, estimating costs and risks of transition, judging likely outcomes under uncertainty. A higher salary elsewhere might come with worse long-term prospects or hidden costs in stress and time.

The decision to start a business is perhaps the clearest investment decision in the career realm. It typically requires investment of both financial capital and human capital. The potential returns are higher than employment but so are the risks.

What all these decisions share is the structure of investment: sacrificing something certain now for something uncertain later, with the goal of improving overall position. Understanding this structure brings discipline to career thinking, encouraging explicit consideration of costs, benefits, risks, and alternatives.

But career decisions are not only investments. They are also choices about how to spend irreplaceable time, about what kind of person to become. A complete approach integrates financial analysis with attention to meaning, values, and flourishing.

**Specialization and Trade**

One of the most powerful principles in economics is comparative advantage: individuals benefit from specializing in what they do relatively well and trading with others who specialize differently. You need not be the best at something to benefit from specializing in it. You need only be relatively better at that thing than at other things, compared to others.

This principle has several practical implications. First, it suggests focusing career development on areas of genuine strength. Attempting to be good at everything leads to being excellent at nothing. The market rewards excellence in specific areas more than mediocrity across many.

Second, it suggests looking for unusual combinations. Comparative advantage often emerges from combinations of skills that are individually common but rarely found together. The engineer who can also sell, the scientist who can also communicate, the analyst who can also lead—these combinations create value precisely because they are rare.

Third, it suggests the importance of knowing your own capabilities clearly. Comparative advantage depends on accurate self-assessment. Overestimating abilities leads to specializing in wrong areas. Underestimating them leaves value on the table.

**The Value of Networks**

Income does not flow only from individual capability. It flows also from relationships, connections, and positioning within networks of exchange. The same skills can command vastly different incomes depending on access to opportunity, and access often depends on who you know.

This is sometimes dismissed as unfair—a departure from pure meritocracy. But networks are not merely channels of favoritism. They are information systems. They reduce uncertainty in a world where capabilities are hard to assess and trustworthiness is crucial. When an employer hires through a referral, they use the referrer's knowledge to supplement their own.

Networks also enable collaboration that creates value beyond what individuals could produce alone. The venture capitalist who connects an entrepreneur with key hires and customers adds value beyond capital. The professional who facilitates introductions lubricates transactions that might otherwise not occur.

Building and maintaining networks is therefore an investment in earning capacity. This investment involves time and attention—staying in touch, attending events, participating in communities, being helpful without immediate expectation of return. It also involves building a reputation for competence and integrity, since networks function on trust.

The quality of networks matters more than quantity. A handful of deep relationships with people who know your work and trust your judgment is more valuable than hundreds of superficial connections. But breadth also has value: weak ties often provide access to information and opportunities that strong ties cannot.

For many people, networking feels distasteful—too transactional, too focused on using others. This discomfort is worth examining. Good networking is not manipulation; it is mutual helpfulness extended over time. When networking feels exploitative, the problem may be in the approach, not the activity itself.

**Negotiation and Compensation**

Income does not adjust automatically to reflect value provided. It must be negotiated—explicitly or implicitly, at hiring and throughout a career. The skilled negotiator earns more than the unskilled, even with identical capabilities.

This is uncomfortable for many people. Negotiation involves conflict. It requires advocating for oneself, which can feel immodest. It involves risk of rejection. Many people, particularly those from backgrounds where assertiveness was discouraged, find negotiation deeply aversive.

But avoiding negotiation is costly. Studies consistently show that those who negotiate starting salaries end up significantly ahead over a career, as raises build on the negotiated base.

PRIYA SHARMA HAD NEVER NEGOTIATED anything in her life. Her parents, both academics, had considered such discussions unseemly. When she received her first job offer after business school, she accepted immediately, grateful to be wanted.

Three years later, she discovered that a male colleague hired the same month, with the same degree and similar performance reviews, earned eighteen percent more. He had negotiated. She had not.

The discovery burned. But what burned more was recognizing her own complicity. No one had forbidden her from negotiating. She had forbidden herself, internalizing rules that served others' interests. The company had offered what she would accept, and she had accepted immediately.

Her next review, she prepared for weeks. She researched market rates. She documented her contributions. She practiced asking for more until the words no longer caught in her throat. When the conversation came, her manager looked surprised—Priya had never pushed back before. But he also looked, she thought, slightly more respectful. She got most of what she asked for.

"The thing I learned," she told her younger sister, "is that no one will value you more than you value yourself. If you won't advocate for your own worth, why would anyone else?"

SEVERAL PRINCIPLES IMPROVE NEGOTIATION OUTCOMES. Understanding your alternatives is paramount—the best leverage is a genuine option to walk away. Before negotiating, develop alternatives that strengthen your position. Knowing the market matters equally: research what others with similar capabilities earn, establishing a reference point and providing justification for requests.

When possible, letting the other party make the first offer creates advantage. The first number anchors the entire process. If you state a number below what they would have offered, you leave value on the table. Focus on interests rather than positions—the demand for a specific salary is less effective than exploration of underlying interests like security, recognition, or growth opportunity. Often creative solutions can satisfy both parties better than either initial position.

Most importantly, maintain relationship while advocating interests. The most effective negotiators create value through collaboration rather than merely claiming value through competition. They find ways to make both parties better off.

**Multiple Income Streams**

Reliance on a single income source creates vulnerability. If that source disappears, the entire financial foundation is at risk. Diversification of income, like diversification of investments, reduces this risk.

Multiple income streams can take various forms: a primary job supplemented by freelance work, a career combined with investment income, a business with several product lines, a professional practice alongside teaching or writing. The specific form matters less than the principle.

Beyond risk reduction, multiple income streams often create synergies. The teacher who also consults brings practical experience into the classroom. The consultant who also writes builds reputation that attracts clients. These synergies can make the combination more valuable than the sum of parts.

Developing multiple income streams requires investment of time that might otherwise go to primary income. This tradeoff must be managed carefully. Diversification pursued too aggressively can prevent excellence in any area. The goal is to optimize the overall portfolio—primary income sufficient for needs, secondary income providing security and optionality.

For many people, the path begins with converting existing skills into additional revenue. The professional with marketable expertise can consult or teach or write. Starting with what you already know minimizes additional investment required.

**Entrepreneurship**

Entrepreneurship represents a distinctive approach to earning—one that involves not just providing labor but organizing production, bearing uncertainty, and capturing the returns (or losses) that result. The entrepreneur accepts unhedged exposure to outcomes in exchange for possibilities that employment cannot provide.

Mises placed the entrepreneur at the center of economic theory. The entrepreneur perceives opportunities others miss, organizes resources to exploit them, and either profits from success or absorbs losses from failure. Entrepreneurship is not about risk-taking per se; it is about judgment under uncertainty, about imagining possible futures and acting on those imaginings.

The returns to entrepreneurship, when it succeeds, can vastly exceed employment returns. The entrepreneur captures not just wages for labor but profits from judgment and organization. When they are right about opportunities others missed, gains can be enormous.

But risks are commensurate. Most new ventures fail. The entrepreneur who is wrong absorbs the losses—financial, temporal, psychological. What is certain is that variance is higher than employment.

Entrepreneurship also offers non-financial returns: autonomy to direct one's own efforts, opportunity to build something new, engagement that comes from building something you believe in. For some people, these returns make entrepreneurship preferable even when financial calculus is unfavorable.

The decision to pursue entrepreneurship should be made with clear eyes about both potential and risks. The romanticization of entrepreneurship in contemporary culture obscures how difficult and uncertain it actually is. But so does excessive caution that leads capable people to remain in employment when they could create more value—and find more fulfillment—building something of their own.

**The Ethics of Earning**

Not all ways of earning money are equally good. The market provides income for activities that range from deeply beneficial to actively harmful. The question of how to earn—not just how much—is inescapably ethical.

Nietzsche would approach this in terms of self-creation and affirmation of life. What kind of person are you becoming through your work? Does your earning express strength and creativity? Or does it express conformity and denial of life? The work we do shapes us as much as we shape it. The salesperson who spends years manipulating customers becomes practiced in manipulation. The craftsperson who spends years perfecting their work becomes practiced in excellence. These formations happen gradually but they are real.

The market will pay you to do things that help others, harm others, or are neutral. It does not distinguish. The pharmaceutical company that develops life-saving drugs and the one that aggressively markets addictive opioids both generate profits. The choice of which activities to engage in is yours.

This does not mean only obviously altruistic work is ethically acceptable. Most work is neither heroic nor villainous; it simply provides goods or services people want. The accountant, the plumber, the software developer—these are not saving the world, but neither are they harming it.

But there are edges where ethical questions become pointed. Industries that profit from addiction or manipulation. Work that involves deception, even if legal. Roles that require compromising integrity. These situations call for judgment that economic analysis cannot provide.

DAVID CHEN HAD BEEN a successful marketing executive for a vaping company. The pay was exceptional, the work interesting, and he told himself he was marketing to adults who made their own choices. The product was legal. His work was legal.

Then his daughter turned fourteen and came home talking about kids at school who vaped in the bathrooms. She asked him what he did at work. He found himself giving a vague answer, and the vagueness revealed something he had been avoiding.

He did not quit immediately—there were mortgages and tuition and practical realities. But he began looking for other positions. When he finally left for a job that paid thirty percent less marketing medical devices, he felt something shift.

"I'm not a saint," he told his wife. "The new company isn't saving the world either. But I can tell my daughter what I do without editing. I can look at my work and not need to look away. That's worth something. It turns out it's worth about thirty percent of my salary."

MISES WOULD INSIST that such judgments are subjective—that no economist can determine correct values for another person. This is true. But it does not mean judgments are arbitrary or all choices equal. Each person must make their own evaluation, but the evaluation matters. Living with integrity requires that how you earn aligns with what you believe.

The costs of ethical compromise are not only moral; they are psychological. The person who spends working hours in activities they cannot respect often experiences dissonance in their sense of self, relationships, and mental health.

**Work-Life Integration**

The phrase "work-life balance" suggests work and life are separate domains to be kept in equilibrium. But for many people, this framing misleads. Work is not outside life; it is part of life. The question is not how to balance them but how to integrate them into a coherent whole.

This integration looks different for different people and life stages. The young professional building a career may rightly devote enormous energy to work, knowing this investment will pay dividends for decades. The parent with young children may need to constrain work to protect family time. The older person approaching retirement may shift energy from earning to other pursuits.

What can be said generally is that extreme imbalance in either direction causes problems. The person who devotes everything to work often finds relationships atrophying, health declining, sense of meaning narrowing. The person who devotes nothing to productive work often finds themselves adrift, without structure or the self-respect that comes from adding value.

Daniel Kahneman's research illuminates these dynamics. The experiencing self is affected by quality of daily experience, which work heavily shapes. Long commutes, conflictual workplaces, boring tasks, and lack of autonomy reduce experienced wellbeing. Engaging work, pleasant colleagues, meaningful tasks, and appropriate challenge enhance it.

The remembering self cares about achievement, progress, and narrative coherence. Work that contributes to goals, involves growth, and fits into a story of a life well-lived satisfies the remembering self even when particular moments are difficult.

Integrating work and life well requires attention to both selves. The experiencing self needs work that is not miserable, that contains engagement and satisfaction, that does not consume so much time nothing else remains. The remembering self needs work that is going somewhere, that contributes to a life that makes sense.

**Earning Over a Lifetime**

Earning follows patterns over a life. In early career, income is typically low but growing. Skills are being developed, reputation built, human capital accumulated. This is the investment phase, when sacrifice of present income for future capacity often makes sense.

In mid-career, earnings typically peak. Accumulated human capital pays its highest dividends. Responsibilities are often heaviest. This is the harvest phase, when early investments produce returns.

In late career and retirement, earning typically declines or ends. Human capital depreciates as skills become less current. The question shifts from earning more to deploying accumulated resources wisely.

Understanding this arc helps with planning at each stage. In early career, it justifies accepting lower current income for investments in future earning capacity. In mid-career, it highlights the importance of capturing peak earning years while building assets that will fund later life. In late career, it suggests planning the transition from earning to spending.

The arc is not fixed. Some careers peak early; some late. The gig economy and longer lifespans are changing traditional patterns. But the general shape—investing early, harvesting in the middle, spending later—provides a useful framework.

**Practical Wisdom for Earning More**

Certain principles tend to increase earning over time. The foundation is continuous investment in human capital. Learning should not end with formal education. The best earners continuously develop capabilities through reading, courses, practice, and challenges that stretch them. This investment compounds, creating ever-greater capability gaps between those who invest and those who coast.

Closely related is developing rare and valuable skills. Following Mises's insight that value is subjective and determined by market participants, the wise person focuses on skills both rare and in demand. Common skills face competition that suppresses compensation. Rare skills command premiums.

Reputation compounds in ways that mirror financial returns. Excellent work builds reputation; reputation attracts opportunities for more excellent work. Early career is the time to prioritize reputation-building, even at the cost of current compensation.

Cultivating relationships expands opportunity. Investment in relationships with people who can help you grow—mentors who guide, peers who challenge, connections who open doors—pays dividends for decades. Being genuinely helpful without immediate expectation of return is not merely ethical but strategic.

Positioning matters as much as capability. Seek situations where contributions are scalable—where you create value for many rather than one at a time. Seek situations where you participate in upside rather than just receiving fixed compensation. Seek situations where you build assets that continue producing even when you stop working.

Negotiate deliberately. Don't accept the first offer without consideration. Research market rates. Develop alternatives. Small differences in negotiated compensation compound over a career into large differences in lifetime earnings.

Manage career transitions actively rather than drifting with circumstance. Periodically assess whether your current trajectory is best available, and make changes when better options emerge. The costs of inertia accumulate; benefits of active management compound.

These principles are not equally applicable to everyone. Circumstances differ; personalities differ; priorities differ. But they provide a framework from which to draw based on individual situation.

**Conclusion**

Earning is where the abstract meets the concrete, where economic principles take on flesh in the daily reality of work. The core truth is simple: income flows from value provided to those who can pay. Increasing income requires increasing value, reaching more people, serving those with more resources, or differentiating from competitors. This is the market logic that shapes earning.

But earning is more than market logic. It is how we spend our days, what we contribute to the world, who we become through work. Nietzsche understood that we create ourselves through actions, that there is no essential self waiting to be discovered but rather a self forged through choices and consequences. The choices we make about earning are among the most important acts of self-creation we undertake.

Kahneman would add the empirical dimension: how we earn affects wellbeing in ways we often fail to predict. The high-paying job with the miserable commute and toxic boss may look good on paper but feel terrible in practice. The lower-paying work that engages us may produce more actual happiness than its modest salary suggests. Understanding what actually makes us flourish—rather than what we think should—is essential for earning wisely.

The goal is integration: earning that is both economically effective and personally meaningful, that generates resources for the life you want while constituting, in itself, a life worth living. This integration requires clarity about what you value, honesty about tradeoffs, and willingness to make choices that purely economic thinking might not recommend.

SUMMARY: **Key Takeaways from Chapter Three**

**The Economics of Earning:** Income depends not on hard work, need, or virtue, but on value provided to those who can pay for it. The market's valuation is information, not moral judgment. Increasing income requires some combination of providing more value, reaching more people, serving those with greater resources, or differentiating from competitors.

**Human Capital:** Your earning capacity is an asset—often your most valuable one—that requires continuous investment and maintenance. Skills depreciate if not maintained. Diversification of human capital provides protection against the risk that any single skill set becomes obsolete.

**Career as Investment:** Career decisions involve tradeoffs between risk and return, present sacrifice and future gain. Viewing these choices through an investment lens brings discipline to career thinking, but a complete approach also considers meaning, values, and flourishing.

**Comparative Advantage:** Focus development on areas of genuine strength rather than attempting to be good at everything. Unusual combinations of individually common skills often create distinctive value because they are rare.

**Networks:** Access to opportunity depends significantly on relationships and connections. Good networking is mutual helpfulness extended over time, not manipulation. Quality of relationships matters more than quantity.

**Negotiation:** Income must be negotiated; it does not adjust automatically to reflect value. Those who negotiate earn significantly more over a career. Key principles include understanding your alternatives, knowing market rates, focusing on interests rather than positions, and maintaining relationship while advocating for yourself.

**Multiple Income Streams:** Diversification of income reduces vulnerability and often creates synergies. The goal is not to maximize the number of streams but to optimize the overall portfolio.

**Ethics of Earning:** Not all ways of earning are equally good. The work we do shapes who we become. Living with integrity requires that how you earn aligns with what you believe. The costs of ethical compromise are psychological as well as moral.

**Work-Life Integration:** Work is part of life, not separate from it. Extreme imbalance in either direction causes problems. The experiencing self needs work that is not miserable; the remembering self needs work that is going somewhere.

**Earning Over a Lifetime:** Earning typically follows an arc —investing early, harvesting in the middle, spending later. Understanding this pattern helps with planning at each stage.

# SIX
# THE ART OF SPENDING

The moment money leaves your possession, it reveals what you truly value. Not what you say you value, not what you believe you should value, but what you actually value when faced with the concrete choice of exchanging limited resources for something in the world. Spending is where financial life becomes moral life, where economic abstractions resolve into the particular texture of how you live.

This chapter examines spending not as a technical problem of budgeting—though practical wisdom has its place—but as a domain of human choice that deserves philosophical attention. How should we think about the endless decisions that constitute our spending lives? What does economics reveal about these choices, and what does it obscure? How can we spend in ways that serve our flourishing rather than undermining it?

The answers are less obvious than they might appear. Spending well is genuinely difficult, and the difficulty is not merely a matter of willpower or information. It involves deep questions about what constitutes a good life, how we relate to our future selves, what we owe to others, and how we navigate a commercial culture designed to influence our choices in ways we rarely perceive.

**The Economics of Consumption**

In the framework of economic theory, spending is straightforward. The consumer has preferences, faces prices, and chooses the combination of goods and services that maximizes utility given their budget constraint. This model, elegant and powerful, has generated enormous insight into how markets function.

But Ludwig von Mises understood that the apparent simplicity of this model conceals profound complexity. Preferences are not given from outside; they are formed, changed, and sometimes contradictory within the same person. The "utility" that economists invoke is not a measurable substance but a way of describing the fact that people choose—that they reveal, through their choices, what they prefer in that moment, in that context, with that information.

What remains true and important in the economic framework is the reality of tradeoffs. Every dollar spent on one thing is a dollar not spent on another. Every choice to consume now is a choice not to save for later. The budget constraint, whatever its level, forces choices that reveal priorities. This forcing is not merely a regrettable limitation; it is the mechanism through which value is expressed and discovered.

The economic perspective also illuminates how prices coordinate spending decisions across an entire economy. When you buy bread, you are participating in a vast network of cooperation that brings together farmers, millers, bakers, truckers, and retailers—none of whom know you or care about you personally, but all of whom serve your needs because prices make it profitable for them to do so.

Understanding this system breeds a certain gratitude. The abundance available to ordinary people in market economies is historically unprecedented. Options that would have been unimaginable luxuries for kings a few centuries ago—fresh fruit in winter, instant global communication, pain-free dentistry—are now available to the masses. Spending is not merely depleting resources; it is participating in and benefiting from the greatest engine of material prosperity ever created.

### What Spending Cannot Buy

Yet the economic perspective, for all its insight, is radically incomplete when it comes to understanding spending as a human activity. It tells us that people choose what they prefer, but it cannot tell us what they should prefer. It analyzes efficiency in satisfying wants but remains silent on which wants are worth satisfying.

The most important things in life cannot be purchased. Love, friendship, meaning, self-respect, integrity, wisdom—these are not for sale, and no amount of spending can secure them. This is not a pious platitude but a practical truth with profound implications. Money is a tool for acquiring certain goods, but the deepest goods lie outside its reach.

This does not mean that money is unimportant. Material sufficiency matters. The person struggling to afford food and shelter faces deprivations that money could relieve. Health care, education, security, opportunity—all of these have monetary dimensions. Pretending that money does not matter is a luxury available only to those who have enough of it.

The point, rather, is that money's importance is bounded. Beyond a certain level of material sufficiency, additional spending contributes less and less to genuine flourishing. The research is consistent: income correlates with wellbeing up to a point, after which the relationship weakens dramatically. The difference between poverty and middle-class security is enormous; the difference between affluence and great wealth is modest at best.

Kahneman's work is particularly illuminating here. He distinguishes between life evaluation—how people judge their lives when they reflect on them—and emotional wellbeing—how people feel as they live their days. Income affects life evaluation substantially and continuously; people with more money report higher satisfaction when asked to rate their lives. But emotional wellbeing plateaus much earlier. Beyond roughly $75,000 to $100,000 in household income (in contemporary American terms, adjusted for location), additional income has little effect on daily emotional experience.

This finding has profound implications. If what we ultimately care about is how we feel as we live our lives, then spending beyond the point of comfortable sufficiency should be viewed skeptically. The additional consumption may raise our assessment of our lives in the abstract while doing little to improve our actual lived experience.

**The Psychology of Spending**

Understanding how humans actually make spending decisions requires moving beyond the rational actor model of economics into the messier territory of psychology. We are not the calculating optimizers that textbooks describe. We are creatures of habit, emotion, social influence, and cognitive limitation, making countless small decisions that aggregate into patterns we may never consciously choose.

Kahneman's distinction between System 1 and System 2 thinking is essential here. Most spending decisions are made by System 1—fast, automatic, intuitive. We grab the familiar brand, click the suggested purchase, respond to the sale sign, buy what our friends are buying. These decisions feel effortless because they bypass deliberation. They are efficient for routine choices but vulnerable to manipulation and error.

System 2—slow, deliberate, analytical—is what we imagine ourselves using when we think about "making decisions." But System 2 is lazy. It requires effort and consumes limited cognitive resources. For most of the hundreds of small spending decisions we make each week, System 2 never engages. We default to habit, impulse, and environmental cues.

This has practical implications. If you want to change your spending patterns, changing your environment and habits is more effective than trying to exercise willpower in each moment of choice. The person who cancels their cable subscription does not have to resist watching television every evening; the option is simply gone. The person who automates savings does not have to choose to save each month; the default handles it. The person who avoids entering stores where they tend to overspend does not have to resist temptation they never encounter.

The hedonic treadmill presents another psychological challenge. We adapt to new levels of consumption with remarkable speed. The new car that thrills us in the first week becomes merely normal within months. The larger house that seemed so spacious becomes cluttered and ordinary. The raise that felt like a windfall gets absorbed into a slightly higher lifestyle that feels no more satisfying than what came before.

This adaptation is asymmetric in ways worth understanding. We adapt more completely to positive changes than to negative ones. The pleasure of gaining fades more quickly than the pain of losing. Losses loom larger than gains. This asymmetry has implications for spending: the pleasure of acquiring is fleeting, but the pain of giving up what we have become accustomed to is lasting.

MARGARET HOLLOWAY HAD DONE everything right, by the standards of her peers. The house in the good suburb, the luxury cars, the private schools, the club membership, the vacations that photographed beautifully. At fifty-three, she and her husband had accumulated what would have seemed, to their younger selves, a dream life.

But the dream had a peculiar emptiness at its center. The house required constant maintenance and worry. The cars were merely transportation dressed in status anxiety. The schools were fine, but her children seemed no happier than she had been in public school. The club was an obligation as much as a pleasure. The vacations were exhausting performances of leisure.

The turning point came during a power outage that lasted three days. No internet, no television, no work. Just candles and conversation and board games with her children, who were home from college for the holidays. They talked—really talked—for hours. They laughed at things that were actually funny rather than performing amusement for an audience. When the power returned, something had shifted.

She began experimenting with subtraction. Canceled the club membership—no one missed it. Sold the vacation house that they visited twice a year and felt obligated to maintain. Traded the luxury car for something ordinary and felt, oddly, relieved. Each subtraction revealed how much maintenance the additions had required, how much life had been devoted to sustaining a lifestyle rather than living a life.

"I thought I was building something," she told her sister. "But I was really just accumulating—things that needed cleaning, insuring, worrying about, replacing. The stuff owned me more than I owned it. Now I'm trying to figure out what I actually want, rather than what I was supposed to want."

## SPENDING ON FREEDOM

There is a category of spending that deserves special attention, one that does not fit neatly into the usual framework of buying goods or even experiences. This is spending that purchases freedom itself—the capacity to do what you want, when you want, on your own terms. Such spending does not acquire things; it acquires options. It does not fill life with possessions; it opens life to possibilities.

The most obvious form of this spending is the accumulation of savings that permits choice. The person with a year's expenses in the bank can walk away from a job that has become intolerable. The person with no savings cannot. This difference in spending—choosing to save rather than consume—translates directly into a difference in freedom. The saved money buys nothing tangible, but it buys something more valuable: the ability to say no, to wait, to choose from a position of strength rather than desperation.

But spending on freedom extends beyond mere savings. It includes any expenditure that expands your capacity for autonomous choice in how you live your days. The person who spends money to live close to work buys back hours of commuting time—hours that become available for whatever they choose. The person who spends on tools that enable remote work buys geographical freedom. The person who pays for household help buys time that would otherwise go to chores. The person who invests in skills buys the freedom to pursue different kinds of work.

This framing inverts the usual understanding of spending. We typically think of spending as consuming resources, reducing what we have. But spending on freedom is investing in capacity—reducing financial resources while increasing life resources. The relevant question is not "what did I get?" but "what can I now do that I could not do before?"

Mises understood that the ultimate purpose of economic activity is not accumulation but the living of life according to one's own values. Money is instrumental; freedom is closer to the goal itself. The person who accumulates wealth but remains trapped—by obligations, by lifestyle inflation, by the expectations of others—has achieved something hollow. The person with modest means but genuine freedom to direct their days has achieved something real.

DANIEL OKAFOR HAD BEEN a successful attorney for fifteen years, and he had little to show for it except exhaustion and a growing sense that his life was not his own. He made excellent money, but the money disappeared into a lifestyle that had somehow become mandatory—the apartment in the expensive building, the suits that signaled status, the dinners and vacations that his colleagues expected. He was wealthy on paper and trapped in practice.

The calculation that changed his life was simple once he finally made it. He tracked where his money actually went and asked, for each category, what freedom it was purchasing. The expensive apartment bought proximity to an office he wished he could leave. The suits bought the approval of colleagues he did not particularly like.

The dinners bought obligations, not friendships. He was spending enormous sums to remain imprisoned.

He began redirecting his spending toward freedom itself. He moved to a modest apartment and banked the difference. He took a sabbatical, then negotiated a part-time arrangement at reduced salary. He discovered that his actual needs were far smaller than his previous spending suggested—that much of what he had thought essential was merely habitual.

Within three years, he had accumulated what he called "freedom money"—enough to live modestly for several years without working. He was still an attorney, but now by choice rather than necessity. He took cases that interested him and declined those that did not. He worked intensely for periods, then took months to travel, to read, to visit family in Nigeria, to do nothing at all. His income had dropped by more than half, but his sense of wealth had increased immeasurably.

"People think I made a sacrifice," he told friends. "But I gave up things I never wanted in order to have something I always did. That's not sacrifice. That's the best trade I ever made."

THE CONNECTION between spending and freedom illuminates why lifestyle inflation is so dangerous. As income rises, spending typically rises to match—the nicer car, the larger house, the more expensive habits. Each of these upgrades may provide genuine pleasure, at least initially. But each also raises the baseline of what feels necessary, which means each reduces the freedom that the higher income might otherwise provide.

Consider two people who both receive substantial raises. One upgrades their lifestyle accordingly, spending the additional income on improved consumption. The other maintains their previous lifestyle and saves the difference. In terms of current consumption, the first person is better off. But in terms of freedom—the ability to quit, to change, to take risks, to weather setbacks—the second person is far wealthier. The first has spent their raise on things; the second has spent it on options.

This is not an argument against all lifestyle improvement. Some upgrades genuinely enhance life quality in lasting ways. Better health care, a safer neighborhood, education for oneself or one's children—these may be worth the increased spending and the reduced freedom that comes with higher fixed costs. The point is that each lifestyle upgrade should be evaluated not just for what it provides but for what it forecloses. Every increase in fixed costs is a decrease in flexibility, a reduction in the ability to respond to opportunity or adversity.

The deepest form of spending on freedom is spending on experiences and capabilities that expand who you are and what you can do. Travel to unfamiliar places does not just provide pleasant memories; it expands your understanding of how life can be lived. Learning a language opens access to entire cultures. Developing a skill creates options that did not exist before. These expenditures are not consumed and depleted like ordinary purchases; they become part of you, permanently enlarging your capacity for life.

**Spending on Experiences**

The research on spending and happiness converges on a finding that should reshape how we think about consumption: spending on experiences produces more lasting satisfaction than spending on material goods. This finding is robust across cultures, income levels, and types of experiences.

Why should experiences outperform things? Several mechanisms appear to be at work. First, experiences become part of our identity and life story in ways that possessions do not. The trip to Japan, the concert where you met your spouse, the course that changed your thinking—these become chapters in the narrative of who you are. The couch, however comfortable, remains merely a couch.

Second, experiences are more resistant to hedonic adaptation. We get used to things quickly; they fade into the background of ordinary life. But memories of experiences can maintain or even increase in value over time. We remember the highlights and forget the discomforts. The vacation that involved delayed flights and a mediocre hotel becomes, in memory, the beautiful beach and the evening when the children laughed until they cried.

Third, experiences connect us to other people in ways that possessions rarely do. We share experiences with companions, and we share stories of experiences with everyone else. The social dimension of experience—anticipating together, undergoing together, remembering together—creates bonds that material consumption cannot match.

Fourth, experiences are less vulnerable to comparison. The car you bought is constantly compared to other cars; there is always a better one, and the comparison diminishes satisfaction. But your experiences are yours, unique in their particulars, not directly comparable to what others have done.

YUKI TANAKA HAD SPENT her twenties accumulating—the right apartment, the right furniture, the right wardrobe for a young professional ascending in Tokyo's corporate world. By thirty-two, she had an impressive collection of possessions and an unimpressive collection of memories. Her apartment looked like a magazine spread and felt like a waiting room.

The shift began when a college friend was diagnosed with cancer. Visiting her in the hospital, Yuki listened to her friend talk about what she regretted. It was not what she had failed to buy. It was what she had failed to do—the trips postponed, the reunions skipped, the experiences deferred until a future that was now uncertain.

Yuki returned home and looked at her carefully curated possessions with new eyes. She did not see security or success; she saw evidence of misallocated life. She began, systematically, to trade things for experiences. She sold the designer bags and used the money for a month in South America. She downsized her apartment and used the savings for a sabbatical to study ceramics in Kyoto. She declined the promotion that would have meant more money but less life.

The transformation was not instant, and it was not free of difficulty. She lost status among colleagues who measured success by visible consumption. Her mother worried she was throwing away her future. But her days became more vivid, more memorable, more genuinely hers. She could describe her last year in rich detail; previously, her years had blurred together, indistinguishable sequences of work and acquisition.

"I realized I was collecting the wrong things," she said. "I had closets full of stuff I barely remembered buying. Now I have less and I am more. The experiences are inside me; no one can take them away, and they never become clutter."

THE CASE for experiential spending comes with important nuances. Not all experiences are equal. Passive consumption—watching television, scrolling through feeds—provides experience of a sort but rarely the lasting satisfaction that active, engaged experience provides. The experience that transforms is typically one that involves challenge, novelty, engagement, or connection. Merely having experiences is not the point; having experiences that expand, connect, or develop is.

Furthermore, some material purchases facilitate experiences. The hiking boots enable the mountain trek. The kitchen equipment enables the dinner party. The musical instrument enables the joy of playing. These purchases have experiential value beyond their material function. The question is not things versus experiences in a rigid dichotomy, but whether spending—on things or experiences—enriches lived life or merely fills space.

The timing of experiences also matters. Research suggests that experiential spending early in life produces particularly high returns. Experiences undertaken when young become part of the foundation of identity, influence subsequent choices and relationships, and provide decades of memory and meaning. The trip taken at twenty-five pays dividends for fifty years; the same trip at seventy-five, while still valuable, has a shorter horizon for returns.

This suggests a spending priority that runs counter to conventional financial advice. The typical guidance is to save when young and spend when old—accumulate in the earning years, consume in retirement. But if experiential spending produces lasting value that compounds over a lifetime, the logic is less clear. The experiences foregone at thirty cannot be had at seventy, at least not in the same form.

**Spending and Identity**

What we buy signals who we are—to others and to ourselves. This signaling function of consumption is not merely vanity; it is a deep feature of human social psychology. We are intensely social creatures who establish and maintain identity partly through what we consume.

Thorstein Veblen identified this over a century ago with his concept of conspicuous consumption—spending designed to demonstrate wealth and status rather than to satisfy direct needs. But the phenomenon extends far beyond the wealthy displaying their riches. Every spending choice participates in systems of meaning that communicate something about the spender.

The person who buys organic food is not only seeking nutrition; they are expressing values about health, environment, and perhaps social class. The person who drives a pickup truck is not only seeking transportation; they are expressing something about identity that differs from the person who drives a Prius. The person who wears designer labels, or deliberately avoids them, is making a statement either way.

This identity dimension of spending is neither good nor bad in itself. We are social beings, and expressing identity through consumption is a natural extension of expressing identity through dress, speech, and behavior. The question is whether our identity-expressive spending serves our authentic self-understanding or distorts it, whether it connects us to genuine community or merely performs connection.

Nietzsche would push us to ask: whose values are you expressing through your consumption? Are they values you have chosen after genuine reflection, or values you have absorbed from a commercial culture that profits from your absorption? The person who spends to impress others with their sophistication may be expressing the herd values they claim to transcend. The person who conspicuously rejects consumerism may be equally trapped in defining themselves by opposition.

Authentic spending—if such a thing is possible—would express values that are genuinely one's own, chosen through the kind of self-examination that genuine flourishing requires. This does not mean spending in ways that ignore social context; we are unavoidably social beings. It means spending in ways that reflect who you actually are and want to become, rather than who advertisers or social pressures suggest you should be.

### The Commercial Environment

We do not make spending decisions in a vacuum. We make them in an environment saturated with commercial influence—an environment designed, with extraordinary sophistication, to shape our choices in directions profitable for sellers.

Advertising is only the most visible manifestation of this influence. Beyond the explicit messages of advertisements lies a vast infrastructure of persuasion: product placement, package design, store layout, pricing psychology, social media influence, algorithmic recommendation, and the entire apparatus of modern marketing. Billions of dollars and some of the best minds of our generation are devoted to influencing how we spend.

This influence operates largely below conscious awareness. We believe we are choosing freely, but our choices are shaped by defaults we did not set, options we did not select, frames we did not construct. The supermarket places impulse purchases at checkout for a reason.

The streaming service autoplays the next episode for a reason. The shopping website shows "only 3 left in stock" for a reason.

Recognizing this environment is not an argument for helpless victimhood. We remain capable of choice, capable of resisting influence, capable of structuring our own environments to counteract commercial pressures. But realistic self-assessment requires acknowledging that we are not the sovereign rational consumers that economic theory imagines. We are influenceable beings operating in an environment designed to influence us.

The practical response is not paranoid rejection of all commercial culture—an impossible stance in modern society—but conscious curation of the influences we allow. Limiting exposure to advertising. Being skeptical of urgent prompts to buy. Creating friction between impulse and purchase. Building habits and environments that serve our considered values rather than our momentary impulses.

**Spending and Happiness**

If the goal of spending is to increase wellbeing—and for most spending, this is at least part of the goal—then what does research tell us about which spending actually accomplishes this? The findings are remarkably consistent and often counterintuitive.

Spending on experiences tends to produce more lasting satisfaction than spending on material goods. The vacation, the concert, the dinner with friends—these generate memories that maintain their value over time, become part of our identity and life story, and provide social connection and conversational material.

Spending on others tends to produce more happiness than spending on ourselves. The gift, the donation, the treating of friends—these tap into our social nature and generate wellbeing through connection and generosity. Self-focused spending satisfies, but the satisfaction is more transient and less meaningful.

Spending that buys time tends to improve wellbeing more than spending that buys things. The housecleaning service, the meal delivery, the convenient location that shortens commutes—these free up hours for what we actually want to do with our lives. Time is the ultimately scarce resource, and spending that creates more of it has outsize effects on how life feels.

Spending that aligns with core values produces more satisfaction than spending that does not. The person who values adventure and spends on travel feels the money was well used. The person who values learning and spends on education feels similarly. Misalignment—spending in ways that do not connect to what one actually values—produces the hollow feeling that something was wasted.

ROBERTO VASQUEZ HAD ALWAYS ASSUMED he wanted a boat. His father had talked about getting a boat someday, and the someday had never come. When Roberto made enough money, he swore he would not make the same mistake. He bought the boat.

The first summer was wonderful. Weekends on the water, friends aboard, cold drinks and sunshine. This was what money was for. But by the second summer, the magic had faded. The maintenance was constant and expensive. The logistics of each outing were complicated. His friends were less available than they had been. He found himself going through the motions of using the boat because he had it, not because he wanted to be on the water.

The third summer, the boat sat in the marina. He paid storage and insurance and maintenance for something that represented not pleasure but obligation. When he finally sold it—at a significant loss—the relief was immediate. He had bought his father's dream, not his own.

What he actually enjoyed, he realized, was simpler: cooking elaborate meals for friends, long hikes in the mountains, reading on his patio with a good cup of coffee. None of these required a boat or significant money. They required time, attention, and the people he loved. The boat had been an obstacle to these things, not a path toward them.

. . .

## FRUGALITY **and Its Limits**

Frugality—the practice of careful, economical spending—has an honorable tradition and genuine virtues. The frugal person makes resources go further, wastes less, maintains greater independence, and often achieves financial security that profligate spenders never reach. In a culture of thoughtless consumption, frugality can be a form of resistance.

But frugality can become pathological. The miser who has wealth but cannot enjoy it, who saves compulsively while denying themselves and others legitimate pleasures, has not achieved the good life. They have sacrificed the purpose of money (what it can provide) for the mere accumulation of money itself. This is means-end confusion of a particularly sad variety.

Mises understood that the purpose of economic activity is consumption—present or future. Saving is deferred consumption, not an end in itself. The person who can never consume, who can never enjoy the fruits of their labor and saving, has missed the point of the entire enterprise.

The goal is neither profligacy nor miserliness but wisdom—spending that serves genuine wellbeing without waste, that enjoys legitimate pleasures without excess, that provides for the future without sacrificing the present entirely. This is a matter of balance and judgment, not rigid rules.

### Major Spending Decisions

Most spending is small and habitual—the coffee, the groceries, the gas, the subscriptions that recur without decision. But periodically, major spending decisions arise that deserve explicit deliberation: the home, the car, the education, the wedding, the major purchase that will lock in patterns for years to come.

These decisions merit more analysis than they typically receive. The house purchase, often the largest financial decision of a lifetime, is frequently made on the basis of emotion, social comparison, and realtor persuasion rather than careful analysis of needs, costs, and alternatives. The car purchase, heavily influenced by marketing and identity signaling, often neglects the total cost of ownership.

For major decisions, several principles deserve attention. First, understand the full costs, not just the purchase price. The house has property taxes, insurance, maintenance, and opportunity cost of the down payment. The car has insurance, fuel, maintenance, and depreciation. The prestigious university has not just tuition but also the opportunity cost of potentially cheaper alternatives.

Second, separate the decision from the emotion of the moment. Major purchases often come with high-pressure sales tactics, time limits, and emotional intensity designed to short-circuit deliberation. Creating space—sleeping on it, discussing with trusted advisors, explicitly analyzing alternatives—counteracts these pressures.

Third, consider the ongoing commitments, not just the initial acquisition. The house locks you into a location, a community, a commute, a lifestyle. The car locks you into transportation costs and, often, an identity you will maintain. The education creates path dependencies in career and life. These ongoing implications may matter more than the initial choice.

Fourth, beware of spending that solves the wrong problem. The bigger house will not fix a troubled marriage. The fancy car will not create self-respect that is absent. The expensive vacation will not repair relationships neglected throughout the year. Major spending sometimes serves as a substitute for addressing problems that require attention, not money.

### Budgeting and Conscious Spending

Given the difficulty of spending well—the psychological biases, the commercial pressures, the tendency toward drift and default—some structure for conscious spending is valuable. This is where practical budgeting enters, not as the whole of spending wisdom but as a tool that supports it.

A budget, at its simplest, is a plan for spending that reflects priorities. It translates abstract values into concrete allocations. It forces tradeoffs to be confronted explicitly rather than handled by default and drift. It provides a framework for saying no to spending that does not serve priorities.

The value of budgeting lies not in the document itself but in the process of creating and maintaining it. The act of deciding how much to allocate to various categories requires confronting what you actually value. The act of tracking spending against the plan reveals the gap between intention and behavior. The act of adjusting when reality departs from plan develops the skill of realistic assessment.

Different people need different levels of structure. Some thrive with detailed tracking of every expense; others find this oppressive and counterproductive. Some need rigid categories with strict limits; others do better with general guidelines and periodic review. The goal is not a particular system but spending that is conscious rather than automatic, aligned with values rather than driven by impulse.

Several frameworks have proven useful. Pay yourself first—saving and investing before spending on anything else—automates the most important allocation and removes it from constant decision. Spending on needs before wants ensures that essential categories are covered before discretionary spending begins. Tracking and reviewing periodically, even if not in real time, creates awareness that shapes subsequent choices.

For many people, the most effective approach is to create systems and environments that make good spending automatic. Direct deposit to savings accounts. Automatic investment contributions. Unsubscribing from marketing emails. Removing saved credit cards from shopping websites. Avoiding stores and situations that trigger unnecessary spending. These environmental modifications reduce reliance on willpower, which is unreliable.

**Spending and Relationships**

Money is one of the most common sources of conflict in relationships, and spending is where much of this conflict manifests. Partners who have different values, different habits, different expectations around spending can find money a constant source of friction.

Some of this conflict reflects genuine differences in values that deserve direct attention. If one partner values security and the other values experience, their natural spending patterns will differ in ways that budgeting alone cannot resolve. These value differences need discussion, negotiation, and sometimes acceptance that partners will not perfectly align.

But much conflict around spending reflects not value differences but failures of communication, trust, or respect. Secret spending undermines trust. Unilateral major purchases show disrespect. Criticism of a partner's spending often masks control issues or value judgments about the partner themselves.

WHEN ELENA AND JAMES MARRIED, they assumed their similar incomes and backgrounds meant financial compatibility. They were wrong. Elena had grown up with scarcity and saved compulsively; money in the bank was safety, and spending felt like risk. James had grown up with abundance and spent freely; money was for use, and saving felt like deprivation.

Their early conflicts were typical. She thought he was irresponsible; he thought she was miserly. Each spending decision became a referendum on character. Resentment accumulated in a ledger neither wanted to examine.

What saved them was a therapist who pointed out that they were each making sense from their own perspective. Elena was not wrong to want security; her childhood had taught her that security could disappear. James was not wrong to want enjoyment; his childhood had taught him that money was meant to be used. Neither needed to convert the other.

They developed a system that honored both perspectives: a large savings buffer that gave Elena peace of mind, discretionary funds for each that James could spend without scrutiny. She stopped policing his purchases; he stopped resenting her caution. They still did not fully understand each other's relationship with money, but they had stopped trying to fix what was not broken—only different.

. . .

THE PRACTICAL WISDOM here is straightforward even if execution is difficult. Transparency about finances builds trust, while secrecy erodes it. Joint decisions on major spending show mutual respect, even when partners have different preferences. Separate discretionary funds can provide autonomy within an overall framework of shared responsibility. Regular financial conversations—not triggered by crisis but scheduled for calm review—keep partners aligned and prevent small differences from becoming large conflicts.

**Charitable Giving**

Any complete discussion of spending must address giving—the allocation of resources to benefit others without expectation of direct return. Charitable giving is spending, but it operates by a different logic than consumption for oneself.

The case for giving rests on several foundations. There is the simple ethical claim that we owe something to others, particularly those less fortunate than ourselves. There is the observation that giving increases the giver's wellbeing—the research on this is consistent and robust. There is the practical reality that some problems can only be solved through collective contribution, and someone must contribute. There is the religious and spiritual dimension present in virtually every tradition.

How much to give is a deeply personal question that depends on resources, obligations, values, and beliefs. Various traditions suggest various figures—the tithe of ten percent, the zakat of Islam, the effective altruist's calculation of maximizing impact. No single answer applies universally, but the complete absence of giving deserves scrutiny. The person who gives nothing, ever, has made a statement about their relationship to the broader human community.

How to give raises practical questions about effectiveness. The charity that spends most of its budget on fundraising and administration provides less benefit per dollar than one that operates efficiently. The cause that seems emotionally compelling may have less impact than one that seems less dramatic. The effective altruism movement has brought analytical rigor to these questions, and their insights deserve attention even for those who do not embrace the framework entirely.

**Spending Across the Lifecycle**

How we spend should change as our lives change. The spending appropriate to a young single person differs from that appropriate to a family with children, which differs from that appropriate to retirees.

In early adulthood, spending typically emphasizes building—establishing a household, developing capabilities, investing in experiences and relationships that will shape the decades ahead. Resources are often limited, but so are obligations. This is when frugality builds the savings that provide future security and when experiences build the memories and relationships that will be valued forever.

In the family years, spending typically emphasizes provision—housing, education, health care, the myriad expenses of raising children. Resources may be greater, but obligations are certainly greater. The tradeoffs between consumption and saving are sharpest here, as current needs press against future security.

In later life, spending typically emphasizes security and legacy—ensuring resources will last, providing for health needs that increase with age, perhaps giving to heirs or causes. Resources may be substantial but finite; the question shifts from accumulation to wise deployment. Many find that their spending needs actually decrease as children leave, mortgages are paid, and lifestyles simplify.

Throughout these stages, the underlying principles remain constant: spend in ways that serve genuine wellbeing, align spending with values, maintain awareness of what spending is actually accomplishing. But the application of these principles changes as life changes.

**Conclusion**

Spending is moral choice made concrete. Every purchase is a small statement about what matters, a vote cast in the marketplace of values. The patterns of our spending, accumulated over time, reveal who we are more honestly than our proclaimed beliefs.

This is not an argument for tortured deliberation over every coffee or newspaper. Life must be lived, and much of it is legitimately routine. But the examined life that Socrates commended includes examining how we spend—periodically stepping back to assess whether our patterns of consumption actually serve the lives we want to live.

Mises would remind us that spending is the endpoint of all economic activity, the purpose toward which production and saving and investment all aim. There is no virtue in earning money that is never spent, either on oneself or on others. The point of economic life is what money can provide—the goods, the experiences, the security, the help to others.

Kahneman would add the empirical caution that we are poor predictors of what spending will actually make us happy. We overestimate the impact of material purchases and underestimate the impact of experiences and relationships. We adapt to new levels of consumption more quickly than we expect. We are influenced by social comparison and commercial manipulation in ways we rarely acknowledge. Spending well requires correcting for these systematic biases.

Nietzsche would push us toward authenticity—spending that expresses values we have truly chosen rather than values we have merely absorbed. The person who spends to impress others, who consumes according to the script written by advertisers and social pressures, has not achieved freedom.

The integration of these perspectives yields an approach to spending that is neither ascetic nor indulgent but wise. Spend on what genuinely matters to you, having examined what genuinely matters. Spend on experiences and relationships more than things. Spend on freedom—on options, on time, on the capacity to choose. Spend on others as well as yourself. Spend in ways that express your authentic values rather than values imposed from outside. Maintain awareness of the commercial environment that seeks to influence your choices. Create systems and environments that support good spending without constant willpower battles.

And remember that spending is not the whole of financial life or the whole of life itself. The ultimate purpose of building wealth is to spend it, wisely and well, on the things that make a human life worth living.

SUMMARY: **Key Takeaways from Chapter Four**

**The Economics of Consumption:** Spending involves real tradeoffs—every dollar spent on one thing cannot be spent on another. Understanding this forces clarity about priorities. The market system that enables our spending represents an extraordinary engine of prosperity and cooperation.

**What Spending Cannot Buy:** The most important things in life—love, friendship, meaning, self-respect—are not for sale. Beyond a level of comfortable sufficiency, additional spending contributes less and less to genuine wellbeing. Emotional wellbeing plateaus far earlier than life evaluation.

**The Psychology of Spending:** Most spending decisions are made automatically by System 1, not deliberatively by System 2. Changing environments and habits is more effective than relying on willpower. The hedonic treadmill ensures we adapt quickly to new levels of consumption, with the pleasure of acquiring fading faster than the pain of losing.

**Spending on Freedom:** The most valuable spending may be what purchases options rather than things—savings that allow you to say no, time bought back from commutes, skills that open new possibilities. Every increase in fixed costs is a decrease in flexibility.

**Spending on Experiences:** Experiences produce more lasting satisfaction than material goods because they become part of identity, resist hedonic adaptation, connect us to others, and are less vulnerable to comparison. Experiential spending early in life may produce particularly high returns.

**Spending and Identity:** Consumption signals who we are, to others and ourselves. Authentic spending expresses values genuinely chosen rather than absorbed from commercial culture.

**The Commercial Environment:** We make spending decisions in an environment designed to influence us in ways we rarely perceive. Conscious curation of influences and creation of friction between impulse and purchase can counteract these pressures.

**Spending and Happiness:** Research consistently shows that spending on experiences, on others, on time, and in alignment with core values produces more lasting wellbeing than spending on material goods for oneself.

**Frugality and Its Limits:** Frugality has genuine virtues, but miserliness defeats the purpose of economic activity. The goal is wisdom—spending that serves wellbeing without waste.

**Major Decisions:** Large purchases deserve deliberate analysis including full costs, separation from emotion, ongoing commitments, and whether the spending addresses the right problem.

**Budgeting:** Structure for conscious spending—whatever form it takes—helps align behavior with values. Systems and environments that make good spending automatic reduce reliance on willpower.

**Relationships:** Financial conflict often reflects value differences or failures of communication. Transparency, joint decisions on major matters, and separate discretionary funds can reduce friction.

**Charitable Giving:** Giving benefits both recipients and givers. Questions of how much and where to give deserve thoughtful attention.

**Lifecycle Changes:** Spending priorities should shift across life stages—from building and experiencing in youth, to provision in family years, to security and legacy later.

# SEVEN
# THE ART OF SAVING

To save is to refuse the present moment its full claim on your resources. It is an act of faith in a future you cannot see, performed on behalf of a self you have not yet become. This makes saving one of the more peculiar behaviors in economic life—a voluntary sacrifice of certain present pleasure for uncertain future benefit, requiring both imagination and discipline in measures that do not come naturally to our species.

Yet saving is also one of the most consequential choices in financial life. The person who saves accumulates options, security, and eventually freedom. The person who does not remains vulnerable to every shock, dependent on continued income, trapped in circumstances they cannot change because they lack the resources to change them. The mathematics are simple; the psychology is not.

This chapter examines saving as both an economic and a human phenomenon. What does saving actually accomplish, and how should we think about the tradeoff between present and future? What psychological barriers make saving difficult, and how can they be overcome? How should saving change across a lifetime, and what is enough?

## The Nature of Saving

Saving, in its essence, is deferred consumption. Income arrives, and rather than exchanging all of it for present goods and services, some portion is set aside—not destroyed, not abandoned, but held for future use. This holding takes various forms: currency, bank deposits, bonds, stocks, real estate, or any other store of value. The form matters for investment purposes, which the next chapter will address. Here we focus on the more fundamental act of choosing not to consume.

This choice has a peculiar structure. The present is certain, vivid, and immediately felt. The future is uncertain, abstract, and experienced only in imagination. When you decline to spend money today, you give up something real for something hypothetical. The pleasure you would have derived from the purchase is foregone. The pleasure you may derive from future use of the saved funds is speculative—dependent on your survival, your future preferences, the stability of institutions, and countless other contingencies.

Economists capture this asymmetry through the concept of time preference—the degree to which people prefer present goods over future goods. A positive time preference, which appears to be universal, means that a good available today is valued more highly than the same good available tomorrow. This is not merely impatience or short-sightedness; it reflects the genuine uncertainty of the future and the genuine reality of the present.

Mises placed time preference at the center of his economic theory. The interest rate, in his framework, is fundamentally an expression of time preference—the premium required to induce people to defer consumption. The saver who forgoes present consumption and makes resources available to others is compensated for this deferral through interest. The borrower who gains access to resources before they have earned them pays this premium for the privilege of accelerating consumption.

This framework illuminates why saving is neither natural nor automatic. It requires overcoming an inherent preference for the present, a preference that served our ancestors well in environments where the future was genuinely uncertain and present resources genuinely needed. The problem is that our psychology, shaped by evolutionary pressures very different from modern economic life, makes saving harder than it should be.

**Why Saving Matters**

The importance of saving operates at two levels: the individual and the social. At the individual level, saving provides security, options, and eventually freedom. At the social level, saving provides the capital that makes economic growth and rising prosperity possible.

For the individual, the most immediate benefit of saving is security. Life is unpredictable. Income can disappear through job loss, illness, economic disruption, or countless other shocks. Expenses can spike through medical emergencies, family crises, necessary repairs, or legal troubles. The person with savings can weather these storms without catastrophe. The person without savings faces every disruption as a potential crisis, forced to borrow at unfavorable terms, liquidate assets at inopportune moments, or accept help on others' terms.

This security function of saving is sometimes called an emergency fund, and conventional advice suggests holding three to six months of expenses in liquid form for this purpose. The specific number matters less than the principle: some buffer between income and expenses is essential for navigating the ordinary unpredictability of life.

Beyond security, saving provides options. The person with accumulated resources can take opportunities unavailable to the person without them. They can accept a lower-paying job that offers better prospects. They can start a business, pursue education, move to a new city, or take a risk on an uncertain venture. They can leave situations that have become intolerable—a bad job, a bad relationship, a bad location—because they have the resources to survive the transition. This optionality is a form of freedom, perhaps the most practical form that money can buy.

Eventually, sufficient saving provides freedom from the need to earn at all. This is the goal of retirement planning, of course—accumulating enough that investment returns can replace employment income. But the freedom of sufficient savings extends beyond the traditional retirement framework. It includes the freedom to work less, to work differently, to take extended breaks, to pursue meaningful work that pays poorly, or to give generously. Saving is not an end in itself but a means to living on one's own terms.

At the social level, saving is the source of capital, and capital is the engine of economic progress. When you save, you make resources available that would otherwise be consumed. These resources—whether held as bank deposits, invested in bonds or stocks, or otherwise deployed—become available for use by others. Businesses borrow to invest in equipment, research, and expansion. Entrepreneurs borrow to start new ventures. Investment, in turn, is what makes economies more productive. This increased productivity is the source of rising wages and living standards—not redistribution of a fixed pie but expansion of the pie itself.

Mises emphasized that this process cannot be short-circuited. Capital cannot be conjured through monetary manipulation or government decree. It must be saved—accumulated through the genuine sacrifice of present consumption. This means that saving has a moral dimension beyond the individual benefits it provides. The saver is not merely securing their own future; they are contributing to the pool of resources that makes economic progress possible for everyone.

### The Psychology of Saving

If saving is so beneficial, why is it so difficult? The answer lies in the mismatch between our evolved psychology and the demands of modern economic life. We are equipped with mental machinery designed for a very different environment.

The most fundamental challenge is hyperbolic discounting—our tendency to discount the future more steeply in the short run than in the long run. When choosing between $100 today and $110 in a month, many people choose the immediate $100. But when choosing between $100 in a year and $110 in thirteen months, the same people often choose to wait for the larger amount. The inconsistency reveals that we are not applying a consistent discount rate but are instead giving special weight to the immediate present.

This pattern shows up in saving decisions constantly. The abstract commitment to save is easy; the concrete act of saving, when the money is actually available to spend, is hard. We plan to save "starting next month" indefinitely, because next month's saving is abstract and easy to commit to, while this month's spending is concrete and tempting.

Kahneman's work illuminates other psychological barriers. Present bias leads us to give disproportionate weight to immediate costs and benefits. Saving involves an immediate cost (foregone consumption) and a delayed benefit (future resources). Present bias makes the cost loom larger than the benefit, even when the benefit exceeds the cost in objective terms.

Mental accounting can work both for and against saving. On the positive side, earmarking money for specific future purposes can make saving feel more concrete and motivated. On the negative side, treating money in different mental accounts as non-fungible can lead to irrational choices—keeping low-interest savings while carrying high-interest debt, for instance.

Loss aversion also affects saving behavior. Reducing current spending feels like a loss, and losses are psychologically weightier than equivalent gains. The person asked to cut spending by $200 per month experiences this as more painful than the future benefit of $200 per month in additional savings feels pleasurable.

MARCUS CHEN HAD KNOWN for years that he needed to save more. He made good money as a software engineer, but somehow the money disappeared each month, absorbed into a lifestyle that felt modest but evidently was not. He would read articles about retirement planning, feel a pang of guilt, resolve to do better, and then continue exactly as before.

The breakthrough came from an unexpected direction. His company offered a behavioral economics workshop—a half-day session on how cognitive biases affect financial decisions. The instructor did not moralize or lecture about responsibility. She simply described, with clinical precision, the mental patterns that make saving difficult: the hyperbolic discounting, the present bias, the tendency to treat savings as optional and spending as fixed.

Marcus recognized himself in every example. He was not weak-willed or irresponsible. He was a normal human being with normal psychology, operating in an environment that made poor choices easy and good choices hard. The recognition was somehow liberating. The problem was not his character but his systems.

He left the workshop and immediately restructured his finances. He increased his 401(k) contribution to 20 percent, which he had always told himself he could not afford. He set up automatic transfers to a savings account on the day after each paycheck—not at the end of the month when he would "save what was left over." He moved his emergency fund to a bank with no ATM card, adding friction to any withdrawal. He canceled the subscriptions he never used and unsubscribed from the retail emails that generated impulses to spend.

None of these changes required ongoing willpower. That was the point. He had designed an environment where saving was the default and spending required deliberate action. Within a year, his savings rate had tripled—not through heroic self-denial but through structural changes that worked with his psychology rather than against it.

"I used to think saving was about discipline," he told friends. "But discipline is a limited resource. Systems are unlimited. I just built better systems."

. . .

## STRATEGIES FOR SAVING

Given the psychological barriers to saving, what practical strategies actually work? The research and accumulated wisdom converge on several approaches.

The most powerful strategy is automation. When saving requires a decision each pay period, each decision is an opportunity for present bias and hyperbolic discounting to win. When saving is automatic—deducted before you see the money, transferred without your intervention—the decision is made once and then executed repeatedly without further willpower expenditure. This is why 401(k) participation increases dramatically when enrollment is automatic rather than opt-in.

Closely related is the principle of paying yourself first. Conventional budgeting suggests spending on necessities, then discretionary items, and then saving "what's left over." But there is rarely anything left over, because spending expands to fill available resources. Inverting this—saving first, then spending what remains—ensures that saving actually occurs.

Commitment devices can help overcome time-inconsistent preferences. These are arrangements that make it difficult or costly to access saved funds, thereby countering the temptation to spend them. Retirement accounts with early withdrawal penalties are a form of commitment device. So are certificates of deposit with fixed terms, savings accounts at inconvenient banks, or even informal arrangements like giving control of funds to a trusted person.

Framing effects can be harnessed for saving. Thinking of saving as "spending on the future" rather than "not spending" can make it more palatable. Visualizing concrete future goals—the house, the retirement, the freedom—makes the abstract benefits of saving more vivid. Naming accounts after their purposes invokes mental accounting in service of saving rather than against it.

Social accountability helps some people. Sharing savings goals with friends or family, joining groups focused on financial improvement, or working with a financial coach creates external expectations that reinforce internal motivation.

**How Much to Save**

The question of how much to save has no single correct answer. It depends on age, income, obligations, goals, risk tolerance, and values. But it is possible to reason about the question in ways that clarify the tradeoffs.

The conventional retirement planning framework asks: how much wealth will you need to fund your desired retirement lifestyle, and how much must you save each year to accumulate that amount? Various rules of thumb emerge—save 10 percent, 15 percent, 20 percent of income—but these are rough approximations that may or may not fit individual circumstances.

A more fundamental approach starts with the question of what saving is for. If the goal is security, then saving enough to weather several months of income loss may be sufficient. If the goal is optionality, then saving enough to fund a career transition or major opportunity matters. If the goal is eventual freedom from employment, then saving enough to replace employment income from investment returns is necessary.

The "financial independence" framework focuses on this last goal. The basic calculation is straightforward: if you can live on 4 percent of your invested assets annually (a withdrawal rate that has historically been sustainable over long periods), then you need 25 times your annual expenses in invested assets to be financially independent. If you spend $50,000 per year, you need $1.25 million. If you spend $100,000, you need $2.5 million.

This framework has the virtue of clarity. It makes explicit the relationship between spending levels and the savings required for independence. It reveals that reducing spending accomplishes two things simultaneously: it increases the amount available to save, and it decreases the amount needed for independence.

But the framework assumes that financial independence—freedom from the need to work—is the goal. Not everyone shares this goal as a priority. Some people find deep meaning in work and have no desire to stop. Some have other obligations that take precedence over personal independence. Some simply prefer to enjoy more consumption during their working years, accepting the need to work longer in exchange.

HELENA PAPADOPOULOS HAD ENCOUNTERED the financial independence movement in her late twenties and found it compelling. The math was clear, the goal was attractive, and she had the income to make real progress. She threw herself into optimization —tracking every expense, maximizing her savings rate, investing aggressively. Her savings rate climbed to 50 percent, then 60 percent.

By her late thirties, she was more than halfway to her independence number. But she was also exhausted, and not just from work. The optimization itself had become draining. Every spending decision was freighted with calculation. Every social invitation prompted evaluation of its cost-effectiveness. She had optimized for future freedom so aggressively that she had eliminated present freedom.

The recalibration came gradually. She realized that her extreme savings rate was driven partly by genuine desire for independence but partly by anxiety—a fear of being trapped, of being dependent, of being vulnerable. The fear was not irrational; her parents' financial struggles had left deep marks. But fear was running the show more than she wanted to admit.

She eased back. Her savings rate dropped to 40 percent, then 35 percent—still high by any conventional standard, but no longer punishing. She spent more on experiences, on travel, on generosity to friends. She stopped tracking every expense with obsessive precision. The path to financial independence lengthened by a few years, but the path itself became more pleasant.

"I was treating my present self as an obstacle to my future self," she reflected. "But my present self is also a self who deserves to live, not just to prepare for living someday. The goal is to live well across the whole span, not to sacrifice everything for a finish line."

## SAVING AND LIFE **Stages**

The appropriate level and purpose of saving changes across the arc of life. Saving at twenty serves different functions and faces different constraints than saving at fifty.

In early adulthood, income is typically modest, expenses often include debt repayment from education, and the future seems impossibly distant. These factors conspire against saving. But early adulthood is also when saving has its greatest power, because time allows compound growth to work its magic. A dollar saved at twenty-five has decades to grow; a dollar saved at fifty-five has perhaps ten years before retirement draws. This argues for prioritizing saving in early adulthood despite the difficulty.

The practical approach for young savers is often to start small but start immediately. Even modest contributions to retirement accounts matter enormously if started early. Building the habit of saving matters as much as the initial amounts. And in early adulthood, the most important investment may be in oneself—education, skills, experience—which is a form of saving even if it does not show up in a bank account.

In the middle years, income typically rises, family obligations often increase, and the future becomes more concrete and pressing. This is when serious wealth accumulation typically occurs. The challenge is often preventing lifestyle inflation from absorbing all the gains—maintaining or increasing savings rate even as income grows.

In later working years, earning power may plateau or decline, but obligations often decrease as children become independent and major purchases are complete. This can be a period of accelerated saving as the reduced expenses of empty nest life free up resources that were previously absorbed by family needs.

In retirement itself, the relationship to saving inverts. The purpose is no longer to accumulate but to deploy—to draw on accumulated resources to fund life without employment income. This requires a different mindset, as spending savings can feel psychologically uncomfortable to those who have spent decades building them.

### The Relationship Between Saving and Spending

Saving and spending are not separate domains but two aspects of the same fundamental choice about how to allocate resources across time. Every dollar saved is a dollar not spent; every dollar spent is a dollar not saved.

Several points from the previous chapter bear repetition in the context of saving. First, reducing spending accomplishes saving directly—a dollar not spent is a dollar saved, regardless of income level. This is why high savers often focus as much on expense management as on income maximization.

Second, the composition of spending affects the ease of saving. Fixed costs—rent, car payments, subscriptions, insurance—create ongoing claims on income that are difficult to reduce month by month. Variable costs can be adjusted more easily. A lifestyle heavy in fixed costs is inflexible; even high income leaves little room for saving if it is already committed to obligations.

Third, spending that generates genuine wellbeing may be worth the foregone saving, while spending that fails to generate wellbeing should be cut ruthlessly. The point of saving is eventual spending—consumption deferred, not consumption denied. Saving too much, at the cost of genuine present happiness, is as much a mistake as saving too little.

DAVID AND MARIA SANTOS had saved diligently throughout their working lives. He was an engineer, she a teacher, and their combined income was comfortable without being exceptional. They had lived below their means, maximized retirement contributions, paid off their home, funded their children's educations without debt.

By their mid-sixties, they had accumulated more than enough to retire comfortably.

But they could not spend it. Decades of saving had created habits of mind that resisted reversal. Every expenditure beyond the basics triggered anxiety. The cruise their children encouraged them to take felt extravagant. The home repairs they genuinely needed felt unnecessary. They had a seven-figure portfolio and the spending habits of people worried about making rent.

Their daughter finally confronted them. "You saved for this. This is what it was for. If you can't enjoy it, what was the point of all those years of sacrifice?"

The question lodged in David's mind. What was the point? He had told himself the saving was for security, for independence, for options. But now that he had all of those things, the saving had become its own purpose, divorced from any actual use. He was hoarding resources he would never deploy, while time—the truly scarce resource—continued to run out.

They worked with a financial planner who specialized in retirement spending—helping people shift from accumulation mindset to spending mindset. They created a budget that required them to spend a minimum amount each month on experiences and enjoyment. They took the cruise, visited grandchildren more often, upgraded the house. Each expenditure still felt slightly wrong, but the wrongness faded as they began to receive what they had saved for: life lived richly while they were still able to live it.

## SAVING AND FREEDOM

Beyond security, saving enables freedom—the capacity to make choices unconstrained by immediate financial necessity. This is the deeper promise of saving.

Freedom through saving operates on multiple levels. At the most basic level, savings enable you to say no. No to the job that has become intolerable. No to the living situation that does not serve you.

No to the relationship that has turned exploitative. Each of these refusals requires the ability to survive the transition period, and savings provide that ability.

At a higher level, savings enable you to say yes. Yes to the opportunity that requires a period of low or no income. Yes to the move to a new city. Yes to the startup idea that might fail. Yes to the sabbatical that would restore your energy.

At the highest level, sufficient savings enable you to stop. To stop working for money, to stop organizing your time around earning, to stop deferring life until later. The person who reaches this level has achieved a form of freedom that was available only to the wealthy throughout most of history.

Mises understood that the purpose of economic activity is ultimately the living of life according to one's own values. Saving is instrumental to this purpose. It converts present earnings into future freedom, present sacrifice into future choice.

AFTER FIFTEEN YEARS in corporate law, Janet Morrison knew with certainty that she wanted out. The work had lost any meaning it once held. The hours were brutal, the culture was toxic. But she also had a mortgage, car payments, private school tuition for two children, and a lifestyle that consumed essentially all of her substantial income.

She was trapped—not by external force but by her own accumulated choices. Each individual decision had seemed reasonable, but together they formed a cage. She earned more than she had ever imagined earning, yet she was less free than she had been as a first-year associate with no obligations.

The escape took five years of deliberate preparation. She paid off the car loans and did not replace the cars. She moved the children to public schools after researching options and finding one that was excellent. She refinanced the mortgage to a lower payment. She cut lifestyle expenses that had seemed essential but turned out to be merely habitual. Her savings rate climbed from near zero to 40 percent.

At forty-seven, she had enough. Not enough for the same lifestyle —that would have taken decades more—but enough for a different life. She resigned from the firm, took six months to decompress, then started a solo practice taking only cases she believed in. Her income dropped by two-thirds, but her life opened up immeasurably.

"The money wasn't making me rich," she said later. "It was keeping me poor—poor in time, in freedom, in the ability to choose. Real wealth isn't income. It's options. And you can only buy options through saving."

## SAVING AND GENEROSITY

Saving is sometimes framed as selfish—prioritizing one's own future over present claims including the needs of others. But this framing is mistaken. Saving enables generosity in ways that living paycheck to paycheck does not.

The person with savings can give without destabilizing their own life. They can respond to emergencies in their family or community. They can support causes they believe in. They can help friends in crisis. They can be generous spontaneously, without calculating whether they can afford it, because they have resources beyond immediate needs.

The person without savings faces every request for help as a potential threat to their own security. Their generosity is constrained by necessity rather than enabled by abundance.

This does not mean that saving should replace giving. Generosity is a present obligation, not merely a future option. But building resources enables greater generosity over time. The person who saves and then gives from abundance may contribute more, over a lifetime, than the person who gives from scarcity and never builds the capacity for larger gifts.

### Common Mistakes in Saving

Certain errors in saving are so common that they deserve explicit attention.

Starting too late is perhaps the most consequential mistake. The power of compound growth means that early saving dominates late saving. A person who saves $5,000 per year from age twenty-five to thirty-five (ten years, $50,000 total) and then stops will often have more at retirement than a person who saves $5,000 per year from age thirty-five to sixty-five (thirty years, $150,000 total). This mathematical reality argues for prioritizing saving in early adulthood, even in small amounts.

Saving without purpose often undermines persistence. Abstract saving—putting money aside without clarity about why—is psychologically difficult to maintain. Concrete goals, with specific amounts and timelines, create motivation that sustains saving through tempting moments.

Letting lifestyle inflate with income is the most common reason that high earners fail to build wealth. As income rises, expectations rise to match. Each upgrade becomes the new baseline, requiring still higher income to maintain. The person on this treadmill earns more each year but saves no more.

Holding too much in low-return savings vehicles is a mistake once emergency funds are established. Money sitting in a savings account earning minimal interest is losing purchasing power to inflation. Once security is established, additional savings should be invested to grow.

Failing to account for taxes can undermine saving efforts. Retirement accounts offer significant tax advantages that substantially increase the effective value of contributions. Ignoring these advantages leaves significant value on the table.

### The Limits of Saving

Saving is important, but it is not everything. A financial life organized entirely around saving would miss much of what makes life worth living.

First, saving requires income. For those whose income barely covers necessities, advice to save more can feel like mockery. The problem is not insufficient discipline but insufficient resources.

Second, saving requires time to work. The person who saves so aggressively for a future they never enjoy has made a tragic miscalculation. Saving is deferred consumption, but deferral makes sense only if there will be a future in which to consume.

Third, some goods cannot be saved for. The experiences available at twenty-five cannot be had at sixty-five. The time with children while they are young cannot be recovered after they are grown. Saving should not come at the cost of goods that are only available now.

Fourth, saving can become pathological. The miser who accumulates wealth but cannot enjoy it, who lives in deprivation despite abundant resources, who dies with money that was never used—this is not financial wisdom but financial illness. Saving is a tool for living well, not a substitute for living.

**Conclusion**

Saving is one of the fundamental acts of financial life, and one of the most consequential. The person who saves builds security, options, and eventually freedom. The person who does not remains vulnerable to every shock, dependent on continued income, constrained in ways that limit both present choices and future possibilities.

Yet saving is neither natural nor easy. Our psychology pulls toward the present and away from the abstract future. Commercial culture surrounds us with invitations to spend. Lifestyle inflation absorbs income increases before they can be saved. The act of saving requires working against substantial forces, both internal and external.

The response to these forces is not willpower alone—willpower is too unreliable for a task that extends across decades. The response is systems: automatic transfers, commitment devices, environmental modifications that make saving the default and spending the exception. The person who designs their financial environment well can save consistently without constant struggle.

How much to save depends on goals, circumstances, and values. Security requires some baseline of emergency funds. Freedom requires more substantial accumulation—enough that employment becomes optional rather than necessary. But saving is not an end in itself. It is a means to the living of a good life, and saving that prevents good living has defeated its own purpose.

Mises would remind us that saving is what makes capital formation possible, and capital formation is what makes economic progress possible. The saver contributes not only to their own future but to the productive capacity of the entire economy.

Kahneman would add that our intuitions about saving are systematically biased. We discount the future too steeply, weight present costs too heavily, and fail to appreciate how adapted we will become to whatever we have. Correcting for these biases means saving more than feels natural, especially early in life when compound growth has the most time to work.

Nietzsche would push us to ask whether our saving—or our failure to save—reflects our authentic values or merely absorbed conventions. Genuine saving, like genuine spending, requires knowing what you value and aligning your choices accordingly.

The integration of these perspectives yields an approach to saving that is neither obsessive nor negligent but wise: save enough for security and freedom, through systems that work with your psychology rather than against it, in service of a life genuinely worth living.

## SUMMARY: **Key Takeaways from Chapter Five**

**The Nature of Saving:** Saving is deferred consumption—choosing to hold resources for future use rather than spending them now. This requires overcoming our inherent time preference, which values present goods over future goods.

**Why Saving Matters:** At the individual level, saving provides security against life's unpredictability, options to pursue opportunities, and eventually freedom from the need to earn. At the social level, saving provides the capital that makes economic growth and rising prosperity possible.

**The Psychology of Saving:** Hyperbolic discounting, present bias, and loss aversion make saving psychologically difficult. We are not weak-willed; we are normal humans with evolved psychology ill-suited to modern financial decisions.

**Strategies for Saving:** Automation is the most powerful tool —make saving the default by having it happen before you see the money. Pay yourself first. Use commitment devices that make accessing savings difficult. Frame saving as "spending on the future" and visualize concrete goals.

**How Much to Save:** There is no single right answer. Security requires an emergency fund of several months' expenses. Financial independence requires approximately 25 times annual expenses. But saving goals should align with your actual values, not just conventional wisdom.

**Saving and Life Stages:** Early saving has the greatest power due to compound growth. Middle years are typically when serious accumulation occurs. Later working years may allow catch-up saving. Retirement requires shifting from accumulation to spending—a psychological transition as much as a financial one.

**The Relationship Between Saving and Spending:** These are two sides of the same choice. Reducing spending directly enables saving. Low fixed costs preserve flexibility. But saving that prevents genuine wellbeing has defeated its purpose.

**Saving and Freedom:** Savings enable you to say no to intolerable situations, say yes to opportunities, and eventually stop working for money entirely. Real wealth is options, not income.

**Saving and Generosity:** Saving enables rather than prevents generosity. Resources beyond immediate needs allow giving without destabilizing your own life.

**Common Mistakes:** Starting too late sacrifices the power of compound growth. Saving without purpose undermines motivation. Lifestyle inflation absorbs income gains. Holding too much in low-return vehicles loses to inflation. Ignoring tax advantages leaves value on the table.

**The Limits of Saving:** Saving requires income to work with. Some goods—experiences, time with loved ones—cannot be saved for and must be enjoyed when available. Pathological saving that prevents living well is as much an error as failing to save.

# PART 4
# INVESTING

*The mechanics of growing wealth*

# EIGHT
# THE PHILOSOPHY OF INVESTING

The previous chapters addressed what might be called the defensive side of personal finance: earning, budgeting, eliminating debt, building reserves. These are the foundations without which investing is premature. But defense alone does not win the game. At some point, you must deploy your capital—put your money to work so that it grows.

This chapter begins the offensive portion of your financial life. It addresses not the mechanics of investing, which will come later, but the philosophy that should guide every investment decision you make. Philosophy may seem an odd starting point. You might prefer to know which stocks to buy or which funds to choose. But the investor who understands principles can adapt to any market environment. The investor who knows only tactics is lost when conditions change.

The Nature of Investing

Investing is the act of committing resources today in expectation of greater resources tomorrow. This simple definition conceals considerable complexity. The commitment is real and immediate; the expectation is uncertain and distant. Between the commitment and the payoff lies time, and time is where everything happens—where returns are generated, where risks materialize, where patience is tested and psychology matters.

The investor exchanges certainty for uncertainty. Cash in hand is certain; its future purchasing power is not, but its nominal value is known. An investment's future value is unknown. It may grow substantially, grow modestly, stagnate, or decline. The investor accepts this uncertainty in exchange for the probability of higher returns.

This exchange is the fundamental bargain of investing. You give up the known for the unknown, the certain for the uncertain, the present for the future. The compensation for this sacrifice is the expected return—the average outcome across all possible futures, weighted by their probabilities.

Not all sacrifices are equally compensated. Some risks are rewarded by the market; others are not. Understanding this distinction is essential.

Risk and Return: The Central Relationship

The relationship between risk and return is the closest thing investing has to a physical law. Higher expected returns require accepting higher risk. Lower risk means accepting lower expected returns. There is no escape from this tradeoff, no clever strategy that offers high returns without commensurate risk. Anyone promising otherwise is either ignorant or dishonest.

This relationship exists because of competition. If an investment offered high returns with low risk, everyone would want it. The rush of buyers would bid up the price, reducing the future return until it matched the risk. Conversely, if an investment offered low returns with high risk, no one would want it. The lack of buyers would push down the price, raising the future return until it compensated for the risk.

Markets are not perfect, and mispricings occur. But the competitive process constantly corrects them. By the time you hear about an opportunity, the price has almost certainly adjusted to reflect the opportunity's true risk-return profile. The edges that remain are small, fleeting, and difficult to capture reliably.

Different types of risk earn different compensation. The risk that matters for expected returns is not the total volatility of an investment but the portion that cannot be diversified away—the systematic risk tied to broad economic conditions. An investor holding a single stock faces enormous risk. Much of that risk is specific to the company: a product failure, a lawsuit, a management scandal. By holding many stocks, this company-specific risk washes out; some companies do better than expected, others worse, and the effects cancel. What remains is market risk—the exposure to factors that affect all companies.

Only market risk commands a premium. Company-specific risk can be eliminated for free through diversification; the market does not pay you for bearing it. This is why diversified portfolios are not merely less risky than concentrated ones—they offer better risk-adjusted returns. Diversification is the rare free lunch in finance.

The Tyranny of Compounding

Albert Einstein is said to have called compound interest the eighth wonder of the world. Whether he actually said this is uncertain, but the sentiment is accurate. Compounding is the most powerful force in investing, and understanding it is essential to sound financial thinking.

Compounding means that your returns generate their own returns. If you earn ten percent on a thousand dollars, you have eleven hundred dollars. If you earn ten percent again, you earn ten percent on eleven hundred, not on the original thousand. The gain is one hundred ten dollars, not one hundred. The difference seems small. It is not small over time.

At seven percent annual returns, money doubles roughly every ten years. A twenty-five-year-old investing ten thousand dollars will see that sum become twenty thousand by thirty-five, forty thousand by forty-five, eighty thousand by fifty-five, and one hundred sixty thousand by sixty-five. The original investment grew sixteenfold without any additional contributions—purely through the compounding of returns.

This example uses modest assumptions. With regular contributions, the results are transformative. Someone investing five hundred dollars monthly from age twenty-five to sixty-five, earning seven percent annually, accumulates over 1.2 million dollars. Their total contributions of two hundred forty thousand become over a million through compounding alone.

The corollary is equally important: costs compound too. A one percent annual fee seems trivial. It is not. Over forty years, it consumes roughly a third of what your wealth would otherwise have been. A two percent fee consumes more than half. The investment industry is well aware of this mathematics and relies on investors not understanding it.

This is why the single most reliable way to improve your investment returns is to reduce your costs. You cannot control the market. You can control what you pay.

Time in the Market

The phrase "time in the market beats timing the market" is repeated so often that it risks becoming meaningless. But it captures a profound truth.

Markets are unpredictable in the short term. Daily, monthly, even yearly movements are essentially random, driven by news, sentiment, and noise that no one can consistently forecast. Over longer periods, the picture changes. The stock market has delivered positive real returns over every thirty-year period in American history, including periods that encompassed depressions, world wars, and financial crises.

This does not mean stocks are safe over thirty years. The range of outcomes remains wide. But the probability of a positive outcome rises dramatically with time, and the probability of a severely negative outcome falls. Time diversifies across market conditions just as holding many stocks diversifies across companies.

The implication is clear: start early. An investor who begins at twenty-five has forty years to retirement. An investor who begins at forty has twenty-five years. The difference in outcomes, assuming identical contributions, can be millions of dollars.

Starting early is difficult. Young people have lower incomes, higher demands on their money, and often student debt to manage. These constraints are real. But even modest early investments have outsized effects. One thousand dollars invested at twenty-five becomes more than ten thousand by sixty-five at seven percent returns. The same thousand invested at forty-five becomes barely four thousand. The mathematics do not negotiate.

The Philosophy of Ownership

When you buy a stock, you become a part owner of a business. This is not metaphor; it is legal reality. Shareholders own the company, are entitled to their share of profits, and have voting rights on major decisions.

This ownership perspective transforms how you think about investing. Stock prices fluctuate daily, sometimes wildly. If you view stocks as tickets whose prices bounce around, this volatility is alarming. If you view yourself as a business owner, the perspective shifts. The value of a business depends on its future cash flows, not on what someone will pay for a piece of paper tomorrow.

The owner's mindset encourages patience. Businesses do not transform overnight. Competitive advantages are built over years. Earnings grow gradually. The owner who checks stock prices hourly is like the farmer who digs up seeds to see if they are growing. The activity does not help and may cause harm.

The owner's mindset also encourages selectivity about ownership. If you were buying a local business—a restaurant, a dry cleaner—you would investigate carefully. You would want to understand the economics, the competition, the management. Public stocks deserve the same scrutiny, which is one reason why broad diversification is so valuable: you own small pieces of many businesses, acknowledging that you cannot possibly investigate each one deeply.

The Nature of Markets

Markets are mechanisms for aggregating information. Millions of buyers and sellers, each with their own views and circumstances, trade with each other. The prices that emerge reflect the collective wisdom—and sometimes the collective foolishness—of all participants.

Most of the time, markets are remarkably efficient at this aggregation. The price of a stock reflects everything publicly known about the company, plus the informed guesses of professionals who study it full-time. To beat the market, you must know something that this vast collective does not, or interpret known information in a way that this vast collective has failed to.

This is not impossible, but it is extremely difficult. The professionals studying each company have more resources, more data, more experience than you. When you trade against them, you are the underdog. Occasionally underdogs win. Usually they do not.

The implication is humility. Approach the market not as a puzzle to be solved or an opponent to be defeated, but as a system to be harnessed. The market offers a return for bearing risk. Accept that return rather than trying to outsmart the other participants. This approach will be explored in depth when we discuss index investing in Chapter 10.

Speculation Versus Investment

The line between investing and speculation is blurry but important. Both involve committing capital with hope of gain. The difference lies in the basis for that hope.

Investment relies on the productive capacity of assets. You buy a stock because the company generates profits. You buy a bond because the issuer will pay interest. You buy real estate because tenants will pay rent. The returns come from the asset's fundamental economic activity.

Speculation relies on price movements divorced from fundamentals. You buy something because you expect its price to rise, regardless of whether it produces any cash flow. The return comes not from the asset itself but from finding someone willing to pay more than you did. This is sometimes called the greater fool theory: your profit depends on finding a greater fool to buy from you.

Pure speculation is a zero-sum game. One participant's gain is another's loss, and after transaction costs, the average speculator loses. Investment, by contrast, is positive-sum. The economy grows, companies generate profits, and the aggregate wealth of investors increases over time.

The distinction is not always clear-cut. Real estate can be both investment (rental income) and speculation (price appreciation divorced from rents). Stocks can be both investment (dividend and earnings growth) and speculation (buying based on momentum or tips). The question to ask yourself is: would I still want to own this if I could never sell it? If the answer is yes—if the asset generates value on its own—you are investing. If the answer is no—if you need someone else to buy it from you at a higher price—you are speculating.

Some speculation is inevitable in any portfolio. Growth stocks, by definition, pay less in current dividends and more in expected future appreciation. But the core of your portfolio should be grounded in investment, not speculation. The expected returns are more reliable, and the odds are in your favor.

Why Investing Feels Wrong

Human psychology evolved in environments utterly different from financial markets. Our ancestors faced physical threats requiring immediate response. Those who hesitated when a predator appeared did not become ancestors. We are descended from people who reacted quickly, emotionally, and decisively to perceived threats.

Financial markets trigger these ancient responses. A falling portfolio feels like a threat. The urge to act—to sell, to flee, to do something—is powerful. But acting on this urge is usually wrong. The threat is not physical; selling does not ensure survival. In fact, selling during declines locks in losses and forfeits the recovery.

This is just one example of how our psychological wiring conflicts with sound investing. The full landscape of behavioral pitfalls—and strategies for navigating them—will be examined in Chapter 13. For now, the essential point is that successful investing often requires acting against instinct. It requires patience when you feel impatient, calm when you feel anxious, inaction when you feel the urge to act.

This is why philosophy matters. In the moment of crisis, rational calculation fails. Only principles deeply internalized beforehand can guide behavior. The investor who has thought carefully about what she owns and why is less likely to panic than one who bought on a tip and has no framework for understanding a decline.

The Investor's Edge

If professional investors struggle to beat the market, what hope does the individual have? Paradoxically, quite a lot—but not in the way most people expect.

The individual investor has advantages that professionals lack. Professionals must justify their fees by doing something—trading, selecting stocks, timing markets. The individual can simply hold. Professionals face quarterly performance pressure and career risk if they underperform. The individual answers to no one but herself. Professionals manage large sums that limit their flexibility and move markets when they trade. The individual trades in sizes too small to matter.

These advantages do not help you beat the market. They help you capture the market's return more fully. By holding rather than trading, you minimize transaction costs and taxes. By ignoring short-term performance, you can ride out volatility. By staying small, you can execute any strategy without market impact.

The individual's edge is the freedom to be patient, cheap, and passive. Embracing this edge requires surrendering the fantasy of beating the market through superior analysis. It means accepting that market returns, captured at minimal cost over long periods, will build substantial wealth.

The Framework for What Follows

This philosophy—respect for risk, humility about prediction, patience through volatility, ownership of productive assets, minimization of costs—underpins everything in the chapters ahead.

Chapter 9 will survey the investment universe: the different types of assets available and their characteristics. Chapter 10 will examine how to own those assets efficiently. Chapter 11 will build literacy for interpreting economic and company data—not to pick stocks, but to understand the context in which your investments operate. Chapter 12 will address derivatives, instruments you should largely avoid but should understand. Chapter 13 will explore investor psychology and the behavioral traps that ensnare even sophisticated investors. Chapter 14 will bring these threads together into practical portfolio construction. Chapter 15 will address the tax and legal framework that shapes your actual returns.

Through it all, the principles established here remain constant. Risk and return are linked. Costs matter. Time is your ally. Diversification is free insurance. Markets are hard to beat. Behavior determines outcomes.

## SUMMARY

Investing means exchanging present certainty for future uncertainty in expectation of growth. The relationship between risk and return is inviolable: higher expected returns require accepting higher risk, and no strategy escapes this tradeoff. Diversification eliminates company-specific risk for free, leaving only the market risk that commands a premium.

Compounding transforms modest sums into substantial wealth over time—but also transforms small costs into enormous drags on returns. Starting early dramatically improves outcomes because time allows compounding to work.

Owning stocks means owning businesses. This perspective encourages patience and reduces the impulse to trade based on price fluctuations. Markets efficiently aggregate information, making them extremely difficult to beat consistently; the wise approach is to harness market returns rather than attempt to outperform.

Investment relies on the productive capacity of assets; speculation relies on finding someone to pay a higher price. The core of your portfolio should be grounded in investment.

Human psychology conflicts with sound investing. The urge to act during market declines, among other instincts, leads to poor outcomes. Principles internalized before a crisis can guide behavior when emotions run high.

The individual investor's true edge lies not in superior analysis but in the freedom to be patient, minimize costs, and hold for the long term. The chapters ahead will build on this foundation to create a practical framework for building and maintaining wealth.

# NINE
# THE INVESTMENT UNIVERSE

Before you can invest wisely, you must understand what you are choosing among. The financial world offers a bewildering array of places to put your money, each with its own mechanics, risks, potential returns, and role in a portfolio. This chapter maps the terrain. It surveys the major asset classes, explains how each works, and helps you understand why investors hold them. The goal is not to tell you what to buy but to give you the conceptual framework to understand what you are buying when you make any investment decision.

Think of this as learning geography before planning a journey. You need to know what countries exist, what their climates are like, what dangers and opportunities each presents. Only then can you design an itinerary that makes sense for where you want to go.

**Stocks: Owning Pieces of Businesses**

When you buy a stock, you become a part owner of a company. This is not metaphor. It is legal reality. A share of stock represents a fractional claim on the company's assets and earnings. If the company has one million shares outstanding and you own one thousand, you own one-tenth of one percent of everything the company has and everything it earns.

This ownership stake entitles you to a proportional share of profits, typically distributed as dividends, and to vote on major corporate decisions. In practice, small shareholders rarely exercise meaningful control, but the ownership is real. When the company prospers, the value of your stake rises. When it struggles, your stake declines. When it fails entirely, your shares become worthless.

The mechanics of stock trading are straightforward. Companies issue shares to raise capital. Those shares then trade on exchanges where buyers and sellers meet, either directly or through electronic systems. The price at any moment reflects the collective judgment of market participants about what the company is worth. This judgment incorporates expectations about future earnings, assessments of risk, and the general mood of the market.

Historically, stocks have delivered the highest returns of any major asset class over long periods. Since reliable records began in the late nineteenth century, American stocks have returned roughly nine to ten percent annually before inflation, or six to seven percent after inflation. This return has persisted through world wars, depressions, panics, and countless predictions of doom. Over any given decade, stocks usually rise. Over any given century, they always have.

But this long-term return comes with substantial short-term volatility. Stocks can and do lose half their value in a matter of months. They can remain depressed for years. The investor who bought American stocks at the peak in 1929 waited until 1954 to recover their nominal value, and longer still to recover in inflation-adjusted terms. The investor who bought Japanese stocks in 1989 still has not recovered their peak value more than three decades later.

Stocks represent claims on the productive capital of the economy. When you own stocks broadly, you own a slice of human enterprise itself—the factories, the intellectual property, the organizational knowledge, the ongoing effort to create value through production and exchange. The returns to stocks reflect the returns to entrepreneurship, the profits that accrue to those who deploy capital successfully in the face of uncertainty.

The psychological difficulty of holding stocks should not be underestimated. Their volatility triggers loss aversion, the tendency to feel losses more acutely than equivalent gains. When stocks fall, every instinct screams to sell, to stop the pain, to flee to safety. This instinct, if followed, locks in losses and forfeits the recovery that historically follows. The successful stock investor must override their emotional responses repeatedly, sometimes for years at a stretch.

**Categories of Stocks.** Stocks come in various categories that behave somewhat differently. Large-capitalization stocks, those of the biggest companies, tend to be more stable than small-capitalization stocks but offer somewhat lower expected returns over time. Growth stocks, those of companies expected to expand rapidly, behave differently than value stocks, those of mature companies trading at lower prices relative to their earnings. International stocks diversify away from any single country's economic fortunes but introduce currency risk and different regulatory environments. Emerging market stocks offer higher potential returns with higher volatility and political risk.

For most investors, the way to own stocks is through diversified funds rather than individual securities. Owning one company's stock concentrates your fortunes with that company. Owning hundreds or thousands of companies through an index fund spreads your risk across the entire market. The individual company may fail. The entire market, while it fluctuates, has never gone to zero and reflects the aggregate success of human economic activity.

**Bonds: Lending Your Money**

If stocks represent ownership, bonds represent lending. When you buy a bond, you are lending money to the issuer, whether a government, a corporation, or another entity. In return, the issuer promises to pay you interest, typically at regular intervals, and to return your principal at a specified maturity date.

The mechanics are simple in principle. A ten-year Treasury bond with a face value of one thousand dollars and a coupon rate of four percent will pay you forty dollars per year for ten years, then return your thousand dollars at maturity. You know exactly what you will receive if you hold to maturity and if the issuer does not default.

This predictability is the primary attraction of bonds. Unlike stocks, whose future returns are uncertain, bonds promise specific cash flows. If you need a known amount of money at a known future date, bonds can provide it with high confidence, assuming the issuer remains solvent.

**Interest Rate Risk.** Bond prices move inversely with interest rates. If you buy a bond paying four percent and rates subsequently rise to six percent, no one will pay full price for your bond when they could buy a new one at the higher rate. Your bond's market value declines. If you hold to maturity, you still receive everything promised. But if you need to sell before maturity, you may take a loss. The longer a bond's maturity, the more sensitive its price to interest rate changes.

**Credit Risk.** The issuer might fail to pay. Government bonds from stable countries carry minimal credit risk because governments can tax and, in the case of debt denominated in their own currency, create money. Corporate bonds carry more risk because corporations can and do go bankrupt. Bonds from financially stressed governments carry risk because default, while rare, is possible. Higher credit risk means higher interest rates to compensate investors for bearing that risk. Credit rating agencies assess this risk, though their judgments are imperfect.

**Inflation Risk.** The fixed payments you receive may buy less over time as prices rise. A bond paying four percent when inflation runs five percent is losing purchasing power every year. You receive more dollars, but those dollars buy less. This is why bonds have historically delivered lower real returns than stocks. Their safety is partly illusory if inflation erodes their value.

Historically, high-quality bonds have returned roughly four to five percent annually before inflation, or one to two percent after inflation. This is substantially less than stocks, but the path is smoother. Bonds rarely lose half their value in a year. They provide ballast to a portfolio, reducing overall volatility even as they reduce expected returns.

**Types of Bonds.** Treasury bonds, issued by the federal government, are considered the safest and serve as the benchmark against which other bonds are measured. Municipal bonds, issued by state and local governments, often offer tax advantages. Corporate bonds range from investment-grade issues of stable companies to high-yield or "junk" bonds of shakier issuers. Treasury Inflation-Protected Securities, or TIPS, adjust their principal for inflation, providing direct protection against rising prices.

For most investors, bonds serve as a stabilizing element in a portfolio. They tend to rise when stocks fall, or at least fall less. During market panics, investors flee to the safety of government bonds, driving their prices up. This negative or low correlation with stocks makes bonds valuable for reducing portfolio volatility, even if their returns are modest. Bond index funds offer broad exposure at minimal cost.

**Cash and Cash Equivalents**

Cash, in investment terms, means not just physical currency but any highly liquid, stable-value asset. Money market funds, Treasury bills, bank savings accounts, and certificates of deposit all qualify as cash or cash equivalents. They offer immediate availability and near-zero risk of losing nominal value.

The return on cash is typically low, often below inflation. In some environments, cash returns are essentially zero or even negative in real terms. This is the price of safety and liquidity. You sacrifice return for the certainty that your money will be there when you need it, worth approximately what you put in nominally.

Cash serves essential functions despite its low returns. It provides an emergency fund, money available immediately when unexpected needs arise. It serves as dry powder for opportunities, capital ready to deploy when investments become attractively priced. It covers near-term spending needs without requiring you to sell volatile assets at potentially unfavorable times.

The danger of cash is holding too much for too long. Inflation erodes purchasing power relentlessly. One hundred dollars held in cash for thirty years at three percent inflation becomes worth only forty-one dollars in today's purchasing power. Cash is not truly safe over long periods. It is merely stable in nominal terms while declining in real terms.

Money's value derives from its exchange function, its ability to command goods and services. When inflation outpaces the return on cash, holding money becomes a losing proposition. The prudent approach is to hold enough cash for immediate needs and invest the rest in assets that can outpace inflation.

For most investors, cash should represent a modest portion of total assets—enough for emergencies and near-term needs but not so much that it drags down long-term returns. The precise amount depends on personal circumstances, income stability, and upcoming known expenses.

### Real Estate

Real estate represents ownership of land and the structures built upon it. As an investment, it comes in two primary forms: direct ownership of property and indirect ownership through securities like real estate investment trusts.

**Direct Ownership.** This means buying a home, an apartment building, commercial property, or land. The returns come from two sources: rental income if the property is leased to tenants, and appreciation if the property's value rises over time. Real estate offers tangible utility that financial assets do not. You can live in a house. You cannot live in a stock certificate.

The historical returns to real estate are surprisingly modest when measured rigorously. Home prices, adjusted for inflation, have risen only about one percent annually over the very long term in most developed countries. The apparent wealth created by homeownership often reflects leverage (mortgages magnify gains and losses), maintenance costs that are forgotten, and the imputed rent of living in the property rather than paying a landlord. Still, real estate has generated positive real returns over time, and for many families, home equity represents their primary wealth.

Rental properties can generate attractive returns but require active management. Tenants must be found, rents collected, repairs made, vacancies absorbed. The returns compensate for this labor as much as for the capital invested. Real estate is not purely passive in the way stock ownership is.

**Real Estate Investment Trusts.** REITs offer a way to own real estate without the burdens of direct ownership. These publicly traded companies own portfolios of properties, from office buildings to shopping centers to apartment complexes to data centers. They must distribute most of their income as dividends, providing regular cash flow. Their shares trade on exchanges like stocks, offering liquidity that direct real estate ownership lacks.

Real estate diversifies a portfolio because its returns are not perfectly correlated with stocks or bonds. Property values reflect local economic conditions, interest rates, and supply and demand for physical space—factors that differ from those driving stock prices. Owning some real estate, whether directly or through REITs, can reduce overall portfolio volatility.

**Risks of Real Estate.** These include illiquidity for direct holdings (selling a property takes months, not seconds), sensitivity to interest rates (higher rates increase mortgage costs and reduce buyer demand), local economic conditions that can devastate particular markets, and the concentration that comes from owning one or a few properties. The investor whose wealth is tied up in a single rental property faces catastrophic risk if that property burns, if the local economy collapses, or if a lawsuit results in a massive judgment.

Real estate functions as a form of capital good, producing ongoing services of shelter or commercial space. The returns to real estate reflect the value of these services and the scarcity of desirable land. In a world of growing population and limited geography, well-located real estate tends to appreciate over the very long term.

**Commodities**

Commodities are raw materials and primary goods: oil, gold, wheat, copper, cattle, coffee. They are the physical inputs to economic production and consumption. As investments, they behave quite differently from stocks and bonds.

Commodities do not generate earnings like a company or pay interest like a bond. A barrel of oil sitting in storage produces nothing. Its value comes solely from what someone will pay for it in the future. Commodity prices are volatile, driven by supply and demand dynamics, weather, geopolitics, and speculation.

Historically, commodities have delivered returns slightly above inflation over very long periods, but with enormous volatility and long stretches of disappointing performance. They do not compound the way productive assets do. Their primary investment appeal lies in diversification and inflation protection.

Commodities tend to rise when inflation is high because they are the physical goods whose prices define inflation. When paper currency loses value, tangible goods become more valuable in currency terms. This makes commodities a potential hedge against unexpected inflation, complementing bonds, which suffer when inflation rises unexpectedly.

Investing in commodities directly is impractical for most people. You cannot store crude oil in your garage. Instead, investors access commodities through futures contracts, exchange-traded funds, or the stocks of commodity-producing companies. Each approach has different characteristics. Futures involve rolling contracts and can deviate from spot prices. ETFs may use futures or hold physical commodities. Producer stocks are influenced by company-specific factors beyond commodity prices.

**Gold** deserves special mention because of its historical role as money and its enduring psychological appeal. Gold has preserved purchasing power over very long periods. An ounce of gold bought roughly the same amount of goods in ancient Rome as it does today. But over shorter periods, gold can be extremely volatile and has experienced long bear markets. It pays no dividend and produces nothing.

Its value rests entirely on the belief that others will value it in the future.

Gold emerged historically as the market's choice for money through spontaneous order rather than government decree. Its monetary properties—divisibility, durability, portability, recognizability—explain its persistent appeal. But value is subjective. Gold is worth what people will pay for it, no more and no less. The investor who expects gold to serve as a reliable store of value should understand that its price can halve and stay depressed for decades.

For most investors, commodities should represent a small allocation, if any. Their volatility, lack of income, and modest long-term returns make them unsuitable as core holdings. They may provide diversification benefits in specific circumstances but should not be the foundation of a portfolio.

**Alternative Investments**

Beyond the traditional asset classes lie alternatives: private equity, hedge funds, venture capital, and more exotic instruments. These investments are typically available only to wealthy or institutional investors, carry higher fees, offer less liquidity, and promise potentially higher returns.

**Private Equity** means ownership of companies that do not trade on public exchanges. Private equity funds buy companies, attempt to improve their operations or financial structure, and sell them later at a profit. The returns can be attractive, but the investments are illiquid—often locked up for a decade—and fees are substantial, typically including both management fees and a share of profits. Access is limited to accredited investors meeting income or net worth thresholds.

**Venture Capital** is a specialized form of private equity focused on young, high-growth companies. The potential returns are enormous if an investment becomes the next transformative company. But most venture investments fail entirely. The asset class is characterized by extreme outcomes: a few huge winners subsidizing many total losses. Returns to venture capital are highly dependent on access to the best funds, which are typically closed to new investors.

**Hedge Funds** employ strategies unavailable to traditional funds: short selling, leverage, derivatives, arbitrage. The best hedge funds have delivered strong risk-adjusted returns, but the average hedge fund has underperformed simple index funds, especially after fees. The industry is vast and varied, making generalization difficult. Fees typically include two percent of assets annually plus twenty percent of profits.

**Cryptocurrency** represents a newer category that defies easy classification. Bitcoin, Ethereum, and thousands of other digital tokens use cryptographic technology to create scarce digital assets. Proponents see them as revolutionary money, a hedge against government currency debasement, or platforms for decentralized applications. Critics see them as speculative manias with no intrinsic value. The volatility has been extreme, with drawdowns of eighty percent or more followed by recoveries to new highs. The asset class is too young for reliable conclusions about long-term returns.

**Derivatives**—options, futures, and related instruments—allow investors to take leveraged positions, hedge existing holdings, or speculate on price movements. These instruments are powerful tools in sophisticated hands but dangerous for the uninformed. They can multiply gains but also multiply losses, sometimes beyond the initial investment. Chapter 12 will explore derivatives in more detail.

The psychological appeal of alternatives is worth noting. They seem sophisticated, exclusive, and exciting compared to boring index funds. They offer the narrative of beating the market, of accessing opportunities unavailable to the masses. This narrative appeals to our desire to feel special and skilled, even when the average investor in alternatives underperforms simple strategies.

For most investors, alternatives should be approached with extreme caution or avoided entirely. The complexity, fees, illiquidity, and access barriers make them unsuitable for building foundational wealth. The wealthy investor who has already secured their financial future may find them interesting for a small allocation. The person building wealth is almost always better served by the traditional asset classes, simply and cheaply accessed.

**The Role of Each Asset in a Portfolio**

Understanding asset classes individually is necessary but not sufficient. What matters is how they combine into a portfolio. Each asset serves a purpose, and the combination determines both the expected return and the volatility of your wealth over time.

**Stocks** are the growth engine. Over long periods, they deliver the highest returns. But they are volatile, capable of losing half their value in a year. A portfolio without stocks will likely fail to outpace inflation and build real wealth. A portfolio of only stocks will experience terrifying declines that test the investor's resolve.

**Bonds** are the stabilizer. They provide modest, reliable returns and tend to hold value or rise when stocks fall. A portfolio without bonds exposes you to the full violence of market declines. A portfolio of only bonds will grow too slowly to meet most long-term goals and offers no protection against unexpected inflation.

**Cash** is the buffer. It provides immediate liquidity for emergencies and opportunities. Too little cash leaves you vulnerable to forced selling at bad times. Too much cash drags down long-term returns as inflation erodes its value.

**Real estate** provides diversification and, for homeowners, a tangible asset that serves as both investment and shelter. It behaves differently from financial assets and can smooth portfolio returns.

**Commodities and alternatives** may offer additional diversification or specific characteristics like inflation protection. But they are not essential, and their complexity and costs often outweigh their benefits for individual investors.

The art of portfolio construction lies in combining these assets in proportions suited to your goals, time horizon, and temperament. There is no single correct allocation. There are only tradeoffs. More stocks means higher expected returns and higher volatility. More bonds means lower expected returns and lower volatility. The right balance depends on when you need the money and how much uncertainty you can tolerate along the way. Chapter 14 will address portfolio construction in detail.

**Creating Your Mental Map**

The investment universe is vast, but its essential structure is comprehensible.

Ownership assets—primarily stocks and real estate—give you a stake in productive enterprises. You share in their success and bear their risks. Their returns are variable but have historically exceeded inflation substantially over long periods.

Lending assets—primarily bonds—make you a creditor. You receive fixed payments and face the risk that the borrower cannot pay or that inflation erodes your returns. Their returns are more predictable but more modest.

Cash provides stability and liquidity at the cost of growth. It is essential for short-term needs but destructive of wealth if held excessively over long periods.

Alternatives offer varied characteristics but usually add complexity and cost without commensurate benefit for most investors.

With this map in mind, you can evaluate any investment opportunity. When someone proposes an investment, ask: Is this ownership or lending? What are the sources of return? What are the risks? How does it fit with what I already own? How liquid is it? What does it cost? How is the person proposing it compensated?

Most investments fit somewhere on this map. Those that do not—those that claim to offer high returns with low risk, that cannot be explained in simple terms—should be approached with skepticism or avoided entirely. The fundamental relationships between risk and return, between different asset classes, between complexity and cost, hold across time and circumstance. Understanding them protects you from the countless schemes that depend on your ignorance.

**Summary**

The investment universe divides into several major asset classes, each with distinct characteristics.

**Stocks** represent ownership of businesses and have delivered the highest long-term returns of any major asset class—roughly six to seven percent annually after inflation. This return comes with substantial volatility; stocks can lose half their value in months and take years to recover. Diversification across many stocks through index funds eliminates company-specific risk while capturing market returns.

**Bonds** represent lending to governments or corporations. They offer predictable cash flows and lower volatility than stocks but also lower expected returns—historically one to two percent after inflation. They face interest rate risk (prices fall when rates rise), credit risk (the borrower may default), and inflation risk (fixed payments lose purchasing power). Bonds serve as portfolio stabilizers.

**Cash** provides safety and liquidity but earns returns that typically fail to keep pace with inflation. It is essential for emergencies and near-term needs but destructive of wealth if held excessively over long periods.

**Real estate** offers diversification, tangible utility, and modest long-term returns above inflation. Direct ownership requires active management; REITs provide liquid, passive exposure.

**Commodities** provide potential inflation protection and diversification but generate no income and have delivered modest long-term returns with high volatility. Gold, despite its historical role as money, can experience decades-long bear markets.

**Alternatives**—private equity, hedge funds, venture capital, cryptocurrency—are typically illiquid, expensive, and inaccessible to most investors. Average returns often fail to compensate for their complexity and costs.

Portfolio construction combines these assets based on goals, time horizon, and risk tolerance. Stocks drive long-term growth; bonds reduce volatility; cash provides liquidity; real estate and commodities may offer diversification. The right mix involves tradeoffs, not a single optimal answer.

# TEN
# THE CASE FOR SIMPLICITY

In 1976, a fund manager named John Bogle launched a product that his competitors mocked as "Bogle's Folly." The premise seemed almost offensive to the investment profession: instead of trying to pick winning stocks, the fund would simply buy every stock in the S&P 500 index, in proportion to each company's size, and hold them. No analysis. No judgment. No attempt to distinguish promising companies from doomed ones. Just passive ownership of the entire market.

The fund gathered a mere eleven million dollars in its initial offering, a humiliating result. Wall Street professionals dismissed it as un-American, a surrender to mediocrity. Why would anyone settle for average returns when skilled managers could deliver superior performance?

Four decades later, index funds hold more than half of all U.S. equity fund assets. Bogle's folly became the most successful innovation in the history of retail investing. The professionals who mocked him have spent their careers being beaten by the strategy they derided.

This chapter explains why. The answer is not complicated, but it is counterintuitive enough that most investors still resist it. Understanding the case for index investing—truly understanding it, not just nodding along—is one of the most valuable intellectual achievements available to anyone who wants to build wealth.

**The Arithmetic Nobody Can Escape**

Before we discuss theory or evidence, let us establish a mathematical truth that requires no assumptions about market efficiency or investor skill. This truth holds regardless of whether markets are rational or irrational, whether some investors are geniuses or all are fools.

Here it is: the aggregate return of all investors, before costs, must equal the return of the market.

This is not an empirical finding. It is arithmetic. The market is simply the sum of all invested dollars. If the market returns ten percent in a given year, then the dollar-weighted average return of all investors must also be ten percent. For every investor who beats the market, another investor must trail it by an equal amount. Outperformance and underperformance must sum to zero.

Now introduce costs. Active investors pay more than passive investors. They pay higher management fees to fund managers who employ analysts and make decisions. They pay more in trading costs because active strategies require buying and selling. They pay more in taxes because frequent trading generates taxable events.

If all investors collectively earn the market return before costs, and active investors pay higher costs than passive investors, then active investors must collectively earn less than passive investors after costs. This is not a tendency or a probability. It is a certainty.

The investor who buys an index fund that charges 0.03 percent annually receives the market return minus 0.03 percent. The investor who buys an actively managed fund charging 1.0 percent annually must, on average, receive the market return minus 1.0 percent. The active investor starts nearly a full percentage point behind before any stock is selected.

William Sharpe, a Nobel laureate in economics, formalized this logic in a 1991 paper titled "The Arithmetic of Active Management."

His conclusion is worth quoting directly: "After costs, the return on the average actively managed dollar will be less than the return on the average passively managed dollar."

This holds in any period, for any market, under any conditions. It is not a statement about efficient markets or unskilled managers. It is pure arithmetic.

**The Evidence Nobody Can Dismiss**

Arithmetic tells us that the average active investor must lose to the average passive investor. But perhaps skilled investors can consistently beat the average? Perhaps the losers are unsophisticated retail investors, while professionals reliably outperform?

This is an empirical question, and the evidence is devastating to the active management industry.

The S&P Dow Jones Indices publishes a semi-annual study called SPIVA—the S&P Indices Versus Active scorecard—that tracks how actively managed funds perform relative to their benchmark indices. The results have been remarkably consistent across decades, countries, and market conditions.

Over rolling fifteen-year periods, approximately ninety percent of actively managed U.S. stock funds fail to beat their benchmark index. The numbers are similar for bond funds, international funds, and emerging market funds. This is not a narrow failure; it is near-universal underperformance.

Perhaps more damning: past success does not predict future success. The funds that beat their benchmarks over one five-year period are no more likely than random chance to beat them over the next five years. Top-quartile performance does not persist. Skill, if it exists, is either too rare to identify in advance or too unstable to exploit.

The professionals manage billions of dollars. They employ armies of analysts with elite credentials. They have access to company executives, sophisticated research, real-time data feeds. They devote their entire working lives to the task of selecting investments. And they lose, reliably and overwhelmingly, to a strategy that requires no skill whatsoever.

This outcome becomes less puzzling once you understand what the professionals are competing against.

**The Paradox of Skill**

Here is the subtle truth that explains professional failure: the market is hard to beat precisely because so many skilled people are trying to beat it.

Imagine a poker game where all the players are amateurs. The one professional at the table will clean up. Now imagine a poker game where all the players are professionals. No one has an edge. Skill still exists—everyone at the table is excellent—but skill is evenly distributed, so outcomes depend largely on chance.

Financial markets are that second poker game. The investors trying to beat the market are not random members of the public. They are professionals who have survived a brutal selection process. They are smart, hardworking, well-resourced, and intensely motivated by large financial incentives. They study the same companies, read the same reports, use similar analytical frameworks.

Any advantage one investor discovers is quickly discovered by others. Any mispricing is rapidly corrected. The collective effect of all these smart people trying to beat the market is a market that is very difficult to beat.

This is the paradox of skill: the more skill that exists in a competitive arena, the less skill determines outcomes. Michael Mauboussin, who has studied this phenomenon extensively, notes that as absolute skill levels rise across competitors, luck becomes the primary differentiator of results.

It is possible that some investors possess genuine skill. But skill has diminishing marginal returns when everyone is skilled. And whatever skill exists must overcome the arithmetic handicap of higher costs. A manager must be not just good, but sufficiently better than the competition to offset the fee disadvantage. Very few can clear that hurdle consistently.

**What We Mean by Efficiency**

The academic framework for understanding these patterns is called the Efficient Market Hypothesis, developed primarily by economist Eugene Fama. The hypothesis comes in several strengths, but the core insight is simple: prices reflect available information.

In a market populated by intelligent, profit-seeking investors, new information is quickly incorporated into stock prices. When a company announces better-than-expected earnings, the stock price adjusts within minutes or seconds. There is no leisurely opportunity to analyze the news and trade on it. By the time you read the headline, the adjustment has already occurred.

This does not mean prices are always correct. It means prices are correct enough, often enough, that predicting their direction is extraordinarily difficult. The market can be irrational, but if you cannot predict when and how it will be irrational, you cannot exploit that irrationality.

Critics sometimes attack the Efficient Market Hypothesis by pointing to bubbles and crashes. Surely, they argue, a market that occasionally loses half its value cannot be efficient. But this misunderstands the claim. Efficiency does not mean stability. It does not mean prices always reflect fundamental value. It means that you, the individual investor, are unlikely to outsmart the collective intelligence of the market consistently enough to overcome your cost disadvantage.

The practical question is not whether markets are perfectly efficient. They are not. The question is whether markets are efficient enough that you should expect to beat them after costs. For the overwhelming majority of investors, the answer is no.

**The Cost Equation**

Let us make the cost disadvantage concrete.

The average actively managed stock mutual fund charges approximately 0.70 percent annually in explicit management fees. The average index fund tracking the S&P 500 charges approximately 0.03

percent. This difference of 0.67 percentage points may sound trivial. It is not.

Consider a forty-year investment horizon, starting with one hundred thousand dollars and earning seven percent annually before fees. At the end of forty years, the index fund investor, paying 0.03 percent, has approximately 1,456,000 dollars. The active fund investor, paying 0.70 percent, has approximately 1,178,000 dollars.

The difference—278,000 dollars—is money transferred from the investor to the fund management industry. It purchases no improvement in returns. It is pure leakage.

But explicit management fees are only part of the cost. Active funds also incur higher trading costs, as they buy and sell frequently. They generate more taxable events, reducing after-tax returns. And many active funds have load fees—upfront or back-end charges—that further erode investor capital.

When all costs are included, the hurdle an active manager must clear becomes daunting. An active fund might need to outperform its benchmark by one and a half percentage points annually just to match the net return of an index fund. Sustained outperformance of that magnitude is exceptionally rare.

**The Case for Indexing**

The positive case for index investing follows directly from the arithmetic.

Index funds deliver market returns minus minimal costs. This sounds modest until you recognize that market returns, over long periods, have been excellent. U.S. stocks have returned approximately ten percent annually over the past century. After adjusting for inflation, that is roughly seven percent real return—enough to double purchasing power every decade.

Capturing the market return is not settling for mediocrity. It is capturing one of the most powerful wealth-building forces available to ordinary people. The problem was never that market returns are inadequate. The problem was that investors kept finding ways to earn less than market returns through poor timing, excessive fees, and self-defeating behavior.

Index funds also offer diversification without effort. A single total stock market index fund might hold three or four thousand companies. This diversification reduces company-specific risk to near zero. You will never suffer catastrophic losses because you were concentrated in a single company that failed.

The simplicity of index investing is itself a benefit. You need not spend time researching companies or evaluating fund managers. You need not monitor your investments for signs that your strategy has stopped working. You need not make decisions that create opportunities for behavioral errors. You set your allocation, invest regularly, and let compound growth work.

**The Limitations**

Intellectual honesty requires acknowledging the limitations of index investing.

Index funds guarantee you will never beat the market. If your goal is market-beating returns, indexing cannot achieve it. This is a sacrifice worth making for most investors, because the attempt to beat the market usually produces returns worse than the market. But it is a sacrifice nonetheless.

**The Capitalization-Weighting Critique.** Most index funds weight their holdings by market capitalization—the total market value of each company's shares. This means the fund automatically owns more of larger companies and less of smaller ones. Critics, particularly value investors, point out that this approach has a structural flaw: it guarantees you own more of overvalued companies and less of undervalued companies. When a stock becomes overpriced, its market cap rises, and the index fund buys more of it. When a stock becomes cheap, its market cap falls, and the index fund sells.

This critique is theoretically valid. A capitalization-weighted index does mechanically overweight whatever the market is currently enthusiastic about. In a bubble, index investors ride the bubble up and then ride it down.

However, the practical significance of this flaw is limited. Alternatives exist: equal-weighted indexes that hold the same amount of each company, fundamentally-weighted indexes that weight by earnings or dividends or book value, and various "smart beta" strategies that attempt to correct for capitalization weighting's biases. These alternatives have theoretical appeal. But after accounting for their higher costs and trading expenses, they have not consistently outperformed simple capitalization-weighted indexes over long periods. The theoretical flaw does not translate to practical advantage. The simplest approach remains, for most investors, the best approach.

**Market-Specific Considerations.** Indexing works best in large, liquid, heavily-analyzed markets. The case is strongest for U.S. large-cap stocks, where thousands of analysts scrutinize every company and any mispricing is rapidly corrected. It may be somewhat weaker in less-followed markets—small-cap stocks, frontier markets, obscure bonds—where information is scarcer and fewer professionals compete. Even in these markets, however, the evidence suggests that most active managers fail to add value after costs. The bar for successful active management may be lower, but few clear it.

**Behavioral Requirements.** Index investing requires the discipline to hold through terrifying declines. The investor who abandons their index fund at the bottom of a bear market will not capture long-term market returns. The simplicity of the strategy does not make it easy to execute emotionally. In some ways, passive investing is harder than active investing because it requires you to do nothing when every instinct screams for action.

### When Deviation Might Be Warranted

Given the overwhelming evidence for indexing, when might deviation be justified? The honest answer is: rarely, and with great caution.

The most common reason investors give for active management is access to exceptional managers. In theory, some managers possess genuine skill—the ability to identify mispriced securities or time market movements consistently enough to overcome their cost disadvantage. Such managers exist, but several facts should temper enthusiasm.

First, they are extraordinarily rare. The SPIVA data suggests that perhaps ten percent of managers outperform over long periods, which is roughly what you would expect from chance alone. Identifying the genuinely skilled among the lucky is nearly impossible in advance.

Second, successful managers often close to new investors. A manager with a genuine edge faces diminishing returns as assets grow. The best opportunities are in smaller, less liquid securities that cannot absorb large amounts of capital. Truly skilled managers have strong incentives to limit their asset base, which means the managers accepting your money are less likely to be the exceptional ones.

Third, past performance provides weak evidence of future success. A manager who has beaten the market for ten years may have been skilled or may have been lucky. Distinguishing between these possibilities requires more data than a human lifetime provides.

Fourth, even if you identify a skilled manager, their fee structure may capture most of the value they create. A manager who generates two percent annual outperformance but charges one and a half percent in fees is not particularly valuable to you.

If despite these obstacles you believe you have found an exceptional manager—one with a long track record, a coherent explanation for why their edge should persist, fee structures that share gains fairly, and limited assets under management—a minority allocation might be reasonable. But you should understand that most investors who believe they have found such a manager are wrong.

Some investors deviate from indexing because they enjoy the process of analyzing companies and constructing portfolios. If this describes you, intellectual honesty requires treating active investing as entertainment rather than as a wealth-building strategy. Confine it to a small percentage of your assets—money you can afford to underperform with. Do not let hobby investing infect your core portfolio.

Finally, genuinely specialized knowledge can occasionally provide an edge. A semiconductor engineer may understand technology trends before Wall Street analysts. A commercial real estate developer may recognize local market dynamics invisible to distant investors. But this is different from the vague sense most people have that they understand their industry. Genuine informational advantages are narrow, specific, and rare. Most people who believe they possess them are experiencing overconfidence rather than insight.

In all these cases, the burden of proof rests heavily on the decision to deviate. Indexing is the default, the strategy that wins unless you have compelling, specific, evidence-based reasons to do otherwise. The investor who cannot articulate precisely why their situation differs from the typical case should not deviate.

### Simplicity as the Destination

The most profound argument for index investing is not about returns or costs. It is about simplicity.

The investor who indexes their portfolio eliminates vast categories of decisions that create opportunities for error. They do not choose which stocks to buy or sell. They do not evaluate fund managers. They do not time their entry and exit. They do not respond to market news with adjustments.

Each eliminated decision is a potential mistake avoided. The research on investor behavior shows that investors systematically make poor decisions. They buy high, sell low, chase performance, and abandon strategies at precisely the wrong times. Complexity multiplies the opportunities for these errors.

Simplicity is not a consolation prize for those who cannot master complexity. It is the destination that complexity eventually reaches. The most sophisticated investors in the world, after decades of study, often conclude that simple strategies beat complex ones. The complex strategies sound more impressive. They feel more active, more professional, more worthy of the fees they charge. But they do not deliver better results.

John Bogle lived to see his folly become the industry standard. Before his death in 2019, he estimated that index investing had saved ordinary investors hundreds of billions of dollars in fees they would otherwise have paid for underperformance. He titled his autobiography "Enough," and the word captures something essential about his philosophy. Enough ambition to save and invest. Enough humility to take what the market offers. Enough wisdom to recognize that more is often less.

The index fund is an investment vehicle. It is also a philosophical statement. It says that you do not need to be smarter than everyone else to build wealth. You do not need to beat the market. You need only participate in the market while controlling your costs and your behavior. This is achievable for anyone. And that is the revolutionary idea.

If the case for indexing is so overwhelming, why do most investors still fail to capture market returns? The answer lies not in the strategy but in the strategist—in the psychological patterns that lead us to abandon sound approaches at precisely the wrong moments. Understanding these patterns, and building defenses against them, is the subject of the next chapter.

## SUMMARY

**The arithmetic is inescapable.** All investors collectively earn the market return before costs. Active investors pay higher costs than passive investors. Therefore, active investors must collectively earn less than passive investors after costs. This is mathematical certainty, not empirical tendency.

**The evidence is overwhelming.** Over fifteen-year periods, approximately ninety percent of actively managed funds fail to beat their benchmark indexes. Past outperformance does not predict future outperformance. The fund industry's professional resources do not translate to superior results.

**The paradox of skill explains professional failure.** When all competitors are highly skilled, skill differences shrink and luck dominates outcomes. The market is hard to beat precisely because so many talented people are trying to beat it.

**Costs compound devastatingly.** A seemingly small fee difference of 0.67 percent annually can cost an investor nearly 280,000 dollars over forty years on a 100,000 dollar initial investment. Active management must dramatically outperform just to match index returns after costs.

**The capitalization-weighting critique has theoretical merit but limited practical significance.** Alternative weighting schemes have not consistently outperformed cap-weighted indexes after accounting for their higher costs.

**Index investing offers powerful advantages.** It captures excellent long-term market returns, provides broad diversification, eliminates the need for stock selection or manager evaluation, and reduces opportunities for behavioral errors.

**Deviation from indexing is rarely warranted.** Genuinely exceptional managers are rare, hard to identify in advance, often closed to new investors, and may capture most of their alpha in fees. Most investors who believe they have found exceptions are experiencing overconfidence.

**Simplicity is the destination, not a compromise.** Eliminating decisions eliminates opportunities for error. The most sophisticated investors often conclude that simple approaches beat complex ones.

# ELEVEN
# READING THE NUMBERS
## WHAT ECONOMIC DATA CAN AND CANNOT TELL YOU

Numbers surround us. Economic reports fill the news. Company earnings announcements move markets. Analysts pore over data, drawing conclusions and making predictions. For the average person trying to make sense of financial life, this flood of information can be overwhelming. What do these numbers mean? Which matter? How should they inform decisions?

This chapter provides a foundation for reading economic and financial data. It covers macroeconomic indicators—the vital signs of the broader economy—and microeconomic data about individual companies. It explores what these numbers can tell us and, equally important, what they cannot. The goal is not to make you an economist or financial analyst but to give you enough literacy to understand the conversation and evaluate claims made by those who purport to know.

A warning at the outset: data can illuminate, but it can also mislead. Numbers carry an aura of objectivity that words lack. A claim supported by statistics seems more credible than the same claim made without them. This is sometimes warranted—data can reveal truths that intuition misses. But it is sometimes dangerous—

data can be selected, manipulated, or misinterpreted to support almost any conclusion. Reading data well means reading it critically, understanding its limitations, and resisting the temptation to see precision where there is only estimation.

Before diving into specific indicators, a preview of where we are heading: knowing what GDP or the unemployment rate measures matters less than knowing how to interpret such measures, what their limitations are, and when to ignore them. We will cover the definitions first because you need vocabulary to follow the conversation. But the real payoff comes in learning to read these numbers skeptically and to resist the false confidence that precise-looking figures can inspire.

## Macroeconomic Indicators: The Vital Signs

Macroeconomics concerns the economy as a whole: total output, overall employment, the general price level, aggregate trade. Macroeconomic indicators are measurements of these aggregate phenomena. They tell us how the economy is doing in broad terms—whether it is growing or shrinking, whether jobs are plentiful or scarce, whether prices are stable or rising.

These indicators matter for personal finance in several ways. They affect the job market you operate in, the interest rates you pay and receive, the returns your investments generate, and the purchasing power of your money. Understanding them helps you interpret the economic environment and, perhaps, anticipate changes that affect your plans.

### Gross Domestic Product

Gross Domestic Product, or GDP, is the broadest measure of economic activity. It represents the total value of goods and services produced within a country during a specific period, typically a quarter or a year. When commentators speak of "the economy" growing or shrinking, they usually mean GDP.

GDP can be measured in three equivalent ways: as total spending on final goods and services, as total income earned in producing those goods and services, or as total value added across all industries. In theory, these should be equal; in practice, measurement errors create discrepancies that statisticians reconcile.

The spending approach breaks GDP into components: consumption by households, investment by businesses, government spending, and net exports (exports minus imports). These components reveal the structure of economic activity. In the United States, consumption dominates, typically accounting for about two-thirds of GDP. Changes in consumer spending therefore drive much of GDP fluctuation.

GDP growth is typically reported in two forms: nominal and real. Nominal GDP measures output in current prices, so it increases both when more is produced and when prices rise. Real GDP adjusts for inflation, isolating the change in actual output. Real GDP growth is what economists focus on when assessing economic performance; nominal growth can be misleading in periods of significant inflation.

A positive real GDP growth rate indicates an expanding economy—more goods and services being produced than before. A negative rate indicates contraction. Two consecutive quarters of negative real GDP growth is a common (though not official) definition of recession. The distinction matters: a recession is not merely slow growth but actual shrinkage.

GDP has significant limitations as a measure of wellbeing. It counts all production equally, whether beneficial or harmful—the costs of cleaning up pollution count the same as the production that caused it. It ignores unpaid work, including household labor and caregiving. It says nothing about distribution; GDP can rise while most people's incomes stagnate. It ignores environmental degradation and resource depletion. A country strip-mining its natural resources shows rising GDP even as it destroys future capacity. For these reasons, GDP is better understood as a measure of economic activity than as a measure of welfare or prosperity.

**Employment and Unemployment**

Employment data measure the labor market—how many people are working and how many are seeking work without finding it.

These numbers matter directly to most people because most people depend on work for income.

The unemployment rate is the most widely cited employment indicator. It measures the percentage of the labor force that is unemployed and actively seeking work. The labor force includes employed persons and unemployed persons seeking employment; it excludes those not working and not seeking work, such as retirees, students, and discouraged workers who have given up looking.

This definition creates quirks. The unemployment rate can fall for good reasons (more people finding jobs) or bad reasons (discouraged workers leaving the labor force). During severe downturns, the unemployment rate may understate distress because many people stop looking. The labor force participation rate—the percentage of the working-age population in the labor force—provides complementary information.

Beyond the headline unemployment rate, alternative measures capture different aspects of labor market health. The Bureau of Labor Statistics in the United States publishes several measures, from the narrowest (those unemployed fifteen weeks or longer) to the broadest (including marginally attached workers and those employed part-time for economic reasons). The broadest measure, sometimes called the "real" unemployment rate, is typically much higher than the headline rate and may better capture overall labor market slack.

Employment data also include job creation numbers—how many payroll jobs were added or lost in a given month. This flow measure complements the stock measure of unemployment. An economy can have high unemployment but also high job creation if many people are entering the labor force. Context matters.

Wage data complete the employment picture. Employment can be strong while wages stagnate, as occurred in much of the 2010s. Average hourly earnings, tracked monthly, indicate whether workers are gaining bargaining power. Real wages—nominal wages adjusted for inflation—indicate whether purchasing power is increasing.

**Inflation**

Inflation is the rate at which the general price level rises, eroding the purchasing power of money. Moderate inflation is considered normal and even healthy; deflation (falling prices) is generally considered more dangerous than mild inflation. But high or accelerating inflation disrupts economic life, distorting decisions and harming those on fixed incomes.

The Consumer Price Index, or CPI, is the most widely followed inflation measure. It tracks the cost of a "basket" of goods and services that a typical urban consumer purchases—food, housing, transportation, healthcare, and so on. Monthly changes in the CPI indicate the current pace of inflation.

CPI has known limitations. The basket is updated periodically but may not reflect current consumption patterns. Quality improvements are difficult to capture; a computer today is far more powerful than one twenty years ago, so comparing prices is complicated. Housing costs, a major component, are measured through "owners' equivalent rent," an estimate of what homeowners would pay to rent their homes, which may not track actual housing costs well.

Core inflation excludes food and energy prices, which are volatile and driven by factors outside the domestic economy. When oil prices spike due to geopolitical events, headline CPI may surge while core inflation remains stable. Policymakers often focus on core inflation as a better indicator of underlying trends, though this can seem disconnected from consumer experience when grocery and gasoline prices are rising.

The Personal Consumption Expenditures price index, or PCE, is another inflation measure that the Federal Reserve officially targets. It differs from CPI in technical ways—different weighting, different scope—and tends to run slightly lower. Both tell broadly similar stories but can diverge in particular periods.

Inflation expectations matter as much as current inflation. If people expect prices to rise, they may demand higher wages and raise their own prices, creating a self-fulfilling cycle. Surveys of consumer and business expectations, as well as market-based measures derived from inflation-protected bonds, indicate what people anticipate. The Federal Reserve monitors these closely, as anchored expectations help keep actual inflation stable.

**Interest Rates**

Interest rates are the price of borrowing money and the reward for lending it. They pervade economic life, affecting mortgages, car loans, credit cards, savings accounts, bonds, and business investment. Understanding the interest rate landscape helps you navigate borrowing and saving decisions.

The Federal Reserve sets the federal funds rate, the rate at which banks lend to each other overnight. This rate is the foundation of the interest rate structure; other rates are built upon it. When the Fed raises the federal funds rate, borrowing becomes more expensive throughout the economy. When it lowers the rate, borrowing becomes cheaper.

The Fed adjusts rates to pursue its dual mandate: maximum employment and stable prices. When the economy weakens, the Fed typically lowers rates to encourage borrowing and spending. When inflation rises, the Fed raises rates to cool economic activity. This balancing act is monetary policy's core function.

Market interest rates reflect the federal funds rate plus additional factors: the term of the loan, the creditworthiness of the borrower, and expectations about future rates. The yield curve—a graph of interest rates across different maturities—reveals market expectations. Normally, longer-term rates exceed shorter-term rates because lenders demand compensation for tying up money longer. When short-term rates exceed long-term rates, the yield curve "inverts," historically a signal of impending recession.

Real interest rates—nominal rates minus inflation—indicate the true cost of borrowing and true return to lending. When inflation exceeds nominal interest rates, real rates are negative: borrowers are effectively paying back less in purchasing power than they borrowed. This environment favors debtors over creditors and encourages borrowing.

## Other Key Indicators

Beyond these core indicators, numerous other data series provide insight into economic conditions.

Retail sales measure consumer spending at stores and restaurants, offering a timely read on household consumption. Since consumption drives most economic activity, retail sales often signal broader trends before they appear in GDP.

Industrial production measures output from factories, mines, and utilities. It is a narrower measure than GDP but more timely and a good indicator of the manufacturing sector's health.

Housing data—starts, permits, existing home sales, prices—matter because housing is a major sector and because home purchases are often consumers' largest financial decisions. Housing also leads the business cycle; construction often slows before the broader economy weakens.

Consumer confidence surveys ask households about their current situation and expectations. Confidence affects spending; pessimistic consumers retrench while optimistic ones spend. These surveys are subjective and volatile but provide useful information about household sentiment.

Business surveys, such as the Purchasing Managers' Index (PMI), ask business leaders about current conditions and expectations. A PMI above 50 indicates expansion; below 50 indicates contraction. These surveys often anticipate official data.

Trade data—imports, exports, the trade balance—measure international flows. A trade deficit (imports exceeding exports) is often portrayed negatively but is not inherently bad; it may reflect strong domestic demand and foreign willingness to invest.

Government budget data track revenues, spending, and the deficit or surplus. Federal debt outstanding indicates accumulated borrowing. These matter for fiscal policy's sustainability and potential future impacts on taxes and spending.

## How to Read Macroeconomic Data

Having surveyed the major indicators, we turn to what matters more: how to interpret them. Several principles help.

**Focus on trends rather than individual data points.** Any single month's report may be distorted by weather, seasonal adjustment issues, or random variation. A pattern across several months is more meaningful. Avoid overreacting to one report. The financial media treats each release as breaking news, but most individual reports tell us little we did not already know.

**Look at multiple indicators together.** No single indicator tells the whole story. Strong GDP growth with stagnant wages tells a different story than strong growth with rising wages. Rising unemployment with rising job creation tells a different story than rising unemployment with falling creation. Triangulate across measures to form a more complete picture.

**Understand the lag structure.** Some indicators are leading —they turn before the broader economy. Others are coincident—they move with the economy. Others are lagging—they turn after. Unemployment is famously lagging; it often rises even after recovery begins. Stock prices are leading; they often fall before recession is officially recognized. Housing permits lead construction, which leads employment in construction. Knowing which is which helps interpretation.

**Distinguish levels from changes.** A high unemployment rate is bad, but a falling high rate is better than a rising low rate. Direction often matters more than position. An economy healing from weakness may be better positioned than one deteriorating from strength. The same unemployment rate of 6 percent means something very different if it was 8 percent last year versus 4 percent last year.

**Be skeptical of forecasts.** Economic forecasting is notoriously difficult. Models that worked in the past may fail in the future. Experts routinely miss recessions and turning points. The Federal Reserve, with hundreds of PhD economists and access to nonpublic data, has a poor track record of predicting downturns. Data help you understand the present; they are far less reliable for predicting the future. Make decisions robust to uncertainty rather than betting on predictions.

**Recognize revisions.** Initial data releases are estimates that are revised, sometimes substantially, as more information becomes available. The first GDP report for a quarter is based on incomplete data; final estimates may differ by a full percentage point or more. Employment numbers are routinely revised by tens of thousands of jobs. Policy and market reactions to initial releases may later prove misguided. The data you see today may not be the data recorded in history.

**Account for publication lags.** Economic data describe the past, not the present. GDP for a quarter is released weeks after the quarter ends. By the time revisions are complete, months have passed. The economy you read about in the data may have already changed. This lag between reality and measurement is distinct from the backward-looking nature of data itself; it means that even the recent past is known imperfectly and with delay.

**Separate signal from noise.** Much economic commentary is noise: analysts explaining random fluctuations, pundits extrapolating short-term movements, media dramatizing routine variation. The underlying economic trends change slowly; most of what is reported as news is not particularly meaningful. Develop the discipline to ignore most of it. A monthly jobs report that comes in 30,000 above or below expectations is well within the margin of error and tells us essentially nothing.

For personal financial planning, macroeconomic data provide context rather than direction. They help you understand the environment—whether jobs are plentiful, whether inflation is eroding savings, whether rates are likely to rise or fall. They rarely dictate specific actions; personal circumstances matter more than macroeconomic conditions for most decisions. But understanding the environment helps you interpret your own situation and adjust expectations appropriately.

### Company Financial Data: Understanding the Trees

If macroeconomic indicators describe the forest, microeconomic data describe individual trees. For investors who own shares of companies or who are evaluating employment opportunities, understanding company-level financial data can be valuable.

A caveat before we proceed: earlier chapters argued that most individuals are better served by passive index investing than by picking individual stocks. If you accept that argument, detailed financial statement analysis becomes somewhat academic for your own investment decisions. You will not be poring over balance sheets to select stocks.

Yet understanding the basics remains useful. It helps you comprehend business news and earnings reports. It allows you to evaluate claims made by analysts and commentators. If you work for a company or are considering a job offer, understanding financial statements helps you assess your employer's stability and prospects. And if you run a business, even a small one, these concepts apply directly to your own operations.

Think of this section as understanding the game you are choosing not to play—or at least not to play actively. Knowing the rules and the scoring helps you appreciate what is happening even if you are not on the field.

### The Three Financial Statements

Every public company publishes three core financial statements: the income statement, the balance sheet, and the cash flow statement. Together, they provide a comprehensive picture of the company's financial position and performance.

The income statement reports what happened over a period—typically a quarter or a year. It begins with revenue, the money received from selling goods or services. It then subtracts various costs and expenses to arrive at profit. The cost of goods sold includes the direct costs of production. Gross profit is revenue minus cost of goods sold—a measure of how much the company earns from its core activity before overhead. Operating expenses include salaries, rent, marketing, research and development, and other costs of running the business. Operating income is gross profit minus operating expenses—what the company earns from operations before financing costs and taxes. Interest expense reflects the cost of debt. Pre-tax income is operating income minus interest. Income tax expense reduces this further. Net income, the bottom line, is what remains after all costs, expenses, interest, and taxes.

The income statement shows whether the company is profitable and where profit comes from. A company can have high revenue but low profit if costs are high. It can have high gross margins but low operating margins if overhead consumes the difference. Tracing through the statement reveals the structure of profitability.

The balance sheet reports the company's financial position at a specific moment—a snapshot rather than a movie. It has two sides that must be equal: assets on one side, liabilities and shareholders' equity on the other. Assets are what the company owns: cash, receivables, inventory, property, equipment, intangible assets like patents. Current assets are those convertible to cash within a year; non-current assets are longer-term. Liabilities are what the company owes: accounts payable, short-term debt, long-term debt, other obligations. Current liabilities are due within a year; non-current liabilities are longer-term. Shareholders' equity is the residual—assets minus liabilities—representing the owners' stake.

The balance sheet shows the company's financial structure. How much debt does it carry relative to equity? How liquid is it—can it pay near-term obligations? What assets does it have to generate future income? These questions are answered by the balance sheet.

The cash flow statement bridges the income statement and balance sheet, showing how cash moved during the period. It has three sections. Operating cash flow shows cash generated or used by business operations—essentially net income adjusted for non-cash items and changes in working capital. Investing cash flow shows cash spent on or received from buying and selling long-term assets.

Financing cash flow shows cash raised from or paid to investors and lenders—issuing stock, paying dividends, borrowing, repaying debt.

The cash flow statement matters because profit is not the same as cash. Accounting rules allow revenue recognition and expense matching that diverge from actual cash movement. A company can be profitable on paper while running out of cash, or unprofitable while generating cash. The statement reconciles the two.

**Key Financial Metrics**

From these statements, analysts derive numerous metrics to evaluate company performance. A few are particularly important.

Revenue growth measures how fast the company is expanding its top line. Companies can grow through selling more, raising prices, or acquiring other businesses. The source of growth matters; organic growth from selling more is generally viewed more favorably than growth through acquisition.

Profit margins measure how much of each revenue dollar becomes profit. Gross margin is gross profit divided by revenue. Operating margin is operating income divided by revenue. Net margin is net income divided by revenue. Higher margins indicate more efficient operations or stronger pricing power. Margins vary dramatically by industry; comparing margins across industries is misleading.

Return on equity measures how much profit the company generates relative to shareholders' investment. It is net income divided by shareholders' equity. A high ROE indicates efficient use of capital; a low ROE suggests the company struggles to translate capital into profit. However, high ROE can be achieved through high leverage (debt), which adds risk.

Return on assets measures profit relative to total assets—net income divided by assets. It is a broader measure than ROE, capturing how well the company uses all its resources, not just shareholder capital.

The debt-to-equity ratio measures leverage—total debt divided by shareholders' equity. A high ratio indicates reliance on borrowed money, which amplifies both gains and losses. Some industries (utilities, banks) normally carry high debt; others (technology) normally carry little.

The current ratio measures liquidity—current assets divided by current liabilities. A ratio above one indicates the company can likely meet short-term obligations; below one suggests potential liquidity problems.

Earnings per share (EPS) is net income divided by shares outstanding. It measures profit on a per-share basis, facilitating comparison across companies of different sizes and tracking changes over time when share counts change.

The price-to-earnings ratio (P/E) is the stock price divided by earnings per share. It indicates how much investors pay for each dollar of earnings—a measure of valuation. A high P/E suggests investors expect strong future growth; a low P/E suggests lower expectations or concerns. P/E varies widely by industry and market conditions.

Free cash flow is operating cash flow minus capital expenditures —the cash available after maintaining and expanding the business. It measures the cash the company could distribute to shareholders or use for acquisitions without borrowing. Many analysts consider free cash flow a more reliable measure than net income because it is harder to manipulate.

**Reading Financial Statements Critically**

Numbers on financial statements are not raw facts; they are products of accounting choices and, sometimes, deliberate manipulation. Reading critically means understanding how the numbers are constructed and where they might mislead.

Revenue recognition offers latitude. When does a sale count? Companies selling long-term contracts can recognize revenue upfront or spread it over the contract life. Aggressive recognition inflates current revenue at the expense of future periods. Changes in recognition policies can create apparent growth or decline that does not reflect underlying business change.

Depreciation and amortization affect profit but not cash. These non-cash charges allocate the cost of long-term assets over their useful lives. Companies choose depreciation schedules; different choices produce different reported profits from identical operations. Comparing companies with different depreciation policies requires adjustment.

One-time charges and gains distort trends. Companies may take "restructuring charges" or write down assets, producing unusually low profits in one period. They may sell assets, producing unusually high profits. Adjusted earnings, which exclude these items, may better reflect ongoing operations—or may be manipulated to make results look better. Both reported and adjusted numbers warrant scrutiny.

Non-GAAP measures proliferate. Companies report earnings according to Generally Accepted Accounting Principles (GAAP), but also report alternative measures that exclude various items. These adjusted measures may illuminate or obscure. A company consistently excluding stock compensation, a real cost to shareholders, is presenting a misleading picture. When a company emphasizes non-GAAP earnings that are consistently higher than GAAP earnings, skepticism is warranted.

Off-balance-sheet items can hide obligations. Some liabilities, like certain lease arrangements, have historically been structured to avoid appearing on balance sheets. Companies could appear less leveraged than they were. Accounting rules have tightened, but reading footnotes still reveals obligations not obvious from the main statements.

Related-party transactions signal potential problems. When a company transacts with entities controlled by its executives or directors, the transactions may not be at arm's length. Footnotes disclose these; they warrant attention.

Auditor opinions provide assurance, but limited. Auditors attest that financial statements fairly represent the company's position. But auditors are paid by the companies they audit, creating conflicts. Major frauds—Enron, WorldCom, Wirecard—occurred despite auditor approval. An unqualified opinion does not guarantee accuracy.

### What Financial Data Can and Cannot Tell You

Financial statements tell you what happened in the past. They reveal historical revenue, profit, assets, and cash flows. They show trends over time if you examine multiple periods. They allow comparison across companies in the same industry.

Financial statements do not tell you what will happen in the future. Past performance does not guarantee future results; this cliché is nonetheless true. A company with excellent historical financials can deteriorate; one with poor financials can improve. The statements provide a starting point for analysis, not a conclusion.

Financial statements do not tell you what a company is worth. Valuation requires judgment about future performance, risk, and appropriate discount rates. Two analysts examining identical statements can reach different valuations. The stock price reflects the market's collective judgment, which may be right or wrong.

Financial statements do not fully capture intangible value. A company's brand, customer relationships, employee talent, and competitive position may be its most important assets, yet they appear on the balance sheet only in limited ways. Technology companies with few tangible assets but enormous market values illustrate this gap.

Financial statements may not reflect reality. Despite rules and audits, companies sometimes misrepresent their position. Frauds are discovered only after they have occurred. Unusual patterns, aggressive accounting choices, and divergences between profit and cash flow warrant skepticism but are not definitive red flags.

### Using Company Data

For the individual investor committed to passive indexing, company financial data serve mainly to enhance understanding rather than to drive decisions. You will not be analyzing quarterly reports to decide which stocks to buy. But when you read that a major company missed earnings expectations or that a sector is struggling with margin compression, you will understand what those words mean.

If you are evaluating a job offer, understanding the employer's financials helps you assess stability and prospects. A company burning cash with no path to profitability may not be around to pay your salary in two years. A company with strong margins and consistent growth may offer better long-term career prospects. You can find public company financials in their SEC filings; for private companies, you may have to rely on news reports and your own judgment.

If you are a business owner, understanding financials is essential. You need to read your own statements, manage cash flow, and evaluate customers and suppliers. The concepts apply to businesses of all sizes, from sole proprietorships to multinational corporations.

**The Limits of Data**

Having surveyed macroeconomic and microeconomic data, we should step back and consider their limits more broadly.

Data are backward-looking. They tell you what happened, not what will happen. Extrapolating past trends into the future is tempting but often wrong. The economy surprises; companies disrupt and are disrupted. Data inform judgment but do not replace it.

Data are constructed. Every number reflects choices about what to count and how. Different methodologies produce different results. Revisions change the historical record. Comparisons across countries, time periods, or accounting regimes may be misleading. Understanding how data are constructed is part of using them wisely.

Data are incomplete. They capture what can be measured, missing what cannot. Economic wellbeing, job satisfaction, environmental sustainability, social cohesion—these matter but are not fully reflected in standard statistics. Over-reliance on measurable indicators can lead to optimizing the wrong things.

Data are subject to manipulation. Companies, governments, and analysts have incentives to present data favorably. Cherry-picking, selective disclosure, and outright fraud occur. Critical reading includes considering the source's incentives.

Data can create false confidence. Precise numbers suggest precise knowledge. But many economic statistics have wide margins of error. GDP estimates are revised for years. Employment surveys have sampling error. The appearance of precision masks genuine uncertainty.

Data overload can paralyze. There is always more data, another indicator, a different perspective. At some point, additional information does not improve decisions; it merely delays them. Knowing when you have enough information to act is part of practical wisdom.

For personal finance, these limits counsel humility. Read the numbers to understand context, not to predict the future. Recognize that experts with far more data and sophistication regularly fail to forecast accurately. Build plans robust to uncertainty rather than dependent on predictions. Use data as one input among many, not as the answer.

# TWELVE
# DERIVATIVES
## UNDERSTANDING WHAT TO AVOID

We turn now to a corner of finance that many people find intimidating: derivatives. The word itself sounds complex, and the instruments it describes—options, futures, swaps, and their many variations—are indeed more complicated than stocks and bonds. Derivatives have been blamed for financial crises and associated with spectacular losses. They are the province of specialists, or so it seems.

Yet derivatives, at their core, are simple in purpose: they are tools for managing risk. Understanding their basic logic illuminates how financial markets work and helps you evaluate whether they have any place in your own financial life. For most people, the answer is that they do not—but understanding why is valuable.

This chapter explains what derivatives are, why they exist, how the most common types work, and what their uses and dangers are. It concludes with reflections on day trading and speculation more broadly. The goal is not to make you a derivatives trader but to give you the knowledge to understand this part of the financial landscape and to recognize when you are being encouraged to enter territory where you do not belong.

### What Are Derivatives?

A derivative is a financial contract whose value derives from something else—an underlying asset, index, rate, or event. The "something else" can be almost anything: stocks, bonds, commodities, currencies, interest rates, even the weather. The derivative's value moves with the underlying, but the derivative is distinct from it.

Consider a simple example. You own a house. You worry that its value might fall before you sell it. Someone offers you a contract: if your house falls below a certain value in a year, they will pay you the difference. In exchange, you pay them a fee now. This is a derivative—its value depends on your house's future value. You have transferred the risk of price decline to someone else.

The key insight is that derivatives separate risk from ownership. The person who sold you that contract does not own your house or want to. They are taking on a risk—betting that prices will not fall—in exchange for the fee. You have reduced your risk in exchange for paying that fee. Both parties may be better off: you have security you value more than the fee; they have income they value more than the risk.

This separation of risk from ownership is derivatives' essential function. It allows risks to move to those most willing and able to bear them, and it allows economic actors to manage exposures that would otherwise constrain their activities.

**Why Do Derivatives Exist?**

Derivatives emerged from real economic needs. Farmers face uncertainty about future prices for their crops. A wheat farmer planting in spring does not know what wheat will sell for at harvest. If prices fall, they may lose money despite a good harvest. This uncertainty makes planning difficult and may discourage planting.

Futures contracts solve this problem. The farmer can sell a futures contract, agreeing now to deliver wheat at harvest for a specified price. This locks in the price, eliminating uncertainty. The buyer of the contract—perhaps a flour mill that needs wheat—gains certainty too. Both can plan with confidence.

The farmer has hedged—reduced risk by taking an offsetting position. The mill has also hedged. Neither is speculating; both are managing their core business risks. This is derivatives' original and most legitimate purpose.

Beyond hedging, derivatives enable speculation—betting on price movements without owning the underlying asset. A trader who believes oil prices will rise can buy oil futures without taking physical delivery of barrels. If right, they profit; if wrong, they lose. Speculation is often portrayed negatively, but it serves functions: it provides liquidity (someone for hedgers to trade with), it incorporates information into prices, and it connects current prices to expected future conditions.

Derivatives also enable arbitrage—profiting from price discrepancies without risk. If a stock trades at different prices in different markets, traders can buy low and sell high simultaneously. Arbitrage activity eliminates these discrepancies, keeping markets efficient. Derivatives facilitate complex arbitrage strategies that connect different markets.

Finally, derivatives enable access. An investor who cannot or does not want to buy the underlying asset can still gain exposure through derivatives. Someone who cannot store barrels of oil can trade oil futures. Someone who cannot short stocks directly can achieve similar effects through options. This access expands the universe of available strategies—for those with the expertise to use them.

**Futures and Forwards**

A futures contract is an agreement to buy or sell an asset at a specified price on a specified future date. The buyer agrees to purchase; the seller agrees to deliver. Both are obligated to perform unless they close their positions before expiration.

Futures contracts are standardized and trade on exchanges. The Chicago Mercantile Exchange, for example, lists futures on commodities (corn, wheat, oil, gold), financial instruments (stock indices, Treasury bonds, currencies), and other underlyings. Standardization enables liquidity; buyers and sellers can find each other easily.

Futures require margin—a deposit that demonstrates ability to perform. This margin is small relative to the contract's full value, creating leverage. A 10 percent margin means a $10,000 deposit controls $100,000 of underlying exposure. This leverage amplifies gains and losses: a 10 percent move in the underlying creates a 100 percent gain or loss on the margin.

Futures are marked to market daily. Gains and losses are settled each day, with margin accounts adjusted accordingly. If your position loses money, you must add margin; if it gains, you can withdraw. This mechanism prevents large losses from accumulating unaddressed.

A forward contract is similar but trades over the counter (directly between parties) rather than on an exchange. Forwards can be customized—any quantity, any delivery date, any terms the parties agree upon. This flexibility suits specific hedging needs. But forwards carry counterparty risk: if the other party cannot perform, you may not receive what was promised. Exchange-traded futures eliminate this risk through the exchange's clearinghouse, which guarantees performance.

The relationship between spot prices (current prices) and futures prices reveals market expectations. If futures prices exceed spot prices, the market expects prices to rise (or storage costs exceed the convenience yield of holding the physical asset). If futures prices are below spot prices, the reverse. This relationship, called the term structure, contains information about supply, demand, and expectations.

For most individuals, futures are not appropriate investment vehicles. The leverage is dangerous; small mistakes become large losses. The need to post margin and manage rollovers (replacing expiring contracts with later ones) creates complexity and cost. The specialized knowledge required to trade effectively is considerable. Futures are tools for professionals and for hedging specific commercial exposures, not for ordinary investing.

## Options: The Right but Not the Obligation

Options are derivatives that give the holder a right without an obligation. This asymmetry is their defining feature. You can exercise the option if it benefits you; you can let it expire if it does not. This flexibility has value, and that value is the option's price.

A call option gives the holder the right to buy the underlying asset at a specified price (the strike price) before or on a specified date (the expiration). If the asset's price rises above the strike, the call is valuable; you can buy at the lower strike price and sell at the higher market price. If the asset's price stays below the strike, the call expires worthless; you simply do not exercise it.

A put option gives the holder the right to sell the underlying asset at the strike price. If the asset's price falls below the strike, the put is valuable; you can sell at the higher strike price even though the market price is lower. If the asset's price stays above the strike, the put expires worthless.

Options have two types distinguished by exercise timing. American options can be exercised any time before expiration. European options can be exercised only at expiration. Most stock options are American; most index options are European. The names are historical and do not reflect geography.

The option buyer pays a premium to the option seller (also called the writer). This premium is the option's price. The buyer's maximum loss is the premium paid; if the option expires worthless, that is all they lose. The seller's maximum loss can be very large (for calls on assets that can rise significantly) or substantial (for puts on assets that can fall). This asymmetry explains why option selling is considered riskier than option buying, despite the fact that options often expire worthless.

## What Determines Option Prices

Option prices depend on several factors, formalized in pricing models. Understanding these factors helps you comprehend option behavior even if you never trade them.

The underlying price matters most. A call becomes more valuable as the underlying rises; a put becomes more valuable as the underlying falls. The relationship between current price and strike price determines whether the option is in the money (valuable to exercise), at the money (strike equals current price), or out of the money (not valuable to exercise).

Time to expiration matters. More time means more opportunity for the underlying to move favorably. Options lose value as expiration approaches—a phenomenon called time decay. An out-of-the-money option with a week to expiration is worth less than the same option with a year to expiration. This time decay is relentless; it works against option buyers every day.

Volatility matters critically. Options profit from large moves in the underlying; calls profit from large rises, puts from large falls. Higher expected volatility makes large moves more likely, making options more valuable. Implied volatility is the volatility that makes the model price equal to the market price; it reflects the market's expectation of future volatility. Changes in implied volatility can move option prices even when the underlying does not move.

Interest rates and dividends affect option prices more modestly, through mechanisms involving the present value of the strike price and the expected stock price drops when dividends are paid.

**The Greeks**

Professional option traders track the sensitivities of option prices to various factors using measures called "the Greeks." Two are particularly important for understanding basic option behavior.

Delta measures sensitivity to the underlying price. A delta of 0.5 means the option price moves about $0.50 for each $1.00 move in the underlying. Calls have positive delta (they gain when the underlying rises); puts have negative delta. Delta also approximates the probability of expiring in the money.

Theta measures time decay—how much the option loses each day, all else equal. Theta is negative for option buyers (time works against them) and positive for option sellers. The closer to expiration, the faster the decay. This is why buying options is often described as fighting the clock.

Other Greeks—gamma, vega, rho—measure sensitivity to other factors and matter for sophisticated trading strategies. The key insight for non-traders is that option prices depend on multiple factors interacting in complex ways. Even a correct prediction about direction can produce a losing trade if time decay or volatility changes work against you.

**Basic Option Strategies**

Options can be combined in numerous ways to create specific risk-return profiles. A few basic strategies illustrate the possibilities.

Buying a call is a bullish bet. You profit if the underlying rises above the strike plus the premium paid. Your maximum loss is the premium. The payoff is asymmetric: limited loss, potentially large gain. You might buy calls if you expect a rise but want to limit downside.

Buying a put is a bearish bet. You profit if the underlying falls below the strike minus the premium. Your maximum loss is the premium. You might buy puts to protect a stock position (this is called a protective put) or to speculate on decline.

Covered call writing involves owning the underlying and selling a call against it. You collect the premium but give up gains above the strike. If the stock rises above the strike, your stock is called away; you sell at the strike price regardless of how high it went. If it stays below, you keep the stock and the premium. This strategy generates income in flat or slightly rising markets but limits upside.

These strategies only hint at the complexity possible. Multi-leg strategies with different strikes and expirations can create nearly any payoff pattern. But complexity brings danger: the more complex the strategy, the more ways it can go wrong and the harder it is to understand the true risk.

**The Dangers of Options**

Options are risky, and most individuals who trade options lose money. The dangers are substantial.

Time decay erodes value constantly. An option that is out of the money loses value every day as expiration approaches. Buying options is a race against time; you need the underlying to move not just in the right direction but far enough and fast enough to overcome time decay and the premium paid.

Leverage amplifies losses. The same leverage that magnifies gains can produce total losses. An option can go from valuable to worthless quickly. Unlike stocks, which rarely go to zero, options frequently expire worthless. Studies suggest that a significant majority of options held to expiration expire worthless.

Complexity invites mistakes. Understanding how multiple factors interact requires sophistication. Strategies that seem attractive may have hidden risks. Many retail traders employ strategies they do not fully understand.

Volatility changes surprise. A position may be correctly positioned for direction but incorrectly for volatility. A drop in implied volatility can cause losses even when the underlying moves as expected.

Bid-ask spreads consume capital. Options, especially less liquid ones, often have wide spreads between what buyers pay and sellers receive. Frequent trading in options erodes capital through spreads.

For most people, options are best avoided. They are not necessary for achieving financial goals. Their complexity, leverage, and time decay create traps that few retail traders navigate successfully. The rare exceptions—perhaps protective puts on concentrated positions, or covered calls for income by sophisticated investors—are limited and require care.

### Other Derivatives

Beyond futures and options, derivatives include swaps, credit default swaps, and numerous exotic instruments. These are primarily institutional tools, but brief understanding illuminates financial news.

An interest rate swap exchanges fixed-rate payments for floating-rate payments. One party pays a fixed rate; the other pays a rate that floats with market interest rates. Neither principal changes hands; only the interest payments are swapped. Companies use interest rate swaps to manage their exposure to rate changes. A company with floating-rate debt that fears rate increases can swap into fixed payments, achieving certainty.

A currency swap exchanges payments in different currencies. Companies with foreign operations use currency swaps to manage exchange rate exposure. Again, the purpose is hedging underlying business risk.

A credit default swap is essentially insurance against default. The buyer pays premiums to the seller; if a specified credit event (default, restructuring) occurs, the seller compensates the buyer. These instruments allow investors to hedge credit exposure or speculate on creditworthiness. Credit default swaps became notorious in the 2008 financial crisis; they amplified losses and interconnected institutions in ways that were not fully understood.

Exotic derivatives have customized features: barrier options that activate or deactivate at certain price levels, Asian options whose payoff depends on average prices, weather derivatives whose payoff depends on temperature or rainfall. These serve specialized hedging needs but are far from ordinary investing.

The derivatives market is enormous. The notional value of outstanding derivatives dwarfs global GDP. But notional value overstates true exposure; it represents the face value of contracts, not the actual capital at risk. Still, the scale indicates derivatives' centrality to modern finance. They are the plumbing through which risk flows from those who have it to those willing to bear it.

### Day Trading: A Word of Caution

Having discussed derivatives, we should address a related phenomenon: day trading. Day trading is the practice of buying and selling financial instruments within the same trading day, seeking to profit from short-term price movements. It is not specific to derivatives—people day trade stocks as well—but derivatives' leverage makes them common day trading instruments.

Day trading is seductive. Stories of people making fortunes from their laptops circulate widely. The activity seems exciting, immediate, and within reach. Markets are open; anyone with a brokerage account can participate. The implied promise is that skill, intelligence, or hard work can produce consistent profits.

The reality is grimmer. Research consistently finds that most day traders lose money. One study of Taiwanese day traders found that more than 80 percent lost money over a six-month period. The more frequently people traded, the worse their returns. Another study found that only about 1 percent of day traders earned profits exceeding minimum wage after costs. The very active traders—those doing what we might call full-time day trading—were the most likely to lose.

Why do day traders lose? Several factors combine.

Transaction costs consume capital. Every trade has a cost: commissions (even if nominally zero, costs are embedded in execution quality), spreads, and slippage. For day traders making many trades, these costs compound. You must not merely be right about direction but right by enough to cover costs.

Competition is fierce. Day traders compete against professionals with better information, faster execution, more sophisticated analysis, and advantageous cost structures because they provide liquidity rather than consume it. The playing field is not level. What looks like opportunity to the amateur is often the crumb left by institutions.

Markets are efficient in the short term. While long-term mispricings can exist, short-term price movements are close to random. Predicting whether a stock will rise or fall over the next hour is essentially impossible. Day traders who believe they have skill are usually experiencing luck, which eventually reverses.

Behavioral biases work against you. Overconfidence leads traders to overtrade. Loss aversion leads them to hold losers too long and sell winners too quickly. The mind finds patterns in randomness. Emotional decision-making undermines discipline. All the psychological traps discussed in earlier chapters are amplified by day trading's rapid pace.

Leverage magnifies errors. Day trading with options or futures means small mistakes become large losses. A few bad days can wipe out an account. The mathematics of loss work against recovery: a 50 percent loss requires a 100 percent gain to break even.

Survivorship bias distorts perception. We hear about the winners because they talk. The losers disappear quietly. This creates the impression that success is more common than it is. The day trader showing off returns on social media is one of thousands who lost.

For these reasons, day trading is not a path to financial success for nearly anyone. It is, for most participants, a form of gambling with poor odds—entertainment that happens to be expensive. If you enjoy the activity and can afford to lose the money, that is a personal choice. But it should not be confused with investing or with building wealth.

The distinction is worth making explicit. Investing is the allocation of capital to productive enterprise over time; you provide resources to businesses that create goods and services, and you share in the value created. Day trading is the attempt to extract value from price fluctuations without contributing capital to enterprise. The former creates wealth over the long term. The latter redistributes it—mostly to professionals and intermediaries.

The same applies, though somewhat less extremely, to active trading in general. Attempting to time the market, to pick winning stocks, to identify mispricings—these activities reliably underperform passive indexing for most participants. Some people do outperform; whether through skill or luck is hard to determine, and the odds that you will be one of them are low.

**Why Understanding This Matters**

If futures and options are mostly inappropriate for individual investors, and day trading is a losing game, why spend a chapter on them?

Understanding derivatives helps you comprehend financial news and market events. When headlines announce a "volatility spike" or discuss "options market activity," you can follow the discussion. When crises involve derivatives—as in 2008—you can understand what happened. Financial literacy includes knowing what you should avoid and why.

Understanding derivatives protects you from harmful advice. Aggressive brokers and self-styled gurus promote options trading to unsophisticated investors. Knowing the risks allows you to recognize bad advice and resist pressure to engage in strategies you do not understand.

Understanding derivatives illuminates market structure. The existence of futures and options affects the assets that underlie them. Hedging activity affects supply and demand. Options expiration dates affect price behavior. Even if you never trade a derivative, the derivatives market shapes the markets you do participate in.

Understanding derivatives completes the picture of risk. Earlier chapters discussed insurance and hedging in personal finance. Derivatives are the market's tools for transferring and pricing risk. Seeing how professionals manage risk puts personal risk management in context.

Finally, understanding derivatives reveals the distance between sophisticated finance and personal finance. The institutions that trade derivatives have resources, expertise, and objectives different from yours. Recognizing this distance helps you focus on what matters for your situation rather than imitating what is appropriate for others.

**The Core Message**

Derivatives are powerful tools with legitimate uses. Hedging genuine risks, managing business exposures, and enabling market efficiency are valuable functions. For those with the expertise to use them properly, derivatives solve real problems.

But for most individuals, derivatives are inappropriate. The complexity, leverage, and time decay create traps. The competition is fierce. The potential for loss is substantial. The skills required are specialized and developed over years, not weeks or months.

The same applies to day trading and active speculation more broadly. The evidence overwhelmingly shows that most participants lose. The psychological appeal—excitement, the dream of quick riches, the illusion of control—works against sound financial behavior.

This is not a counsel of despair but of focus. By recognizing what you should not do, you can devote your attention to what you should: earning income, controlling spending, saving steadily, investing passively, protecting against catastrophe, and using money to build a good life. These activities are less glamorous than trading but far more likely to produce the outcomes you seek.

The greatest risk in finance is often not the risk you consciously take; it is the risk you take without understanding. Options, futures, and day trading are domains where the unwitting assume risks that the knowing avoid. Knowing enough to stay away is itself a form of financial wisdom.

# THIRTEEN
# MONEY WITHOUT INSTITUTIONS
## CRYPTOCURRENCY AND YOUR PORTFOLIO

In 2017, I was driving when I heard an interview that would change how I thought about money itself.

Every Saturday since 2005, I have watched Consuelo Mack's WealthTrack on PBS. My daughter, who was ten when we started this ritual, has grown up with it. She teases me that Consuelo is her stepmother. That particular week I was catching up via podcast, and Mack was speaking with Matt Hougan about something called Bitcoin. I had heard the name before—associated vaguely with hackers, drug markets, and speculation—but had dismissed it as I suspect you might have. Hougan, who would go on to become Chief Investment Officer of Bitwise Asset Management, explained it differently. He described Bitcoin not as a get-rich-quick scheme but as a technological solution to a problem humans had struggled with for centuries: how to create something digitally scarce.

Think about that for a moment. Every digital file you have ever encountered can be copied infinitely at zero cost. Your photographs, your documents, your music—all of it reproducible without limit. This is wonderful for sharing information but fatal for creating money. Money requires scarcity. If anyone could copy a dollar, dollars would be worthless. This is why physical cash has elaborate anti-counterfeiting measures, why banks maintain careful ledgers, why the entire financial system depends on trusted institutions verifying that you cannot spend the same dollar twice.

Bitcoin solved this problem without trusted institutions. Through cryptography and a distributed network of computers, it created digital scarcity for the first time in human history. Only twenty-one million bitcoins will ever exist—not because a government promises restraint, but because the mathematics make creation beyond that limit impossible.

I did not invest my life savings that afternoon. But I listened carefully, did my own research over the following weeks, and eventually allocated a small amount—less than one percent of my portfolio—to Bitcoin and a few other cryptocurrencies. That decision, and the discipline with which I managed it over the subsequent years, taught me lessons I want to share with you.

**The Problem of Trust**

Every monetary system before cryptocurrency required trust in institutions. You trust that the Federal Reserve will not print so many dollars that your savings become worthless. You trust that your bank actually holds the money it claims you have deposited. You trust that when you send a wire transfer, the intermediaries processing it will not steal your funds or make errors. This trust is usually warranted—but not always, and not everywhere.

In 2008, that trust shattered for millions of people. Banks that were supposed to be prudent had made catastrophic bets. Regulators who were supposed to protect the public had failed. Governments responded by creating money on a scale previously unimaginable, bailing out the institutions whose recklessness had caused the crisis. If you held your savings in dollars, your wealth was diluted to rescue those who had gambled irresponsibly.

Satoshi Nakamoto's Bitcoin whitepaper, published in October 2008 as Lehman Brothers' corpse was still warm, proposed an alternative: a peer-to-peer electronic cash system that required no trusted third party. The timing was not coincidental.

**How Cryptography Creates Trust**

Cryptography, the science underlying cryptocurrency, is ancient in concept but modern in implementation. At its core, cryptography allows you to prove something is true without revealing the underlying information. When you log into your bank's website, cryptography verifies your identity without transmitting your password in readable form. When you make an online purchase, cryptography protects your credit card number from interception.

Two cryptographic concepts are essential for understanding cryptocurrency.

The first is public-key cryptography. Imagine a mailbox with two keys: one that only locks and one that only unlocks. You publish the locking key freely—anyone can put mail in your box. But only you possess the unlocking key, so only you can retrieve what others have deposited. In cryptocurrency, your public key is your address, visible to all. Your private key is your proof of ownership, known only to you. When you send cryptocurrency, you use your private key to create a digital signature proving you authorized the transaction. Anyone can verify this signature using your public key, but no one can forge it without your private key.

The second concept is the hash function. A hash function takes any input—a word, a document, an entire library—and produces a fixed-length output that appears random but is entirely determined by the input. Change a single character in the input, and the output changes completely and unpredictably. This has a crucial property: given an output, there is no way to work backward to find the input except by trying possibilities until one matches. Hash functions create digital fingerprints—unique identifiers that verify data has not been altered.

**The Blockchain as Shared Ledger**

A blockchain is simply a record of transactions that is distributed across thousands of computers worldwide, with each new batch of transactions linked cryptographically to all previous batches.

Here is how it works in practice. When you send Bitcoin to someone, you broadcast a message to the network: "I am transferring one bitcoin from my address to this other address," signed with your private key. Computers around the world—called miners or validators—collect these pending transactions. Approximately every ten minutes, one computer solves a difficult mathematical puzzle, earning the right to add the next batch of transactions to the permanent record. This batch, called a block, includes a hash of the previous block, creating a chain. To alter any historical transaction, you would need to redo the mathematical work for that block and every subsequent block—a feat requiring more computing power than the rest of the network combined.

This is the breakthrough. Without any central authority, without any institution you must trust, the network reaches consensus on who owns what. The ledger is public, so anyone can verify any transaction. The ledger is distributed, so no single point of failure can destroy it. The ledger is immutable, so history cannot be rewritten. For the first time, digital scarcity exists.

### Bitcoin as Digital Gold

Bitcoin's fixed supply of twenty-one million coins is not an arbitrary choice but a deliberate design to mimic the scarcity of gold while improving on its limitations.

Gold became money across civilizations because it was scarce, durable, divisible, portable, and verifiable. But gold has drawbacks. It is heavy, making large transactions cumbersome. It requires physical verification to detect counterfeits. It cannot be transmitted electronically without involving trusted intermediaries who might be corrupted or coerced.

Bitcoin shares gold's scarcity—enforced not by geology but by mathematics—while solving its practical problems. Bitcoin can be sent anywhere on earth in minutes. It can be verified by anyone with internet access. It can be divided into one hundred million units called satoshis, allowing transactions of any size. It can be stored in your memory as a string of words, crossing any border invisibly.

This is why Bitcoin's advocates call it digital gold: a store of value for the internet age, immune to the inflationary pressures that erode fiat currency over time. The Federal Reserve can create dollars with a keystroke; no one can create bitcoins beyond the predetermined schedule.

Whether this vision will prove correct remains uncertain. But the thesis is coherent, and after more than fifteen years, Bitcoin has not been hacked, has not been shut down, and has grown from a curiosity discussed by cryptographers to an asset class with exchange-traded funds approved by the Securities and Exchange Commission.

**Beyond Bitcoin**

Bitcoin was first, but it was not last. Thousands of cryptocurrencies now exist, most worthless, some significant. Understanding the landscape helps you avoid the worthless and evaluate the significant.

Ethereum, launched in 2015, extended Bitcoin's innovation from money to computation. Where Bitcoin asks "who owns this coin," Ethereum asks "what should happen when certain conditions are met." These conditional instructions, called smart contracts, enable applications impossible on traditional financial infrastructure: loans that execute automatically when collateral is deposited, insurance that pays instantly when a flight is delayed, ownership records that transfer without lawyers or title companies. Ethereum is less digital gold than digital infrastructure—a platform on which others build.

XRP, created by Ripple Labs, targets a different problem: the friction and delay of international payments. When you wire money abroad, your transaction passes through correspondent banks, each taking time and fees. XRP proposes to serve as a bridge currency, converting your dollars to XRP, transmitting them in seconds, and converting to the recipient's local currency on arrival. Whether banks will adopt this technology remains contested, but major financial institutions have tested it.

Solana, launched in 2020, addresses a limitation of earlier

blockchains: speed. Bitcoin processes roughly seven transactions per second, Ethereum around thirty. Solana claims capacity for tens of thousands. This speed comes with tradeoffs—greater centralization, less battle-tested security—but enables applications requiring rapid settlement that earlier blockchains cannot support.

Most other cryptocurrencies are not worth your attention. Many are outright scams designed to enrich their creators at your expense. Others are sincere experiments that failed or will fail. The four I have named—Bitcoin, Ethereum, XRP, Solana—represent different theses about what blockchain technology might achieve. I own all four, in varying proportions, because I find each thesis plausible without certainty about which will prove correct.

**The Investment Thesis**

You might reasonably ask why anyone should invest in something so volatile, so uncertain, and so removed from the traditional assets I have discussed throughout this book. Let me offer several reasons, none of which constitute certainty.

First, diversification. Cryptocurrency has historically shown low correlation to stocks and bonds, meaning it sometimes rises when traditional assets fall and vice versa. This imperfect correlation can reduce portfolio volatility even when the added asset is itself highly volatile. Whether this low correlation will persist as institutional adoption increases remains unclear, but the mathematical argument for including uncorrelated assets holds regardless.

Second, asymmetric returns. When you buy a stock, your upside is theoretically unlimited but practically constrained by the company's growth potential. When you buy Bitcoin at current prices, you are betting on an asset that might become a global reserve currency—or might go to zero. The range of outcomes is wider than for almost any traditional investment. If you size your position appropriately, you can participate in the upside while surviving the downside.

Third, a hedge against monetary debasement. Since 2008, central banks worldwide have created money at unprecedented rates. If you believe this will eventually produce significant inflation—not the moderate inflation of recent years but something more serious—then an asset with a fixed supply offers protection that bonds and cash cannot provide. I do not make predictions about inflation, but I acknowledge the risk and allocate accordingly.

Fourth, technological optionality. Blockchain technology may transform finance, contracts, identity verification, supply chain management, and domains not yet imagined. By owning cryptocurrency, you own a stake in that potential transformation. Even if specific coins fail, the technology they represent may succeed, and early exposure positions you to benefit.

**Institutional Adoption**

When I first invested in 2017, cryptocurrency was largely the province of technologists, libertarians, and speculators. Institutional involvement was minimal and often dismissive. That has changed dramatically.

In January 2024, the Securities and Exchange Commission approved spot Bitcoin exchange-traded funds, allowing ordinary investors to gain exposure through their brokerage accounts without managing wallets or private keys. Within months, these ETFs accumulated tens of billions of dollars. Major asset managers including BlackRock, Fidelity, and Invesco now offer cryptocurrency products to their clients.

Publicly traded companies hold Bitcoin on their balance sheets. MicroStrategy, a software company, has made Bitcoin accumulation central to its corporate strategy. Tesla held Bitcoin briefly before selling. Sovereign wealth funds have disclosed cryptocurrency positions.

This institutional adoption does not guarantee success. Institutions have been wrong before, sometimes catastrophically. But it does mean that cryptocurrency can no longer be dismissed as a fringe phenomenon. The same serious investors who allocate to stocks, bonds, real estate, and commodities now allocate to digital assets. You may choose not to join them, but you should understand that the ground has shifted.

**The Risks—Stated Plainly**

I would not respect your intelligence if I presented cryptocurrency without confronting its risks honestly. They are substantial.

Volatility is the most obvious. Bitcoin has fallen eighty percent from its highs multiple times—in 2014, in 2018, in 2022. If you cannot watch eighty percent of an investment disappear without panic-selling, you should not own cryptocurrency, or should own so little that the decline does not matter. This volatility is not a bug to be fixed. It is a feature of an emerging asset class finding its value through market discovery. Expect it to continue.

Regulatory risk is real but diminishing. Governments have taken varying approaches to cryptocurrency—from El Salvador adopting Bitcoin as legal tender to China banning mining and trading entirely. The United States has moved toward regulatory clarity with ETF approvals and proposed legislation, but future administrations could reverse course. I consider outright prohibition in developed democracies unlikely but not impossible.

Technological risk persists despite Bitcoin's track record. A flaw in the cryptography, a successful attack on the network, or a superior technology that makes current cryptocurrencies obsolete all remain theoretically possible. The probability decreases with each passing year but never reaches zero.

Custody risk is unique to cryptocurrency. If you hold your own coins and lose your private key, your funds are gone forever—not frozen, not recoverable through customer service, but mathematically inaccessible for eternity. If you trust an exchange to hold your coins and that exchange is hacked or commits fraud, your funds may similarly vanish. The collapse of FTX in 2022 cost customers billions. "Not your keys, not your coins" is a mantra in the cryptocurrency community for good reason.

Environmental concerns have been raised about Bitcoin's energy consumption. The computers securing the network consume electricity comparable to medium-sized countries. Whether this is wasteful or valuable depends on your assessment of what that security provides. Some newer cryptocurrencies use less energy-intensive mechanisms, but Bitcoin's security model remains energy-dependent by design.

Scams are endemic. For every legitimate cryptocurrency project, dozens exist solely to separate you from your money. Celebrities promote coins they were paid to endorse. Anonymous developers launch projects, attract investment, and disappear. Elaborate frauds mimic legitimate exchanges. If an opportunity seems too good to be true, it is. Stick to established cryptocurrencies trading on regulated exchanges, and treat everything else with extreme skepticism.

**Position Sizing**

After that 2017 interview with Matt Hougan, I did not rush to invest my retirement savings. I allocated less than one percent of my portfolio to cryptocurrency—an amount I could lose entirely without meaningful impact on my financial life.

This was not timidity. It was discipline.

Position sizing is the most important decision you will make in cryptocurrency investing. Get it wrong, and no amount of analytical skill will save you. Invest too much, and an eighty percent drawdown becomes financially or psychologically devastating, leading you to sell at the worst possible moment. Invest too little, and gains that should be meaningful become trivial.

My suggestion: start with an allocation you could watch go to zero without losing sleep. For most people, this means somewhere between one and five percent of investable assets. If you are new to cryptocurrency and uncertain of your conviction, start at one percent. If you have studied the technology, understand the thesis, and trust your ability to hold through volatility, you might begin at three to five percent.

I started under one percent. Today, through appreciation rather than additional allocation, cryptocurrency represents roughly five percent of my portfolio. I did not chase this growth—I let it happen while managing risk along the way.

**The Discipline of Regular Investment**

No one knows where cryptocurrency prices will be next month

or next year. Anyone claiming otherwise is either lying or self-deceived. This uncertainty makes timing the market not merely difficult but impossible.

Dollar-cost averaging solves this problem by removing timing from the equation. Instead of investing a lump sum and hoping you chose the right moment, you invest fixed amounts at regular intervals regardless of price. When prices are high, your fixed investment buys fewer coins. When prices are low, it buys more. Over time, your average cost reflects the full range of prices, protecting you from the catastrophe of investing everything at a peak.

I have purchased cryptocurrency every two weeks since 2017. Some purchases were at prices that now look absurdly cheap. Others were at prices that still look expensive years later. In aggregate, my average cost is reasonable, and I never experienced the regret of poor timing because I never tried to time at all.

For someone beginning today, I would suggest a similar approach. Decide on a monthly amount that fits your budget and risk tolerance —perhaps one hundred dollars, perhaps one thousand, depending on your circumstances. Set up automatic purchases through a reputable exchange. Then forget about it. Do not watch the price daily. Do not second-guess your decision when markets fall. Trust the process and let time work in your favor.

**Taking Profits**

Dollar-cost averaging addresses the problem of buying. Taking profits addresses the problem of selling.

When cryptocurrency prices rise dramatically, euphoria takes hold. Online communities overflow with predictions of imminent new highs. The temptation to hold indefinitely, to let winners run without limit, becomes overwhelming. This is when discipline matters most.

My approach: when my cryptocurrency holdings appreciate significantly—say, doubling from my cost basis—I sell a portion, typically enough to recover my original investment plus some profit. I then allocate one-third of those proceeds back into cryptocurrency on the next meaningful decline, keep one-third in traditional investments, and reserve one-third for taxes and personal use.

This system accomplishes several things. It locks in real gains that cannot be taken away by subsequent declines. It maintains exposure to further upside through the portion reinvested. It forces me to sell when greed urges holding and buy when fear urges selling—exactly contrary to the emotional impulses that destroy most investors.

You need not adopt my specific formula. What matters is having a formula at all, decided in advance and executed without negotiation when conditions are met. Rules made in calm moments protect you from decisions made in chaos.

### Reinvesting During Declines

The counterpart to taking profits is reinvesting during declines. When cryptocurrency falls significantly—thirty percent, fifty percent, eighty percent from recent highs—the same online communities that predicted endless gains now predict terminal collapse. Fear replaces greed. The temptation to abandon your position entirely becomes overwhelming.

This is when the profits you took earlier become powerful. You have cash available to deploy at lower prices, improving your average cost and increasing your position for the eventual recovery. You can act rationally precisely because you acted rationally before.

I do not invest blindly during every decline. A thirty percent drop might not warrant additional investment if it follows a speculative mania. An eighty percent decline over eighteen months, with leverage flushed from the system and weak hands capitulated, presents a different opportunity. Judgment is required, but the judgment is easier when you have dry powder and a plan.

### Where to Buy and How to Hold

Practical mechanics matter. Buy cryptocurrency through regulated exchanges with established track records: Coinbase, Kraken, and Gemini in the United States, with equivalents in other jurisdictions. Avoid obscure exchanges offering better prices or lower fees—the savings are not worth the counterparty risk.

For most investors, keeping cryptocurrency on a reputable exchange is acceptable despite the "not your keys, not your coins" warning. The major exchanges have security practices, insurance policies, and regulatory oversight that mitigate—though do not eliminate—custody risk. If your holdings grow substantial, consider moving a portion to a hardware wallet, a physical device that stores your private keys offline. Ledger and Trezor are the dominant providers.

The spot Bitcoin and Ethereum ETFs approved in 2024 offer another option: cryptocurrency exposure through traditional brokerage accounts with no wallets, keys, or exchanges required. You sacrifice some theoretical benefits—you cannot use your ETF holdings to transact on the blockchain—but gain simplicity and the familiar protections of the regulated securities market. For investors who want exposure without complexity, ETFs are increasingly attractive.

**Volatility and Your Nervous System**

Everything I wrote earlier about behavioral finance applies to cryptocurrency, amplified to an extreme degree.

Recency bias convinces you that recent trends will continue. After a rally, you believe cryptocurrency will rise forever. After a crash, you believe it will never recover. Both beliefs are wrong, but they feel true in the moment.

Loss aversion makes declines hurt more than equivalent gains feel good. An eighty percent loss is psychologically devastating even if you sized your position to survive it financially. The pain tempts you to sell, to stop the bleeding, to make the discomfort end—precisely when holding would be most rewarded.

Social proof surrounds you with others whose beliefs mirror your own. In bull markets, cryptocurrency communities celebrate with memes and predictions of million-dollar Bitcoin. In bear markets, the same communities fracture into bitter recrimination or delusional denial. Neither environment supports clear thinking.

The availability heuristic makes recent, vivid events dominate your judgment. The friend who got rich buying cryptocurrency in 2020 is more salient than the statistical base rate of cryptocurrency investors who lost money. The news story about someone who lost everything to a scam is more memorable than the boring reality of steady, disciplined accumulation.

### Systems That Protect You From Yourself

The solution is not to overcome these biases through willpower. You cannot think your way to rationality under emotional stress. Instead, create systems that make good decisions automatic and bad decisions difficult.

Automate your purchases. If cryptocurrency is bought every two weeks without your active involvement, you cannot talk yourself out of buying during declines when buying is most valuable.

Write down your rules before you need them. Decide in advance at what appreciation level you will take profits, at what decline you will reinvest, and at what loss you will exit entirely. Write these numbers down. When conditions are met, execute without reconsideration.

Limit your exposure to real-time information. Checking prices hourly serves no purpose except to agitate your nervous system. Once weekly is sufficient for an investor with a long time horizon. If you cannot resist checking more frequently, delete the apps from your phone.

Find a trusted person to hold you accountable. Tell someone your rules and ask them to remind you when you are tempted to violate them. The mere act of articulating your intentions to another person strengthens your commitment.

### My Own Psychology

I confess that holding cryptocurrency through multiple eighty-percent drawdowns was not easy. In late 2018, my holdings were worth a fraction of what I had paid. The same was true in late 2022. Each time, the voice in my head suggested that this time was different, that the thesis had failed, that I should salvage what remained.

I did not listen because I had systems that made not listening easier. My position was small enough that its collapse would not derail my life. My rules were written down before the declines began. My automatic purchases continued regardless of my emotional state. And I had absorbed, through decades of investing, the lesson that selling during panics is almost always wrong.

Your mileage may vary. If you are someone who checks prices obsessively, who cannot sleep when investments decline, who makes impulsive decisions under stress, cryptocurrency may not be for you. There is no shame in this. Self-knowledge is more valuable than exposure to any asset class. But if you can build systems to protect yourself from yourself, the rewards for discipline in this volatile market are substantial.

**Possible Futures**

I hold cryptocurrency because I believe the expected value is positive, not because I know the future. Let me sketch the range of possibilities.

In the optimistic scenario, Bitcoin becomes a globally recognized store of value, a digital gold held by central banks, corporations, and individuals as a hedge against currency debasement. Ethereum becomes the infrastructure layer for a new financial system, with trillions of dollars in value transacting on its blockchain. Other cryptocurrencies find their niches: XRP for payments, Solana for high-speed applications, others not yet invented for purposes not yet imagined. In this scenario, current prices are a small fraction of eventual value.

In the pessimistic scenario, cryptocurrency proves to be a speculative bubble that deflates over years or decades. Regulatory hostility, technological obsolescence, or simple loss of interest causes prices to decline until only die-hard believers remain. The technology persists in some form but never achieves mainstream adoption. In this scenario, current prices represent most or all of the value that will ever exist.

In the middle scenario—perhaps most likely—cryptocurrency becomes a permanent but niche asset class. Bitcoin survives as digital gold, held by a subset of investors seeking inflation protection, but never achieves mass adoption as money. Ethereum hosts financial applications useful to a technical minority but irrelevant to most people. Prices fluctuate wildly but trend modestly upward over decades, rewarding patient holders without making anyone spectacularly rich. In this scenario, cryptocurrency is a reasonable portfolio allocation but not a transformative investment.

I do not know which scenario will obtain. No one does.

**Central Bank Digital Currencies**

One wild card is the development of central bank digital currencies, or CBDCs. These government-issued digital currencies would provide some benefits of cryptocurrency—faster payments, programmable money, reduced friction—while preserving central bank control over monetary policy.

Whether CBDCs compete with or complement existing cryptocurrencies is unclear. They might satisfy the demand for digital money, reducing interest in decentralized alternatives. Or they might highlight the value of decentralization by demonstrating government surveillance capabilities that Bitcoin's pseudonymity avoids. Or they might coexist, serving different purposes for different users.

I include this uncertainty not to make predictions but to emphasize how early we are in this technology's development. The landscape fifteen years from now may be unrecognizable.

**What Would Change My Mind**

I continue to hold and accumulate cryptocurrency, but I am not ideologically committed. Evidence could change my position.

If a major cryptocurrency suffered a successful attack that compromised its security model, I would reconsider my holdings. Fifteen years without such an attack is meaningful evidence but not proof of impossibility.

If regulatory hostility made holding or transacting in cryptocurrency illegal in major jurisdictions, I would reduce my exposure to comply with the law and avoid stranded assets.

If a technological successor emerged that rendered current cryptocurrencies obsolete—as email rendered fax largely obsolete—I would reallocate accordingly.

If my own circumstances changed such that I could no longer tolerate the volatility, I would reduce my position to whatever level allowed me to sleep soundly.

None of these conditions currently obtains, so I continue as I have: buying small amounts regularly, taking profits when euphoria peaks, reinvesting when fear dominates, and accepting uncertainty as the price of potential reward.

**The Story Continues**

In the first chapter of this book, I traced money's evolution from barter through precious metals to paper currency to the fiat system we inhabit today. Cryptocurrency represents the next chapter in that story—or perhaps a footnote, or perhaps a revolution. We are too early to know.

What I know is that the same principles that guide prudent investing in traditional assets apply here, perhaps more urgently. Understand what you own. Size your positions to survive the worst outcomes. Diversify across assets and theses. Create systems that protect you from your own worst impulses. Accept uncertainty as inherent to investing in anything.

I did not get rich from cryptocurrency. I got something more valuable: experience navigating an asset class that tests every cognitive bias and emotional weakness an investor possesses. That experience reinforced lessons I thought I had already learned and taught me new ones I had not anticipated.

If you choose to allocate a portion of your portfolio to cryptocurrency, do so with eyes open to both the potential and the risks. Start small, as I did. Invest regularly, as I do. Take profits when greed whispers to hold forever. Reinvest when fear screams to sell everything. Build systems that make good decisions automatic.

And remember that this chapter of money's story is still being written. You are not merely observing it—you are a participant, making choices that will shape your financial life for decades to come.

Choose wisely, act patiently, and hold loosely to certainty. The future is uncertain. It always has been. Cryptocurrency just makes that uncertainty harder to ignore.

## SUMMARY: **Key Takeaways**

Cryptocurrency solves the problem of digital scarcity. For the first time in history, something digital cannot be copied infinitely. Bitcoin's fixed supply of twenty-one million coins is enforced by mathematics, not by institutional promises that can be broken.

The technology rests on cryptography and distributed consensus. Public-key cryptography proves ownership without trusted intermediaries. The blockchain creates an immutable record verified by thousands of computers worldwide. Understanding these mechanisms helps you evaluate what cryptocurrency actually offers.

Position sizing matters more than timing. Start with an allocation small enough to lose entirely without financial or psychological devastation—typically one to five percent of investable assets. Let appreciation grow your position rather than chasing gains with additional capital.

Systems protect you from yourself. Automate purchases to remove timing decisions. Write rules for taking profits and reinvesting during declines before you need them. Limit exposure to real-time price information. These structures make discipline easier when emotions urge otherwise.

The future is genuinely uncertain. Cryptocurrency might become a globally significant asset class, might fade into irrelevance, or might settle into a permanent niche. No one knows. Position yourself to benefit from the upside while surviving the downside, and accept that uncertainty is the price of potential reward.

# FOURTEEN
# THE INVESTOR'S WORST ENEMY

You have now learned the mechanics of finance, the mathematics of compound growth, and the geography of the investment universe. You understand, in principle, what you should do: buy diversified assets, keep costs low, stay invested for the long term, let compounding work its quiet magic. The strategy is not complicated. It is taught in introductory courses, explained in countless books, confirmed by decades of evidence.

And yet most investors fail to follow it.

The gap between knowing and doing is the central problem of investing. It is not a gap of information—the facts are widely available. It is not a gap of intelligence—brilliant people make catastrophic investment mistakes. It is a gap of psychology, the treacherous space between what our rational minds understand and what our emotional minds compel us to do.

This chapter examines the systematic ways human psychology undermines investment success. It draws on Daniel Kahneman's research into cognitive biases and decision-making under uncertainty, work that earned him the Nobel Prize and illuminates why intelligent people consistently make predictable errors. Understanding these patterns will not make you immune to them. But it may help you recognize when your own mind is betraying you and give you the chance to override its worst impulses.

**Two Systems of Thought**

Kahneman's framework begins with a simple but profound observation: the human mind operates through two distinct modes of thinking.

System 1 is fast, automatic, and effortless. It recognizes faces, completes familiar phrases, and recoils from sudden threats. It operates constantly, generating impressions and intuitions without conscious effort. You do not decide to recognize your mother's face or to feel fear at a loud noise. These responses happen to you.

System 2 is slow, deliberate, and effortful. It solves complex problems, follows logical arguments, and makes careful decisions. It requires concentration and can be depleted by sustained effort. When you calculate a tip or evaluate an investment, you are using System 2.

The crucial insight is that System 1 runs the show most of the time. System 2 is lazy, preferring to endorse System 1's impressions rather than do the hard work of questioning them. This arrangement serves us well in everyday life, where most situations do not require careful analysis.

But investing is not everyday life. The intuitions that serve us well in physical and social environments lead us catastrophically astray in financial markets. Our ancestors evolved to respond to immediate threats, follow the crowd, and seek patterns in their environment. These instincts helped them survive predators and navigate tribal politics. They do not help navigate the abstraction of modern markets.

The investor who follows System 1 will buy when prices are high because rising prices feel safe and exciting. They will sell when prices are low because falling prices feel dangerous. They will chase performance, follow the crowd, and mistake recent trends for permanent truths. They will do exactly what the evidence says destroys wealth.

Successful investing requires System 2 to overrule System 1, repeatedly and indefinitely. This is difficult because it feels wrong—it requires acting against emotional responses, trusting abstract reasoning over visceral feeling. Few accomplish this consistently.

## The Core Biases

### Loss Aversion

The most powerful force in investment psychology is loss aversion. Kahneman and Amos Tversky demonstrated that people feel losses roughly twice as intensely as equivalent gains. Losing one hundred dollars hurts more than gaining one hundred dollars feels good.

This asymmetry shapes behavior profoundly. Loss aversion explains why investors hold losing positions far too long—selling crystallizes the loss, makes it real, forces confrontation. As long as you hold, you can tell yourself the loss is only on paper, that recovery is possible. This thinking is economically irrational; the market does not care what you paid. But psychologically, the reluctance to realize losses is nearly universal.

Loss aversion also explains why investors sell winners too quickly. Taking a profit feels good, locks in a gain, provides the pleasure of success. Never mind that the winning investment might have further to run. So investors harvest small gains and nurse large losses —exactly the opposite of what wealth maximization requires. This pattern is so common it has a name: the disposition effect.

Loss aversion also makes investors too conservative. The pain of potential losses looms larger than the pleasure of potential gains, so people hold too much cash, avoid stocks that feel risky, and accept lower long-term returns to avoid short-term volatility. The irony is that this conservatism is itself risky—the investor who avoids stocks may find their savings insufficient for retirement, a different kind of loss but a devastating one.

The possibility of loss is the price of admission to the returns that stocks provide. Those who cannot pay that price in emotional terms are barred from those returns.

**Overconfidence**

Human beings are systematically overconfident about their abilities. This is not arrogance in the moral sense but a cognitive bias affecting almost everyone. We overestimate how much we know, how well we can predict the future, and how much our actions affect outcomes.

In investing, overconfidence manifests in excessive trading. The overconfident investor believes they can identify which stocks will outperform and when markets will turn. They trade frequently, incur costs, and underperform passive strategies. The evidence is overwhelming: higher trading frequency correlates with lower returns for individual investors.

Overconfidence also leads investors to under-diversify. They concentrate portfolios in familiar companies, their employer's stock, their home country's market. They believe familiarity gives them an edge. Usually it does not—familiarity breeds the illusion of insight, not genuine insight.

Studies of brokerage accounts find that men trade more frequently than women and earn lower returns on average. The confidence that serves well in some domains undermines investment performance. Professional investors are not immune; fund managers who believe they can beat the market usually cannot, yet their confidence persists regardless.

Kahneman distinguishes between the illusion of skill and actual skill. In some domains—chess, surgery—practice leads to genuine expertise because feedback is clear and patterns are stable. In stock picking, the environment is too complex, feedback too noisy, patterns too unstable for genuine expertise to develop. Yet practitioners feel just as confident as genuine experts in other fields.

The antidote to overconfidence is humility, but humility is hard to manufacture. You can, however, recognize environmental cues suggesting your confidence is unjustified: making predictions about complex systems, delayed or unclear feedback, others making similar predictions doing no better than chance. In such environments, simple rules and diversified approaches outperform clever strategies.

**The Herd Instinct**

Humans are social animals. We look to others for cues about how to behave and what to believe. The person who noticed the crowd running and joined them survived; the person who stopped to investigate did not.

In financial markets, the herd instinct produces bubbles and crashes. When prices rise, more people buy, driving prices higher still. Rising prices become evidence that buying was correct, drawing in more buyers. At some point, prices become completely detached from underlying value, supported only by the expectation that someone else will pay even more. When that expectation falters, prices collapse as everyone rushes to sell.

The herd instinct makes it psychologically nearly impossible to buy when everyone is selling or to sell when everyone is buying. At market bottoms, the mood is universal despair. Every headline screams danger. Every friend advises caution. Buying at such moments requires acting against every social and emotional signal you receive.

At market tops, the opposite prevails. Everyone has made money. Stories of easy gains circulate. Not investing feels like missing out. The person who counsels caution seems old-fashioned, unable to appreciate the new era. Standing aside requires ignoring the crowd, rejecting social consensus, accepting the possibility that you are wrong while everyone else is right.

The solution is not to always oppose the crowd—sometimes the crowd is right. The solution is to think independently, form your own view based on evidence, and act on that view regardless of what others are doing. This requires a psychological independence that few possess naturally but that can be cultivated through awareness and discipline.

**Recency Bias**

The human mind gives excessive weight to recent experience. What happened last year feels more real than what happened ten years ago. What is happening now seems like it will continue forever.

After stocks have risen for several years, investors expect them to keep rising. They increase stock allocations and feel confident about the future. After stocks have fallen, investors expect more decline. They reduce exposure, move to cash, and brace for further losses. In both cases, they extrapolate the recent past into the indefinite future.

This extrapolation is usually wrong. Returns tend to mean-revert over time. Periods of exceptional returns are followed by mediocre returns, and vice versa. The investor who buys after strong performance and sells after weak performance does the opposite of what long-term success requires.

Recency bias also affects risk perception. After a long bull market, stocks feel safe. After a crash, they feel dangerous. But the actual riskiness of stocks does not change with recent performance. If anything, stocks are safer after they have fallen, when prices are lower and expected returns higher.

The cure is historical perspective. Looking at data spanning decades reminds us that the recent past is just one small sample of possible outcomes. Markets have crashed before and recovered. Bear markets have always ended. Bull markets have always ended too. Whatever is happening now has antecedents that usually inform us better than the vivid present.

But gaining historical perspective is hard because it conflicts with how our minds work. The present is vivid and emotional; the past is abstract and faded. Reading about the crash of 1929 does not feel like living through 2008. We know intellectually that markets recover, but our gut tells us this time might be different.

**Pattern Recognition**

The human brain is a pattern-recognition machine. We see faces in clouds, hear messages in random noise, find meaning in coincidence. This ability helped our ancestors identify predators and navigate complex environments.

In financial markets, pattern recognition is mostly a liability. Markets are noisy; day-to-day movements are largely random. Yet investors relentlessly search for patterns, finding them where none exist and trading on them to their detriment.

Technical analysis—predicting prices from charts of past prices—appeals to our pattern-seeking instincts. The charts look meaningful: head and shoulders, double bottoms, support and resistance levels all seem pregnant with predictive power. Academic research has found that most technical patterns have no statistically reliable predictive value. They are like seeing faces in clouds: real in perception but meaningless in reality.

The persistence of technical analysis despite evidence against it reveals something important: the human need to find patterns is so strong that entire industries are built on satisfying it. The market for pattern-finding is itself evidence of the bias.

Even sophisticated investors fall prey to pattern illusions. A fund manager with three years of strong performance seems skilled. But three years is far too short to distinguish skill from luck. A coin that comes up heads ten times is not special—it is just one of many coins, and it happened to be the one that came up heads. Yet investors pour money into funds with hot streaks and are disappointed when performance reverts to average.

Kahneman calls this the law of small numbers—drawing large conclusions from small samples. We treat tiny samples as fully reliable when they are actually dominated by noise. The skilled investor knows that most patterns are illusory, that past performance genuinely does not predict future results, and that the urge to find patterns must be resisted rather than indulged.

**Anchoring**

When people estimate uncertain quantities, they are heavily influenced by whatever number is available, even if that number is completely irrelevant. Kahneman demonstrated this with experiments where spinning a wheel of fortune affected estimates of the percentage of African countries in the United Nations. The random number pulled estimates toward it—an effect so powerful and irrational it is almost embarrassing.

In investing, the price you paid for a stock becomes an anchor. If it has fallen below your purchase price, it feels cheap and due for recovery. If it has risen, it feels expensive and due for a pullback. These feelings are economically meaningless—the market does not know or care what you paid. Yet the anchor persists, distorting perception and decisions.

Previous high prices anchor expectations. A stock that traded at one hundred dollars feels cheap at sixty, even if sixty is actually expensive relative to earnings and prospects. Round numbers create anchors too; investors pay more attention when indices cross ten thousand or twenty thousand.

The defense is to focus on fundamental value—earnings, cash flows, assets—and ignore arbitrary numbers. But this requires constant effort because anchors are established automatically by System 1 and must be consciously overridden by System 2.

**Mental Accounting**

People do not think of money as fungible, even though it is. A dollar is a dollar. Yet we treat money differently depending on where it came from, where it is held, and what we intend to use it for.

The gambler who separates winnings from their original stake and bets the winnings more recklessly engages in mental accounting. Those winnings are real money, but they do not feel real because they came too easily. Investors do the same with realized gains, treating them as "house money" and taking excessive risks—as if losses from gains hurt less than losses from principal.

Mental accounting leads people to simultaneously carry high-interest debt while maintaining low-interest savings. The debt and savings sit in different mental accounts, so the irrationality of paying eight percent while earning one percent does not register. It also creates reluctance to sell a losing position in a taxable account to harvest the loss, because the loss feels more real once realized—even when realizing it would reduce taxes owed.

Investors partition portfolios into mental accounts—retirement money, college money, vacation money—and make different decisions for each. This can lead to inconsistent risk-taking when a unified approach would be more efficient.

**Confirmation Bias**

People seek information that confirms existing beliefs and avoid or discount information that contradicts them. This tendency is pervasive and powerful.

The investor who believes a particular stock will rise notices every positive article while dismissing negative ones as biased. They remember when predictions were right and forget when they were wrong. They surround themselves with agreeing sources. Their belief becomes unfalsifiable, immune to evidence.

Confirmation bias makes it difficult to change your mind even when you should. Evidence that you are wrong is systematically filtered out while evidence that you are right is amplified. You feel increasingly confident in a position that may be increasingly wrong.

The antidote is actively seeking disconfirming evidence. Before making an investment, ask: What would make me wrong? What would the smartest person who disagrees with me say? What am I not seeing? This practice feels uncomfortable because it threatens beliefs you want to protect. That discomfort is a sign you are doing it right.

**The Narrative Fallacy**

Humans understand the world through stories. We find narratives compelling, memorable, and persuasive. Statistics and probabilities are abstract and cold. When story and statistics conflict, story usually wins.

This preference leads investors to weight compelling stories over solid evidence. A company with an exciting story—a visionary founder, a revolutionary product—feels like a better investment than a boring company with steady earnings. Never mind that the boring company might be better. The story captures imagination and capital.

Financial media exploits this relentlessly. Every market movement gets a narrative explanation. Stocks fell because of trade concerns. Stocks rose on earnings optimism. These explanations are usually invented after the fact, retrofitting stories to explain essentially random movements. Yet they feel satisfying because they give meaning to chaos.

Hindsight bias reinforces the narrative fallacy. Looking back, we can always construct an explaining story. The housing bubble was obvious in retrospect. But in the moment, the future was radically uncertain. The story that explains the past so neatly did not exist until after the fact.

The defense is to demand evidence beyond story. What do the numbers say? What does history suggest about similar situations? What is the base rate of success for investments with this profile? These questions are harder than spinning a narrative, but the answers are more reliable.

### Building Defenses

Awareness of biases is necessary but insufficient. Knowing you are susceptible to loss aversion does not make losses hurt less. Knowing you follow the herd does not grant courage to stand apart. The biases operate beneath conscious thought and cannot be defeated by knowledge alone.

What can be circumvented is the opportunity for biases to express themselves. The practical solution is not to become a better decision-maker in the moment but to make fewer decisions in the moment. Systems remove choices from your fallible real-time judgment and place them in structures designed during calmer, more rational hours.

**Automation is the first line of defense.** When money flows automatically from paycheck to investment account, you never face the monthly decision of whether to invest. Loss aversion cannot stop a transfer you never see. Recency bias cannot discourage contributions that happen without involvement. The investor who automates removes themselves from the equation at precisely the moments when their involvement would be most destructive.

**Rules-based rebalancing prevents emotional drift.** A simple rule—rebalance every June and December, or whenever any asset class drifts more than five percentage points from target—removes the question of when to act. You act on schedule, regardless of what markets are doing or how you feel. The rule does not care that stocks have been falling and feel dangerous. The rule executes, and your biases are bypassed.

**Cooling-off periods introduce valuable friction.** A personal rule requiring seventy-two hours between any decision to trade and execution allows System 2 time to engage. Most impulses do not survive three days of reflection. The panic that seemed urgent on Monday feels less compelling by Thursday.

**Pre-commitment devices bind your future self to present intentions.** Retirement accounts with early withdrawal penalties are a form of pre-commitment—you cannot easily access money during a panic, so you do not sell at the bottom. Written investment policy statements serve similarly: drafted during calm periods, they articulate your strategy and rules. When markets become turbulent and emotions clamor for action, the statement speaks with the voice of your rational self.

**Decision checklists force System 2 to engage.** Before selling any holding, require yourself to answer in writing: Why am I selling? What has changed about fundamental value? Am I reacting to price movements or genuine new information? Would I buy this investment today at current prices? If the answers do not support the sale, you do not sell.

**Accountability structures leverage social nature against biases.** Sharing decisions with a trusted friend or advisor creates external oversight. The knowledge that you will have to explain choices makes impulsive action less likely.

These systems share common logic: they recognize that you cannot reliably win the battle against biases through willpower alone. Willpower depletes. Emotions surge. Ancient instincts overwhelm recent resolutions. The solution is to design systems that work whether you are feeling rational or irrational, whether markets are calm or chaotic.

The investor who relies on discipline will eventually fail. The investor who relies on systems can succeed even when discipline fails. We cannot change what we are, but we can change the environment in which we operate.

**Countermeasures for Specific Biases**

Against loss aversion, reframe the time horizon. Losses feel devastating when viewed daily. Over decades, they become mere fluctuations in an upward trajectory. The investor who checks their portfolio daily subjects themselves to frequent small losses. The investor who checks annually experiences mostly gains, because stocks rise in most years. Same portfolio, same returns, radically different emotional experience.

Against overconfidence, enforce humility through structure. Position limits prevent any single bet from becoming catastrophic. The rule that no individual stock may exceed five percent of the portfolio means even complete conviction cannot produce complete ruin. Diversification is not just mathematical optimization; it is behavioral safeguard against unjustified certainty.

Against herding, employ contrarian forcing mechanisms. Before following any popular investment trend, write a memorandum arguing the opposite case. What would the smartest skeptic say? Why might the crowd be wrong?

Against recency bias, embed historical perspective in your process. Keep a written record of past panics and recoveries. When the present feels unprecedented, review that record. The panic of 2008 felt like the end of capitalism. It was not. The crash of 2020 felt like depression's beginning. It was not.

Against anchoring, evaluate holdings without reference to purchase price. The market does not know your cost basis. Evaluate based on current earnings, current prospects, current price relative to intrinsic value. If you would not buy today at today's price, the only reason to hold is tax efficiency.

Against confirmation bias, mandate exposure to opposing views. Before any significant decision, read the best argument against it. Seek out the analyst who hates the stock you love. Understand their reasoning fully before dismissing it.

Against the narrative fallacy, impose quantitative discipline. Require that every investment story be accompanied by specific, measurable predictions. If the story is that a company will dominate its industry, what revenue must it achieve by when? Pin narrative to numbers, and you can evaluate against reality.

**The Internal Battle**

These biases explain why most investors underperform simple strategies. They explain why bubbles form and crashes occur. They explain why intelligent people make predictable mistakes with their money.

You cannot eliminate these biases. They are built into cognitive architecture, products of millions of years of evolution. But you can recognize them, design systems to mitigate them, and cultivate awareness of when they are likely to strike.

**Trade rarely.** Every trade is an opportunity for bias to influence decisions. The less you trade, the less damage your biases can do. The best approach for most investors is to establish a sensible allocation and change it only when life circumstances change, not when markets move or mood shifts.

**Automate where possible.** Automatic contributions remove decisions from your hands. You cannot talk yourself out of investing if money moves before you see it.

**Ignore financial news.** The news is designed to trigger System 1 responses—fear, greed, excitement, outrage. It provides entertainment, not useful information. Reading financial news will make you worse at investing, not better.

**Commit in advance.** Decide on your strategy when calm and commit to following it regardless of later feelings. Write down your plan. Tell someone about it. Create barriers to changing it.

**Seek opposing views.** Before any major decision, find

someone who disagrees and listen genuinely. Not to argue, but to understand. What are they seeing that you are not?

**Focus on process, not outcomes.** Any single decision can turn out well or badly regardless of whether it was wise. Luck plays an enormous role in short-term results. Judge yourself on whether you followed sound process, not whether outcome was favorable.

**Know your history.** Study past bubbles and crashes, past euphoria and despair. See how people behaved and what happened next. This provides context for whatever is happening now and inoculates against the feeling that the present is unprecedented.

The investor's worst enemy is not the market, not Wall Street, not the economy. It is the investor themselves. Every failure of discipline, every capitulation to fear or greed, every deviation from a sound plan represents a victory of ancient instinct over modern reason. The battle is internal, fought daily, never fully won.

But it can be fought to a draw. You can recognize when emotions are driving decisions. You can override them often enough to stay on course. You can build systems that protect you from your worst impulses. And you can, over time, accumulate the wealth that patient discipline delivers.

The enemy is formidable. But knowing its tactics is only the beginning. The real work is in the daily practice of resistance, the unglamorous discipline of doing what you know is right when everything in you screams to do otherwise.

## SUMMARY

The gap between knowing the right investment strategy and actually following it is primarily psychological, not informational. Daniel Kahneman's research reveals that our minds operate through two systems: a fast, intuitive System 1 that generates immediate responses, and a slow, deliberate System 2 that requires effort to engage. System 1 dominates most decisions, and its instincts—evolved for physical survival and social navigation—systematically undermine investment success.

The core biases that damage investors include loss aversion, which causes us to hold losers too long and sell winners too quickly; overconfidence, which leads to excessive trading and inadequate diversification; herding, which produces bubbles and crashes; recency bias, which causes us to extrapolate recent trends indefinitely; pattern recognition applied to random noise; anchoring to irrelevant numbers like purchase prices; mental accounting that treats money differently based on its source; confirmation bias that filters out disconfirming evidence; and the narrative fallacy that makes compelling stories more persuasive than solid data.

Because these biases operate beneath conscious thought, awareness alone cannot defeat them. The practical solution is building systems that remove decisions from real-time judgment: automating contributions, establishing rules-based rebalancing, imposing cooling-off periods, creating pre-commitment devices, using decision checklists, and maintaining accountability structures. The investor who relies on willpower will eventually fail; the investor who relies on systems can succeed even when discipline fails.

The enemy is not external but internal. Victory comes not from eliminating biases but from designing an environment where they have fewer opportunities to cause harm.

# FIFTEEN
# BUILDING YOUR PORTFOLIO

The previous chapter armed you against your own psychology. You understand now that the enemy is internal, that biases and emotions conspire against wealth accumulation, and that systems must substitute for willpower. But systems require content. They must be built around something. That something is your portfolio—the specific collection of assets you own, in the specific proportions you choose to hold them.

This chapter addresses the most consequential decision you will make as an investor: how to allocate your capital across different asset classes. This decision, more than any individual security selection, more than any market timing, will determine your long-term results. It is the architecture within which everything else operates.

But architecture admits of different styles. The allocation appropriate for a young professional with a 401(k) differs from that appropriate for a university endowment with a perpetual horizon. The investments available to someone with modest savings differ from those available to someone who meets regulatory thresholds for sophisticated investors. Understanding these differences—and where you fit within them—is essential to building a portfolio suited to your situation.

**The Primacy of Asset Allocation**

Studies of institutional portfolio returns have consistently found that asset allocation explains the vast majority of return variability over time. The decision to hold sixty percent stocks and forty percent bonds matters far more than which stocks or which bonds you select. The broad strokes dominate the fine details.

This finding surprises many investors. They spend hours researching individual companies, comparing fund managers, timing entries and exits. These activities feel productive—they engage System 2 in what seems like careful analysis. But the evidence suggests this effort is largely misdirected. The investor who gets asset allocation right and everything else wrong will outperform the investor who gets asset allocation wrong and everything else right.

The reason is straightforward. Different asset classes have fundamentally different risk and return characteristics. Stocks have historically returned far more than bonds, but with far greater volatility. Bonds provide stability and income but limited growth. Cash preserves principal but loses purchasing power to inflation. The proportions in which you combine these assets determine the risk and expected return of your overall portfolio. No amount of clever security selection can transform a conservative allocation into an aggressive one, or vice versa.

Asset allocation is also the decision most within your control. You cannot control what the market does. You cannot reliably predict which stocks will outperform or when recessions will occur. But you can decide, deliberately and in advance, how much risk you are willing to bear and construct a portfolio reflecting that decision. In a world of radical uncertainty, asset allocation is your one reliable lever.

**The Risk-Return Tradeoff**

Every investment involves a tradeoff between risk and expected return. Assets offering higher expected returns do so because they carry higher risk. This relationship is not accidental—it reflects the basic logic of markets.

Consider why anyone would hold stocks if bonds were equally attractive. They would not. For stocks to find buyers, they must offer something bonds do not: the prospect of higher returns. But that prospect comes bundled with the possibility of severe losses. The higher expected return is compensation for bearing that risk.

This tradeoff holds across asset classes with reasonable consistency. Treasury bills, the safest assets, offer the lowest returns. Government bonds offer somewhat more. Corporate bonds offer more still. Stocks offer the highest expected returns but with the greatest volatility. Within stocks, smaller companies and those in financial distress have historically offered higher returns than large, stable companies—again, compensation for higher risk.

The implication is that you cannot have high returns without accepting high risk, and you cannot eliminate risk without accepting low returns. Any strategy promising otherwise is either misrepresenting its risks or is fraud. The investor who understands this tradeoff can make informed decisions. The investor who does not will be perpetually disappointed, chasing returns without accepting the risks that produce them.

Expected return deserves careful definition. It is not a guarantee or even a prediction. It is an average across many possible outcomes, weighted by their probabilities. An asset with a ten percent expected return might deliver thirty percent in a good year and lose twenty percent in a bad year. Over many years, the average might approach ten percent, but any single year could diverge dramatically.

Risk, typically measured by volatility, matters for two reasons. First, practical: the investor who needs to withdraw money during a down year sells assets at depressed prices, locking in losses. Second, psychological: the biases discussed in the previous chapter are triggered by losses, and volatile assets produce more frequent losses.

### Time Horizon: The Great Modifier

The relationship between risk and return is profoundly affected by time. What is risky over one year may be relatively safe over thirty years, and what seems safe over one year may be dangerous over thirty.

In any given year, stocks might lose thirty percent or more. For the investor who needs their money next year, this risk is intolerable. But for the investor who will not touch their money for three decades, a single bad year is merely a blip in a long upward trajectory. The same asset presents entirely different risk profiles depending on when you need the money.

Over short periods, stock returns are dominated by unpredictable fluctuations. Over long periods, the fundamental return of corporate earnings growth dominates, and fluctuations average out. The probability of stocks outperforming bonds over any single year is perhaps sixty percent. Over ten years, it rises to perhaps eighty percent. Over thirty years, it approaches near certainty based on historical data.

This is why time horizon is the single most important input into asset allocation. The young investor with decades until retirement can afford to hold mostly stocks. The retiree who needs income next month cannot. Time horizon is not merely about age, though age is a useful proxy—it is about when you will need the money. Each goal has its own time horizon and therefore its own appropriate allocation.

**Risk Capacity Versus Risk Tolerance**

Two concepts govern how much risk you should take: risk capacity and risk tolerance. They are often confused but are entirely distinct.

Risk capacity is objective. It measures how much risk you can afford given your financial situation. A young professional with decades of earning ahead, no dependents, and modest expenses has high risk capacity. If their portfolio falls fifty percent, they have time to recover and future income to invest at lower prices. A retiree with no labor income and high expenses has low risk capacity—the same decline might mean running out of money.

Risk capacity depends on time horizon, income stability, existing wealth, future obligations, and other safety nets. It can be calculated, at least approximately.

Risk tolerance is subjective. It measures how much risk you can emotionally bear. Some people lie awake if their portfolio declines five percent. Others shrug off thirty percent declines. This difference reflects personality and psychological makeup, not financial circumstances. Risk tolerance cannot be calculated—it must be discovered through experience or, imperfectly, through questionnaires probing hypothetical reactions.

The crucial insight is that your appropriate level of risk is the minimum of your risk capacity and your risk tolerance. Having high risk capacity does you no good if you will panic and sell during every decline. Having high risk tolerance does you no good if you cannot afford the losses you are willing to accept.

The goal is to find an allocation you can both afford and tolerate—one appropriate for your financial circumstances that you can maintain through inevitable periods of market stress. This allocation may not maximize expected return. That is acceptable. The best portfolio is not the one with the highest expected return but the one you can actually stick with.

**The Role of Human Capital**

Your portfolio is only part of your total wealth. The other part, often larger for younger people, is your human capital—the present value of your future earning ability.

A young professional has decades of future earnings ahead. This human capital functions somewhat like a bond: it provides relatively stable future income. Because their human capital is bond-like, young investors can afford to hold more stocks in their financial portfolio—the stocks provide growth and diversification against their human capital.

As you age, human capital depletes. You have fewer earning years ahead. Your financial portfolio becomes a larger fraction of total wealth. Simultaneously, your remaining time horizon shortens. Both factors argue for shifting gradually toward more conservative investments.

The character of your human capital also matters. A tenured professor has very stable human capital, almost bond-like, and can afford more aggressive financial investments. An entrepreneur has highly variable human capital, more stock-like, and should hold more conservative financial investments to diversify against income risk.

If your human capital is tied to a particular industry, diversifying away from that industry in your financial portfolio is prudent. The technology employee should not hold most of their portfolio in technology stocks—if the industry suffers, both their job and portfolio would decline together.

**The Total Balance Sheet**

Your investment portfolio is only one component of your total wealth. To understand your true asset allocation, you must account for everything you own and every claim you have on future income. This broader perspective, emphasized by Charles Ellis and other thoughtful financial planners, often reveals that investors are more conservative—or more aggressive—than they realize.

Consider home equity. For many households, the primary residence represents the largest single asset. A paid-off home worth five hundred thousand dollars is, in effect, a large bond-like holding. It provides stable, imputed income in the form of housing services. It does not fluctuate daily like stocks. It will not go to zero. When you add this home equity to your balance sheet, your true allocation to stable assets may be far higher than your brokerage statement suggests.

The homeowner with a five hundred thousand dollar house and a five hundred thousand dollar investment portfolio split evenly between stocks and bonds might believe they have a balanced allocation. But their true balance sheet tells a different story: five hundred thousand in home equity (bond-like), two hundred fifty thousand in bonds, and two hundred fifty thousand in stocks. Their actual allocation is roughly seventy-five percent stable assets and twenty-five percent stocks. If this investor has decades until retirement, they may be dramatically underexposed to growth assets. Their "balanced" portfolio is, in reality, quite conservative.

Future savings work similarly. If you are early in your career and expect to save consistently for thirty more years, the present value of those future contributions is substantial. These future savings function like a bond—a series of predictable future cash flows. The investor who will add twenty thousand dollars annually for thirty years has, in present value terms, perhaps three or four hundred thousand dollars in future contributions. This is wealth that does not yet appear in any account but is nonetheless real. It provides a cushion that allows for more aggressive allocation of current savings.

Pensions and annuities are explicit bond-like claims. A defined benefit pension promising forty thousand dollars annually for life is equivalent to holding roughly eight hundred thousand to one million dollars in bonds, depending on interest rates and life expectancy. The retiree receiving this pension can afford to hold their remaining portfolio almost entirely in stocks, because the pension already provides the stability that bonds would otherwise supply.

Social Security functions identically. The present value of future Social Security benefits for a typical American household ranges from three hundred thousand to over a million dollars. This is a government-guaranteed, inflation-adjusted annuity—the safest bond imaginable. Failing to count it as part of your fixed income allocation leads to portfolios that are more conservative than necessary.

Even job security enters the calculation. The tenured professor, the career civil servant, the physician with specialized skills in constant demand—all have human capital that resembles a bond. Their income is stable and predictable. They can afford volatility in their financial portfolios because their income provides ballast. The commissioned salesperson, the startup founder, the freelancer with variable income—their human capital resembles a stock. They should hold more conservative financial portfolios to diversify against their already volatile income streams.

The practical implication is that you should inventory your complete balance sheet before determining your portfolio allocation. Add up the present value of your home equity, future savings, pension benefits, Social Security, and annuity income. Consider the stability of your employment. Only then can you see your true exposure to stable versus growth assets.

Many investors who perform this exercise discover they can afford to be more aggressive than they thought. The retiree with a government pension, Social Security, and a paid-off home may have seventy or eighty percent of their true wealth in bond-like assets before investing a single dollar. For such a person, holding one hundred percent of their investment portfolio in stocks might produce a total balance sheet allocation of only thirty or forty percent equities. What seems aggressive when viewed in isolation is actually moderate when viewed in context.

Others discover the opposite. The entrepreneur whose entire net worth is tied up in their business—itself a highly volatile, equity-like asset—may think they are being conservative by holding a balanced portfolio. But when the business is included, their true equity exposure might exceed ninety percent. Such a person should hold bonds and stable assets in their investment portfolio, not because they are risk-averse but because their total balance sheet is already dominated by equity-like risk.

The balance sheet perspective also clarifies the treatment of real estate beyond your primary home. Investment properties generate income and appreciate over time, but they also carry risk—vacancies, repairs, local market declines. They are neither pure bonds nor pure stocks but something in between. They should be counted as part of your allocation, typically as a real asset category distinct from both stocks and bonds.

This framework is not precise. Estimating the present value of future Social Security requires assumptions about discount rates and life expectancy. Valuing human capital is inherently uncertain. But precision is not the point. The point is to think holistically about your wealth rather than focusing narrowly on the brokerage account. The investor who grasps this broader picture will make better allocation decisions than one who optimizes a single account in isolation.

**Two Approaches to Portfolio Construction**

For most investors, the optimal portfolio is remarkably simple. A combination of low-cost index funds covering domestic stocks, international stocks, and bonds provides diversification across asset classes and geographies. The exact proportions depend on your age, risk tolerance, and goals, but the structure remains constant.

This is the standard portfolio—available to everyone with a brokerage account or retirement plan. It requires no special access, no minimum wealth, no sophisticated analysis. Target-date funds automate this approach entirely: you choose a fund matching your expected retirement year, and it gradually shifts from aggressive to conservative as that date approaches. For investors who want simplicity above all, a single target-date fund is a complete portfolio.

This approach is not merely adequate—it is optimal for most people. After fees and taxes, after behavioral mistakes and transaction costs, the simple portfolio reliably outperforms the complex one. The investor who spends an hour per year on their finances and owns three index funds will likely retire wealthier than the investor who spends an hour per day on research and trades individual securities.

But another approach exists, pioneered by large institutional investors—university endowments, pension funds, sovereign wealth funds—who play a different game. They have perpetual or multi-decade time horizons, access to investments unavailable to individuals, and professional staff to evaluate complex strategies. The endowment model, developed most famously by David Swensen at Yale, exploits these advantages.

The endowment approach diversifies beyond stocks and bonds into asset classes that behave differently from public markets: private equity, venture capital, real assets like timber and farmland, and hedge funds employing strategies uncorrelated with traditional assets.

The endowment model's core insight is that time horizon determines opportunity set. An investor who can lock up capital for ten years can access investments closed to someone who needs liquidity. The illiquidity premium—extra return earned for accepting lockup—is real and substantial. But exploiting it requires the ability to wait and skill in selecting managers, as dispersion between top-quartile and bottom-quartile private equity managers is far wider than in public markets.

**Core and Satellite Investing**

The case for index funds is overwhelming. Most active managers underperform their benchmarks after fees. Even those who outperform in one period usually fail to repeat in the next. Costs compound relentlessly. For these reasons, this chapter has emphasized low-cost index funds as the foundation of a sound portfolio.

But some investors have genuine interest in individual companies. They enjoy reading annual reports, following industry developments, and forming views about which businesses will thrive. For these investors, a hybrid approach offers the best of both worlds: the reliability of indexing combined with the opportunity to act on conviction.

The core-satellite model divides the portfolio into two components. The core consists of broad market index funds—perhaps seventy to eighty percent of the total portfolio. This core provides diversification, low costs, and market returns. It ensures that even if every individual stock selection fails, the portfolio will still participate in the long-term growth of the economy.

The satellite consists of individual stocks—perhaps twenty to thirty percent of the portfolio. These are positions in specific companies where the investor has done research, developed conviction, and is willing to deviate from the index. The satellite allows the investor to express views and potentially enhance returns, while the core limits the damage if those views prove wrong.

I have followed this approach myself. The bulk of my portfolio started in index funds, providing broad exposure to domestic and international markets. But alongside this core, I have held individual positions in companies I believed had exceptional prospects. Amazon, when it was primarily a bookseller transforming into a cloud computing giant. Google, as its advertising dominance and technological capabilities became clear. Microsoft, during its renaissance under new leadership. Tesla, as electric vehicles moved from niche to mainstream. Nvidia, as artificial intelligence drove unprecedented demand for its chips.

Not every position worked immediately. Some required patience through extended periods of underperformance or volatility. Tesla in particular tested conviction through dramatic price swings. But the thesis behind each investment was grounded in observable business fundamentals: durable competitive advantages, large addressable markets, strong management, and reasonable valuations relative to growth prospects. These were not speculative gambles but considered positions in businesses I had studied.

What I did not anticipate, and what many successful stock-pickers discover, is how dramatically winning positions can reshape a portfolio. A stock that rises tenfold does not remain a modest satellite—it becomes a dominant holding. The investor who allocated five percent to a company that subsequently grows ten times now finds that single position comprising perhaps a third of their portfolio. The careful core-satellite structure, designed to limit risk, has organically transformed into something far more concentrated.

This is the rebalancing dilemma. Traditional portfolio theory says to rebalance: sell the winners, buy the laggards, restore the original proportions. This approach manages risk and enforces the discipline of buying low and selling high. But it also means repeatedly trimming your best investments. The investor who rebalanced out of Amazon in 2015, or Nvidia in 2020, captured gains but forfeited the extraordinary returns that followed.

There is no universally correct answer. The case for rebalancing rests on risk management. Concentrated positions, however successful, expose you to company-specific risk. Even great businesses stumble. Regulatory changes, technological disruption, management missteps, or simple mean reversion can devastate a stock that once seemed invincible. The investor who holds fifty percent of their wealth in a single company is not diversified, regardless of how that concentration arose.

The case against mechanical rebalancing rests on the nature of exceptional investments. Truly great companies are rare. Their outperformance is not random but reflects genuine competitive advantages that may persist for decades. Selling simply because a position has grown may cut off the very returns that made it exceptional. As the saying often attributed to various investors goes, the best time to sell a great company is never.

A middle path exists. Rather than rebalancing mechanically to original percentages, you might set wider bands for successful positions. A stock that grows from five percent to fifteen percent might be left alone, while one that reaches twenty-five or thirty percent triggers partial trimming. You might also rebalance into tax-advantaged accounts, using new contributions to buy underweighted assets rather than selling winners and incurring capital gains.

Another consideration is the changing thesis. If your original investment rested on specific expectations that have now been realized, the case for continued holding weakens. The investor who bought Nvidia anticipating the artificial intelligence boom might reasonably ask whether that thesis is now fully reflected in the price. Conversely, if the company's prospects have expanded beyond your original vision, continued holding may be justified.

My own approach has evolved through experience. I have learned to tolerate more concentration in positions where my conviction remains high and the business fundamentals continue to strengthen. I have also learned, sometimes painfully, that no position deserves infinite faith. Partial trimming—taking some profits while allowing the remainder to run—offers a psychological compromise that captures some gains while preserving upside. There is no formula, only judgment applied to each situation as it unfolds.

The core-satellite approach succeeds only with discipline. Several principles govern its execution.

First, size the satellite appropriately. If individual stocks constitute more than twenty-five or thirty percent of your portfolio, you are no longer an index investor with satellites—you are a stock picker with some index exposure. This may be appropriate for professional investors or those with exceptional skill, but it increases risk substantially for everyone else.

Second, limit position sizes. No single stock should exceed five to ten percent of your total portfolio. Concentration creates the possibility of outsized gains but also outsized losses. Even if your analysis is correct, you may be wrong about timing, or external events may intervene. Diversification within the satellite protects against these risks.

Third, invest only in companies you understand. The advantage of individual stock selection, if it exists, comes from knowledge—understanding a business better than the market does. If you cannot explain how a company makes money, who its customers are, and why it will outcompete rivals, you have no business owning it as an individual position. Buy the index instead.

Fourth, have a thesis and monitor it. Each satellite position should rest on a specific investment thesis—a view about why this company will outperform. Perhaps you believe its technology is superior, its market is underappreciated, or its management is exceptional. Write down this thesis. Periodically revisit it. If the thesis breaks—if the competitive advantage erodes, if management stumbles, if the market changes—sell the position. Do not hold out of inertia or hope.

Fifth, be honest about your results. Track the performance of your satellite positions against the relevant index. If your individual stocks consistently underperform, you are not adding value—you are subtracting it. Acknowledge this and shift more toward the core. There is no shame in concluding that you cannot beat the market; most professionals cannot either.

Sixth, account for taxes. Individual stocks in taxable accounts create tax events when sold. Gains are taxable; losses can offset gains. This friction should enter your decision-making. Sometimes holding a position slightly longer to qualify for long-term capital gains treatment is worthwhile. Sometimes harvesting losses to offset gains elsewhere makes sense. Tax considerations should not drive investment decisions, but they should inform them.

The satellite portion of your portfolio also serves a psychological function. Many investors feel the urge to do something—to act on news, to chase performance, to express views. Channeling this urge into a bounded portion of the portfolio protects the core from interference. The investor who scratches the itch by buying an individual stock they have researched is less likely to panic-sell their index funds during a market decline. The satellite becomes a release valve for the impulse to tinker.

Some will object that this hybrid approach contradicts the efficient market hypothesis or the evidence against active management. But the evidence is about averages. Most active managers underperform—this does not mean all do. And the individual investor selecting a handful of stocks based on genuine knowledge is playing a different game than the mutual fund manager who must deploy billions while conforming to benchmark constraints.

The realistic assessment is this: most investors will not outperform through stock selection. But some will. If you have genuine interest, knowledge, and discipline—and if you size your satellite positions appropriately—the attempt costs little and might add meaningfully to returns. The index core ensures you will do well regardless. The satellite allows for the possibility of doing better.

What the satellite does not allow is reckless speculation. Day trading, options gambling, meme stock chasing—these belong nowhere in a serious portfolio. The satellite is for positions you intend to hold for years, in companies you have studied carefully, sized to be meaningful without being catastrophic. Anything else is not investing but entertainment, and should be funded, if at all, from money you can afford to lose entirely.

**The Qualified Investor Gateway**

Between the standard portfolio and the endowment model stands a regulatory barrier: the concept of the qualified or accredited investor. Securities regulations restrict access to certain investments—private placements, hedge funds, venture capital—to investors meeting wealth or income thresholds. In the United States, an accredited investor generally has net worth exceeding one million dollars (excluding primary residence) or income exceeding two hundred thousand dollars annually.

For those who do not meet thresholds, most alternative investments are unavailable. This is not necessarily a disadvantage—the standard portfolio has performed admirably, many alternatives have disappointed after fees, and complexity creates new opportunities for error.

For those who do meet thresholds, the question becomes whether to pursue alternatives at all. Access is not wisdom. Many wealthy investors have lost money in private placements and hedge funds that their wealth entitled them to enter but their judgment should have avoided.

**Allocation Across Life Stages**

The principles discussed translate into different strategies at different life stages.

In early career, from twenties through thirties, the investor typically has decades until retirement, high human capital, low current wealth, and ability to recover from setbacks. This stage calls for aggressive allocation—perhaps eighty or ninety percent stocks and ten or twenty percent bonds. The priority at this stage is not return on existing investments but rate of saving. A young investor with modest savings who increases their savings rate gains far more than the same investor who marginally improves their returns.

In mid-career, from forties through fifties, the investor has accumulated meaningful wealth but still has significant human capital and sees retirement approaching. Time heals fewer wounds now. This stage calls for gradual moderation of risk, perhaps shifting to sixty or seventy percent stocks as retirement approaches. Specific retirement planning should begin in earnest.

In late career, the five to ten years before retirement, preservation of capital becomes increasingly important. A major loss now might require delaying retirement for years. Something like fifty-five or sixty percent stocks might be appropriate, though this depends on individual circumstances.

In early retirement, the investor has stopped earning labor income and begun drawing on their portfolio. A balanced allocation of perhaps fifty percent stocks and fifty percent bonds provides growth potential while limiting damage from poor early returns. Bucket strategies can help: holding two or three years of expenses in cash and short-term bonds provides a buffer, allowing the rest to remain invested.

In late retirement, the remaining time horizon shortens but does not disappear. A seventy-five-year-old might still have fifteen or twenty years ahead, and the portfolio needs some growth to maintain purchasing power. An allocation of perhaps forty percent stocks and sixty percent bonds might be appropriate. Legacy considerations may also matter—assets intended for heirs have a longer effective time horizon.

**Sample Portfolios**

The following illustrate how principles translate into practice. They are not recommendations for any individual.

**Young Investor (twenties to early thirties):** Ninety percent stocks, ten percent bonds. Within stocks, perhaps sixty percent domestic equities through a total market index fund and forty percent international. This portfolio will experience significant volatility—perhaps declining twenty-five percent or more in bad years—but historically has averaged eight to nine percent annually over long periods.

**Mid-Career Investor (forties to early fifties):** Seventy percent stocks, thirty percent bonds. The bond allocation might include some inflation-protected securities. Expected volatility is lower, with worst years typically seeing losses of fifteen to twenty percent.

**Late-Career Investor (late fifties):** Fifty-five percent stocks, forty-five percent bonds. The investor might begin building a cash reserve for early retirement expenses.

**New Retiree (mid-sixties):** Fifty percent stocks, fifty percent bonds, plus two years of expenses in cash. The cash reserve allows withdrawals during downturns without selling depressed assets.

**Late Retirement (mid-seventies):** Forty percent stocks, sixty percent bonds. Some stock exposure remains prudent to maintain purchasing power over perhaps fifteen or twenty remaining years.

**Core-Satellite Variant:** For investors who wish to combine indexing with individual stock selection, the portfolio might allocate seventy to eighty percent to index funds (divided between domestic and international stocks and bonds as appropriate for age) and twenty to thirty percent to individual stock positions. Within the satellite, no single position should exceed five to ten percent of the total portfolio. This structure provides the benefits of diversification while allowing room for conviction-based investing.

**Total Balance Sheet Adjustment:** Any of these portfolios should be adjusted based on the investor's complete balance sheet. The retiree with substantial pension income and Social Security might hold a higher stock allocation in their investment portfolio, since their total wealth already includes significant bond-like assets. The homeowner with substantial equity might similarly tilt toward stocks. The entrepreneur with volatile business income should tilt toward bonds. The sample percentages assume a typical balance sheet; your specific situation may warrant meaningful adjustments.

**Accredited Investor Variant:** For those who meet the thresholds and choose to venture beyond the standard portfolio, a modified version might allocate eighty-five percent to the core portfolio (stocks, bonds, and cash as appropriate for age) and fifteen percent to alternatives—perhaps five percent to private equity, five percent to real estate beyond what is captured in stock indices, and five percent to other alternatives like cryptocurrency or hedge funds. This structure keeps the core intact while allowing exposure to asset classes with different return drivers. The key is sizing alternatives modestly and understanding that they add complexity and risk alongside any potential benefits.

All these portfolios share features: diversification across asset classes, both domestic and international stocks, low-cost index funds as building blocks, no attempt to time markets or identify superior managers.

### Implementation Mechanics

Building a portfolio requires practical decisions beyond target allocation.

On fund selection, costs matter enormously. Low-cost index funds tracking broad market indices are suitable for most investors. The difference between a fund charging 0.03 percent and one charging 1.00 percent compounds to enormous sums over decades.

On account location, taxes matter. Stock index funds generate relatively little taxable income; bond funds generate regular interest taxed at ordinary rates. Holding bonds in tax-advantaged accounts and stocks in taxable accounts often makes sense.

On rebalancing, simplicity trumps optimization. Pick a rule—once or twice annually, or when any asset class drifts more than five percentage points from target—and follow it mechanically. Rebalancing automatically enforces buying low and selling high.

Review the portfolio periodically, perhaps annually, to confirm allocation still matches circumstances. But review should not become an excuse for tinkering. Most of the time, the right action is to rebalance to your target and leave everything else alone.

### What Asset Allocation Cannot Do

Asset allocation is powerful but not magic. It cannot eliminate risk—a well-diversified portfolio still declines during crashes. It cannot predict the future—historical returns guide but do not guarantee. And most importantly, it cannot override psychology. The previous chapter detailed biases that lead investors astray. A perfectly designed portfolio does no good if you abandon it during a panic.

This is why asset allocation must be accompanied by systems: automation, rules-based rebalancing, cooling-off periods, written policy statements. The allocation provides architecture. The systems ensure you inhabit it as intended.

**What Belongs in Your Portfolio**

For most readers, the answer is simpler than you might hope: low-cost index funds covering domestic and international stocks, a bond allocation appropriate to your age and risk tolerance, and consistent contributions over decades. This is not a consolation prize for those who cannot access sophisticated investments. It is the strategy that works.

If you have genuine interest in individual companies and are willing to do the research, the core-satellite approach allows you to pursue that interest while protecting the bulk of your wealth. Size the satellite modestly, invest only in businesses you understand, maintain discipline about position sizes, and be honest about your results. Let the core do the heavy lifting while the satellite provides opportunity for enhanced returns—and a constructive outlet for the impulse to engage more actively with markets.

If you meet accredited investor thresholds and choose to venture further, size alternative investments modestly—single-digit percentages, not the core. If you choose to hold cryptocurrency or other speculative assets, size them as speculation: meaningful enough to matter if successful, small enough to survive if they fail.

Before finalizing your allocation, inventory your complete balance sheet. Count your home equity, your pension, your Social Security, your future savings capacity, and the stability of your income. Your investment portfolio is only one piece of your total wealth. The allocation that makes sense for your brokerage account depends on what else you own and what claims you have on future income.

Do not abandon the core for the satellites. The index fund portfolio has earned its place through decades of evidence. Everything else is addition, not replacement.

## SUMMARY

Asset allocation—the division of your portfolio across stocks, bonds, and other asset classes—is the most consequential investment decision you will make. Studies show it explains the vast majority of return variability over time, far outweighing the impact of individual security selection or market timing.

The fundamental principle is the risk-return tradeoff: assets offering higher expected returns carry higher risk. You cannot have high returns without accepting volatility, and you cannot eliminate volatility without accepting lower returns. This tradeoff is modified by time horizon—what is risky over one year may be relatively safe over thirty years, as short-term fluctuations average out and fundamental returns dominate.

Two factors determine appropriate risk: risk capacity (how much you can afford to lose given your financial situation) and risk tolerance (how much volatility you can emotionally bear). Your appropriate risk level is the minimum of these two. Human capital—your future earning ability—also matters: young investors with decades of earnings ahead can afford aggressive portfolios, while those whose human capital is depleted need more conservative allocations.

Your investment portfolio is only part of your total balance sheet. Home equity, pensions, Social Security, annuities, future savings capacity, and job stability all function as bond-like assets. Before determining your portfolio allocation, inventory your complete wealth. Many investors discover they can afford more aggressive investment portfolios because their total balance sheet already includes substantial stable assets.

For most investors, the optimal portfolio is remarkably simple: low-cost index funds covering domestic and international stocks and bonds, with proportions adjusted for age and circumstances. Target-date funds automate this entirely. For those with genuine interest in individual companies, the core-satellite approach offers a middle path: seventy to eighty percent in index funds provides the foundation, while twenty to thirty percent in carefully researched individual stocks allows for conviction-based investing. Success in individual positions creates its own challenge, as winning stocks grow to dominate a portfolio; the rebalancing decision—whether to trim winners or let them run—requires judgment rather than mechanical rules.

Those meeting accredited investor thresholds may venture into alternatives like private equity, but these should remain modest satellites around an index fund core. The key is sizing all satellite positions—whether individual stocks or alternative investments—modestly enough that failure is survivable while success is meaningful.

The allocation should shift gradually over life stages: heavily stock-weighted in early career, moderately balanced in mid-career, more conservative approaching retirement, and stability-focused during retirement. Implementation requires attention to costs, tax-efficient account location, and disciplined rebalancing. But the best portfolio is ultimately the one you can stick with through inevitable market stress—which is why asset allocation must be paired with the behavioral systems discussed in the previous chapter.

# SIXTEEN
# TAXES, ACCOUNTS, AND RULES

The previous chapter established your portfolio's architecture—the proportions of stocks, bonds, and other assets appropriate for your circumstances. But a portfolio exists within a legal and institutional framework that profoundly affects your actual returns. Two investors with identical portfolios can achieve dramatically different outcomes depending on how they navigate this framework.

Taxes are the most significant drag on investment returns that you can actually control. You cannot control what the market does. You can control, within limits, how much of your return you surrender to the government. The difference between tax-efficient and tax-inefficient investing compounds over decades into differences of hundreds of thousands of dollars.

This chapter addresses the institutional landscape: the accounts available to you, how different investments are taxed, where to place which assets, the basics of estate planning, and when professional guidance is worth its cost. These topics lack the drama of market movements or the intellectual appeal of portfolio theory. They are administrative, technical, sometimes tedious. They are also among the highest-value areas of personal finance, where attention to detail pays handsomely.

**The Logic of Tax-Advantaged Accounts**

Governments want citizens to save for retirement. Retirees who have accumulated wealth do not depend on public assistance. They consume goods and services, supporting the economy. They leave bequests that fund the next generation. For these reasons, governments offer tax advantages to encourage retirement saving.

These advantages come in two basic forms. Tax deferral means you contribute pre-tax money, it grows without annual taxation, and you pay taxes only when you withdraw. Tax exemption means you contribute after-tax money, it grows without taxation, and you withdraw tax-free. Both forms are valuable. Which is more valuable depends on your tax rates now versus in retirement.

The traditional IRA exemplifies tax deferral. You contribute money before paying income tax on it. The money grows for decades without any tax on dividends, interest, or capital gains. When you withdraw in retirement, you pay ordinary income tax on the full amount. The benefit is that decades of compounding occur on the pre-tax amount rather than the after-tax amount.

The Roth IRA exemplifies tax exemption. You contribute money after paying income tax. It grows for decades without taxation. When you withdraw in retirement, you owe nothing—no tax on the contributions, no tax on the growth. The benefit is that all growth escapes taxation entirely.

The mathematics illuminates the choice. Suppose you have ten thousand dollars of pre-tax income and a twenty-five percent tax rate both now and in retirement. With a traditional IRA, you invest the full ten thousand, it grows to forty thousand over thirty years, and you withdraw forty thousand, paying ten thousand in taxes, netting thirty thousand. With a Roth IRA, you pay twenty-five hundred in taxes now, invest seventy-five hundred, it grows to thirty thousand, and you withdraw thirty thousand tax-free. The result is identical.

This equivalence holds when tax rates remain constant. If your tax rate will be lower in retirement—as is typical for many people whose income drops when they stop working—the traditional IRA wins. You defer taxes from a high-rate period to a low-rate period. If your tax rate will be higher in retirement—possible if you accumulate substantial wealth or if tax rates rise generally—the Roth wins. You pay taxes at the lower rate now.

For most investors, a blend makes sense. You cannot know future tax rates with certainty. Holding both traditional and Roth accounts provides flexibility—you can draw from whichever is more advantageous given the tax environment at the time of withdrawal. This is diversification not across asset classes but across tax treatment.

**The Menu of Account Types**

The American retirement system offers a bewildering variety of account types. Each has its own rules, limits, and quirks.

The 401(k) is the workhorse of retirement saving for employees. Offered by employers, it allows pre-tax contributions up to a substantial annual limit—twenty-three thousand dollars in 2024 for those under fifty, with an additional catch-up contribution for those older. Many employers match a portion of contributions, providing an immediate return that no market investment can match. If your employer offers a match, contributing enough to capture the full match should be among your highest financial priorities. The 401(k) comes in traditional and Roth versions, and many plans offer both options.

The Individual Retirement Account exists for those without workplace plans or as a supplement to them. Contribution limits are lower—seven thousand dollars in 2024, with a catch-up for those over fifty. Traditional IRAs offer a deduction if you meet income limits or lack a workplace plan. Roth IRAs have income limits that phase out eligibility for high earners.

The Health Savings Account deserves special mention as perhaps the most tax-advantaged account available. If you have a high-deductible health insurance plan, you can contribute to an HSA. Contributions are pre-tax. Growth is tax-free. Withdrawals for qualified medical expenses are tax-free. This triple tax advantage is unique. After age sixty-five, you can withdraw for any purpose, paying only ordinary income tax—making the HSA function like a traditional IRA with the bonus of tax-free withdrawals for medical expenses.

The 529 plan addresses education rather than retirement. Contributions are after-tax, but growth is tax-free if used for qualified education expenses. Many states offer deductions for contributions to their own 529 plans.

Taxable brokerage accounts offer no tax advantages but also no restrictions. You can contribute unlimited amounts, withdraw at any time, and invest in anything. Taxable accounts are where you save for goals before retirement, where you invest after maxing out tax-advantaged space, and where you hold assets unsuitable for retirement accounts.

**How Investments Are Taxed**

Different investments generate different types of taxable income, and the tax code treats these types differently.

Ordinary income includes wages, interest, and short-term capital gains. It is taxed at your marginal rate, which can exceed thirty-seven percent for high earners, plus state taxes. Bond interest and dividends from real estate investment trusts typically count as ordinary income.

Qualified dividends from stocks held more than sixty days receive preferential treatment—fifteen percent for most taxpayers, twenty percent for high earners. This makes stock dividends less burdensome than bond interest at the same dollar amount.

Long-term capital gains—profits from selling assets held more than one year—receive the same preferential rates as qualified dividends. Short-term gains are taxed as ordinary income. This creates a powerful incentive to hold investments for the long term.

Unrealized gains are not taxed until you sell. You can hold an appreciated stock for decades and owe nothing until you dispose of it. This deferral allows the full pre-tax amount to compound.

At death, the step-up in basis eliminates unrealized gains

entirely. Your heirs receive appreciated assets with a basis equal to value at your death. The gain during your lifetime is never taxed.

Losses can offset gains. If losses exceed gains, you can deduct up to three thousand dollars against ordinary income, carrying forward any remainder.

**Asset Location**

Asset location is the strategic placement of investments across account types to minimize taxes. It is distinct from asset allocation, which determines what you hold. Asset location determines where you hold it.

The principle is straightforward: place tax-inefficient investments in tax-advantaged accounts and tax-efficient investments in taxable accounts.

Bonds are tax-inefficient—they generate interest taxed as ordinary income. In a taxable account, a bond yielding five percent might net only three percent after taxes for a high earner. The same bond in an IRA yields the full five percent with taxes deferred. Real estate investment trusts are similarly tax-inefficient, as their dividends are generally taxed as ordinary income.

Stock index funds are tax-efficient. They generate modest qualified dividends and rarely distribute capital gains. The bulk of the return comes from unrealized appreciation, which is not taxed until you sell. These funds can reside comfortably in taxable accounts.

International stock funds are moderately efficient. In taxable accounts, you can claim a credit for foreign taxes paid by the fund. In retirement accounts, this credit is lost, making taxable accounts slightly preferable for international holdings.

The overall strategy is to fill your tax-advantaged space with tax-inefficient assets, then hold tax-efficient assets in taxable accounts. Asset allocation should not be distorted to fit asset location—if your target calls for forty percent bonds, hold forty percent bonds across your total portfolio regardless of where they sit.

**Tax-Loss Harvesting**

When investments decline, they create an opportunity. By selling at a loss, you realize that loss for tax purposes. You can use it to offset gains elsewhere or deduct against ordinary income.

Tax-loss harvesting is the systematic practice of capturing these losses. When an investment falls significantly, you sell it, realize the loss, and immediately purchase a similar but not identical investment to maintain your market exposure. The loss reduces your current taxes while your portfolio remains invested.

The wash sale rule constrains this practice. If you buy a substantially identical security within thirty days before or after the sale, the loss is disallowed. But you can sell one provider's index fund and buy another provider's similar fund tracking a different index.

Tax-loss harvesting is most valuable early in your investing career, when losses can be carried forward for decades, and for high earners facing the highest marginal rates. One caution: harvesting reduces your cost basis in the replacement investment, so you will owe more tax when you eventually sell. The benefit is tax deferral, not permanent elimination—though holding the investment until death captures the step-up in basis.

**Required Minimum Distributions**

Tax-advantaged accounts come with strings attached. At a certain age, you must begin withdrawing from traditional accounts, paying the taxes you deferred.

Required minimum distributions begin at age seventy-three for those born between 1951 and 1959, and age seventy-five for those born in 1960 or later. Each year, you must withdraw a minimum amount calculated by dividing your account balance by a life expectancy factor. Failure to take RMDs triggers a severe penalty—twenty-five percent of the amount you should have withdrawn, reduced to ten percent if corrected promptly.

Roth IRAs have no RMDs during the owner's lifetime, allowing money to compound tax-free indefinitely. Inherited Roth accounts do have distribution requirements for non-spouse beneficiaries.

Planning for RMDs should begin years before they start. If you reach retirement with large traditional balances, RMDs may push you into higher tax brackets than necessary. Strategic Roth conversions in lower-income years between retirement and age seventy-three can smooth your tax liability and reduce future RMDs.

**Estate Planning Basics**

Death is not merely a biological event. It is a tax event, an administrative event, and a legal event. How you prepare for it determines what your heirs receive and how smoothly they receive it.

The federal estate tax exemption is currently very high—over thirteen million dollars per individual—so most estates owe no federal estate tax. However, this exemption is scheduled to drop roughly in half in 2026 unless Congress acts, and some states impose their own estate or inheritance taxes at much lower thresholds.

Beneficiary designations are the most important estate planning tool for investment accounts. Retirement accounts and life insurance pass directly to named beneficiaries, outside probate. Keeping these designations current is essential—a decades-old designation naming an ex-spouse could direct your retirement account to someone you have not spoken to in years. Review designations whenever circumstances change.

The step-up in basis has profound estate planning implications. If you hold both appreciated stocks and other assets, spend down the other assets first, preserving appreciated stocks for the step-up. When you must sell, sell assets with losses or minimal gains rather than those with large unrealized gains.

Trusts serve various purposes—avoiding probate, providing for minor children, managing assets for beneficiaries who cannot manage them themselves—but most investors of moderate wealth do not need complex trusts. Wills remain necessary to address assets outside trusts, name guardians for minor children, and provide instructions for matters trusts do not cover. Powers of attorney and healthcare directives address incapacity, allowing someone to manage your affairs and make medical decisions if you cannot.

**Financial Advisors**

The question of whether to hire a financial advisor is itself a financial decision. Like all such decisions, it requires understanding what you're buying, what it costs, and whether the benefit exceeds the price.

The financial advice industry is rife with conflicts of interest. Many people calling themselves financial advisors are primarily salespeople compensated for selling products—insurance policies, loaded mutual funds, annuities—that benefit them more than their clients. Titles like financial consultant, wealth manager, and financial planner are unregulated and mean nothing specific. Understanding the underlying structure matters more than the title on the business card.

The most important distinction is between fiduciary and suitability standards. A fiduciary is legally obligated to act in your best interest, even when it conflicts with their own. A suitability standard requires only that recommendations be suitable for your situation—not optimal, not best, merely not inappropriate. A broker operating under suitability can recommend a high-commission product when a low-cost alternative would serve you better, as long as the expensive product is not wholly unsuitable. When evaluating any advisor, ask directly: are you a fiduciary, and will you put that in writing? Hesitation or evasion is informative.

Compensation structures create incentives you should understand. Fee-only advisors are compensated solely by their clients, through hourly fees, flat fees, or a percentage of assets under management. They sell no products and receive no commissions. Commission-based advisors are compensated by the companies whose products they sell, creating obvious conflicts. Fee-based is a hybrid term that often obscures more than it reveals.

The assets-under-management model, common among fee-only advisors, typically charges around one percent of your portfolio annually. On a million-dollar portfolio, that's ten thousand dollars per year—a substantial sum that compounds against you over decades. Whether this fee is justified depends on what you receive in return. For complex situations requiring ongoing attention—tax optimization, estate planning coordination, behavioral coaching during market turmoil—the fee may be worthwhile. For a simple portfolio requiring only occasional attention, you are likely paying for services you don't need.

Hourly and flat-fee advisors offer an alternative for those who need occasional guidance rather than ongoing management. You might pay for consultation to establish your investment plan, implement it yourself, and return every few years for a check-up. Roboadvisors—automated services that construct and manage portfolios—charge far less, often around 0.25 percent of assets. They provide basic portfolio management and automatic rebalancing but not personalized advice on complex situations or behavioral coaching.

When does professional advice add value? The situations where advisors most clearly earn their fees include complex tax planning across multiple account types, coordination between investment strategy and estate planning, major life transitions such as retirement or the sale of a business, and behavioral coaching for investors who might otherwise make costly emotional decisions. If your situation is straightforward—regular contributions to a workplace retirement plan, a simple asset allocation, standard beneficiary designations—you likely do not need ongoing advisory services.

If you decide to hire an advisor, verify credentials through FINRA's BrokerCheck and the SEC's Investment Adviser Public Disclosure database. Ask about compensation structure, fiduciary status, and potential conflicts. Request a sample financial plan to evaluate the quality of their work. The best advisors integrate investment management with tax planning, estate planning, and major financial decisions, translating principles into personalized strategy. The worst are product salespeople in professional clothing. The difference justifies careful selection.

**The Administrative Discipline**

Tax-efficient investing requires administrative discipline. Records must be kept, deadlines met, elections made.

Keep records of all contributions to retirement accounts,

including the basis of any after-tax contributions. These records are necessary to calculate taxes on distributions and may be needed decades later. Track your cost basis in taxable accounts—for purchases after 2011, brokers report this to the IRS, but for older purchases you must maintain records yourself.

Meet deadlines. IRA contributions for a given tax year can be made until the following April. Roth conversions must be completed by December 31. Required minimum distributions must be taken by December 31, with a special extension to April 1 for the first RMD year. Missing these deadlines has consequences ranging from lost tax benefits to substantial penalties.

Consider automation where possible. Have RMDs calculated and distributed automatically. Set calendar reminders for annual reviews. An annual review of accounts, beneficiaries, and tax strategies, combined with disciplined record-keeping, is sufficient for most investors. Those with complex situations should engage professionals —recognizing that fees are usually recovered many times over in tax savings.

**The Investor's Framework**

The legal and tax landscape is the water in which your portfolio swims. Understanding it allows you to structure your investments to keep more of what you earn.

The core principles are durable even as details change. Use tax-advantaged accounts to their limits before investing in taxable accounts. Place tax-inefficient assets in tax-advantaged accounts and tax-efficient assets in taxable accounts. Hold investments long enough to qualify for preferential capital gains rates. Harvest losses when available to offset gains. Plan for RMDs before they begin. Keep beneficiary designations current. Hold appreciated assets until death when possible to capture the step-up in basis.

None of this changes what you should invest in. Your asset allocation is determined by your time horizon, risk capacity, and risk tolerance. The tax and account considerations determine where you hold those assets and how you manage them.

. . .

## SUMMARY

Taxes represent the most significant controllable drag on investment returns. Two investors with identical portfolios can achieve dramatically different outcomes depending on how they navigate the tax and account landscape.

Tax-advantaged accounts come in two forms: traditional accounts offering tax deferral (contribute pre-tax, pay taxes on withdrawal) and Roth accounts offering tax exemption (contribute after-tax, withdraw tax-free). Traditional accounts favor those expecting lower tax rates in retirement; Roth accounts favor those expecting higher rates. Holding both provides flexibility across uncertain future tax environments. If your employer offers a 401(k) match, capturing the full match should be among your highest priorities.

Asset location—where you hold investments—matters independently of asset allocation. Tax-inefficient assets like bonds and REITs belong in tax-advantaged accounts. Tax-efficient assets like stock index funds can reside in taxable accounts. International stocks are slightly favored in taxable accounts to capture foreign tax credits.

Tax-loss harvesting captures losses during market declines to offset gains, reducing current taxes while maintaining market exposure through similar replacement investments. The benefit is tax deferral rather than elimination, though holding investments until death captures the step-up in basis.

Required minimum distributions force withdrawals from traditional accounts beginning at age seventy-three or seventy-five. Strategic Roth conversions in lower-income years before RMDs begin can smooth tax liability.

Estate planning ensures smooth wealth transfer. Beneficiary designations must be kept current. The step-up in basis at death eliminates unrealized gains. Most investors need current wills, powers of attorney, and healthcare directives.

Financial advisors can add value for complex situations—tax optimization, estate coordination, major transitions, behavioral coaching—but most straightforward portfolios do not require ongoing professional management. When hiring an advisor, prioritize fiduciary duty, understand compensation structures, and verify credentials. Fee-only advisors with fiduciary obligations have fewer conflicts of interest than commission-based salespeople.

Administrative discipline—record-keeping, meeting deadlines, periodic review—captures the full value of these strategies. The principles are durable even as specific rules change: maximize tax-advantaged contributions, locate assets efficiently, hold for the long term, harvest losses opportunistically, and plan for distributions and estate transfer well in advance.

# PART 5
# SPENDING WISELY

*The art of using money well*

# SEVENTEEN
# THE HEDONIC TREADMILL

**h**We have spent fifteen chapters discussing how to accumulate wealth. This chapter asks a different question: what is wealth for?

The obvious answer—happiness—turns out to be complicated. The relationship between money and well-being is real but nonlinear, subject to adaptation, and dependent on how money is spent rather than merely how much is accumulated. Understanding this relationship is not a philosophical indulgence. It is practical knowledge that should shape both your saving decisions and your spending decisions.

The person who saves relentlessly for decades, accumulating far more than needed, sacrificing experiences and relationships along the way, has made an error. So has the person who spends freely on things that provide only fleeting pleasure, never building the security that enables lasting well-being. Both errors stem from misunderstanding what money can and cannot do for human happiness.

This chapter synthesizes what researchers have learned about money and well-being. The findings are often counterintuitive. They challenge assumptions embedded in both consumer culture and frugality culture. They suggest that the good life is available at lower cost than advertising implies, but that it requires more intentionality than simply spending less.

**What the Research Shows**

For decades, economists assumed that more money meant more happiness, with no upper limit. This assumption was convenient for economic models and flattering to the wealthy. It was also wrong.

The modern study of money and happiness began with economist Richard Easterlin's observation in 1974 that rising national income did not produce rising national happiness. Countries grew wealthier over decades, but their citizens did not report greater life satisfaction. This became known as the Easterlin Paradox, and it launched a research program that continues today.

Within countries, at any given time, richer people report higher life satisfaction than poorer people. This finding is robust and unsurprising. But the relationship is logarithmic, not linear. The difference in well-being between earning twenty thousand dollars and forty thousand dollars is much larger than the difference between earning one hundred thousand and one hundred twenty thousand. Each doubling of income produces roughly the same increment of well-being. Going from poor to middle class transforms life. Going from affluent to wealthy changes it only modestly.

A widely cited study by Daniel Kahneman and Angus Deaton, published in 2010, found that emotional well-being—the quality of everyday experience—stopped rising at an annual income of about seventy-five thousand dollars. Above that threshold, people did not report more happiness, less stress, or greater enjoyment of daily life. They did report higher life evaluation—their abstract assessment of how their life was going—but their actual experienced happiness plateaued.

This finding captured public attention and entered popular discourse as "money can't buy happiness above seventy-five thousand dollars." The truth is more nuanced. The threshold varies by location and family size; seventy-five thousand in Manhattan is not seventy-five thousand in rural Mississippi. More recent research by Matthew

Killingsworth, using real-time experience sampling, found that experienced well-being continued rising with income even above this threshold, though at a diminishing rate. The relationship may also differ for people who are already unhappy for other reasons.

What emerges from the research is not a single threshold but a general pattern. Money matters a great deal for happiness when it relieves genuine deprivation and insecurity. It matters less and less as income rises beyond sufficiency. The person earning thirty thousand dollars who gets a raise to fifty thousand experiences a meaningful improvement in well-being. The person earning three hundred thousand who gets a raise to five hundred thousand experiences much less change in daily happiness, whatever they might tell themselves.

### The Mechanics of Adaptation

Why doesn't happiness keep rising with income? The answer lies in a fundamental feature of human psychology: adaptation.

Humans adapt to their circumstances with remarkable speed and thoroughness. The new car that thrilled you in the first week becomes merely transportation within months. The larger house that felt palatial when you moved in becomes simply home. The raise that seemed transformative is absorbed into a new baseline within a year. This process is automatic, unconscious, and nearly universal.

Psychologists call this the hedonic treadmill. Like a person walking on a treadmill, you keep moving but stay in the same place. Each acquisition or improvement provides temporary pleasure, then becomes the new normal, requiring further acquisition to produce further pleasure. The treadmill keeps turning, and you keep walking, but your happiness remains roughly constant.

The evolutionary logic is clear. A creature that remained perpetually satisfied with its circumstances would lack motivation to improve them. The dissatisfaction that follows adaptation drives continued striving, which may have been advantageous for survival and reproduction. But in a modern context of abundant consumer goods, this drive can become pathological—an endless chase for satisfaction that remains perpetually just out of reach.

Adaptation is not uniform across all domains. Research suggests that people adapt more completely to material improvements than to experiential ones. The new television becomes invisible within weeks; the memory of a meaningful trip persists for years. People adapt more to stable circumstances than to variable ones; a steady high income produces less ongoing pleasure than a lower income with occasional windfalls. People adapt more to positive changes than to certain negative ones; chronic pain, for instance, produces less complete adaptation than a new home.

Understanding adaptation should change how you think about spending. The purchase that provides lasting value is one that resists adaptation. The purchase that provides only temporary pleasure is one that adapts quickly. The challenge is that at the moment of purchase, both feel equally compelling. The car dealer does not tell you that the new-car feeling will fade within ninety days. The real estate agent does not mention that the larger house will feel normal within a year.

**Experienced Happiness and Remembered Happiness**

Kahneman drew a distinction that illuminates the money-happiness relationship: the difference between the experiencing self and the remembering self.

The experiencing self lives in the present moment. It feels pleasure and pain, engagement and boredom, moment by moment throughout the day. If you sampled its experience at random intervals, you would get a picture of actual lived happiness.

The remembering self constructs narratives about the past. It tells stories about how your life has been, what experiences were meaningful, how satisfied you are with your choices. When asked how happy you are with your life, the remembering self answers.

These two selves often disagree. A vacation might involve many moments of discomfort—flight delays, bad weather, unfamiliar beds—but be remembered as wonderful because of a few peak experiences and a pleasant ending. A period of life might involve many moments of contentment but be remembered as unhappy because of how it ended or because it lacked memorable peaks.

Money affects these two selves differently. Higher income improves the remembering self's life evaluation quite consistently, even at high income levels. When wealthy people assess their lives abstractly, they conclude that things are going well. But higher income stops improving the experiencing self's moment-to-moment happiness at a much lower level. The wealthy person's Tuesday afternoon is not appreciably more pleasant than the middle-class person's Tuesday afternoon.

This distinction matters for spending decisions. Some purchases improve experienced happiness—the comfortable mattress that provides better sleep every night, the short commute that reduces daily stress, the coffee that you genuinely enjoy each morning. Other purchases improve remembered happiness—the once-in-a-lifetime trip, the special celebration, the experience that becomes a cherished memory. Both have value, but they are different kinds of value.

The most effective spending improves both. A hobby that provides daily engagement and creates lasting memories. A home that is comfortable to live in and that hosts gatherings you will remember. Time with people you love, which is pleasant in the moment and meaningful in retrospect.

**What Money Can Buy**

Money can reliably purchase certain things that contribute to well-being.

Security is perhaps the most important. The person with adequate savings sleeps better, worries less, and can absorb setbacks without catastrophe. This benefit does not require wealth, but it does require enough. Having six months of expenses in reserve changes your relationship with uncertainty. It allows you to take appropriate risks, leave bad situations, and weather inevitable storms. This is why the early chapters of this book emphasized building reserves before investing.

Freedom is closely related. Money buys options. The person with savings can leave a toxic job, take a sabbatical, move to a new city, start a business. These options may never be exercised, but knowing they exist provides psychological benefit. The absence of options—being trapped by financial necessity—is a reliable source of unhappiness.

Time is purchasable to a degree that people often underestimate. Hiring help with time-consuming tasks you do not enjoy frees hours for activities you do enjoy. Living close to work shortens your commute. Financial independence, achieved after years of saving, converts all of your time from mandatory employment to discretionary use. Research by Ashley Whillans and colleagues finds that people who spend money to buy time report higher life satisfaction than those who do not.

Health benefits from financial resources in multiple ways. Better healthcare, healthier food, safer environments, and—perhaps most importantly—lower chronic stress all contribute to physical well-being. The relationship between socioeconomic status and health outcomes is among the most robust findings in public health research.

Quality in possessions that are used daily can improve experienced happiness. The comfortable shoes, the reliable car, the well-made tools and furniture that function smoothly year after year. These are not status goods but functional goods, and their quality provides ongoing value. The cheap item that must be replaced repeatedly may cost more in money and frustration than the quality item that lasts.

Experiences, particularly social experiences, provide value that persists after the experience ends. Research by Thomas Gilovich and colleagues consistently finds that experiential purchases produce more lasting satisfaction than material purchases. A dinner with friends, a concert, a trip—these become part of your identity and your relationships in a way that possessions do not.

Giving provides benefits to the giver that are well-documented. Spending money on others or donating to causes produces a warm glow that enhances the giver's well-being. Elizabeth Dunn and colleagues have shown that these benefits appear across income levels and across cultures. Money spent on others often produces more happiness than money spent on oneself.

Connection is facilitated by money in various ways—hosting gatherings, traveling to see distant friends and family, participating in communities that have associated costs. Relationships are the strongest predictor of human happiness, and money can support them even if it cannot directly purchase them.

**What Money Cannot Buy**

Money cannot purchase certain things that are essential to well-being, and misunderstanding this leads to some of the most common financial mistakes.

Adaptation-proof satisfaction is not available at any price. No purchase remains novel forever. No possession provides permanent pleasure. Seeking lasting happiness through acquisition is a category error, like trying to quench thirst by eating. The hungry feeling returns because that is what hunger does. The desire for more returns because that is what hedonic adaptation does.

Status is particularly treacherous. Status is a positional good—your status depends not on your absolute position but on your position relative to others. If everyone gets richer, no one gains status. The arms race for status symbols is therefore zero-sum at best. The resources spent chasing status could provide actual well-being if spent differently, but instead they flow into competition that leaves everyone in roughly the same relative position, only poorer.

Meaning and purpose are not purchasable. The wealthy person can be aimless and miserable; the person of modest means can have profound purpose. Money might enable activities that provide meaning, but it does not generate meaning itself. The retiree with millions but no sense of purpose is not happier than the person still working at something they care about.

Relationships cannot be bought, only supported. The person who uses wealth to impress or manipulate others finds their relationships hollow. The person who uses wealth to give time and attention to relationships finds them enriched. Money is an amplifier of relational tendencies, not a substitute for genuine connection.

Health has limits that no amount of money can transcend. The wealthy person can access excellent healthcare, but cannot purchase immortality or immunity from all illness. Beyond a certain point, additional spending on health produces minimal returns. The marginal value of a slightly better doctor is much smaller than the value of exercise, sleep, and stress reduction, which are available at low or no cost.

Happiness itself—the subjective experience of well-being—seems to be only modestly responsive to circumstances and strongly influenced by factors outside conscious control, including genetics. Studies of twins suggest that roughly half of the variation in happiness is heritable. This does not mean effort is useless, but it does mean that no amount of money can transform a dispositionally unhappy person into a naturally cheerful one.

**A Hierarchy of Spending**

Not all spending is created equal. Understanding which categories provide lasting satisfaction and which provide only temporary pleasure can reshape how you allocate resources.

The research suggests a rough hierarchy. At the top are spending categories that resist adaptation, provide both experienced and remembered happiness, and align with deep human needs. At the bottom are categories that adapt quickly, provide only experienced pleasure without lasting memory, and meet superficial wants rather than deep needs.

Spending on relationships consistently produces well-being. Hosting dinners, giving gifts, traveling to see distant loved ones, participating in community activities. These expenditures create shared memories and strengthen bonds. They often cost less than solitary consumption of equivalent pleasure, yet produce more lasting satisfaction.

Spending on experiences, particularly novel and challenging experiences, produces lasting memories that become part of identity.

The learning vacation, the skill-building course, the adventure that tests your limits. These resist adaptation because they are not permanent possessions that become familiar, but discrete events that remain fresh in memory.

Spending on time ranks high for those who have the option. Paying for housecleaning, laundry service, meal preparation, or other tasks you do not enjoy converts money into the most precious resource. For high earners who trade time for money at favorable rates, buying back time often provides excellent returns in well-being.

Spending on functional quality—durability, reliability, and comfort in daily-use items—provides ongoing experienced happiness that, while subject to some adaptation, delivers value day after day. The ergonomic chair, the quality mattress, the well-designed tool.

Spending on health and fitness produces both immediate and long-term benefits. The gym membership actually used, the quality food, the equipment for activities you enjoy. These expenses pay dividends in energy, longevity, and daily well-being.

Lower on the hierarchy, spending on visible upgrades provides diminishing returns. The luxury car, the designer clothes, the prestigious address. These provide initial pleasure and social signaling, but adaptation is rapid and the positional arms race is unwinnable. Within months, the upgrade feels normal, and attention shifts to the next level.

Spending on passive consumption—more channels, more gadgets, more entertainment options—tends to provide less well-being per dollar than active engagement. Watching is less satisfying than doing. Consuming is less satisfying than creating. This is not a moral judgment but an empirical observation about what produces lasting satisfaction.

Spending on conspicuous display primarily serves to signal status to others, with limited benefit to the purchaser beyond that signal. The oversized house, the flashy accessories, the visible luxury. If the expenditure would feel wasted were no one else to see it, it is probably a status purchase, and status purchases are subject to both rapid adaptation and the futility of positional competition.

**Implications for Financial Planning**

These findings have practical implications for how you should think about money across your lifetime.

Reaching sufficiency should be the primary financial goal. Having enough to meet your needs, provide security, and enable meaningful experiences is transformative for well-being. The gap between insufficiency and sufficiency is vast. Cross this gap as a priority.

Beyond sufficiency, more money helps less. The effort required to earn an additional hundred thousand dollars above an already comfortable income might better be spent on relationships, health, or purpose. This is not an argument against ambition, but a reminder that financial ambition has diminishing returns while other forms of investment—in people, in self, in meaning—may offer better returns.

How you spend matters more than how much you spend, beyond a certain point. Two people with identical incomes can have very different levels of well-being depending on their spending patterns. The person who spends on experiences, relationships, and time is likely to be happier than the person who spends on status and stuff.

Saving is not sacrifice if you understand adaptation. The money not spent on an upgrade you would adapt to within months is available for something that provides lasting value—security, freedom, future experiences. The short-term pleasure forgone is real but small; the long-term benefit is real and large.

The purpose of wealth is not wealth but what wealth enables. Accumulation beyond sufficiency should serve identifiable goals. The person who saves mindlessly, reaching seven million when three million would have been plenty, has traded years of potential flourishing for numbers on a statement. The person who spends mindlessly, never reaching sufficiency, has traded future security for transient pleasures already forgotten.

**Redefining Enough**

The concept of enough is central to a healthy relationship with money, yet consumer culture systematically undermines it. Advertising exists to create dissatisfaction, to make you feel that what you have is insufficient. Social comparison, amplified by social media, exposes you to selective displays of others' consumption, recalibrating your sense of normal upward. The hedonic treadmill ensures that each acquisition creates space for new desire.

Resisting these forces requires conscious effort. You must decide what enough means for you before external forces decide it for you. This is not a one-time decision but an ongoing practice of attention and intention.

Some questions can help. What spending in the past year produced lasting satisfaction versus fleeting pleasure? What possessions do you actually use and value versus what sits unused? What experiences remain vivid in memory versus what has already faded? What would you need to feel genuinely secure? What would you need to feel genuinely free? These questions point toward a personal definition of sufficiency that may be quite different from cultural defaults.

The research suggests that enough, for most people in developed countries, is less than they think. The lifestyle that maximizes well-being is comfortable but not luxurious, secure but not extravagant. It involves adequate space but not excessive space, reliable transportation but not status transportation, quality but not luxury. It prioritizes experiences over things, relationships over display, freedom over accumulation.

This is good news. It means that the good life is accessible to far more people than advertising implies. It means that the years of saving required to reach genuine financial security may be fewer than you feared. It means that the treadmill can be escaped—not by reaching some destination of enough stuff, but by stepping off entirely and walking somewhere of your own choosing.

**The Examined Financial Life**

We end where we began: asking what money is for.

Money is a tool. It is a claim on future goods and services, a store of value, a medium of exchange. It can purchase security, freedom, time, health, experiences, and the ability to give. These purchases contribute to well-being in real and measurable ways.

But money is not well-being itself. The confusion of money with what money can buy leads to errors in both directions—the over-working and under-saving that leaves people financially precarious, and the overworking and over-saving that leaves people experientially impoverished.

The research on happiness provides a map, but you must walk the territory yourself. No study can tell you what experiences will be meaningful for you, what relationships matter most, what work is worth doing. These are questions only you can answer, and answering them is part of the work of living well.

What the research can tell you is that the cultural narrative about money and happiness is largely false. More is not always better. Stuff does not satisfy. Status is a trap. Adaptation is relentless. But security is valuable, freedom is valuable, time is valuable, and experiences and relationships are valuable. Money can provide these if spent intentionally. It cannot provide them if accumulated mindlessly or spent thoughtlessly.

The investor who understands these findings is better equipped to make sound financial decisions. They save for security and freedom, not for accumulation. They spend on what produces lasting satisfaction, not on what advertising suggests. They recognize the treadmill and choose not to run. They define enough before reaching it, so they know when to stop striving and start living.

This is not the end of the investment journey but its purpose. Everything discussed in previous chapters—the returns and risks, the allocation and diversification, the behavior and discipline—serves this end. The portfolio is not the goal. The goal is a good life, and the portfolio is one tool among many for achieving it.

. . .

## SUMMARY

The relationship between money and happiness is real but nonlinear. Research shows that income matters enormously when moving from deprivation to sufficiency, but each additional dollar produces diminishing returns in well-being. The difference between earning twenty thousand and forty thousand dollars transforms life; the difference between three hundred thousand and five hundred thousand barely registers in daily experience.

The hedonic treadmill explains why happiness does not keep rising with income. Humans adapt rapidly to improvements in circumstances—the new car becomes ordinary transportation, the larger house becomes simply home. This adaptation is automatic and nearly universal, leaving us perpetually pursuing satisfaction that recedes as we approach it.

Kahneman's distinction between the experiencing self and the remembering self illuminates spending decisions. Some purchases improve moment-to-moment experience; others create lasting memories. The most valuable spending accomplishes both, while the least valuable provides brief pleasure that neither enhances daily life nor creates meaningful memory.

Money reliably purchases certain contributors to well-being: security against misfortune, freedom to pursue options, time freed from unwanted tasks, health, functional quality in daily-use items, experiences, the ability to give, and support for relationships. Money cannot purchase adaptation-proof satisfaction, status (which is inherently zero-sum), meaning and purpose, genuine relationships, health beyond certain limits, or happiness itself.

A hierarchy of spending emerges from the research. At the top: relationships, experiences, time, functional quality, and health. At the bottom: visible upgrades subject to rapid adaptation, passive consumption, and conspicuous display that serves only to signal status.

The practical implications are clear. Reaching sufficiency should be the primary goal. Beyond sufficiency, how you spend matters more than how much you earn. Saving is not sacrifice when you understand that the forgone upgrade would have become invisible within months. The purpose of wealth is not accumulation but what wealth enables.

Defining enough before external forces define it for you is essential. The research suggests that enough is less than most people think—comfortable but not luxurious, secure but not extravagant, prioritizing experiences and relationships over things and display. The good life is more accessible than advertising implies, and the treadmill can be escaped by stepping off rather than running faster.

# EIGHTEEN
# SPENDING THAT COMPOUNDS

The previous chapter established that money's relationship to happiness is real but limited. Beyond a threshold of sufficiency, how you spend matters more than how much you have. This chapter explores the practical implications: how to allocate spending toward what produces lasting value rather than fleeting pleasure.

The phrase "spending that compounds" borrows from investment terminology deliberately. Just as invested capital can grow exponentially over time, certain categories of spending produce returns that accumulate and multiply. A skill learned opens doors to experiences unavailable without it. A relationship nurtured provides support during difficulty and joy during celebration for decades. A formative experience shapes identity and perspective in ways that influence countless subsequent choices. These expenditures do not merely provide momentary pleasure and vanish. They build upon themselves.

Other spending does not compound. It provides immediate gratification that dissipates quickly, leaving no residue. The expensive meal is forgotten within days. The upgraded device becomes the new baseline within weeks. The luxury purchase provides a brief thrill, then becomes invisible through familiarity. This spending is not necessarily wrong, but it should be recognized for what it is: consumption rather than investment, pleasure rather than growth.

The distinction is not always clean. Some experiences that seem trivial become treasured memories. Some investments in growth prove worthless. But patterns emerge with sufficient clarity to guide decision-making. This chapter examines those patterns.

**Experiences Over Things**

The research comparing experiential and material purchases is remarkably consistent. When people are asked about past purchases, they report greater satisfaction with experiences than with things. When people are randomly assigned to spend money on experiences or things, those assigned to experiences report higher well-being. When people anticipate future purchases, they report more positive anticipation for experiences. The finding replicates across ages, income levels, and cultures.

Thomas Gilovich, who has studied this phenomenon extensively, identifies several reasons for the experiential advantage.

Experiences become part of identity in ways that possessions do not. You are the sum of what you have done, not the sum of what you own. The person who has traveled, learned, explored, and connected has a richer sense of self than the person who has merely accumulated. When you recall meaningful experiences, you recall who you were and who you became. When you recall meaningful purchases, you recall only the objects.

Experiences resist comparison more than things. The precise specifications of a car or phone invite direct comparison with alternatives. Did you get the best one? Could you have done better? Experiences are harder to rank. Your vacation cannot be directly measured against someone else's vacation because the experiences are fundamentally different. This incomparability protects experiential purchases from the dissatisfaction that comparison breeds.

Experiences connect you with others, while possessions often isolate. Even solo experiences become social through storytelling.

The trip you took becomes a story you tell, a connection you make with others who have similar stories. The thing you bought rarely sparks such connection. Worse, expensive possessions can create distance, signaling status differences that inhibit intimacy.

Experiences are less subject to adaptation because they are not continuously present. The new couch is in your living room every day, becoming invisible through familiarity. The trip to Japan is not continuously present; it exists in memory, where it can be revisited without the dulling effect of constant exposure. The memory may even improve over time as inconveniences fade and highlights sharpen.

Experiences satisfy at a deeper level because they address intrinsic human needs. We need novelty, challenge, growth, connection, and meaning. Experiences can provide all of these. Possessions address different needs—comfort, convenience, status—that are real but perhaps less fundamental to flourishing.

The implication for spending is straightforward: when choosing between an experiential and a material purchase of similar cost, lean toward the experience. The weekend trip rather than the upgraded appliance. The class rather than the gadget. The meal with friends rather than the meal alone with better ingredients.

This does not mean all material purchases are inferior. Possessions that enable experiences share in the experiential advantage. The bicycle that enables rides, the camping gear that enables trips, the musical instrument that enables playing—these material purchases are really investments in future experiences. The key is whether the object is used actively or merely owned passively.

**Spending on Relationships**

If the research on happiness has one finding more robust than all others, it is that relationships predict well-being. People with strong social connections are happier, healthier, and longer-lived than those who are isolated. This finding appears in every population studied, with every methodology used. It is as close to certain as social science gets.

Money can support relationships in ways that are often overlooked in personal finance discussions. The standard advice emphasizes frugality, cutting expenses, optimizing. This advice can be counterproductive when applied too aggressively to relational spending.

Hosting creates connection. The dinner party, the backyard gathering, the holiday celebration—these require expenditure on food, drink, and sometimes space. The money spent is not wasted but invested in social capital. The relationships strengthened through repeated gathering provide returns in support, joy, and meaning that far exceed the cost of the groceries.

Travel to see distant friends and family maintains relationships that would otherwise atrophy. The geographic dispersion of modern life means that many important relationships require planes, trains, or long drives. Treating this travel as optional is treating the relationships as optional. The frugal choice to skip the trip may save money while impoverishing life.

Shared experiences bond more tightly than parallel experiences. Spending money to do things together—the concert attended with a friend, the class taken with a partner, the trip with family—creates shared memory and mutual understanding. These joint experiences become part of the relationship's story, reference points for future connection.

Generosity strengthens bonds. The gift given, the check picked up, the offer made. These small generosities signal investment in the relationship and create positive association. The person who always calculates their precise share, who never treats or gives, who optimizes every transaction, may save money while losing something more valuable.

Time spent with others requires sometimes spending money to create the circumstances. The coffee shop meeting, the restaurant lunch, the activity that costs admission. These expenses purchase not just the coffee or the food or the activity but the context for connection. Refusing all such expenses in the name of frugality impoverishes social life.

The practical implication is that relational spending should be protected from budget cuts that might reasonably be applied elsewhere. When economizing is necessary, cut solitary consumption before social consumption. Downgrade your private pleasures before downgrading your shared ones. The streaming subscription you watch alone provides less value than the dinner out with friends, even if the dinner costs more.

This is not permission for unlimited social spending. Status display masquerading as hospitality provides little relational value. The goal is genuine connection, not impression management. A potluck dinner with close friends may provide more relational value than an expensive restaurant meal with acquaintances. The question is not how much you spend but whether the spending genuinely supports relationships that matter.

**Spending on Time**

Time is the ultimate scarce resource. Money can be accumulated and stored; time cannot. When time is spent, it is gone. Yet people routinely sacrifice time to save money in ways that make no sense upon examination.

The person who earns fifty dollars an hour but spends two hours to save twenty dollars has made a poor trade. They have exchanged a hundred dollars of their time for twenty dollars of savings. This arithmetic is obvious when stated but routinely ignored in practice. People drive across town to save a few dollars on gas, spend hours researching minor purchases, do tasks themselves that could be hired out at rates below their earning power.

The value of time is not only its market rate. An hour of leisure, of connection, of engagement with meaningful activity has value beyond what you might earn during that hour. When you spend money to buy time, you are not merely exchanging money for money-equivalent labor. You are exchanging money for life.

Research by Ashley Whillans and colleagues finds that people who spend money to buy time report greater life satisfaction than those who do not. This effect holds across income levels. Even people of modest means benefit from occasional outsourcing of disliked tasks. The absolute amount spent matters less than the time freed.

Common opportunities to buy time include outsourcing household tasks like cleaning, laundry, and yard work; paying for convenience through delivery, proximity, or faster options; and purchasing tools and services that reduce time required for necessary tasks. Each of these trades money for time. For those whose money is more abundant than their time—which includes most working adults—these trades often make sense.

The resistance to buying time stems partly from the Protestant work ethic embedded in American culture. Doing it yourself is virtuous; paying someone else is lazy. Suffering through unpleasant tasks builds character; paying to avoid them is soft. These moral intuitions are not entirely without basis, but they become harmful when applied indiscriminately. The person who spends their limited free time on tasks they dislike, could afford to outsource, and that provide no growth or satisfaction has not demonstrated virtue. They have merely wasted their life.

A useful test: if you had half as many remaining years to live, would you still spend time on this task? If the answer is no, and you can afford to outsource it, then outsource it. Your remaining years are limited whether you know the number or not.

The most significant time purchase is often housing location. Living close to work eliminates commuting, which research consistently identifies as one of the most reliable sources of daily unhappiness. The additional rent or mortgage payment for a closer location may be more than offset by the time gained, the stress avoided, and the life reclaimed. People routinely underweight commute time when making housing decisions, then spend years paying the price in daily misery.

Another significant time purchase is working less. For those who have accumulated some financial cushion, the option to reduce hours, take sabbaticals, or retire early is an option to buy time. This calculation interacts with the findings from the previous chapter: beyond sufficiency, additional income provides diminishing happiness returns, while additional time retains its value. At some income level, the trade tips, and reducing work hours to buy time becomes the happiness-maximizing choice.

**Spending on Personal Growth**

Growth is the process of becoming more capable, more aware, more fully yourself. It is inherently valuable—most people prefer to be growing rather than stagnating—and instrumentally valuable, opening possibilities that would otherwise be closed.

Money can purchase inputs to growth, though it cannot purchase growth directly. You can buy a book but not understanding. You can buy a course but not mastery. You can buy a coach but not discipline. The spending matters only if you do the work that transforms inputs into growth.

Education in its many forms is the most direct growth expenditure. Formal education at schools and universities, professional development in your field, courses and workshops on topics that interest you, individual instruction in skills you want to develop. The returns to education vary enormously depending on what is learned, how well it is learned, and how it is applied. But the potential returns are high enough that this category deserves significant allocation.

The undereducated should prioritize education aggressively. For those without college degrees who want one, the investment often pays dividends in earnings, options, and self-development. For those in fields requiring ongoing learning, keeping current is not optional. For everyone, the capacity to learn remains available throughout life, and exercising it maintains cognitive function while expanding capability.

Experiences that stretch capacity provide growth as a byproduct. The challenging trip, the unfamiliar culture, the demanding activity. These provide the novelty and difficulty that stimulate growth. Merely comfortable experiences, by contrast, provide pleasure without growth. A resort vacation may be restorative, but it does not develop new capacity. An expedition to unfamiliar territory may be uncomfortable, but it returns you changed.

Health investments provide the foundation for all other growth. The fitness developed through training, the energy provided by good nutrition, the restoration provided by quality sleep. Spending on a gym membership actually used, on food that nourishes rather than merely satisfies, on the mattress and environment that enable deep sleep—these expenditures support every other endeavor.

Equipment for activities that develop skill can compound if the activities are actually pursued. The musical instrument for the person who practices, the tools for the person who builds, the gear for the person who explores. These possessions are investments in capability, not mere consumption. The difference between owning and using is essential.

Books remain among the highest-returning investments available. A book that changes how you think, reveals a new domain, or provides a model for action can influence decades of subsequent life. The cost is trivial; the return can be enormous. The person who spends a thousand dollars annually on books and reads them seriously is likely making one of the best investments in their portfolio.

Coaching and mentoring accelerate growth beyond what is possible alone. The coach who sees your blind spots, the mentor who has walked the path, the therapist who helps you understand yourself. These relationships cost money but provide perspective unavailable any other way. The successful people who employ coaches are not wasting money; they are buying an advantage that compounds.

**Evaluating Spending Decisions**

With these categories in mind, a framework for evaluating spending decisions emerges. When considering a discretionary purchase, several questions help distinguish spending that compounds from spending that merely dissipates.

Will this purchase be remembered or forgotten? The experience that will become a vivid memory differs fundamentally from the item that will soon become invisible. Memory is not a guarantee of value—some memorable experiences are memorable for bad reasons—but it is a useful signal. The purchase that will leave no trace in memory provides only momentary value.

Does this purchase strengthen relationships or is it purely individual? Shared experiences and generous giving compound through relationships. Solitary consumption may still be worthwhile, but it lacks the multiplier that social connection provides.

Does this purchase free up time for things that matter? Spending that buys back time is often worthwhile, provided the time gained is actually used for something better. Buying back time only to spend it on low-value activities provides little benefit.

Does this purchase build capacity or merely provide comfort? Growth expenditures develop skills, knowledge, health, and capability that persist and compound. Comfort expenditures feel good in the moment but leave no residue. Both have a place in a life, but their relative proportions matter.

Does this purchase address an ongoing need or a one-time desire? The ergonomic chair that supports better posture every workday differs from the impulse purchase that addresses a momentary craving. Ongoing needs deserve more investment than passing desires.

Is this purchase about genuine enjoyment or about signaling to others? Status purchases provide their value through others' perception. This value is real but limited and subject to positional competition. Purchases for intrinsic enjoyment provide value independent of what others think.

Will this purchase still seem like a good idea in a month? In a year? In ten years? Temporal distance provides perspective. The purchase that seems compelling now may seem foolish in retrospect. The purchase that would seem like a good idea at any future time probably is a good idea now.

No decision rule is perfect, and applying these questions too rigorously would be exhausting. But holding them loosely in mind, asking them when making significant decisions, shifts spending gradually toward what compounds.

**Genuine Desire, Social Comparison, and Emotional Avoidance**

Not all wants are created equal. Some desires emerge from genuine preference, from knowing yourself and what makes your life good. Others are implanted by social comparison, by observing what others have and feeling inadequate. Still others serve emotional avoidance, using consumption to numb or distract rather than to provide genuine value.

Distinguishing among these motivations is difficult but important. Spending driven by genuine desire tends to compound; spending driven by comparison or avoidance rarely does.

Social comparison operates largely outside conscious awareness. You see a neighbor's new car, a friend's vacation photos, a colleague's home, and something shifts in your sense of what is adequate. Your own car, vacation, home—perfectly satisfactory yesterday—now seems insufficient. The desire to upgrade feels genuine, but it is manufactured by comparison.

Several features distinguish comparison-driven desires from genuine desires. Comparison desires are often triggered by specific observations of others. They focus on visible, comparable goods rather than personal or idiosyncratic ones. They are satisfied not by the thing itself but by having as much as or more than others. They recur endlessly because there is always someone with more.

The test for comparison-driven desire is to ask whether you would want the thing if no one would ever know you had it. If the new car would be equally satisfying parked in a windowless garage where no one would see it, the desire may be genuine. If the appeal depends on others knowing, it is at least partly about comparison.

A more radical test is to ask whether you would want the thing if you were the last person on earth. This strips away all social value and reveals whether intrinsic value remains. Many desires vanish under this test, revealing their social origins.

Emotional avoidance uses consumption as a coping mechanism. The person who shops when sad, who buys to fill a void, who uses acquisition to avoid facing difficulty. Retail therapy, so-called, is therapy in the way alcohol is therapy—it provides temporary relief while worsening the underlying condition.

Emotional avoidance manifests in patterns: buying to improve a bad mood, buying when stressed, buying when lonely, buying when bored. The purchase addresses the immediate discomfort but not its source. The mood improves briefly, then returns, prompting further purchase. The pattern is addictive in structure if not always in intensity.

The features of avoidance-driven spending include impulsivity, a sense of urgency that disappears if the purchase is delayed, and disappointment that sets in quickly after the purchase. The purchase seemed important but turns out not to matter. This is because the purchase was never really about the thing purchased. It was about escaping a feeling.

The corrective for avoidance-driven spending is not better budgeting but better emotional processing. Learning to sit with discomfort rather than immediately fleeing it. Developing other coping mechanisms—exercise, connection, creative work, time in nature—that address mood without the costs of consumption. Therapy to address underlying patterns if they are severe.

Genuine desire, by contrast, is stable over time. It does not depend on what others have. It persists even when mood is stable. It leads to purchases that are used and valued, not forgotten in closets. It is often specific and personal rather than generic and conventional.

Learning to recognize which type of desire is operating takes practice. A useful technique is to impose a waiting period on discretionary purchases. Twenty-four hours for small purchases, a week for medium ones, a month for large ones. Comparison-driven and avoidance-driven desires often fade with time; genuine desires persist. The purchase you still want after waiting is more likely to provide lasting satisfaction than the one that seemed urgent in the moment.

Another technique is to track purchases and, after several months, review which ones were worthwhile. Patterns emerge. Categories that consistently disappoint should be cut. Categories that consistently satisfy should be maintained or expanded. The past is the best guide to the future.

**Spending as Self-Expression**

At its best, spending reflects and reinforces who you are and who you want to become. The person who spends on books and courses is investing in a learning self. The person who spends on experiences and travel is investing in an adventurous self. The person who spends on hosting and giving is investing in a generous, connected self. Each spending pattern shapes identity and is shaped by it.

The alignment between spending and identity is worth examining. What does your spending say about who you are? Does it reflect your stated values and priorities, or does it contradict them? Many people discover, upon examination, that their spending does not match their professed identity. They say they value experiences but buy things. They say they value relationships but spend on solitary consumption. They say they value growth but spend on comfort.

This misalignment often operates beneath conscious awareness. Cultural defaults, advertising influence, and social pressure shape spending patterns more than deliberate choice. Bringing awareness to the mismatch is the first step toward correcting it.

Spending can also shape identity in the other direction. The aspirational purchase—the guitar for the person who wants to become a musician, the equipment for the sport you want to pursue, the books on a subject you want to understand—can pull identity toward a desired future self. This works only if the purchase is actually used, but when it is, spending becomes a commitment device, an investment in becoming.

The question "what would the person I want to become spend on" is a useful guide. It filters out comparison and avoidance while illuminating genuine desire. It connects present spending to future identity in a way that encourages compounding.

**A Philosophy of Spending**

We can now articulate a philosophy of spending that synthesizes these themes.

Spend on what compounds. Experiences that become memories and shape identity. Relationships that deepen and support. Time reclaimed for what matters. Growth that builds capability and opens possibility. These expenditures produce returns that accumulate over years and decades.

Spend on what addresses genuine desire. Learn to distinguish authentic preference from comparison-driven wanting and emotional avoidance. Impose delays that allow superficial desire to fade. Track what actually provides lasting satisfaction.

Spend in alignment with identity. Let spending reflect and reinforce who you are and who you want to become. Examine spending patterns for misalignment with professed values. Use spending as a tool for becoming.

Spend proportionally to value. Things you use every day deserve quality. Things you use rarely do not. Experiences that become defining deserve investment. Experiences that fade immediately do not. Relationships that matter deserve generosity. Status competition deserves nothing.

Spend less on what does not compound. Material goods that adapt quickly. Status symbols that merely position you relative to others. Passive consumption that neither grows nor connects. These are not forbidden, but they should not dominate.

Protect the capacity to spend on what compounds. The savings and investment discussed in earlier chapters are not ends in themselves. They are means to having resources available for spending that matters. The goal is not to minimize spending but to optimize it —to direct resources toward what produces lasting value and away from what dissipates.

This philosophy does not demand frugality in any particular category. It demands awareness and intentionality. Some people should spend more, on experiences and relationships and growth they have been neglecting. Others should spend less, on status and stuff that adds nothing to their lives. The direction depends on the current pattern, not on any absolute rule.

What the philosophy does demand is thought. Mindless consumption, whether of much or little, fails to optimize. Spending that compounds requires awareness of what is being purchased and why. It requires the self-knowledge to distinguish genuine desire from its imposters. It requires the discipline to delay, reflect, and sometimes refuse. It requires the wisdom to know what money can and cannot provide.

**The End of the Beginning**

This chapter, and the one before it, have departed from the technical focus of earlier chapters to address what money is ultimately for. Having learned how to earn, save, invest, and manage money, you must now decide what to do with it.

The answer proposed here is not to accumulate indefinitely, treating the portfolio balance as a score to maximize. Nor is it to spend immediately, treating money as valuable only when converted to consumption. The answer is to use money—both the spending of it and the security provided by holding it—to construct a good life.

A good life includes security and freedom, which money provides. It includes experiences that become memories and shape identity. It includes relationships that support and enrich. It includes growth that expands capability and possibility. It includes time for what matters. It includes meaning and purpose, which money cannot buy but can sometimes enable.

Spending that compounds contributes to this good life by converting money into lasting value. The skill is to recognize which spending compounds and which merely dissipates, then to direct resources accordingly. This skill, like the investment skills discussed earlier, improves with practice and attention. It is never fully mastered but can be continually developed.

The portfolio is a means to this end. The returns generated by sound investment provide the resources for spending that compounds. The security provided by adequate savings enables risk-taking in other domains. The freedom provided by financial independence converts all time into discretionary time. Everything discussed in this book serves, ultimately, the goal of living well.

## SUMMARY

Certain spending produces returns that compound over time, like invested capital. A skill learned opens new experiences; a relationship nurtured provides decades of support; a formative experience shapes countless subsequent choices. Other spending provides immediate gratification that dissipates quickly, leaving no residue. The distinction should guide how you allocate resources.

Research consistently shows that experiential purchases produce more lasting satisfaction than material purchases. Experiences become part of identity, resist unfavorable comparison, connect you with others through storytelling, and avoid adaptation because they exist in memory rather than continuous presence. Possessions that enable experiences share these advantages; the key distinction is active use versus passive ownership.

Spending on relationships deserves protection from economizing. Hosting, traveling to see distant loved ones, shared experiences, and small generosities all strengthen bonds that predict happiness more reliably than any other factor. When cuts are necessary, reduce solitary consumption before social consumption.

Time is the ultimate scarce resource, and money can buy it. Outsourcing disliked tasks, paying for convenience and proximity, and eventually reducing work hours all convert money into life. People who spend money to buy time report higher life satisfaction across income levels. The person who sacrifices time to save small amounts of money has made a poor trade.

Spending on personal growth—education, challenging experiences, health, skill-building equipment, books, coaching—produces returns that compound. The spending matters only if you do the work that transforms inputs into growth.

Not all desires are created equal. Some emerge from genuine preference; others are manufactured by social comparison or serve emotional avoidance. Comparison-driven desires focus on visible goods and depend on others' awareness. Avoidance-driven spending is impulsive, feels urgent, and disappoints quickly. Genuine desire is stable over time, persists regardless of mood, and leads to purchases that are actually used and valued. Waiting periods and retrospective tracking help distinguish among these motivations.

At its best, spending reflects and reinforces identity. Examining whether your spending matches your professed values often reveals misalignment operating beneath awareness. Aspirational purchases can pull identity toward a desired future self, provided they are actually used.

A philosophy of spending emerges from these themes: spend on what compounds, on genuine desire, in alignment with identity, proportionally to value, and less on what dissipates. Protect the capacity to spend on what matters. The goal is not to minimize spending but to optimize it—directing resources toward lasting value and away from what vanishes. The portfolio serves this end: living well.

# NINETEEN
# GENEROSITY AND ITS RETURNS

The previous chapter examined spending that compounds for the person spending. This chapter turns to a particular category of such spending: money given away. Generosity—spending on others rather than oneself—occupies a unique position in personal finance. It appears on the surface to be the opposite of wealth-building, the giving up of resources that might otherwise grow. Yet research and reflection reveal a more complex picture, one in which generosity provides returns that, while different in kind from investment returns, are no less real.

This chapter is not a moral argument for giving, though moral arguments exist. It is an examination of what generosity does—for the giver, for the recipient, and for the society in which both are embedded. Understanding these effects allows for more thoughtful decisions about whether, how much, and to whom to give.

**The Research on Spending on Others**

Elizabeth Dunn and Michael Norton, in their research synthesized in the book *Happy Money*, document a finding that surprises many people: spending money on others produces more happiness than spending money on oneself. This finding replicates across studies, methodologies, and cultures.

In one study, participants were given money and randomly assigned to spend it on themselves or on others. Those assigned to spend on others reported greater happiness at the end of the day than those who spent on themselves. The amount mattered less than the direction—giving away even small sums produced measurable effects.

In another study, employees who received a bonus and spent more of it on others reported greater happiness than those who spent more on themselves. The size of the bonus did not predict happiness; the proportion given away did.

Cross-cultural research finds the relationship between prosocial spending and happiness in countries ranging from Canada to Uganda, from wealthy nations to poor ones. The effect appears to be a human universal rather than a cultural artifact.

The magnitude of the effect is not trivial. In some studies, the happiness boost from giving rivals the boost from significant income increases. This is remarkable given how much effort people expend pursuing income and how little attention they typically give to prosocial spending.

Several mechanisms explain why giving produces happiness. Giving strengthens social connection. When you give to someone, you affirm the relationship, signal investment, and often receive gratitude in return. These social effects reinforce bonds and satisfy the deep human need for connection. Even giving to strangers can create momentary connection—the brief exchange with someone you've helped, the awareness of having contributed to another's welfare.

Giving enhances the sense of efficacy and agency. The capacity to give demonstrates that you have enough, that you are capable of affecting others' lives. This sense of sufficiency and capability is itself a form of wealth, a psychological abundance that accompanies material giving.

Giving constructs and reinforces identity as a generous person. As discussed in the previous chapter, spending shapes identity. Each act of giving confirms that you are the kind of person who gives, which makes future giving more natural and further reinforces the generous identity. The cycle is self-reinforcing.

Giving provides meaning by connecting individual action to larger purposes. When you give to a cause, you become part of something beyond yourself—a movement, an effort, a community of concern. This transcendence of narrow self-interest provides the sense of meaning that purely personal consumption cannot.

The research has important nuances. Giving produces more happiness when it is freely chosen rather than coerced. Mandatory charity or guilt-induced giving does not produce the same effects. Giving produces more happiness when the giver can see the impact, can connect the gift to a tangible outcome. Abstract giving to large bureaucracies produces less satisfaction than concrete giving where effects are visible. Giving produces more happiness when it involves social connection—giving directly to someone, giving with others, or giving in ways that create relationship.

These findings suggest that how you give matters as much as how much you give, at least for the psychological returns. The gift given directly, with connection to the recipient and visibility of impact, produces greater returns to the giver than the equivalent amount given abstractly.

**Different Modes of Giving**

Generosity takes many forms, each with distinct characteristics and effects. Understanding these forms allows for more intentional decisions about how to give.

Direct giving to individuals is the most immediate form. Money given to a family member, a friend, or a stranger in need. This mode provides maximum connection and often maximum visibility of impact. You see the person, see the need, see the effect. The psychological returns are typically highest. The risks include enabling dependency, distorting relationships, and being manipulated.

Informal giving to those in your community operates similarly. Picking up the check, contributing to a friend's medical fundraiser, helping a neighbor with an expense. These gifts strengthen community bonds and often create implicit reciprocity—the helped become helpers when circumstances reverse. This mode builds social capital alongside the direct benefit.

Charitable giving to organizations formalizes generosity through institutional intermediaries. You give money; the organization converts it to impact through programs, staff, and operations. This mode allows for scale and specialization—the charity can accomplish things no individual could. It also interposes distance between giver and recipient, reducing connection but enabling broader reach. The efficiency of this conversion varies enormously across organizations.

Philanthropic giving for systemic change aims not merely to help individuals but to alter underlying conditions. Funding research, advocacy, policy change, or institution-building. This mode seeks leverage—small inputs that produce large changes by shifting systems rather than helping people one at a time. The potential impact is greatest, but the uncertainty is also highest. Most attempts at systemic change fail; those that succeed can affect millions.

Volunteering gives time rather than money but deserves mention because the choice between them matters. For most people with jobs, the opportunity cost of an hour volunteered exceeds the impact of that hour's wages donated. A professional who earns sixty dollars an hour and volunteers at a soup kitchen for two hours has given the equivalent of one hundred twenty dollars—but the soup kitchen could have hired someone for far less than that to do the same work. The math suggests that high-earners should give money, not time, if efficiency is the goal. But efficiency is not the only goal. Volunteering provides connection, understanding, and identity-formation that giving money does not. The volunteer sees poverty directly; the donor sees only the receipt. Both modes have value; they serve different purposes.

Legacy giving through bequests allows for generosity beyond the lifespan. The estate left to charity, the endowment created to fund future work, the foundation established for perpetual giving. This mode provides no psychological returns during life—you will not be there to see the impact—but allows for generosity at scale for those who have accumulated significant wealth. It also raises complex questions about control from the grave and whether the donor's wishes should bind future generations.

Each mode has its place in a generous life. Direct giving for immediate impact and connection. Charitable giving for scaled benefit. Philanthropic giving for systemic change. Volunteering for understanding and engagement. Legacy giving for impact beyond the lifespan. A comprehensive approach might include all of these, weighted according to circumstances and priorities.

**The Tension Between Effective and Emotional Giving**

A movement known as effective altruism has, over the past two decades, brought analytical rigor to charitable giving. Its core insight is that charitable interventions vary enormously in their impact per dollar. Some interventions save lives for a few thousand dollars; others spend millions with little measurable effect. If the goal is to do the most good, the choice of where to give matters as much as how much is given.

The research behind this movement is compelling. Rigorous evaluations find that the most effective interventions in global health, for example, produce hundreds of times more benefit per dollar than the least effective. Distributing insecticide-treated bed nets to prevent malaria produces more health benefit per dollar than most other interventions. Deworming programs, vitamin supplementation, and direct cash transfers to the extremely poor consistently outperform more expensive or more complex interventions.

The implication is stark: where you give is a moral choice with significant consequences. Giving to a less effective charity, when a more effective alternative is available, means less suffering prevented, fewer lives saved, less good done. From this perspective, following emotional attachment or personal connection when choosing charities is a kind of self-indulgence—privileging your feelings over others' welfare.

This logic has power. It has directed billions of dollars toward rigorously evaluated interventions. It has saved lives that would otherwise have been lost to less effective giving. It has brought the methods of science—randomized trials, cost-effectiveness analysis, expected value calculations—to a domain previously guided by intuition and tradition.

Yet the effective altruism framework has limitations that should be acknowledged.

The measurement problem is severe. Many valuable things are difficult to measure. The impact of policy advocacy, the value of art and culture, the importance of maintaining institutions, the benefit of building community. The preference for measurable outcomes biases giving toward interventions where measurement is possible, which may not be where impact is greatest. The most important things are often the hardest to count.

The focus on global poverty, while morally serious, can crowd out local giving that serves different purposes. The donation to the local food bank, the gift to your alma mater, the support for the community theater—these may not save lives in Africa, but they maintain the social infrastructure that makes local life possible. Giving that builds community provides value beyond its direct impact.

The purely consequentialist framework ignores the relational dimension of giving. When you give to a cause because your friend asked, because your community is involved, because the organization matters to people you care about, you are not merely maximizing expected value. You are maintaining relationships, fulfilling social obligations, participating in shared projects. These relational goods have value that the effectiveness calculus does not capture.

The emphasis on impartial beneficence—treating all lives as equally valuable regardless of connection—conflicts with the partial attachments that structure human life. Most people care more about their family than about strangers, more about their community than about distant populations, more about their country than about others. Effective altruism asks people to override these attachments in favor of impartial calculation. Some can and do; most cannot sustain it.

The psychological returns to giving depend partly on connection and visibility, which effective giving often lacks. The donation to the Against Malaria Foundation is objectively impactful but emotionally distant. The gift to the local homeless shelter is less efficient but more felt. If the goal includes the psychological benefits of giving, not only the direct impact, then emotionally resonant giving has value that pure effectiveness analysis misses.

A resolution to this tension might involve portfolio thinking. Just as an investment portfolio includes different assets for different purposes, a giving portfolio might include different types of giving. Some giving optimized for effectiveness—the dollars that go to the most rigorously evaluated, highest-impact interventions. Some giving optimized for connection—the gifts to local organizations, to causes that friends care about, to institutions that have shaped you. Some giving optimized for values beyond measurement—art, culture, democracy, the environment. The proportions depend on individual circumstances and values, but a blended approach captures more of what makes giving valuable than single-minded optimization on any one dimension.

**Strategic Frameworks for Giving**

Beyond the effective-versus-emotional tension, several frameworks can guide giving decisions.

The concentric circles model allocates giving based on proximity and relationship. The innermost circle is family and close friends—not charity in the formal sense but still a form of generosity that deserves recognition. The next circle is community—local organizations, religious institutions, schools, neighborhood associations. The next is causes aligned with personal experience or identity. The outermost is impartial giving to whoever needs it most, regardless of connection. Giving at each circle level serves different purposes and provides different returns. Most people's giving concentrates in the inner circles, which is neither right nor wrong but simply human.

The capacity-matching model gives where your particular capacities are most valuable. If you have expertise in a domain, giving to organizations in that domain allows you to evaluate effectiveness and sometimes provide more than money—advice, connections, skilled volunteering. If you have wealth but not expertise, giving to highly rated organizations doing rigorous work outsources the expertise problem. If you have time but not money, volunteering may be your comparative advantage. The principle is to give what you distinctively can, not just what is generically needed.

The leverage model seeks giving opportunities where your dollars go furthest. This includes matching opportunities, where a donor matches your gift dollar for dollar. It includes giving to organizations that are funding-constrained rather than execution-constrained—places where more money would directly enable more work. It includes giving early in an organization's life when capital is hardest to raise. It includes giving to advocacy that might shift vastly larger government or corporate spending. The leverage model asks not just "is this good?" but "is this where my dollars have the most impact?"

The experimental model treats giving as a search process. Rather than committing all giving to known organizations, it allocates some portion to testing new approaches, supporting new organizations, exploring new cause areas. Most experiments fail, but those that succeed can be scaled. This model is most appropriate for larger givers who can afford many experiments and have the capacity to evaluate results.

The identity model gives in ways that reinforce the person you want to become. If you want to be someone who supports the arts, give to arts organizations. If you want to be someone who cares about your city, give locally. If you want to be someone who takes global poverty seriously, give to effective global health charities. The giving shapes the identity, which shapes future behavior, in the positive cycle discussed in the previous chapter.

These models are not mutually exclusive. A thoughtful giver might use elements of each: giving in concentric circles for relational giving, matching capacity for volunteer and skilled giving, seeking leverage for major gifts, experimenting with a portion of the giving budget, and always with an eye toward identity formation.

**How Much to Give**

The question of how much to give has no single answer. Different traditions and thinkers have proposed different benchmarks, each with its own logic.

The tithe—giving ten percent of income—comes from religious traditions but has been adopted by many secular givers as well. The percentage basis connects giving to capacity. The fixed percentage removes the need for annual negotiation with yourself. The ten percent figure is somewhat arbitrary but represents a meaningful commitment without requiring heroic sacrifice.

The Giving What We Can pledge—giving at least ten percent of income to effective charities—formalizes the tithe within an effective altruism framework. Signers commit publicly, which creates accountability and community. The emphasis on effectiveness directs the giving toward high-impact interventions.

Peter Singer's argument for giving until you reach the point of marginal utility—giving until the next dollar given would reduce your welfare more than it increases the welfare of recipients—implies much more than ten percent for those in wealthy countries. This demanding standard follows logically from utilitarian premises but exceeds what most people are willing or able to sustain.

A more moderate approach might follow a graduated percentage: a baseline percentage of income, increasing with income above certain thresholds. This reflects the principle that marginal dollars are worth less as income grows, so giving them away costs less as wealth increases.

The approach taken in this book suggests considering giving as one category of spending that compounds. Like spending on experiences, relationships, and growth, spending on generosity provides returns—psychological, social, and perhaps moral—that persist beyond the moment. The appropriate amount is that which produces these returns without undermining financial security or other important goals.

Practical considerations also apply. Giving should not compromise the emergency fund, the retirement savings, or the capacity to meet obligations. Giving should not create financial stress that undermines its psychological benefits. For those still building financial stability, modest giving—even one or two percent—can begin the habit and identity without jeopardizing security. The percentage can increase as security is established.

For those who are financially secure, the question becomes not whether you can afford to give but what you are giving up by not giving. The marginal dollar spent on yourself, beyond sufficiency, provides diminishing returns. The marginal dollar given away provides the returns described in this chapter—happiness, connection, meaning, identity. At some point, the returns to giving exceed the returns to keeping, and increasing giving becomes the happiness-maximizing choice.

**Generosity as Investment**

The title of this chapter refers to the returns on generosity, a framing that may seem mercenary. Is giving really about returns? Should it be?

The tension is real but can be resolved. Generosity that is purely instrumental—giving only to get something back—is not really generosity. It is exchange, transaction, investment in the ordinary sense. But generosity that is purely selfless, with no benefit to the giver, may not be psychologically sustainable. The research shows that giving does provide returns. Acknowledging this is not corruption but realism.

The mature view recognizes that the best acts often serve multiple purposes. Giving that helps others and helps the giver is better than giving that helps others while harming the giver, because it is sustainable and reinforcing. The returns to the giver are not the reason for giving—the reason is the benefit to recipients or the expression of values—but the returns are a welcome consequence that enables more giving over time.

Investment is a useful metaphor because it emphasizes the long-term, compounding nature of generosity's returns.

Generosity is an investment in identity. Each act of giving shapes who you are. The person who gives regularly becomes a generous person, for whom future giving is natural rather than effortful. The habit compounds as identity solidifies.

Generosity is an investment in relationships. Giving creates connection, and those connections provide support, meaning, and joy over years and decades. The social capital built through generosity is as real as any financial capital, even if it appears on no balance sheet.

Generosity is an investment in community. The organizations and institutions supported by giving provide benefits beyond direct recipients. The homeless shelter serves not only the homeless but the city that is more humane for having the shelter. The museum enriches not only its visitors but the civic culture. Giving maintains the infrastructure of collective life.

Generosity is an investment in society. Philanthropy funds public goods that benefit everyone—medical research, environmental protection, democratic institutions, artistic creation. The giver benefits from these goods along with everyone else. Even purely selfish actors should support public goods if they have no other way to produce them, and private giving is often the only way.

Generosity is an investment in moral development. The practice of giving—the attention to others' needs, the experience of sacrifice, the growth in compassion—develops moral capacity. This is valuable for its own sake and for its effects on every other relationship and decision.

None of this means giving should be calculated for maximum personal return. The spirit of generosity is outward-looking, focused on recipients and purposes rather than benefits to self. But understanding that generosity provides returns can motivate giving that might not otherwise occur, can justify giving to those who doubt its value, and can shape how and where giving is directed.

**The Limits of Generosity**

Generosity has limits, and recognizing them is part of wisdom.

Self-sacrifice that undermines your own flourishing is not sustainable. You cannot give from an empty cup. The person who gives so much that they cannot meet their own needs will soon have nothing left to give. Taking care of yourself is not selfishness but the precondition for ongoing generosity.

Giving that enables harmful behavior harms rather than helps. The money given to someone who will use it destructively is not generosity but naivety or denial. Sometimes the most generous act is withholding, setting boundaries, allowing someone to face consequences. This requires wisdom to distinguish genuine help from enabling.

Giving to ineffective or corrupt organizations wastes resources that could help elsewhere. Due diligence matters. The impulse to give does not absolve the responsibility to ensure that giving does good. This does not require exhaustive research before every gift, but it does require some attention to where money goes and what it accomplishes.

Giving that is done for show, to impress others or construct a public image, provides less of the psychological benefit than giving done authentically. If the purpose is the appearance of generosity rather than generosity itself, the internal rewards are diminished. This is a reason for anonymous giving, which cannot serve signaling purposes.

Giving that substitutes for other forms of engagement may not be optimal. The person who gives money to political causes but does not vote, who gives to environmental organizations but does not change their own consumption, who gives to education but does not mentor —this person is using money as a substitute for more demanding forms of engagement. Money is easier than action, which is why it can become a way to feel good without really engaging. Balance between financial and personal engagement produces more impact and more meaning.

**Generosity in Context**

The place of generosity in a financial life depends on circumstances.

For those in financial distress, survival takes precedence. The instruction on airplane safety applies: put on your own oxygen mask before assisting others. Getting to stability is the priority. Generosity during distress is not forbidden—sometimes giving even from scarcity reinforces identity and provides psychological benefit—but it should not compromise the path to security.

For those building toward sufficiency, modest generosity can coexist with saving and investing. The tithe or some fraction of it, contributed consistently, builds the habit and identity while the portfolio builds toward independence. The amounts given may be small, but the practice is established.

For those who have achieved sufficiency, the question of generosity becomes central. Beyond the point where additional wealth provides declining happiness returns, the case for giving strengthens. The money kept provides less value than the money given. This does not mean giving everything beyond sufficiency, but it does mean taking generosity seriously as a use of surplus.

For those with significant wealth, generosity becomes not just an option but arguably an obligation. The concentration of resources that produces billionaires is largely a function of systems that benefit from everyone's contribution—infrastructure, education, rule of law, past scientific discovery, cooperative social norms. Those who have accumulated much owe much to the systems that made accumulation possible. Returning a substantial portion to those systems, or to those whom the systems have failed to benefit, is a reasonable expectation.

The giving pledge, signed by many of the world's billionaires, commits signatories to giving away the majority of their wealth during their lifetimes or at death. This represents a recognition that extreme wealth carries extreme responsibility. Whether the pledge is fulfilled, and whether the giving is done wisely, remains to be seen. But the principle—that those who have benefited most from society have the greatest obligation to give back—is sound.

**Creating a Giving Practice**

Intention without structure tends to dissipate. A giving practice provides structure that makes generosity consistent and effective.

The elements of a giving practice include a budget, a schedule, a focus, a process for evaluation, and a community.

A budget answers the question: how much will you give, in total and by category? The budget can be a percentage of income, a fixed dollar amount, or a more complex formula. Having a number makes giving intentional rather than reactive.

A schedule answers the question: when will you give? Monthly contributions to a donor-advised fund or directly to organizations ensure regularity. Annual reviews allow for assessment and adjustment. Scheduled giving is more likely to happen than giving left to impulse.

A focus answers the question: where will you give? Some focus is necessary to have meaningful impact. Spreading small amounts across dozens of organizations accomplishes little. Concentrating giving on a few areas or organizations allows for deeper engagement and greater effect. The focus might be local or global, specific causes or broad portfolios, but some narrowing is usually wise.

A process for evaluation answers the question: how will you assess whether your giving is working? For effective-giving approaches, this means following the research on organizational impact. For relational giving, it means maintaining connection with organizations and recipients. For all giving, it means periodic review of whether the giving is producing the intended effects.

A community answers the question: who will you give with? Giving in community—through a giving circle, a family foundation, a religious congregation, a group of friends—provides accountability, shared learning, and social reinforcement. The lone giver has more freedom but less support. Many people find that shared giving enhances both impact and satisfaction.

These elements can be simple or elaborate depending on giving scale. For someone giving a few hundred dollars a year, a mental note of the budget and a list of preferred organizations may suffice. For someone giving significant amounts, formal structures, advised funds, and systematic evaluation become worthwhile.

### The Meaning of Generosity

Beyond its instrumental effects, generosity expresses something important about what it means to be human.

We are not isolated individuals but members of communities, participants in a shared life. Generosity enacts this membership. It says: I acknowledge that I am connected to others, that their welfare matters, that I have obligations beyond myself. The miser who accumulates without sharing denies this connection; the generous person affirms it.

We are not merely consumers but also creators, contributors, builders. Generosity allows participation in creation beyond personal capacity. The gift to medical research contributes to cures you could never develop. The gift to an artist supports work you could never make. The gift to a movement advances causes you could never advance alone. Through giving, individual capacity is multiplied by collective effort.

We are not permanent but temporary, passing through a world that existed before us and will continue after. Generosity is a way of contributing to that larger story. The giver participates in something that transcends individual lifespan. This is particularly true of giving to institutions, endowments, and causes that will continue beyond the giver's life.

We are not self-made but deeply dependent on others—on those who raised us, taught us, built the infrastructure we use, created the knowledge we apply, maintained the peace we enjoy. Generosity acknowledges this debt. It passes on what was received, contributes to the common store from which future generations will draw.

These meanings are not just ideas but are felt in the practice of generosity. The giver experiences connection, contribution, transcendence, gratitude. These experiences are part of what makes a life good, quite apart from any calculation of impact or return.

**Conclusion**

The case for generosity is not primarily a moral argument, though moral arguments have their place. It is an empirical claim about what produces well-being and meaning. The research is clear: giving makes people happier. The mechanisms are understood: connection, efficacy, identity, meaning. The modes are varied: direct giving, charitable giving, philanthropy, volunteering, legacy giving. The tensions are real: effective versus emotional, impartial versus partial, immediate versus systemic. And the returns compound: identity strengthens, relationships deepen, communities thrive, society improves.

For the person seeking not merely wealth but a good life, generosity is not optional. It is one of the primary means by which money is converted to meaning. The financially sophisticated person who saves diligently, invests wisely, and spends thoughtfully but does not give has mastered the tools while missing part of the purpose.

The question is not whether to give but how. How much, given your circumstances? Where, given your values? In what mode, given your capacities? With what structure, given your tendencies? These questions deserve the same thoughtfulness brought to investing or spending, because the stakes are comparable.

The returns on generosity are not guaranteed, any more than investment returns are guaranteed. But the expected value is positive —for the giver, for recipients, for society. This is one of the better deals available in human life: an act that helps others while helping yourself, that serves your interests while serving interests beyond your own, that makes you richer in the ways that matter while making your money go where it can do good.

## SUMMARY

Research consistently shows that spending money on others produces more happiness than spending money on oneself. This finding replicates across cultures, income levels, and methodologies. The mechanisms include strengthened social connection, enhanced sense of efficacy and agency, reinforced identity as a generous person, and meaning derived from participating in something beyond oneself. How you give matters as much as how much you give—freely chosen giving with visible impact and social connection produces the greatest psychological returns.

Generosity takes many forms: direct giving to individuals provides maximum connection and visibility; informal giving builds community and implicit reciprocity; charitable giving to organizations enables scale and specialization; philanthropic giving seeks systemic change through leverage; volunteering provides understanding and engagement that money cannot; and legacy giving allows impact beyond the lifespan. Each mode serves different purposes and a comprehensive approach might include all of them.

The effective altruism movement has brought analytical rigor to giving, demonstrating that charitable interventions vary enormously in impact per dollar. The most effective interventions in global health produce hundreds of times more benefit than the least effective. Yet this framework has limitations: many valuable things are difficult to measure, local giving serves purposes that global optimization misses, relational dimensions matter, impartial beneficence conflicts with partial human attachments, and psychological returns depend on connection. A portfolio approach—some giving optimized for effectiveness, some for connection, some for unmeasurable values—may capture more of what makes giving valuable than single-minded optimization.

Several frameworks can guide giving decisions: the concentric circles model allocates based on proximity and relationship; the capacity-matching model gives where your particular capacities are most valuable; the leverage model seeks opportunities where dollars go furthest; the experimental model treats giving as a search process;

and the identity model gives in ways that reinforce who you want to become.

The question of how much to give has no single answer. The tithe of ten percent represents meaningful commitment without heroic sacrifice. More demanding standards exist but exceed what most can sustain. Giving should not compromise financial security, but for those who have achieved sufficiency, the returns to giving may exceed the returns to keeping. Generosity is best understood as an investment—in identity, relationships, community, society, and moral development—that compounds over time.

Generosity has limits. Self-sacrifice that undermines flourishing is unsustainable. Giving that enables harmful behavior harms rather than helps. Ineffective or corrupt organizations waste resources. Giving for show provides less benefit than authentic giving. Money can substitute for more demanding engagement. A giving practice with budget, schedule, focus, evaluation process, and community provides structure that makes generosity consistent and effective.

Beyond instrumental effects, generosity expresses connection to community, participation in creation beyond personal capacity, contribution to a story that transcends individual lifespan, and acknowledgment of debt to those on whom we depend. For the person seeking not merely wealth but a good life, generosity is one of the primary means by which money is converted to meaning.

# PART 6
# MONEY ACROSS LIFE

*Navigating the decades*

# TWENTY
# STARTING OUT

The transition to financial independence is one of life's major passages. For most people, it occurs in the years between eighteen and thirty, though the exact timing varies with education, family circumstances, and economic conditions. This chapter addresses those in the early stages of that transition—young adults building the foundation on which the rest of their financial lives will rest.

The principles discussed throughout this book apply to everyone, but their application differs for those starting out. The person with no savings faces different challenges than the person with a portfolio to manage. The person establishing credit for the first time navigates different terrain than the person optimizing an existing credit profile. This chapter addresses these specific circumstances while connecting them to the broader framework.

The central message is one of leverage: decisions made early have disproportionate impact. The habits formed now will persist for decades. The money saved now will compound longest. The mistakes made now will be most costly in lifetime terms. This asymmetry means that attention paid to finances early in life yields higher returns than the same attention paid later.

**The Psychological Transition**

Before discussing mechanics, the psychological dimension deserves attention. The shift from financial dependence to independence involves not just new tasks but a new relationship with money.

During childhood and adolescence, most people experience money as something that appears from parents or guardians, subject to their control and approval. Independence requires a different stance: ownership. You are now responsible for your financial life. No one will rescue you from mistakes, at least not reliably. No one will make sure you save enough or spend wisely. This shift from dependence to ownership is psychological as much as practical.

The transition is not instantaneous. Many young adults exist in a prolonged intermediate state—partially dependent on parents for housing, insurance, or emergency support, while also earning income and managing expenses. This intermediate state is neither shameful nor permanent; it reflects economic realities that have made full independence harder to achieve than in previous generations. But the psychological work of assuming ownership should begin even before practical independence is complete.

Ownership means accepting that your financial outcomes are primarily your responsibility. Not exclusively—luck, circumstance, and systemic factors matter—but primarily. This acceptance is empowering rather than burdensome. If outcomes depend on your choices, then your choices have power.

Ownership means developing an internal locus of control regarding money. Not waiting for circumstances to improve but taking action within current circumstances. Not blaming others for financial problems but examining your own contribution and capacity to change.

Ownership means tolerating the anxiety that comes with responsibility. When parents made financial decisions, any resulting problems were their fault. Now problems are yours to solve. This can provoke anxiety, which can provoke avoidance, which can produce worse problems. Learning to face financial reality rather than avoid it is a core skill.

The psychological transition often involves working through inherited beliefs and patterns. Your family of origin transmitted attitudes toward money—through explicit teaching, through observed behavior, through the emotional atmosphere around financial topics. Some of these attitudes serve you; others do not. Some inherited patterns that commonly require examination include shame or secrecy around money that prevents seeking information or help, anxiety that produces either hoarding or avoidance, entitlement that assumes resources will appear without effort, and contempt for financial concerns as beneath serious attention. The goal is not to reject your upbringing wholesale but to become conscious of its influence and make deliberate choices about what to carry forward.

**Building the Foundation**

The practical foundation for financial independence has several components that should be established as early as possible.

Income is the necessary starting point. Without income, there is nothing to manage. The first priority with any income is to understand what you actually have. Gross income—the headline number on your salary—is not what you have to work with. Taxes, benefit deductions, and other withholdings reduce gross to net. Many young adults are surprised by how much disappears between the offer letter and the bank deposit. Understanding this gap prevents planning based on money that was never really yours.

With income established, the core financial practices can begin. Tracking is the foundation of all financial awareness. You cannot manage what you do not measure. The specific method matters less than consistency. A spending plan follows from tracking. Once you know where money goes, you can decide where it should go. The plan need not be elaborate. For a young adult with simple finances, the essential elements are fixed expenses that must be paid, variable expenses that can be adjusted, savings for the future, and discretionary spending.

A checking account is the hub of daily financial life. Choose a bank or credit union that offers low or no fees and convenient access. A savings account separate from checking provides a place for money not needed immediately. The separation is psychological as much as practical—money in a different account is less likely to be spent casually.

These elements—income, tracking, a spending plan, checking and savings accounts—constitute the minimum viable financial infrastructure. They can be established in days and maintained with minimal ongoing effort. Yet many young adults operate for years without them. The simple act of establishing this foundation distinguishes those who take financial responsibility from those who avoid it.

**Building Credit**

Credit—the ability to borrow money based on a lender's assessment of your likelihood to repay—is a critical component of financial infrastructure. Access to credit affects the ability to rent apartments, buy cars, purchase homes, and sometimes get jobs. Building credit early is important, even if you intend to avoid debt.

The credit system is built on the credit report and credit score. The credit report is a record of your borrowing history, maintained by three major bureaus. The credit score is a numerical summary of that history, most commonly calculated using FICO methodology, ranging from 300 to 850.

For someone with no credit history, the challenge is the cold-start problem. You need credit to build credit, but lenders are reluctant to extend credit to those without history. Several approaches can overcome this. Becoming an authorized user on a parent's credit card is often the easiest path—their payment history is typically reported on your credit report as well. A secured credit card, where you provide a deposit that becomes your credit limit, is designed for those with no history. A credit-builder loan, where payments are made before receiving the funds, also establishes history. Student loans and car loans, if you have them, contribute as well.

Once you have credit, maintaining it requires attention to several factors. Payment history is the most important, accounting for about 35 percent of the score. Paying on time, every time, is essential. Setting up automatic payments for at least the minimum due eliminates the risk of forgetting. Credit utilization—the percentage of available credit that you use—is the second most important factor, accounting for about 30 percent. Keeping utilization below 30 percent helps your score. Length of credit history matters, which is why starting early helps.

The goal of building credit is not to borrow more but to have the option to borrow on good terms when borrowing makes sense. The danger is that the tools for building credit—primarily credit cards—are also tools for accumulating destructive debt. The strategy is to use credit responsibly—small regular purchases paid in full each month—to build the record that opens doors, while never using credit to spend money you don't have.

**Negotiating Compensation**

For most young adults, employment income is the primary income source. The compensation received sets the baseline from which all financial plans proceed. Yet many young adults accept offered salaries without negotiation, leaving substantial money on the table.

The reluctance to negotiate has several sources: inexperience creates uncertainty about what is appropriate, gratitude at receiving an offer can make asking for more feel ungrateful, and discomfort with self-advocacy makes the conversation feel aversive.

Understanding why negotiation matters can help overcome this reluctance. The salary accepted in an early job affects not just that job's income but often the salaries offered in subsequent jobs, since many employers use current salary as an anchor. A few thousand dollars difference in a first job can compound to tens or hundreds of thousands over a career.

The practical approach begins with research. Before any negotiation, know the market rate for the position through sites like Glassdoor, Levels.fyi, Payscale, and LinkedIn Salary. The best time to negotiate is after an offer is made but before you accept. The negotiation itself is simpler than many imagine. The basic move is expressing enthusiasm for the role while asking whether there is flexibility in the compensation. The tone should be collaborative, not adversarial.

If the employer cannot move on salary, other elements may be negotiable: signing bonus, start date, vacation time, flexible work arrangements, professional development budget, or equity. Not every negotiation succeeds, and that is acceptable. The worst likely outcome is hearing "no," after which you can accept the original offer without having lost anything.

The skill of negotiation extends beyond salary to raises, contract terms, purchases, and many situations where the initial offer is not the final word. Learning to negotiate early develops a skill that will be applied throughout life.

**The Unique Power of Starting Early**

Time is the most powerful variable in the compounding equation, and the young have more of it than anyone. Consider the dramatic difference in outcomes: a person who saves $500 per month from age 22 to age 32—a total of $60,000 contributed over ten years—and then never saves another dollar, will have more at age 65 than a person who saves nothing until age 32 and then saves $500 per month for the next 33 years—a total of $198,000 contributed. The early saver contributes one-third as much and ends with more money.

The same principle applies to every dimension of financial life. The credit history started at 20 has fifteen more years of length than the history started at 35. The habits formed in the twenties persist for fifty years rather than thirty.

The objection arises that young adults have little money to work with. Incomes are low, student loans may loom, the cost of establishing independent life is high. But starting modestly is still starting. The person who saves $50 per month develops the habit of saving, sees the account grow, internalizes their identity as a saver, and will increase contributions as income rises.

Another objection is that youth is for living, not for financial optimization. This is true, and experiences have value that declines with age. The resolution is not either saving or living but finding the balance that allows both. Paying yourself first—saving a planned amount before discretionary spending—ensures that future security is funded while leaving room for present experience.

**Common Mistakes and Their Costs**

Certain mistakes are particularly common among young adults, and their costs are amplified by the long time horizon during which consequences unfold.

Lifestyle inflation absorbing all income gains is perhaps the most pervasive mistake. The entry-level salary pays the bills with little left over; each raise is immediately absorbed by a nicer apartment and more dining out; the pattern continues until spending always equals income regardless of how much income grows. The alternative is to save a portion of every raise, allowing lifestyle to improve but not to consume all gains.

High-interest debt, particularly credit card debt, is devastating to young finances. The interest rates make the debt nearly impossible to outrun. Every dollar paid in interest is a dollar not saved. Avoiding credit card debt entirely, through spending only what you can pay in full each month, is far easier than escaping it once accumulated.

Neglecting employer retirement matches is leaving free money on the table. If an employer offers to match contributions up to a certain percentage of salary, contributing at least that amount is an immediate, guaranteed 100 percent return.

Not having an emergency fund leaves you one misfortune away from crisis. Building even a small emergency fund, before focusing on other goals, provides the stability that allows everything else to work.

Delaying investment until you "understand the market" or "have enough to matter" costs years of compounding. Starting with whatever you have, in a simple target-date fund if necessary, is far better than waiting for perfect knowledge or larger balances.

Co-signing loans or financially entangling with unreliable others can destroy credit and finances when those others fail to meet obligations. Maintaining appropriate financial boundaries, especially in early adulthood when relationships are still forming, is protective.

Ignoring benefits enrollment when starting a job can be costly. Treating benefits enrollment as a meaningful financial decision ensures you capture value that is part of your compensation.

Falling for financial products targeted at the young occurs regularly: whole life insurance sold to those with no dependents, high-fee investment products sold by advisors targeting new graduates, credit cards with poor terms marketed as starter cards. Be skeptical of financial products actively marketed to you.

**A Sequence for Those Starting Out**

Given these principles, what sequence of actions makes sense for someone beginning their financial life?

The first priority is establishing positive cash flow. Earning more than you spend is the foundation. Without positive cash flow, nothing else is possible.

The second priority is building a minimal emergency fund. Even a few hundred dollars provides some buffer against minor emergencies and reduces the anxiety that comes from having no reserves.

The third priority is capturing any employer retirement match. This is an immediate, guaranteed return that should not be forgone.

The fourth priority is eliminating high-interest debt. Credit cards, payday loans, other high-interest obligations should be paid aggressively.

The fifth priority is expanding the emergency fund to a more robust level—three to six months of expenses.

The sixth priority is saving for other goals and building long-term investments: retirement savings beyond the match, saving for a home down payment, taxable investment accounts.

This sequence is not rigid. Some steps can happen in parallel. What matters is that the foundation is built before the structure rises above it.

**The Long View**

The transition to financial independence is part of the larger transition to adulthood. It involves taking responsibility, developing identity, learning from mistakes, building the life you want to live. Money is a tool in that larger project, not the project itself.

The young adult who understands this—who sees financial management as serving life rather than dominating it—will make better decisions than the one who either ignores money or becomes consumed by it. The goal is competence, not obsession. Enough knowledge to make good decisions, enough attention to stay on track, enough systems to operate automatically. And then freedom to focus on the things that matter most.

The years of starting out are often challenging. Income is low, experience is limited, mistakes are frequent. This is normal and acceptable. The perspective to maintain is that this is temporary. The entry-level salary will increase. The knowledge gaps will fill. The credit score will rise. The emergency fund will grow. The habits will solidify.

The most valuable asset the young person possesses is time—not just time for compounding but time to learn, time to recover from mistakes, time to build. This asset is depleted every day, which is precisely why starting now, imperfectly but earnestly, matters more than starting later with more resources or knowledge.

Begin with what you have. Learn as you go. Build systems that persist. And trust that the early investments—of money, of attention, of effort—will compound into something substantial.

## SUMMARY

The transition to financial independence typically occurs between ages eighteen and thirty and involves both practical tasks and a psychological shift from dependence to ownership. Ownership means accepting that your financial outcomes are primarily your responsibility, developing an internal locus of control, tolerating the anxiety that comes with responsibility, and examining inherited beliefs about money to decide what to carry forward.

The minimum viable financial infrastructure includes income, tracking, a spending plan, and separate checking and savings accounts. Building credit early matters even for those who intend to avoid debt, since credit affects the ability to rent apartments, buy cars, purchase homes, and sometimes get jobs. The strategy is to use credit responsibly—small regular purchases paid in full—while never using credit to spend money you don't have. Payment history and credit utilization are the most important factors in credit scores.

Salary negotiation matters because compensation in early jobs anchors future offers. Research market rates, negotiate after receiving an offer but before accepting, and maintain a collaborative rather than adversarial tone. If salary cannot move, other elements may be negotiable.

Time is the most powerful variable in compounding. A person who saves for ten years starting at 22 and then stops will have more at 65 than someone who saves three times as much starting at 32. The habits formed early—tracking, saving, living below your means, continuous learning, regular review—require effort to establish but then operate automatically for decades.

Common mistakes include lifestyle inflation that absorbs all income gains, high-interest debt, neglecting employer retirement matches, lacking an emergency fund, delaying investment, financially entangling with unreliable others, ignoring benefits enrollment, and falling for products marketed to the young. The recommended sequence is: establish positive cash flow, build a minimal emergency fund, capture any employer match, eliminate high-interest debt, expand the emergency fund, then save for other goals and long-term investments.

# TWENTY-ONE
# THE MIDDLE YEARS

The middle years of financial life—roughly the period from the early thirties to the mid-fifties—are characterized by complexity. The simplicity of starting out, where the primary challenges were building from nothing and avoiding basic mistakes, gives way to a landscape of competing demands, major decisions, and obligations that pull in multiple directions simultaneously.

This is the period when many people marry and merge financial lives with a partner. When children arrive and reshape every priority. When housing decisions carry the largest price tags of a lifetime. When careers reach their peak earning potential but also face disruption and the possibility of reinvention. When parents age and begin to need care even as children still need support. When the question shifts from "how do I build a foundation?" to "how do I manage everything at once?"

The middle years are also when the consequences of earlier decisions become fully apparent. The person who built good habits and avoided major mistakes in their twenties enters this period with resources and flexibility. The person who accumulated debt and never learned to save enters it already strained. This chapter cannot undo the past, but it can address how to navigate the present, whatever starting point you bring.

The central challenge of the middle years is allocation—of money, of time, of attention—among legitimate competing claims. There is not enough of any resource to satisfy all demands fully. The question is not whether to make tradeoffs but how to make them wisely.

**Marriage and Merged Finances**

Marriage, or its functional equivalents in long-term partnership, introduces a second person into financial life. This changes everything. Decisions that were once unilateral become joint. Spending patterns that were purely personal now affect another. Goals that were individually defined must be reconciled with another person's goals.

The mechanics of merging finances admit several approaches. Some couples combine everything—all income goes into joint accounts, all expenses are paid from joint funds. Some couples keep everything separate—each person maintains individual accounts, expenses are divided by agreement. Many couples adopt hybrid approaches—joint accounts for shared expenses and goals, individual accounts for personal spending. No single approach is correct for all couples. The right choice depends on income similarity or disparity, individual attitudes toward money, and the level of trust in the relationship. What matters more than the specific structure is that both partners understand and agree to it.

The psychological dimension is at least as important as the mechanical. Money is never just money in a marriage; it carries meaning. It can represent power, security, freedom, love, or control depending on how it is handled. Disparities in income can create dynamics of dependence or resentment. Differences in spending patterns can generate conflict. Secrets about money can erode trust as thoroughly as any other kind of deception.

Open communication is the foundation of successful financial partnership. This means discussing money regularly, not just when problems arise. It means disclosing financial situations fully before marriage—debts, assets, obligations, financial history. It means making major financial decisions jointly. It means acknowledging different attitudes and finding accommodation rather than imposing one person's approach on the other.

Some couples find it useful to establish explicit agreements. What counts as a major purchase requiring discussion versus a routine expense? How will windfalls be handled? What are the shared financial goals? How will disagreements be resolved? Having clarity prevents conflicts that arise from unstated expectations.

The legal dimension deserves attention. Marriage creates legal and tax consequences that vary by jurisdiction. In community property states, income earned during marriage is jointly owned regardless of who earned it. In common law states, ownership follows title. Tax filing status changes. Estate planning needs revision. Beneficiary designations should be updated.

For those entering marriage with significant assets or income disparities, or with children from previous relationships, prenuptial agreements may be appropriate. These agreements are simply a way of clarifying expectations and protections before they become contested. Many couples benefit from periodic financial meetings—monthly or quarterly—where they review spending, track progress toward goals, and address any concerns.

Conflict over money is among the most common sources of marital stress. The approaches to managing it are the approaches to managing conflict generally: listening to understand rather than to rebut, seeking underlying concerns rather than debating surface positions, looking for solutions that address both partners' needs. Financial counseling or therapy can help when couples cannot resolve conflicts on their own.

The death of a spouse or divorce are realities that some will face during the middle years. Both require significant financial adjustment and benefit from professional advice—estate attorneys, divorce attorneys, financial planners—and from the support of trusted others.

**Children and Their Costs**

Children transform financial life more thoroughly than any other single factor. The arrival of a child introduces expenses that continue for two decades or more, reshapes work decisions for one or both parents, and introduces goals—like college funding—that did not previously exist.

The direct costs of raising a child are substantial. Government estimates suggest figures in the hundreds of thousands of dollars from birth to age eighteen, varying significantly by income level, location, and choices made. These estimates typically exclude college costs, which can double or more the total depending on educational path.

Childcare is often the largest expense in the early years, sometimes rivaling or exceeding housing costs. Options range from family members providing care to in-home nannies to daycare centers to one parent reducing paid work. Each choice involves financial tradeoffs and values tradeoffs. Two incomes with paid childcare may produce more money but less parental presence. One income with a stay-at-home parent may produce less money but more parental involvement.

The financial impact of a parent leaving paid work extends beyond the immediate loss of income. Career continuity is interrupted, making re-entry more difficult. Retirement savings halt or slow. Social Security credits are reduced. These costs are not arguments against staying home—they are factors to consider and, where possible, mitigate.

Housing costs often increase with children. The one-bedroom apartment gives way to a larger space. Schools become a factor in location decisions, with highly rated school districts commanding premium prices. Education expenses extend beyond college to private school tuition, tutoring, enrichment activities, and sports fees. Healthcare costs increase as well.

College funding presents a major planning challenge. The cost of higher education has risen faster than inflation for decades. Several vehicles exist for college savings: 529 plans offer tax-advantaged growth for educational expenses, Coverdell Education Savings Accounts offer similar benefits with more flexibility but lower contribution limits, and custodial accounts under UGMA or UTMA offer still more flexibility but become the child's property at adulthood.

A critical question is the priority of college savings relative to other financial goals. The common advice is to prioritize retirement savings over college savings—you can borrow for college but cannot borrow for retirement. This advice has merit, but some families prioritize giving children an education free of debt. There is no objectively correct ranking; there is the ranking that reflects your values, applied with awareness of the tradeoffs.

The financial pressure of the middle years is often most acute when children are young—when childcare costs peak, housing has recently expanded, and income has not yet reached its career peak. This period requires particular attention to cash flow, emergency reserves, and avoiding overcommitment.

**Housing Decisions**

Housing is typically the largest single expense for households and the largest single purchase most people make. Decisions about housing—whether to rent or buy, where to live, how much space to acquire—have financial consequences that extend for decades.

The factors that favor buying—stability, building equity, locking in housing costs—often align with life circumstances in the middle years. The person with a stable career, a partner, children in school has more to gain from the stability of ownership.

At the same time, the middle years are when the dangers of overbuying are greatest. The desire to provide children with space and good schools, the social pressure to keep up with peers, the emotional appeal of the dream house—these can drive purchases that strain finances for years. The house that requires both incomes working at maximum intensity to afford leaves no room for setbacks.

The conservative approach to home buying applies with special force in the middle years. Buy less than you can afford. Leave room for one income to be reduced. Do not count on appreciation to make an unaffordable purchase work out.

Location decisions often involve tradeoffs between housing costs, commute times, and school quality. There is rarely a choice that dominates on all dimensions; there are only tradeoffs made according to values and constraints. Some families make location decisions that involve significant geographic moves—for career opportunities, for family proximity, for affordability. These moves involve substantial financial costs (moving expenses, transaction costs, possible dual housing situations) and non-financial costs (uprooting children, leaving extended family).

For homeowners, the question of when to move arises periodically. The transaction costs of real estate—agent commissions, closing costs, moving expenses—mean that frequent moves are financially costly. Stability, when circumstances allow it, is usually preferable.

The question of home improvements arises regularly. Some improvements are necessary maintenance. Some add value that may be recovered in a sale. Some add enjoyment but little resale value. Understanding which category a proposed improvement falls into helps inform the decision.

Downsizing in the later middle years—as children leave and space needs decrease—can free up equity and reduce ongoing expenses. The emotional attachment to the family home can make this transition difficult, but the financial benefits can be substantial.

### Career Pivots and Entrepreneurship

The middle years are often a period of career maturation and peak earning. They are also a period when careers may be disrupted, redirected, or transformed.

Career disruptions in the middle years are particularly stressful because obligations are often at their highest. Job loss requires aggressive response—cutting expenses, intensive job searching, considering options that might have been rejected when circumstances were easier. The emergency fund is most valuable in the middle years, precisely because the consequences of income interruption are most severe.

Career pivots—deliberate changes in direction—are common as people discover that the path they chose in their twenties no longer fits. The lawyer who wants to teach, the corporate manager who wants to start a nonprofit. These transitions can be financially challenging, often involving reduced income during the transition period.

Managing a career pivot financially requires planning. Building savings before the transition creates runway. Reducing fixed expenses creates flexibility. Transitioning gradually, if possible, can reduce the income gap. Having a realistic understanding of likely income in the new career prevents disappointment.

Some career pivots involve additional education or credentials. The cost of this education must be weighed against the expected benefit. Careful research into typical outcomes for graduates of specific programs informs this decision.

Entrepreneurship carries both higher potential rewards and higher risks than employment. The financial principles include having sufficient runway (at least a year of living expenses in reserve), starting while maintaining employment when possible, being honest about financial requirements and likely timeline, separating business finances from personal finances, and understanding the opportunity cost of the investment.

For the employed person, career development continues to matter. Skills become obsolete; industries transform; companies restructure. Continuing to learn, to build skills, to maintain professional networks—these are investments in career insurance.

### Caring for Aging Parents

The term "sandwich generation" describes those who simultaneously support children and aging parents. This dual obligation is increasingly common as lifespans extend and the middle generation delays childbearing.

Aging parents may need support in several forms: financial support if their retirement savings prove insufficient, logistical support with tasks they can no longer manage independently, hands-on care as physical or cognitive decline progresses, and emotional support as they face the losses of aging.

The financial implications can be substantial. Funding a parent's care can cost tens of thousands of dollars per year. Adult children often face the choice of providing care themselves (at the cost of their own income and time) or paying for care (at the cost of their own financial goals).

Several approaches can help manage these demands. Early conversations with aging parents about their financial situation and wishes for care are valuable even though uncomfortable. Understanding what resources exist—retirement accounts, Social Security, pensions, home equity, long-term care insurance—allows for realistic planning. Ensuring legal documents are in place—power of attorney, healthcare directives, updated wills—prevents crisis decision-making later.

Coordinating with siblings distributes the burden and prevents resentment. Understanding available resources reduces the burden: Medicare covers acute medical needs but not long-term care, Medicaid covers long-term care but only for those with very limited assets, and Area Agencies on Aging can connect families with local resources.

Building caregiving costs into your own financial plan acknowledges reality. If it is reasonably likely that you will need to provide financial support to aging parents, that likelihood should affect your savings targets and spending levels.

Caring for yourself while caregiving is essential but often neglected. Respite care, support groups, and taking breaks are not indulgences but necessities for sustainable caregiving.

**Navigating Competing Demands**

The signature experience of the middle years is the simultaneity of demands. Mortgage and children and aging parents and retirement savings and career development. There is not enough money for all of it, not enough time, not enough energy. Something must give.

The framework for navigating competing demands begins with clarity about priorities. What matters most to you? Honest reflection can surface true priorities that may differ from stated priorities. With priorities clarified, allocation follows. The most important things receive resources first; the less important things receive what remains.

The particular challenge of the middle years is that many demands feel non-negotiable. But examining what seems fixed often reveals flexibility that was not apparent. The size of the mortgage was negotiable when you bought the house. The scope of children's activities is negotiable. The form of help to aging parents is negotiable.

Some general guidance applies across most situations. Avoid taking on obligations whose cost you cannot clearly afford. Maintain reserves even when it's hard—the emergency fund is what prevents a crisis from becoming a catastrophe. Communicate with everyone affected by financial decisions. Seek efficiency in spending without sacrificing quality of life.

Recognize that this period is temporary. The acute demands of the middle years—young children, mortgages, aging parents—do not last forever. Planning for what comes after maintains perspective.

**Integration and Balance**

The middle years are demanding but also, often, the years of greatest productivity and capability. Incomes typically peak. Skills and judgment are mature. The resources to meet the demands of this period exist; the challenge is marshaling them effectively.

The integration of financial life with the rest of life is especially important. Money is not the point; money is a tool for building the life you want. A life consumed by earning and managing money at the expense of relationships, health, and meaning is not a successful life. The goal is integration—financial health supporting life well-lived.

This integration requires periodic stepping back from the day-to-day to examine the whole. Some couples find it valuable to conduct annual reviews where they assess not just finances but their life together. The middle years are when long-term planning becomes most important. Retirement is no longer a distant abstraction; it is a decade or two away.

The concept of enough is particularly relevant. How much income is enough? How large a house is enough? Without a sense of enough, the demands of the middle years expand to fill all available resources. With a sense of enough, the demands can be met, trade-offs can be made, and life can be lived.

**Transitions Within the Middle Years**

The middle years contain their own transitions. The transition from two incomes to one, or from one to two, changes everything about household finance. The transition as children age changes the expense profile—the end of childcare is often offset by increased costs of activities and eventually college. Career transitions change income levels and introduce new considerations. Housing transitions are episodic but significant. The transition in health and needs of aging parents can be gradual or sudden.

Each transition is an opportunity to revisit the financial structure and ensure it still fits. The plan appropriate at 35 may not be appropriate at 45 or 55.

**Looking Forward**

The middle years are also when the end of financial life comes into view. Retirement is no longer theoretical; it must be planned for with specificity. The work of those later years rests on the foundation built now.

The perspective to carry through the middle years is that this period is simultaneously demanding and formative. It is demanding because obligations are high. It is formative because the decisions made here shape what follows. The middle years are not something to survive but something to navigate deliberately.

The financial principles that apply throughout life apply here with special force: spend less than you earn, save for the future, avoid destructive debt, invest wisely, protect against catastrophe, plan for what comes next. The challenge is applying these principles amid complexity and competing demands. Meeting that challenge is the work of these years.

## SUMMARY

The middle years of financial life, roughly from the early thirties to mid-fifties, are characterized by complexity and competing demands. This period typically involves marriage and merged finances, children and their substantial costs, major housing decisions, career development and possible disruption, and caring for aging parents while still supporting children. The central challenge is allocation of limited resources among legitimate competing claims.

Marriage introduces a second person into financial life, requiring decisions about how to merge finances (fully joint, fully separate, or hybrid approaches) and ongoing open communication about money. The psychological dimension matters as much as the mechanical: money carries meaning in relationships, and secrets or conflicts about finances can be as damaging as any other form of relationship stress. Regular financial meetings and explicit agreements about major purchases and shared goals help prevent conflict.

Children transform financial life through direct costs (hundreds of thousands from birth to eighteen, potentially doubled by college), childcare expenses that can rival housing costs, and the career impact when a parent reduces work. College funding presents planning challenges, with 529 plans and other vehicles available, though the common advice is to prioritize retirement savings since you can borrow for college but not for retirement.

Housing decisions carry the largest price tags of a lifetime. The conservative approach—buying less than you can afford and leaving room for income reduction—applies with special force given the high obligations of the middle years. Location decisions involve tradeoffs between housing costs, commute times, and school quality.

Career disruptions are particularly stressful in the middle years because obligations are highest, making emergency funds essential. Career pivots require financial planning including building savings and reducing fixed expenses before transition. Entrepreneurship requires sufficient runway (at least a year of living expenses), realistic financial projections, and separation of business and personal finances.

The "sandwich generation" simultaneously supports children and aging parents. Managing this requires early conversations with parents about their situation and wishes, coordination with siblings, understanding available resources like Medicare and Medicaid, and building potential caregiving costs into your own financial plan.

The key to navigating competing demands is clarity about priorities, followed by allocation accordingly. Many demands that seem non-negotiable reveal flexibility upon examination. General guidance includes avoiding obligations you cannot clearly afford, maintaining reserves even when difficult, communicating with everyone affected by financial decisions, and recognizing that this demanding period is temporary.

The middle years are the period when long-term planning becomes most important, as retirement shifts from distant abstraction to approaching reality. The concept of "enough" is particularly relevant—without it, demands expand to fill all resources. The goal is integration of financial health with life well-lived, achieved through periodic stepping back to examine whether you are living according to your values and making progress toward your goals.

# TWENTY-TWO
# APPROACHING RETIREMENT

The approach to retirement—the years roughly from the mid-fifties to the moment of leaving work—is a period unlike any other in financial life. The accumulation phase that has defined decades of saving and investing begins to give way to the distribution phase, when assets must support life rather than simply grow. The identity built around work begins to require supplementation or replacement. The theoretical future becomes the imminent present.

This transition is both practical and psychological, and neither dimension can be addressed without the other. The person who has accumulated sufficient assets but has no vision of what retirement will hold may find the transition paralyzing. The person who has a rich vision of retirement but insufficient assets to support it faces a different kind of crisis. The work of these years is to bring the practical and the psychological into alignment, so that retirement, when it comes, is a beginning rather than an ending.

The questions of this period are both simple and profound. Do I have enough? When should I stop working? What will I do with my time? Who will I be when I am no longer what I do? These questions deserve serious attention, not in the final months before retirement but in the years leading up to it.

**How Much Is Enough**

The question of how much is enough to retire is simultaneously technical and personal. The technical dimension involves calculations about assets, spending, longevity, and returns. The personal dimension involves clarity about what retirement will look like and what it will cost.

The technical approaches to determining retirement sufficiency take several forms. The simplest rules of thumb suggest multiples of final salary—perhaps ten to twelve times annual income accumulated by retirement age—as a rough target. These rules provide a starting point but obscure the variation in individual circumstances. The person whose retirement will cost $40,000 per year needs a different sum than the person whose retirement will cost $150,000 per year, regardless of what either earned while working.

More refined approaches focus on spending rather than income. The conventional guidance suggests that retirees need to replace 70 to 80 percent of pre-retirement income, on the theory that certain expenses—commuting, work clothes, payroll taxes, retirement savings itself—disappear in retirement. This guidance, while useful, also obscures variation. Some retirees spend more than they did while working, at least in the early active years; travel, hobbies, and the leisure to spend money can increase expenses. Some retirees spend much less, having paid off mortgages and simplified lifestyles. Knowing what you will spend matters more than knowing what you earned.

The most rigorous approach involves detailed projection. What will your actual expenses be in retirement? Start with current spending, adjust for what will change, and arrive at an estimated annual need. Then consider how that need will be funded. Social Security provides a foundation; its amount can be estimated through the Social Security Administration's online tools. Pensions, for those fortunate enough to have them, provide another layer. The gap between these guaranteed income sources and total spending needs must be filled by portfolio withdrawals.

The question then becomes: how large must the portfolio be to fill that gap sustainably?

The traditional answer invokes the four percent rule, derived from historical analysis of portfolio returns and longevity. The rule suggests that a retiree can withdraw four percent of the initial portfolio value in the first year of retirement, adjust that amount for inflation in subsequent years, and have high confidence of not exhausting the portfolio over a thirty-year retirement. A portfolio of one million dollars would support initial withdrawals of $40,000; two million would support $80,000.

This rule provides useful orientation but deserves scrutiny. It was derived from historical U.S. market returns that may not repeat. It assumes a particular asset allocation and rebalancing approach. It targets high probability of success over thirty years, which means some probability of failure. It does not account for the reality that spending in retirement is rarely constant—often higher in early active years, lower in the middle, and potentially higher again if health care costs rise late in life.

Contemporary retirement planning often uses more sophisticated approaches. Monte Carlo simulations model thousands of possible market scenarios to estimate the probability that a given portfolio and withdrawal strategy will succeed. Dynamic withdrawal strategies adjust spending based on portfolio performance rather than following a fixed inflation-adjusted path. Floor-and-ceiling approaches establish minimum and maximum spending levels, providing both security and flexibility.

Charles Ellis, in his work on investment strategy, proposed a spending rule that offers an alternative to the fixed four percent approach. Rather than withdrawing a fixed dollar amount adjusted for inflation, the spending rule suggests withdrawing a fixed percentage of the current portfolio value each year—perhaps five percent. In years when the portfolio has grown, spending rises; in years when it has fallen, spending declines. This approach has a significant advantage: it is mathematically impossible to exhaust the portfolio, since you are always taking a percentage of what remains. The trade-off is that spending becomes variable rather than stable. A major market decline means a real reduction in lifestyle, at least temporarily. This approach suits retirees who have flexibility in their spending—who can distinguish between essential and discretionary expenses and adjust the latter based on portfolio performance. It may not suit those whose expenses are largely fixed or who cannot tolerate income variability. Some retirees combine elements of both approaches, establishing a floor of essential spending that is protected and allowing discretionary spending to vary with portfolio performance.

The integration of Social Security into retirement planning requires understanding its options and trade-offs. Benefits can be claimed as early as 62, at full retirement age (currently between 66 and 67 depending on birth year), or as late as 70. Claiming early permanently reduces benefits; claiming late permanently increases them. The difference is substantial—benefits at 70 can be 76 percent higher than benefits at 62. The optimal claiming strategy depends on life expectancy, other resources, marital status, and personal preferences. For many people, delaying Social Security as long as feasible—using portfolio withdrawals to fund the gap—maximizes lifetime income, particularly for the higher earner in a married couple whose benefit will continue for the surviving spouse.

The role of guaranteed income in retirement planning extends beyond Social Security. Pensions, for those who have them, provide similar security. Annuities—insurance products that convert a lump sum into a stream of lifetime income—can create guaranteed income for those without pensions. The psychological value of guaranteed income is substantial: knowing that basic needs will be covered regardless of market performance provides peace of mind that portfolio-based strategies may not.

Healthcare costs require special attention in retirement planning.

Before Medicare eligibility at 65, those who retire early must fund their own coverage, which can be expensive. After 65, Medicare provides substantial coverage but leaves significant gaps—premiums for Medicare Parts B and D, supplemental insurance, dental and vision care, and potentially long-term care, which Medicare does not cover. Estimates of lifetime healthcare costs in retirement reach into the hundreds of thousands of dollars for a couple, and long-term care can add hundreds of thousands more.

Higher-income retirees face an additional Medicare cost that often comes as an unwelcome surprise. The Income-Related Monthly Adjustment Amount, known as IRMAA, imposes surcharges on Medicare Part B and Part D premiums for those whose modified adjusted gross income exceeds certain thresholds. These thresholds are not indexed to inflation and are based on income from two years prior, meaning a high-income final year of work can trigger surcharges in the first years of Medicare eligibility. The surcharges are substantial—at the highest income levels, Part B premiums can be more than three times the standard amount, and Part D surcharges add further cost. Because Medicare premiums are typically deducted from Social Security payments, IRMAA effectively reduces the net Social Security benefit that higher-income retirees receive. This creates an important planning consideration: income spikes in the years before and just after retirement, including large Roth conversions, capital gains realizations, or deferred compensation payouts, can trigger IRMAA surcharges that persist for the years those high-income tax returns remain in the lookback window. Managing income in the years surrounding retirement to minimize IRMAA impact, where feasible, can preserve more of the Social Security benefit.

Long-term care is the great uninsurable risk for most retirees. Medicare does not cover it. Long-term care insurance exists but has become expensive and limited in availability. Medicaid covers long-term care but only after assets are depleted. Self-insurance—simply having enough assets to pay for care if needed—requires substantial wealth. Some combination of these approaches, tailored to individual circumstances, addresses the risk but rarely eliminates it.

The housing dimension of retirement planning involves several considerations. Will the retiree stay in the current home, downsize, relocate, or eventually need assisted living? Each path has different cost implications. Home equity is a form of retirement asset, accessible through sale, downsizing, or potentially reverse mortgage, but it is illiquid and often emotionally charged.

Taxes in retirement differ from taxes during working years. Social Security is partially taxable depending on total income. Withdrawals from traditional retirement accounts are taxed as ordinary income. Withdrawals from Roth accounts are tax-free. Capital gains on taxable investments may be taxed at preferential rates. Required minimum distributions from traditional accounts begin at age 73 (under current law) and may push retirees into higher brackets than expected. The sequence and source of withdrawals can be optimized for tax efficiency, a topic where professional advice often pays for itself.

After all the analysis, the question of how much is enough remains partly subjective. The retiree who can tolerate uncertainty may be comfortable with less. The retiree who requires security may need more. The number that emerges from calculation must be tested against personal risk tolerance.

For those approaching retirement with less than ideal accumulation, the options are limited but real. Working longer increases both savings and the years those savings need not be drawn upon. Reducing expected retirement spending lowers the required portfolio. Delaying Social Security increases guaranteed income. Relocating to a lower-cost area reduces housing and living expenses. Part-time work in retirement supplements portfolio income.

The psychological dimension of enough is as important as the technical. Some people never feel they have enough, regardless of accumulation. The fear of running out can persist even in the face of abundant resources. This fear deserves attention as a psychological matter, not just a financial one. Conversely, some people feel they have enough before they do. Reality-testing these feelings through rigorous analysis is essential.

**Timing the Transition**

The decision of when to retire is rarely purely financial. Work provides not just income but structure, identity, social connection, and purpose. Leaving work means leaving all of these. The right time to retire is when both the financial and non-financial conditions are ready.

On the financial dimension, readiness means having sufficient resources to fund the expected retirement, with margin for uncertainty. It means understanding Social Security options and having a claiming strategy. It means having healthcare coverage. It means having a reasonable plan for long-term care risk. It means understanding the tax implications of retirement income. It means having the practical affairs in order—estate documents, beneficiary designations, insurance policies reviewed.

On the non-financial dimension, readiness means having answers, or at least the beginnings of answers, to the questions of how time will be spent, what will provide purpose and meaning, how social needs will be met, and who the retiree will be in this new phase. The person who has cultivated interests, relationships, and identity outside of work is more ready to leave work than the person for whom work is everything.

The timing of retirement is not always voluntary. Health problems, caregiving needs, job loss, or employer pressure may force earlier retirement than planned. These involuntary departures are more difficult, requiring both practical adjustment and psychological processing of loss of control. They are also more common than many anticipate, particularly after age 55. Plans that assume work until 65 or later should be stress-tested against the possibility of earlier departure.

For those with choice about timing, several factors favor later retirement. Continued income allows continued saving. Continued work delays the start of portfolio withdrawals. Each year of delay may allow further delay of Social Security, increasing lifetime benefits. Healthcare coverage through employment avoids the gap before Medicare. The identity and purpose provided by work continue.

Factors favoring earlier retirement include declining health that makes work difficult or makes the window for active retirement shorter. They include financial sufficiency that makes continued work unnecessary. They include the pull of other activities—travel, hobbies, family, volunteer work—that cannot be fully pursued while working. They include burnout or deteriorating work conditions that make continued employment costly in non-financial terms.

The marginal year question is often the right frame for thinking about retirement timing. Given where you are now, would one more year of work improve your retirement sufficiently to justify the cost of that year? The cost includes not just the work itself but the lost year of retirement, which can never be recovered.

This question requires honest accounting on both sides of the ledger. The benefits of one more year include the salary earned, the retirement contributions made, the investment returns on those contributions over the remaining lifetime, the avoided portfolio withdrawal for that year's expenses, and possibly another year of delay in claiming Social Security. These benefits compound: the money earned and saved in that year continues to grow and support spending for decades. For someone early in the consideration of retirement, with meaningful doubt about sufficiency, the marginal year may add substantially to lifetime security.

But the costs are real and often underweighted. The marginal year costs the year itself—twelve months of life spent working rather than in retirement. For someone in their early sixties, that year represents perhaps four or five percent of remaining life expectancy. It cannot be banked or recovered; once spent on work, it is gone. If health is uncertain, the cost rises further; active, healthy retirement years are not guaranteed, and trading a certain year of work for an uncertain future year of active retirement is a losing exchange. The marginal year also costs whatever would have been done with that time—travel while still vigorous, time with aging parents or young grandchildren, pursuit of deferred dreams.

As resources approach sufficiency and non-work life becomes more appealing, the marginal value of additional work declines while its cost remains constant or rises. At some point, the calculation tips. The person who would benefit greatly from one more year at age 58 may benefit only marginally at 63 and not at all at 66. Recognizing when this tipping point has been reached, rather than working past it out of habit or anxiety, is part of the wisdom of retirement timing.

Phased retirement—reducing work gradually rather than stopping abruptly—appeals to many but is less available than desired. For those who can manage it, phased retirement offers both continued income and a gradual psychological transition. Bridge employment—taking a different, often less demanding job between career employment and full retirement—serves similar functions.

The decision about timing is rarely made once. It is revisited as circumstances evolve. Remaining open to reassessment allows the decision to be made with current information.

For couples, retirement timing involves coordination. Retiring together, retiring sequentially, or having one partner continue working—each pattern has different financial and relational implications. The conversations about retirement timing are conversations about the relationship, not just about the finances.

**Portfolio Shifts**

The investment approach appropriate during accumulation may not be appropriate approaching and entering retirement. The shift from accumulation to distribution changes the relationship between the investor and the portfolio.

During accumulation, time is the investor's ally. A market decline, while painful, is also an opportunity; continued contributions buy more shares at lower prices, and recovery over time restores and grows the portfolio. The investor with decades until retirement can afford to hold an aggressive, equity-heavy portfolio.

As retirement approaches, the time horizon shortens, and the consequences of poor sequence of returns become more severe. Sequence risk—the risk that poor returns early in retirement will deplete the portfolio before it can recover—is among the greatest threats to retirement security. The retiree who experiences a major market decline in the first years of retirement, while simultaneously withdrawing for living expenses, may see the portfolio reduced to a level from which it cannot recover.

The traditional response is to reduce equity exposure as retirement approaches, shifting toward bonds and other more stable assets. The logic is that reduced volatility, even at the cost of reduced expected returns, provides protection against sequence risk. The target-date funds common in retirement accounts embed this glide path automatically.

How much to reduce equity exposure, and when, remains debated. Many advisors suggest higher equity allocations than traditional rules, perhaps 50 to 60 percent even in retirement, on the theory that long retirements require the growth that equities provide. The right answer depends on other sources of guaranteed income, risk tolerance, and planned withdrawal rates.

The bucket approach to retirement portfolios offers a conceptual framework many find helpful. The portfolio is mentally divided into three segments based on time horizon, each with a distinct purpose and investment approach. The first bucket holds cash and cash equivalents—money market funds, short-term treasuries, perhaps certificates of deposit—sufficient to cover two to three years of anticipated withdrawals. This bucket provides the buffer against sequence risk; when markets decline, spending continues from this reserve rather than forcing the sale of depreciated assets. The psychological value is substantial: knowing that near-term needs are covered regardless of what markets do reduces the anxiety of watching portfolio values fall.

The second bucket holds intermediate-term investments, typically bonds and bond funds with durations of several years. This bucket covers perhaps years three through ten of anticipated withdrawals. It provides somewhat higher returns than cash while remaining relatively stable. The third bucket holds equities and other growth-oriented investments, meant to fund spending a decade or more in the future. This bucket can absorb the volatility that comes with equity investing because time remains for recovery before those funds are needed.

The buckets are not static; they require periodic replenishment. When the first bucket is depleted by spending, it is refilled from the second. When the second is depleted, it is refilled from the third. In practice, this replenishment often happens during rebalancing or when one asset class has performed particularly well. The discipline is to refill the near-term buckets from whatever has grown beyond its target, naturally implementing a sell-high approach. During sustained market declines, the first bucket provides runway to avoid selling equities at depressed prices; once markets recover, replenishment resumes.

The bucket approach is more a mental model than a rigid system. The underlying investments might be held in a single account rather than physically separated. The boundaries between buckets need not be precise. The value lies in the discipline it encourages: maintaining adequate liquidity to fund near-term needs while allowing long-term investments the time they require to grow.

Tax management becomes more complex in retirement, with multiple account types to draw from. The conventional wisdom suggests drawing first from taxable accounts, then from tax-deferred accounts, then from Roth accounts, on the theory that this maximizes tax-deferred and tax-free growth. But this may not be optimal in all cases.

Roth conversions—moving money from traditional tax-deferred accounts to Roth accounts, paying tax on the converted amount—represent one of the most significant tax planning opportunities in the years surrounding retirement. The logic is straightforward: if you can pay taxes at a lower rate now than you would pay later, converting saves money. The complexity lies in identifying when this condition holds and how much to convert.

The years between retirement and the start of Social Security and required minimum distributions often present a window of unusually low income and therefore low tax rates. A retiree who stops working at 62 and delays Social Security until 70 may have eight years during which taxable income is minimal—perhaps only the withdrawals needed for living expenses. These years offer the opportunity to convert traditional IRA or 401(k) balances to Roth accounts at rates far below what will apply once Social Security begins, RMDs kick in at 73, and perhaps a surviving spouse files as a single taxpayer at higher rates.

The decision of whether to convert before or after retirement involves several considerations. Converting while still working means the conversion income is added to employment income, likely pushing the total into higher brackets. The immediate tax cost is higher, though the conversion is complete before retirement begins. Converting after retirement but before Social Security allows the conversion to fill the lower brackets that would otherwise go unused. Many retirees benefit from converting enough each year to fill the 12 or 22 percent brackets, stopping before pushing into higher rates.

The limitations on Roth conversions require attention. IRMAA, as noted above, uses a two-year lookback; large conversions can trigger Medicare surcharges that persist for two years after the high-income return drops out of the window. Conversions also increase adjusted gross income, which can affect taxation of Social Security benefits, eligibility for ACA premium subsidies if retiring before 65, and various other income-tested provisions. The optimal conversion amount each year often requires modeling multiple factors, not just the marginal tax rate.

The long-term benefits of Roth conversion can be substantial. Roth accounts are not subject to required minimum distributions during the original owner's lifetime, allowing continued tax-free growth. Withdrawals in later years, when expenses may spike due to healthcare costs, come tax-free. The surviving spouse inherits a Roth without the RMD pressure that forces taxable income from traditional accounts. For heirs other than spouses, inherited Roth accounts must be distributed within ten years but those distributions are tax-free, while inherited traditional accounts face the same ten-year rule with all distributions taxable.

The location of different investments across account types can be optimized for tax efficiency. Generally, investments with high expected returns belong in Roth accounts, where all gains are tax-free. Investments that generate taxable income, like bonds, may belong in tax-deferred accounts. Investments with preferential tax treatment may belong in taxable accounts.

The psychological dimension of portfolio management shifts in retirement. The fear of market declines may intensify when the portfolio is supporting life rather than simply growing. Building emotional discipline, and perhaps working with an advisor who can provide behavioral coaching, helps navigate markets in retirement.

**Finding Structure and Purpose**

Work, for those who have spent decades doing it, provides more than income. It provides structure to days, weeks, and years. It provides identity—the answer to "what do you do?" It provides social connection with colleagues. It provides purpose and meaning. It provides challenge and growth. Leaving work means leaving all of this, and replacing what is lost is the central psychological task of retirement.

Those who retire without having considered what will fill these needs often struggle. The first weeks may feel like vacation, but vacation without end loses its savor. The unstructured days that seemed appealing may come to feel empty. The loss of work identity may feel like loss of self. Depression, purposelessness, and decline are real risks of poorly navigated retirement transitions.

Those who thrive in retirement typically share certain characteristics. They have interests and activities that engage them. They have relationships that provide connection and meaning. They have a sense of purpose or contribution that extends beyond paid work. They have accepted the identity transition from worker to retiree. The work of the years approaching retirement is to cultivate these characteristics.

Structure in retirement must be actively created rather than externally imposed. Some retirees benefit from maintaining routines—regular wake times, scheduled activities, recurring commitments. Others prefer freedom. Either approach can work, but drift—days that pass without intention or satisfaction—is a warning sign. Building activities that require showing up can provide enough structure to prevent drift while preserving flexibility.

Identity in retirement shifts from what you do to who you are, from role to self. This shift can be disorienting for those whose identity was heavily invested in work. The work of this transition is to discover or construct identity that does not depend on professional role. This may involve returning to interests abandoned during busy working years, developing new dimensions of self, or finding new roles—grandparent, volunteer, mentor, artist—that carry meaning.

Social connection requires active maintenance in retirement. The workplace provided constant social contact. Retirement removes this, and the relationships of work often fade without the shared context. Friendships must be actively cultivated. Community involvement, clubs, classes, religious organizations, volunteer work—these provide settings where relationships can form.

Purpose in retirement comes from contribution—the sense of doing something that matters. For some, this continues through paid work. For some, it comes through volunteer work. For some, it comes through family, especially grandchildren. For some, it comes through creative work. For some, it comes through learning and growth. The specific source matters less than having one.

Health becomes a more central focus in retirement. Physical activity can become a core part of retirement life. Attention to diet, sleep, and stress pays dividends in quality and length of retirement.

Cognitive engagement supports brain health—learning new things, social interaction, active rather than passive entertainment.

The transition from work to retirement often involves grief, even when retirement is welcomed. Grief for the loss of role, identity, daily purpose, colleagues, structure. This grief is normal and benefits from acknowledgment.

For couples, retirement changes the relationship. Partners who have spent decades with work structuring their time now face continuous togetherness. Conversations about expectations—how much time together versus apart, how domestic responsibilities will be handled—prevent conflict.

The phased approach to retirement, where possible, allows gradual adjustment. Starting to build non-work life well before retirement eases the transition. The person who has maintained hobbies, friendships, and interests throughout working life has less to build from scratch.

**Practical Dimensions of the Transition**

Beyond the psychological, the practical aspects of the transition require attention.

Healthcare coverage is among the most important practical matters. Those retiring before 65 need a plan for the gap before Medicare eligibility. Options include COBRA continuation of employer coverage, marketplace coverage under the ACA, a spouse's employer coverage, or direct purchase of individual insurance.

At 65, Medicare eligibility begins, but Medicare is not automatic or free. Enrollment in Part B requires action during the enrollment window; late enrollment triggers permanent penalties. Many retirees also purchase supplemental coverage—Medigap policies or Medicare Advantage plans.

Social Security claiming requires decision and action. The claiming strategy should be determined well before the claiming date. Once made, claiming decisions are difficult to reverse.

Employer retirement benefits require attention as employment ends. Understanding what happens to pension benefits, options for employer retirement accounts, and continuation of any employer-provided benefits prevents surprises.

Estate planning review is appropriate at retirement. Wills, trusts, powers of attorney, healthcare directives, beneficiary designations—all should be current.

Insurance needs change in retirement. Life insurance may no longer be necessary once income from work is no longer the plan. Disability insurance becomes irrelevant. Long-term care insurance, if not already in place, deserves consideration.

The budget for retirement differs from the budget for working life. Some expenses disappear; some may increase. Creating a realistic budget prevents discovery that retirement costs more than expected.

The relationship with money itself may change. After decades of accumulation, the shift to spending down can feel unnatural. The frugal habits that built wealth may be difficult to relax, even when resources are ample.

**The Retirement Readiness Assessment**

As retirement approaches, a comprehensive readiness assessment brings together the elements discussed throughout this chapter. This assessment is not a one-time event but an ongoing process.

The financial assessment asks: Do I have enough? This requires clarity on expected retirement spending, Social Security and pension income, portfolio size and sustainable withdrawal rate, healthcare costs, taxes, and contingencies.

The timing assessment asks: When should I retire? This integrates the financial assessment with health status, work circumstances, and the readiness of non-financial dimensions.

The investment assessment asks: Is my portfolio positioned for retirement? This includes asset allocation, tax-efficient asset location, a withdrawal strategy, and cash reserves.

The purpose and structure assessment asks: What will I do? This includes activities, sources of meaning, social connections, and the identity that will replace work identity.

The practical assessment asks: Are the logistics in place? This includes healthcare coverage, Social Security strategy, estate documents, insurance review, and budget.

The relationship assessment, for those with partners, asks: Are we aligned? This includes shared understanding of timing, shared vision for retirement life, and plans for how the relationship will work.

Gaps in any dimension warrant attention before retirement.

**The Transition Itself**

The final days of work and the first days of retirement are a passage worth marking. The end of a career that may have spanned decades deserves acknowledgment—not just the farewell parties others may arrange but personal reflection on what has been accomplished, what has been learned, who you have become through the work.

The first days and weeks of retirement often feel strange. The rhythms of decades do not disappear overnight. These feelings are normal, and they pass. Allowing the transition rather than forcing immediate adjustment is appropriate.

Building the new life happens gradually. The activities that will structure time need trial and adjustment. The identity that will carry you through retirement will emerge, not fully formed at the start but developing with experience.

The risks of early retirement include both under-engagement and over-commitment. Under-engagement leads to drift and purposelessness. Over-commitment leads to exhaustion. Finding the right level of activity is part of the adjustment.

Health habits, if not already established, become urgent to develop. The structure that work provided for meals, movement, and rest disappears. Building exercise, healthy eating, good sleep, and stress management into the new routine protects the health that makes retirement enjoyable.

**Retirement as a Beginning**

Retirement, in the best case, is not an ending but a beginning. It is the beginning of a phase of life with its own possibilities, its own challenges, its own sources of meaning.

The approach to retirement is the bridge between working life and what follows. It is the time to ensure readiness—financial, psychological, and practical. It is the time for planning, but also for anticipation. What will this next phase hold? What do I hope for? What can I do now to make it what I want it to be?

The answers are personal. Retirement is not one thing but many things, shaped by individual circumstances, values, and choices. The person who has done the work of this chapter—assessed resources, considered timing, positioned investments, built purpose and structure, addressed practicalities—enters retirement prepared. Not guaranteed success, because life guarantees nothing, but prepared. Ready to begin.

## SUMMARY

The approach to retirement, roughly from the mid-fifties to leaving work, requires bringing practical and psychological readiness into alignment. This period involves answering fundamental questions: Do I have enough? When should I stop working? What will I do? Who will I be?

Determining whether you have enough requires moving beyond simple rules of thumb to detailed projection of retirement expenses, guaranteed income sources (Social Security, pensions), and the portfolio needed to fill the gap. The four percent rule—withdrawing four percent initially, then adjusting for inflation—provides useful orientation but deserves scrutiny; contemporary approaches often use Monte Carlo simulations and dynamic withdrawal strategies. The spending rule proposed by Charles Ellis offers an alternative: withdrawing a fixed percentage of current portfolio value each year, which makes exhausting the portfolio impossible but creates variable income that rises and falls with markets.

Social Security claiming strategy matters significantly, with benefits at 70 potentially 76 percent higher than at 62. Healthcare costs require special attention, particularly the gap before Medicare at 65 and the long-term care risk that Medicare does not cover. Higher-income retirees face IRMAA surcharges on Medicare Parts B and D premiums, based on income from two years prior, which effectively reduce net Social Security benefits and create incentives to manage income in the years surrounding retirement. The question of enough has a psychological dimension as well: some never feel they have enough regardless of accumulation, while others feel secure before they should.

Timing the transition involves both financial and non-financial readiness. The marginal year question asks whether one more year of work would improve retirement sufficiently to justify its cost—including the lost year of retirement that can never be recovered. The benefits of additional work compound over time, but the costs include the year itself, the possibility that health may not permit active retirement later, and the deferral of whatever would have been done with that time. As resources approach sufficiency, the marginal value of additional work declines. Involuntary retirement through health problems, caregiving needs, or job loss is more common than many expect, particularly after 55.

Portfolio management shifts as retirement approaches. Sequence risk—poor returns early in retirement depleting the portfolio—becomes the primary concern rather than long-term growth. The bucket approach divides the portfolio by time horizon: the first bucket holds cash sufficient for two to three years of withdrawals, providing a buffer against selling equities during downturns; the second bucket holds bonds for intermediate needs; the third bucket holds equities for long-term growth. The buckets are replenished from whatever has grown, implementing a sell-high discipline.

Roth conversions represent a significant tax planning opportunity, particularly in the years between retirement and the start of Social Security and required minimum distributions. Converting during this low-income window allows filling lower tax brackets that would otherwise go unused, reducing lifetime taxes. Considerations include IRMAA surcharges triggered by conversion income, effects on Social Security taxation, and the modeling required to optimize conversion amounts. Tax-efficient asset location places high-growth investments in Roth accounts, income-generating investments in tax-deferred accounts, and tax-advantaged investments in taxable accounts.

Finding structure and purpose is the central psychological task of retirement. Work provides structure, identity, social connection, purpose, and challenge. Those who thrive in retirement have cultivated interests, relationships, and identity outside of work. Structure must be actively created; identity shifts from role to self; social connections require active maintenance; purpose comes from contribution in whatever form resonates. The transition often involves grief for what is lost, which benefits from acknowledgment.

Practical dimensions include healthcare coverage (especially before Medicare at 65), Social Security claiming decisions, employer benefit transitions, estate planning review, and insurance adjustments. The retirement budget differs from working life, with some expenses disappearing and others increasing.

A comprehensive readiness assessment covers financial sufficiency, timing, investment positioning, purpose and structure, practical logistics, and relationship alignment. Gaps in any dimension warrant attention before retirement. The transition itself involves acknowledging the passage, allowing gradual adjustment, and building the new life through trial and refinement.

Retirement, done well, is a beginning rather than an ending—a phase with its own possibilities, challenges, and sources of meaning. The work of the approaching years is to ensure readiness across all dimensions, so that when the moment comes, you are prepared to begin.

# TWENTY-THREE
# LEGACY AND LETTING GO

There comes a point, perhaps gradually, perhaps suddenly, when the orientation of financial life shifts. The accumulation that defined decades gives way to a different set of questions. Not how much can I build, but what will happen to what I have built. Not how do I provide for myself, but how do I provide for others, or for purposes beyond myself. Not what do I want, but what do I want to leave behind.

This shift is not only about money. It is about meaning. The assets accumulated over a lifetime are the tangible residue of work, discipline, luck, and time. What happens to them after death is a question that touches on relationships, values, and the kind of person one has been and wishes to be remembered as. The planning that addresses this question—estate planning, in its technical dimension—is ultimately planning for how a life's work will echo beyond that life.

But legacy is larger than estate planning. It includes the intangible transmissions: the values taught to children, the example set for others, the wisdom shared, the institutions supported, the lives touched. Money is only one medium of legacy, and perhaps not the most important one. The question of what you want your relationship with money to have meant, when the relationship is ending, encompasses both the material and the immaterial, the legal and the personal.

This chapter addresses these intertwined concerns. The practical matters of estate planning provide the foundation, because neglecting them creates problems for those left behind. The questions of inheritance—how much, to whom, under what conditions—are both practical and deeply personal. Charitable giving offers a way to extend values beyond death. The non-material legacy of financial wisdom may matter more than the material inheritance. And the final question—what you want your relationship with money to have meant—invites reflection on the whole of a financial life.

**Estate Planning Basics**

Estate planning is the arrangement of one's affairs so that, at death or incapacity, assets pass as intended and loved ones are protected. It is fundamentally an act of care for others, even though it is often avoided because it requires contemplating one's own mortality. The person who dies without an estate plan leaves behind not just grief but confusion, conflict, expense, and the imposition of default rules that may not match their wishes.

The core documents of estate planning are few but essential. A will directs the distribution of assets at death and names an executor to manage the process. A trust may supplement or replace the will, providing benefits like probate avoidance, privacy, and control over timing and conditions of distribution. Powers of attorney designate someone to make financial decisions if the person becomes incapacitated. Healthcare directives, including a healthcare power of attorney and living will, designate someone to make medical decisions and express wishes about end-of-life care.

Without a will, state intestacy laws determine who inherits, following a formula based on family relationships. These defaults may not match wishes: the unmarried partner receives nothing; the estranged relative inherits equally with the beloved one; the cherished charity gets nothing. The process of intestate administration is often more expensive and time-consuming than it would be with a will. Creating a will is the minimum act of responsibility toward those who will survive.

A will, however, has limitations. It is a public document, accessible to anyone who cares to look. It goes through probate, a court-supervised process that takes time and costs money. It takes effect only at death, providing no protection during lifetime incapacity. It controls only assets that are titled in the individual's name; assets with beneficiary designations or joint ownership pass outside the will. For many people, particularly those with significant assets, complex family situations, or desire for privacy, a trust offers advantages.

A revocable living trust is created during lifetime and can be modified or revoked at any time. Assets are transferred into the trust, which the creator typically controls as trustee during life. At death, the trust becomes irrevocable, and assets pass according to its terms, without probate and without public record. The trust can include provisions for management during incapacity, control over timing and conditions of distribution, and multi-generational planning. The complexity and cost of establishing and funding a trust are greater than a simple will, but the benefits often justify them.

Beneficiary designations on retirement accounts, life insurance, and sometimes other accounts pass assets directly to named beneficiaries, outside the probate process and regardless of what the will says. These designations are powerful and convenient but also dangerous if neglected. The ex-spouse who was never removed as beneficiary inherits the retirement account. The deceased child who was never replaced leaves assets to their estate, complicating distribution. The contingent beneficiary who was never named leaves assets without clear direction if the primary beneficiary predeceases. Reviewing and updating beneficiary designations is a simple but essential task.

Joint ownership with right of survivorship passes assets directly to the surviving owner, outside probate. This is convenient for spouses and may be appropriate in other situations, but it creates risks if used carelessly. The joint owner has immediate access to the asset and could misuse it. Adding a joint owner is a gift that may trigger gift tax. The joint owner's creditors may be able to reach the asset. Joint ownership is a tool with uses but also with dangers.

Powers of attorney for financial matters designate someone to act on your behalf if you become unable to manage your own affairs. Without this document, if you become incapacitated, your family may need to seek court appointment as guardian or conservator—an expensive, time-consuming, and public process—before they can pay your bills, manage your investments, or handle your financial affairs. The power of attorney should be durable, meaning it remains effective even after incapacity, and should be carefully drawn to include the necessary powers while including appropriate safeguards.

Healthcare directives address what happens if you cannot make your own medical decisions. The healthcare power of attorney designates someone to make decisions on your behalf. The living will expresses wishes about life-sustaining treatment and end-of-life care. These documents relieve loved ones of the burden of guessing what you would want and prevent conflict among family members with different views. They also ensure that your values, not others' assumptions, guide the decisions.

Estate taxes affect only a small fraction of estates, given current exemption levels, but this could change with future legislation. The federal estate tax exemption as of this writing exceeds thirteen million dollars per person, with portability allowing spouses to combine their exemptions. Estates below the exemption owe no federal estate tax. Some states have their own estate or inheritance taxes with lower thresholds. For estates that exceed applicable thresholds, planning to minimize taxes is appropriate; for those below, the focus should be on other goals.

The estate planning process typically involves working with an attorney who specializes in this area. The attorney drafts the documents, ensures they comply with state law, and advises on structuring to achieve goals. The cost is typically modest relative to the value of most estates, and the consequences of poor or absent planning can be substantial. This is not a domain for pure do-it-yourself approaches, except for the simplest situations.

Once created, estate planning documents require maintenance. Life changes—marriage, divorce, birth of children or grandchildren, death of beneficiaries, significant changes in assets, moves to different states—may require updates. Beneficiary designations should be reviewed periodically. The people named as executors, trustees, and agents should still be appropriate and willing to serve. Estate planning is not a one-time event but an ongoing responsibility.

The conversation about estate planning with those who will be affected by it—particularly the executor or trustee who will be asked to serve—is important. The person who will administer the estate should know they have been named and should understand your wishes. The location of documents and important information should be communicated. Surprises in estate planning—discovering after death that you have been named executor, or that the will contains unexpected provisions—create difficulty for the living.

A legacy letter or ethical will, though not a legal document, can supplement formal estate planning. This is a letter to loved ones expressing values, hopes, life lessons, and the meaning behind bequests. It provides context that legal documents cannot. It is the personal message that persists beyond death. Many people find writing this letter to be a meaningful exercise in reflecting on their lives and what they want to transmit.

### The Role of Professional Advisors

Estate planning and legacy decisions rarely happen in isolation. They intersect with investment management, tax planning, insurance, and the full range of financial concerns. For many people, particularly those with significant assets or complex situations, working with professional advisors becomes important during this phase of life—and may have been important throughout.

The financial advisory landscape can be confusing. Titles proliferate—financial advisor, financial planner, wealth manager, investment advisor, broker—and the distinctions among them are not always clear. Understanding these distinctions matters because the obligations advisors owe to clients differ significantly.

The most important distinction is between fiduciary and non-fiduciary advisors. A fiduciary is legally obligated to act in the client's best interest, to disclose conflicts of interest, and to put the client's interests ahead of their own. Registered Investment Advisors (RIAs), who are regulated by the SEC or state regulators, owe a fiduciary duty to their clients. In contrast, broker-dealers and their registered representatives have traditionally been held to a lower "suitability" standard, requiring only that recommendations be suitable for the client, not necessarily in the client's best interest. Recent regulations have narrowed this gap somewhat, but the distinction remains meaningful. When choosing an advisor, understanding what standard of care they owe is essential.

Compensation models also vary and create different incentive structures. Fee-only advisors are compensated solely by fees paid by clients, typically as a percentage of assets under management, a flat fee, or an hourly rate. They do not receive commissions from selling products, which removes one source of conflict. Fee-based advisors receive both fees and commissions, creating a hybrid model with potential conflicts. Commission-based advisors are compensated primarily through commissions on products sold, which creates incentives to sell products that generate higher commissions regardless of client suitability. Understanding how an advisor is compensated illuminates whose interests they are structured to serve.

The value that good financial advisors provide extends beyond investment selection, where their value is often overstated. The evidence on whether advisors add value through investment outperformance is mixed at best; after fees, many clients would do as well or better with simple index fund portfolios they could construct themselves. Where advisors add clear value is in the domains that require human judgment, coordination, and behavioral coaching.

Behavioral coaching may be the most valuable service advisors provide. The advisor who prevents a client from panic-selling during a market crash, or from chasing performance into overvalued assets, or from making other emotionally-driven errors, can add returns far exceeding their fees. This is not about intelligence; highly intelligent people make behavioral mistakes with money. It is about having a trusted voice who provides perspective when emotions run high.

Comprehensive financial planning is another domain of value. The good financial planner helps clients think through goals, creates integrated plans addressing retirement, taxes, estate, insurance, and other domains, and coordinates these elements. The plan itself has value; the discipline of creating it forces clarity about priorities and trade-offs. The ongoing relationship has value; the planner who knows a client's full situation can spot opportunities and risks that the client might miss.

Tax planning often generates concrete, measurable value. Strategies like tax-loss harvesting, Roth conversion optimization, asset location across account types, and timing of income and deductions can save amounts that exceed advisory fees. This is particularly true for higher-income clients and those with complex situations.

Estate planning coordination, while the legal documents are drafted by attorneys, benefits from financial advisor involvement. The advisor who understands both the client's financial situation and their family dynamics can help think through inheritance decisions, charitable giving strategies, and the integration of estate plans with lifetime financial plans. The advisor serves as a coordinator among the attorney, accountant, and insurance professionals who may all be involved.

For those approaching the legacy phase of life, advisors can facilitate difficult conversations. The advisor who has built trust over years can help initiate discussions about inheritance, about values around money, about preparations for incapacity or death. These conversations are easier with a trusted professional facilitating than as purely family discussions.

The decision about whether to use an advisor, and what type, depends on individual circumstances. Those with simple situations, the discipline to maintain a sensible investment approach, and the time and interest to manage their own finances may not need ongoing advisory relationships. Those with complex situations, limited time or interest, behavioral tendencies that lead to poor decisions, or the desire for professional guidance often benefit from working with advisors.

If you choose to work with an advisor, several principles apply. Seek a fiduciary who is legally obligated to act in your interest. Understand and evaluate the fee structure; fees compound over time and can significantly impact wealth. Look for advisors with relevant credentials such as the CFP (Certified Financial Planner) designation, which requires education, examination, and ethical commitments. Verify credentials through FINRA BrokerCheck or the SEC's Investment Adviser Public Disclosure database. Be wary of advisors who recommend complex or proprietary products that you do not understand. Trust your instincts about whether the relationship feels right; you will be sharing intimate financial details and need to feel comfortable.

The relationship with a financial advisor, when it works well, is a long-term partnership. The advisor comes to understand not just the numbers but the person—the values, fears, hopes, and family dynamics that shape financial decisions. This understanding allows advice that is truly personalized rather than generic. Finding such an advisor, and maintaining the relationship over time, is an investment that can pay dividends throughout financial life and particularly in its later stages.

### The Question of Inheritance

How much to leave to children, and under what conditions, is among the most personal decisions in estate planning. There is no single right answer, and the range of reasonable choices is wide. The question touches on views about money, about parenting, about fairness, about what helps and what harms.

The case for leaving substantial inheritance rests on the desire to provide for children's security and opportunity. The parent who has built wealth may want to share that wealth with children, giving them options and resources that the parent did not have. The inheritance may fund education for grandchildren, support during difficult times, the ability to pursue meaningful work rather than merely lucrative work. The parent who faced financial struggle may especially want to spare children that struggle.

The case for limiting inheritance rests on concerns about what wealth does to recipients who did not earn it. Substantial inheritance may remove the motivation to develop skills and work ethic. It may create entitled adults who lack resilience and purpose. It may attract problematic relationships and encourage poor decisions. The person who built wealth through effort may recognize that effort itself was valuable, and may worry that shielding children from the need for effort harms them. Warren Buffett's formulation—enough to do anything but not enough to do nothing—captures this concern.

The question of fairness among children is often fraught. Equal division is simple and avoids the message that some children are valued more than others. But equal division may not be equitable if children have different needs, different resources, or different relationships. The child with disabilities may need more. The child who provided care during illness may deserve recognition. The child who received substantial support during life may have already received their share. The child who is estranged may raise questions about whether inheritance should be automatic.

Unequal division requires careful thought. It may be appropriate, but it carries risks. It may create or deepen conflict among siblings. It may be experienced as a final judgment on relative worth. It may cause lasting harm to relationships. If unequal division is chosen, the reasons should probably be communicated during life, so that the will does not deliver a surprise that cannot be discussed.

The timing and conditions of inheritance are as important as the amount. Leaving assets outright and immediately gives recipients maximum control but also maximum risk. The young adult who inherits a large sum may not have the maturity to manage it. The middle-aged child with a spending problem or substance abuse issue may be harmed more than helped. The child in a troubled marriage may see the inheritance become part of a divorce settlement.

Trusts can address these concerns by imposing structure on inheritance. A trust might distribute income but not principal, protecting the principal while providing support. A trust might distribute at specified ages—a portion at 25, more at 30, the remainder at 35—allowing recipients to mature before receiving full control. A trust might include incentive provisions, distributing more to those who earn income, pursue education, or engage in charitable work. A trust might give a trustee discretion to distribute based on needs and circumstances, providing flexibility without giving the beneficiary outright control.

These structures are not without cost. They require ongoing administration and the expense of a trustee. They limit recipients' autonomy. They may feel controlling or paternalistic. They reflect the judgment that the creator knows better than the beneficiary how the money should be used. Whether these costs are justified depends on the beneficiaries, the amounts involved, and the creator's values.

The question of whether to tell children about their expected inheritance, and how much to share, is also personal. Some parents prefer transparency, believing that children should be able to plan and that surprises are unfair. Some parents prefer privacy, believing that knowledge of expected inheritance may distort children's motivation and behavior. Some share general information without specific amounts. The right approach depends on the family, the children, and the amounts involved.

When one parent survives the other, the question of how to handle the deceased spouse's wishes adds complexity. Particularly in second marriages with children from prior relationships, the surviving spouse's interests may conflict with the deceased spouse's wishes for their children. Trusts can structure this, providing for the surviving spouse while ultimately passing assets to the deceased spouse's intended beneficiaries. But these structures require advance planning and clear documentation.

Special situations require special planning. Children with disabilities may need trusts structured to provide support without disqualifying them from government benefits. Children with addiction or mental health issues may need protective structures and appropriate fiduciaries. Children who are themselves elderly may need planning that considers their own estate situation. Blended families may need careful attention to whose assets pass to whose children.

The conversation with children about inheritance, if it happens, is an opportunity for broader conversation about money, values, and family. It can be an opening to discuss the family's financial history, the values that guided wealth building, the hopes for how wealth will be used. It can be a chance to hear children's perspectives and concerns. These conversations are often more valuable than the dollars that will eventually pass.

Beyond children, the question of who else deserves inclusion in the estate plan arises. Grandchildren may receive direct bequests or trusts. Other relatives who have been close or who have needs may be included. Friends who have been like family may be remembered. Caregivers who have provided devoted service may receive recognition. The estate plan is an opportunity to acknowledge all the relationships that have mattered.

### Charitable Giving as Legacy

For some, leaving assets to charity is as important as, or more important than, leaving assets to family. Charitable giving is a way to extend values beyond death, to support causes and institutions that matter, to make a lasting difference. It may also reflect a judgment that heirs have enough, or that wealth should return to the community rather than creating dynasty.

The motivations for charitable giving are various. Religious traditions that emphasize stewardship and tithing may shape giving. Gratitude for benefits received—education, healthcare, community support

—may motivate gifts to the institutions that provided them. Passion for particular causes—environmental protection, medical research, arts, poverty alleviation—may direct giving. The simple desire to do good with resources that can no longer be personally used may be sufficient.

Charitable giving during life allows the giver to see the impact, to be involved in the work, to build relationships with the organizations supported. It provides tax benefits that reduce the cost of giving. It establishes a habit and identity of generosity. For many, lifetime giving is more satisfying than waiting until death.

Charitable giving at death, through bequests, extends the legacy beyond what was given during life. A bequest may be a specific amount, a percentage of the estate, or the residue after other bequests. It may be unrestricted, allowing the charity to use funds as needed, or restricted to specific purposes. Large bequests may fund endowments that support the charity perpetually, create named funds or facilities, or launch new initiatives.

Donor-advised funds offer a hybrid approach. Contributions during life receive immediate tax benefits, but distributions to charities can be made over time, during life or after death. The fund can continue after death, with successors directing distributions according to the donor's wishes or values. This provides flexibility and family involvement in giving.

Private foundations offer another vehicle for those with substantial wealth and desire for control. A foundation can be structured to continue indefinitely, managed by family members across generations. It can pursue a focused mission, employ staff, and make grants with donor oversight. The administrative and compliance requirements are significant, making foundations appropriate only for substantial giving programs.

Charitable trusts can combine giving with other goals. A charitable remainder trust provides income to the donor or other beneficiaries for life, with the remainder passing to charity; it provides income tax benefits at creation and removes assets from the estate. A charitable lead trust provides income to charity for a period, with the remainder passing to heirs; it can reduce gift and estate taxes for transfers to heirs. These vehicles are complex but powerful for those with significant assets and charitable intent.

The choice of which charities to support deserves the same thoughtfulness as other financial decisions. Not all charities are equally effective. Due diligence about organizational effectiveness, financial management, and alignment with values is appropriate. Resources like charity rating organizations can inform these decisions. For significant gifts, conversations with charity leadership about how funds will be used can ensure alignment.

For those who wish to support charity but also provide for family, a common approach is to fund charitable bequests with retirement account assets, which would be fully taxable if left to non-spousal heirs but pass tax-free to charity. Family receives other assets with more favorable tax treatment. This coordination can increase the total value delivered to intended recipients.

The decision about how much to leave to charity versus family is deeply personal. Some feel the primary obligation is to family, with charity receiving what remains. Some feel that family has enough and that marginal dollars do more good through charity. Some balance the two according to formulas or feelings. There is no objectively correct answer, only the answer that reflects the individual's values and circumstances.

Charitable giving can also be a family activity, engaging children and grandchildren in philanthropic decisions. Family foundations, donor-advised funds with successor advisors, or simply family discussions about giving can transmit values of generosity across generations. The act of giving together may be as important as the money given.

### The Non-Material Legacy of Financial Wisdom

The inheritance of assets is the obvious legacy, but it may not be the most important one. The transmission of financial wisdom—the values, habits, knowledge, and attitudes that lead to financial well-being—may matter more than the transmission of dollars.

Consider the counterfactual. The child who inherits substantial assets but lacks financial wisdom may squander the inheritance, ending up worse off than if they had received less and learned more. The child who inherits modest assets but has absorbed wisdom may build security and pass that security to the next generation. The intangible inheritance of wisdom compounds across generations in ways that assets alone cannot.

What does this wisdom include? It includes the habits addressed earlier in this book: living within means, saving consistently, investing patiently, avoiding destructive behaviors with money. It includes the knowledge: how compound interest works, how investing works, how to avoid fraud and folly. It includes the attitudes: seeing money as a tool rather than an end, neither fearing it nor worshiping it, understanding its proper place in a life.

This wisdom is transmitted primarily through example. Children who grow up watching parents make sound financial decisions absorb those patterns. Children who see parents avoid debt, save regularly, discuss financial choices openly, and maintain perspective on money's role learn these behaviors without formal instruction. The lived example is more powerful than any lecture.

The wisdom is also transmitted through conversation. Talking with children about money, in age-appropriate ways, shares knowledge and invites engagement. Explaining why certain choices are made, discussing financial news and its implications, involving children in family financial decisions as they mature—these conversations normalize financial competence and transmit values.

Formal financial education supplements example and conversation. Ensuring children understand basic financial concepts, either through school, structured programs, or parental teaching, provides the knowledge base. But knowledge alone is insufficient without the habits and attitudes that make knowledge useful.

Allowing children to make financial decisions and experience consequences builds capability. The allowance that must be budgeted, the part-time job that provides spending money, the contribution to a desired purchase—these experiences develop financial muscles. Mistakes made with small stakes teach lessons that prevent mistakes with large stakes.

For adult children, the transmission of financial wisdom takes different forms. Conversations about financial planning, sharing the reasoning behind estate plans, discussing the challenges and choices of financial life—these can all transmit wisdom. The adult child who understands why a parent made certain choices is better equipped to make their own.

The experience of serving as executor or trustee, or of being involved in a parent's financial affairs during illness or aging, teaches through direct experience. This involvement, when handled as an opportunity to learn rather than merely a burden to bear, transmits practical wisdom about financial management.

The legacy of financial wisdom extends beyond direct descendants. Mentoring others—young colleagues, community members, those who lack the advantages of financial education—extends the ripple of wisdom. Teaching, writing, volunteering in financial literacy programs—all transmit wisdom beyond the family circle.

The non-material legacy also includes the example of generosity. Children who see parents give—to family in need, to community, to charity—absorb generosity as a value. The inheritance of generous spirit may shape beneficiaries more than the inheritance of assets.

And the legacy includes the example of perspective—money as servant rather than master, means rather than end, tool rather than identity. Children who see parents maintain this perspective, who witness lives well-lived with money in its proper place, inherit something invaluable.

### What You Want Your Relationship with Money to Have Meant

This book has been about money, but it has not really been about money. It has been about life—how to live well in a world where money matters, how to make money serve rather than dominate, how to build security without becoming enslaved to accumulation, how to be generous without being foolish, how to navigate the practical demands of financial life while keeping sight of what actually matters.

The final question is not about dollars or strategies or plans. It is about meaning. When you look back on your financial life, what do you want it to have meant?

For some, the answer centers on security. I want to have provided for myself and my family, to have been neither a burden nor a source of burden. I want to have met obligations, kept commitments, maintained independence. The meaning of money, in this framing, is the peace of mind that comes from having enough and not worrying.

For some, the answer centers on generosity. I want to have given freely—to family, to friends, to causes I believe in. I want my wealth to have done good in the world, not merely accumulated in accounts. The meaning of money, in this framing, is the good it enables for others.

For some, the answer centers on freedom. I want money to have freed me—to pursue work I love, to spend time with people I love, to say no to what I don't want and yes to what I do. The meaning of money, in this framing, is the liberation it provides from constraint.

For some, the answer centers on example. I want to have shown others, especially my children, how to relate to money well. I want to have modeled responsibility, restraint, and generosity. The meaning of money, in this framing, is the wisdom transmitted through living example.

For some, the answer centers on accomplishment. I want to have built something—a business, a portfolio, a legacy that reflects what I was capable of. The accumulation itself, the discipline and skill it required, has meaning independent of what the money provides.

For most, the answer combines these elements in some proportion. Security and generosity. Freedom and example. Accomplishment and service. The specific combination reflects individual values and circumstances.

What unites these framings is the recognition that money is instrumental, not ultimate. It is valuable for what it enables, what it represents, what it makes possible—not for its own sake. The person who treats money as ultimate has lost perspective. The person who ignores money has lost practicality. The wise relationship with money holds it in its proper place: important but not supreme, requiring attention but not obsession, a tool to be used rather than a master to be served.

The approach of death concentrates these questions. What has my relationship with money meant? What do I want it to mean to those who survive me? What wisdom have I learned that is worth transmitting? What regrets do I have, and what satisfactions?

For some, this reflection will surface regrets. The sacrifice of health or relationships for earning. The failure to give when giving was possible. The anxiety and grasping that poisoned years. The mistakes that cannot be corrected. These regrets deserve acknowledgment without wallowing. They may inform how the remaining time is spent, or how wisdom is transmitted to others.

For many, this reflection will surface satisfaction. The security built through discipline. The family provided for and protected. The generosity that made a difference. The freedom purchased through prudent choices. The wisdom gained and shared. This satisfaction deserves to be felt without complacency.

For all, this reflection can inform legacy. The estate plan that reflects values. The conversations with heirs that transmit wisdom. The charitable giving that extends meaning. The example that continues to teach after death. The relationship with money, at its end, becomes the legacy of that relationship for others.

**Letting Go**

There is a final dimension to legacy that goes beyond planning and transmission. It is letting go.

Letting go of control over assets that will pass to others, trusting that they will be used well or accepting that they may not be. The trust that includes provisions and conditions reflects a desire to control from beyond death. Such control may be wise in some circumstances, but it also reflects difficulty with letting go. The simpler bequest—here is what I have built, it is now yours, do with it what you will—requires more trust and more acceptance.

Letting go of worry about whether there is enough. The approach of death reveals that the question of enough was never about the number but about the anxiety. At some point, whether there was enough is decided; further worry serves nothing. The wisdom is to reach that letting go while there is still time to enjoy the release.

Letting go of identity bound up with wealth. For some, net worth has become confused with self-worth. The approach of death clarifies that these are different. What remains when the assets pass to others? What is the self that is not defined by the account balances? Discovering this before death allows life rather than death to answer the question.

Letting go of the future, which will unfold without us. The estate plan attempts to shape the future, but the future will not be controlled. The heirs will make their own choices. The charities will pursue their own directions. The institutions will evolve. The world will change in ways we cannot anticipate. Letting go means accepting this, making the best plans we can while recognizing their limits.

Letting go is not resignation or passivity. It is the active acceptance that completes a life well-lived. The person who cannot let go clings to control that was always illusory. The person who lets go too easily fails to engage with the real choices that remain. The wisdom is in the balance: doing what can be done, accepting what cannot be changed, knowing the difference.

**A Financial Life**

A financial life spans decades, from the first earned dollar to the last. It includes the building years and the spending years, the working years and the retirement years, the accumulation and the distribution. It includes mistakes and corrections, anxieties and satisfactions, learning and teaching. It is a thread woven through the whole of life.

This book has traced that thread from beginning to end. The early chapters addressed the psychology and philosophy that underlie all financial behavior. The middle chapters addressed the practical matters of earning, saving, investing, and protecting. The later chapters addressed the lifecycle of financial decisions, from early adulthood through retirement. This final chapter addresses legacy and letting go—how the financial life ends and what it leaves behind.

The hope is that readers, wherever they are in their own financial lives, have found something useful. For the young, perhaps a framework for thinking about money that will serve for decades. For those in mid-career, perhaps insights into the mistakes that are avoidable and the opportunities that remain. For those approaching retirement, perhaps practical guidance for the transition. For those at the end, perhaps wisdom about legacy and meaning.

Money is not the most important thing in life. Relationships, health, purpose, love, meaning—these matter more. But money is not unimportant either. It is the medium through which we meet material needs and pursue many goals. It is a tool that, used wisely, enables much of what matters. It is a test of values and discipline, revealing who we are by how we handle it.

The goal of a financial life is not to accumulate the most. It is to have enough—enough for security, enough for freedom, enough for generosity—and to hold that enough with wisdom and perspective. It is to let money serve rather than dominate. It is to build a life in which money plays its proper role, important but not supreme.

And at the end, the goal is to let go. To pass on what was built, in assets and in wisdom. To trust those who come after. To accept that control always had limits. To find meaning not in the number that remains but in how it was built, how it was used, and what it enabled.

This is a financial life, well-lived.

. . .

## SUMMARY

As life shifts from accumulation to legacy, the central questions change from building wealth to determining what will happen to it. Legacy encompasses both the material—estate planning and inheritance—and the immaterial—values, wisdom, and example. The planning for this phase is ultimately about how a life's work will echo beyond that life.

Estate planning is fundamentally an act of care for others. The core documents include wills, trusts, powers of attorney, and healthcare directives. Without a will, state intestacy laws impose defaults that may not match wishes. Revocable living trusts offer advantages including probate avoidance, privacy, and control over distribution timing. Beneficiary designations on retirement accounts and insurance pass assets outside probate but require regular review. Powers of attorney prevent the need for costly guardianship proceedings if incapacity occurs. Healthcare directives ensure medical decisions reflect personal values rather than others' assumptions. A legacy letter or ethical will, though not legally binding, provides personal context that legal documents cannot.

Professional advisors often play an important role in legacy planning. The key distinction among advisors is between fiduciaries, who are legally obligated to act in clients' best interests, and those held to lower standards. Fee structures—fee-only, fee-based, or commission-based—create different incentive structures. Where good advisors add value is less in investment selection than in behavioral coaching, comprehensive planning, tax optimization, and facilitating difficult family conversations. Those with complex situations or behavioral tendencies that lead to poor decisions often benefit from advisory relationships, while those with simpler situations and strong financial discipline may not need ongoing professional guidance.

Inheritance decisions are deeply personal, touching on views about money, parenting, and fairness. The case for substantial inheritance emphasizes security and opportunity for children; the case for limiting inheritance emphasizes concerns about motivation and character development. Equal division among children is simple but may not be equitable given different needs and circumstances. Unequal division carries risks of family conflict and should probably be explained during life. Trusts can impose structure—distributing at specified ages, including incentive provisions, or giving trustees discretion—but at the cost of ongoing administration and limitations on recipient autonomy.

Charitable giving extends values beyond death. It may be motivated by religious stewardship, gratitude for benefits received, passion for causes, or simply the desire to do good. Lifetime giving allows the giver to see impact and build relationships with organizations. Charitable bequests, donor-advised funds, private foundations, and charitable trusts offer different vehicles with varying levels of control, complexity, and tax benefits. Coordinating charitable and family bequests—for example, funding charitable gifts with retirement account assets that would be fully taxable to non-spousal heirs—can maximize the total value delivered to intended recipients.

The non-material legacy of financial wisdom may matter more than the material inheritance. This wisdom includes habits of living within means, saving, and investing patiently; knowledge of how money works; and attitudes that treat money as tool rather than end. Transmission occurs primarily through example, supplemented by conversation and formal education. Allowing children to make financial decisions and experience consequences builds capability. The legacy also includes the example of generosity and of keeping money in proper perspective.

The final question is what you want your relationship with money to have meant. The answer may center on security, generosity, freedom, example, or accomplishment—or some combination. What unites these framings is recognizing that money is instrumental, not ultimate, valuable for what it enables rather than for its own sake. Reflection on this question may surface regrets that inform remaining time, or satisfactions that deserve to be felt.

Letting go is the final dimension of legacy. This means letting go of control over assets that will pass to others, of worry about whether there is enough, of identity bound up with wealth, and of the future that will unfold without us. Letting go is not resignation but active acceptance—doing what can be done while accepting what cannot be changed. The goal at the end is to pass on what was built, in assets and wisdom, to trust those who come after, and to find meaning not in the number that remains but in how it was built, used, and what it enabled. This is a financial life, well-lived.

# PART 7

# THE LARGER CONTEXT

*Money, society, and meaning*

## TWENTY-FOUR
# INEQUALITY AND RESPONSIBILITY

A book about personal finance necessarily focuses on individual choices: how to save, how to invest, how to build security within the circumstances one faces. This focus is appropriate because individual choices matter and because they are what individuals can control. But a book that addresses only individual choices, without acknowledging the broader context in which those choices are made, would be incomplete.

That context includes economic inequality—the vast differences in wealth and income that exist within societies, particularly within the United States. Some people begin life with every advantage: wealth, education, connections, stable families, safe neighborhoods, good health. Others begin with few or none of these. The financial paths available to these different starting points are not the same. The advice that makes sense for someone with a trust fund and an Ivy League degree may be irrelevant or even cruel when offered to someone working two minimum-wage jobs while caring for a sick parent.

This chapter addresses what the previous chapters largely bracketed: the structural conditions that shape financial outcomes, the debate over how to understand inequality, and the relationship between individual financial success and broader social conditions. It does not offer policy prescriptions—that is beyond this book's scope—but it invites reflection on questions that personal finance literature too often ignores.

The goal is neither to induce guilt in those who have done well nor to provide excuses for those who have not. It is to see more clearly: to understand the interplay between structure and agency, between luck and effort, between individual stories and aggregate patterns. This clearer seeing may inform both how we pursue our own financial lives and how we think about our responsibilities to others.

**Economic Inequality: The Data**

The facts of economic inequality are not seriously disputed, though their interpretation is. In the United States, wealth and income are distributed with extreme unevenness, and this unevenness has increased substantially over the past half-century.

The top one percent of households by wealth hold approximately one-third of all wealth in the country. The top ten percent hold roughly two-thirds. The bottom half of households hold approximately two percent of total wealth. These are not abstractions; they describe a world in which some families have resources measured in hundreds of millions while others have negative net worth, owing more than they own.

Income inequality, while less extreme than wealth inequality, is still pronounced. The top one percent of earners receive roughly twenty percent of all income. The ratio of CEO compensation to typical worker pay, which was around thirty to one in the 1970s, now exceeds three hundred to one at large companies. Wages for workers without college degrees have stagnated in real terms for decades, while compensation at the top has grown dramatically.

These disparities have widened over time. In the decades following World War II, economic growth was broadly shared, with incomes across the distribution rising at similar rates. Beginning in the late 1970s and accelerating since, the pattern changed. Growth increasingly accrued to those at the top, while those in the middle and bottom saw much slower gains or none at all. The economic experience of different segments of the population diverged.

Social mobility—the likelihood that someone born into a poor family will rise to higher economic status—has declined. Children born in 1940 had a ninety percent chance of earning more than their parents in real terms. Children born in 1980 had a fifty percent chance. The expectation that each generation will do better than the last, long central to American self-understanding, has become less reliable.

These patterns are not unique to the United States, but they are more pronounced here than in most other wealthy nations. The United States has higher inequality and lower social mobility than most European countries, Canada, or Australia. The American dream of rags to riches, while not mythical, is statistically less common in America than in countries with smaller gaps between rich and poor.

Inequality varies significantly across demographic lines. Median wealth for white families is approximately eight times that of Black families and five times that of Hispanic families. These gaps persist even when controlling for education and income. They reflect centuries of history—slavery, segregation, discriminatory housing and lending practices, unequal access to education and employment—whose effects compound across generations.

Gender gaps in income and wealth, while narrowing, persist. Women earn less than men in most occupations, and the gap widens for women of color. Caregiving responsibilities fall disproportionately on women, affecting earnings and wealth accumulation. Single mothers face particularly challenging financial circumstances.

Geographic inequality has also grown. Prosperous metropolitan areas with knowledge-economy jobs have pulled away from regions dependent on manufacturing or extraction. The cost of living in places with the best opportunities—housing above all—has risen faster than incomes, limiting access to those opportunities. Where you live increasingly determines what opportunities are available.

These data describe the landscape in which individual financial lives unfold. They do not determine any individual outcome, but they shape the probabilities. The person born into the bottom quintile faces a statistical headwind; the person born into the top quintile enjoys a tailwind. Individual effort and choice matter enormously, but they operate within conditions that vary dramatically.

**What Inequality Feels Like**

Statistics describe patterns across populations. They do not capture what it feels like to live at different points in the distribution. But that lived experience shapes financial behavior in ways that matter for understanding personal finance.

Financial precarity has a distinctive phenomenology. When money is scarce and unpredictable, the present dominates consciousness. The bill that is due, the expense that cannot be met, the crisis that might happen—these occupy mental space that might otherwise go to planning and longer-term thinking. Research on scarcity suggests that financial stress consumes cognitive bandwidth, reducing the capacity for careful decision-making precisely when such decisions matter most. The person who makes a poor financial choice under conditions of scarcity is not simply less disciplined than the person with margin; they are operating with fewer cognitive resources available for the decision.

Time itself feels different under financial stress. The advice to "invest for the long term" presupposes a relationship to the future that precarity undermines. When survival is uncertain, the future becomes abstract, less real, less motivating. The trade-off between present and future consumption, which economic theory treats as a matter of preference, is partly a matter of how real the future feels—and that depends on circumstances.

Precarity also forecloses options. The person without savings cannot take the unpaid internship that leads to the good job, cannot move to the city with better opportunities, cannot weather the period of unemployment while searching for the right position, cannot take the entrepreneurial risk. What looks like a choice not to pursue opportunity may be the absence of the conditions that make pursuit possible. The path not taken may have been closed, not merely unchosen.

By contrast, financial security creates psychological conditions that favor good financial decisions. The person with margin can think about the long term because the short term is handled. They can take calculated risks because failure would not be catastrophic. They can delay gratification because they are not constantly reminded of what they lack. The cognitive bandwidth that precarity consumes is available for planning, learning, and careful choice.

This is not to say that the wealthy automatically make good financial decisions—this book has catalogued the many ways they do not—but rather that they make decisions under more favorable psychological conditions. The discipline required to save when money is scarce is greater than the discipline required when money is abundant. The person who saves from a low income deserves more credit, not less, than the person who saves from a high one.

Understanding this changes how we interpret financial behavior. The person who spends rather than saves, who takes the payday loan, who fails to plan for retirement may not be less rational or disciplined than the person who does these things well. They may be facing conditions—external and internal, material and psychological—that make these behaviors harder. This does not eliminate the importance of choice, but it contextualizes it.

### Intergenerational Transmission

Inequality persists across generations. The children of wealthy parents are likely to be wealthy; the children of poor parents are likely to be poor. This pattern holds even in societies with formal equality of opportunity, suggesting that something beyond legal barriers is at work.

The transmission of advantage operates through multiple channels. The most obvious is inheritance of assets—the wealth passed from parents to children at death or during life. But this is far from the only channel and may not be the most important.

Parents transmit financial knowledge and habits. Children who grow up in households where budgeting, saving, and investing are practiced and discussed absorb these practices. They learn not just information but dispositions: how to think about money, how to relate to it, what is normal and possible. The previous chapter discussed the non-material legacy of financial wisdom; here we note that this wisdom is unequally distributed. Children of the wealthy inherit not just money but the knowledge of how to manage, preserve, and grow it.

Parents transmit networks. The child who grows up with parents who know people in desirable professions, who can provide introductions and vouch for character, faces a different job market than the child without such connections. Many opportunities are not publicly posted but flow through networks. The person inside those networks has access that the person outside does not.

Parents transmit psychological security. The child who knows that their parents could help in a crisis—who has a safety net, even if never used—approaches risk differently than the child who knows they are on their own. This is not about actual wealth but about the security of knowing it exists. This security allows risk-taking, investment in education, and pursuit of opportunity that might not pay off immediately. The child without this security may be more risk-averse out of necessity, not preference.

Parents transmit cultural capital. The knowledge of how to present oneself, how to navigate institutions, what references to make, how to speak and dress—these vary by class background and affect outcomes in education and employment. The interview in which one candidate seems "polished" and another does not may reflect not inherent quality but learned behaviors that depend on upbringing.

Parents transmit beliefs about what is possible. Children who grow up seeing adults with successful careers, stable finances, and achieved goals internalize that such things are possible for people like them. Children who grow up seeing struggle and failure may internalize different expectations. These beliefs affect motivation, effort, and persistence.

All of these channels mean that the child of wealthy parents receives not just wealth but the conditions for creating wealth. The child of poor parents may have equal native ability but lacks these conditions. Equal opportunity, in the formal sense of no legal barriers, does not create equal starting positions. The race begins from different points, with different provisions and different knowledge of the course.

This analysis does not mean that individuals cannot overcome their starting points—many do. It does not mean that individual effort is pointless—it is essential. But it does mean that individual outcomes reflect more than individual merit. The child who rises from poverty to wealth through effort and talent has achieved something remarkable. So, in a different way, has the child who merely maintains the wealth inherited—maintaining is harder than it appears. But the paths are not equally difficult, and recognizing this is simply honest.

**The Perspectives**

The facts of inequality are largely agreed upon. The interpretation of those facts is fiercely contested. Understanding the debate clarifies the conceptual landscape without requiring that we resolve questions that remain contested among serious thinkers.

One perspective emphasizes markets, merit, and individual responsibility. In this view, inequality largely reflects differences in talent, effort, and choices. Those who earn more do so because they contribute more value—they have scarce skills, work harder, take more risks, or make better decisions. Those who earn less have made different choices or have less to offer. This is not unjust but simply how markets work: they reward value creation. Attempts to reduce inequality through redistribution distort incentives, reduce overall prosperity, and punish success.

From this perspective, the appropriate response to inequality is to ensure equal opportunity—equal access to education, to markets, to legal protection—while accepting that equal opportunity will produce unequal outcomes. If everyone has a fair chance to compete, the resulting distribution, whatever it is, is legitimate. The focus should be on removing barriers to opportunity and ensuring that success is available to those who earn it.

This perspective has genuine force. Individual choices do matter; they are not merely epiphenomenal reflections of structure. Incentives do matter; policies that punish success or reward failure create perverse effects. Personal responsibility is both morally important and practically necessary; no arrangement of social structures eliminates the need for individuals to make good choices. And some inequality may be necessary and productive, providing motivation for effort and innovation that benefits everyone.

A second perspective emphasizes structures, history, and power. In this view, inequality reflects not simply differences in individual merit but differences in advantages that individuals did not earn: the family they were born into, the neighborhood they grew up in, the schools they attended, the connections they inherited, the race and gender that shaped how they were treated. Those at the top enjoy compounding advantages; those at the bottom face compounding disadvantages. Markets do not operate in a vacuum but within institutional arrangements that favor some and disadvantage others.

From this perspective, equal opportunity is partly illusory. The child who attends underfunded schools, grows up amid violence and instability, lacks connections to opportunity, and faces discrimination does not have the same opportunity as the child who attends excellent schools, grows up in a stable and supportive environment, inherits connections, and faces no discrimination. Formal equality of opportunity—anyone can apply for the job, anyone can take the test—does not equate to substantive equality of opportunity when starting points differ so dramatically.

This perspective too has genuine force. Starting points do differ dramatically, and those differences are not earned. The correlation between parental income and child outcomes demonstrates that something beyond individual merit is at work. Historical injustices—slavery, discrimination, exclusion—have effects that persist across generations. Market outcomes depend on market rules, and those rules are made by political processes that reflect power, not just efficiency.

A third perspective focuses on the effects of inequality itself, whatever its causes. In this view, extreme inequality is problematic not only if it reflects unfairness in how it arose but because of what it does to society. High inequality correlates with worse health outcomes, lower social trust, more crime, less civic participation, and weaker economic growth. It gives the wealthy disproportionate political power, undermining democracy. It segregates people into different worlds, eroding common experience and common purpose. Even if every dollar were earned fairly, a society in which some have yachts while others cannot afford insulin would have problems.

From this perspective, the question is not only how inequality arose but whether we want to live in a society with these levels of inequality. The effects of extreme inequality may be bad enough to justify addressing it regardless of questions about desert and merit.

These perspectives are not mutually exclusive, and most thoughtful people hold some combination of them. Markets and individual choices matter; structures and history matter; the effects of inequality matter. The question is not which one is right but how to weigh them and what follows for policy and for personal conduct.

This book will not resolve these debates. They involve empirical uncertainties, value conflicts, and genuine difficulty. But recognizing that these perspectives exist and that none is obviously foolish helps us think more clearly about our own situations and our responsibilities.

### Structural Barriers and Individual Agency

The tension between structural barriers and individual agency runs through all discussions of inequality and personal finance. Both are real. The question is how to hold them together without collapsing into either fatalism or victim-blaming.

Structural barriers are the obstacles that individuals face not because of their own choices but because of how society is organized. They include the obvious: discrimination based on race, gender, or other characteristics; unequal schools and neighborhoods; lack of access to healthcare; criminal justice system involvement that follows people for life. They include the less obvious: the cultural capital that comes from growing up in educated households; the financial literacy transmitted in families with wealth; the networks that connect people to opportunities.

These barriers are not merely historical. They operate now, affecting people making financial decisions today. The person denied a mortgage because of neighborhood redlining decades ago passes on the consequence—no home equity, no wealth—to the next generation. The person who attended underfunded schools lacks the credentials and skills that open doors. The person with a criminal record, even for minor offenses, faces closed doors in employment and housing. The person without family wealth cannot take unpaid internships or weather unemployment or take entrepreneurial risks.

Acknowledging structural barriers does not mean denying individual agency. Agency is real too. Within any structural context, individuals make choices that affect outcomes. Two people facing identical circumstances may end up in very different places based on their decisions. The person who saves something from a low income builds more security than the one who does not. The person who seeks out opportunities, develops skills, and persists through setbacks improves their chances.

The stories of individuals who have overcome tremendous obstacles through effort and ingenuity are not false or irrelevant. They demonstrate that structure is not destiny, that human agency is powerful, that giving up guarantees failure while effort creates possibility. These stories matter, and the people who live them deserve recognition for what they have achieved.

The error is in treating these stories as proof that anyone could do the same, that structural barriers are merely excuses, that those who remain poor have simply failed to try. This conflates what is possible for some individuals with what is probable for populations. It ignores the role of luck in which individuals' efforts succeed. It places on individuals the full burden for outcomes that are partly beyond their control.

A more balanced view recognizes that structure and agency interact. Structure shapes the options available and the probabilities of success. Agency operates within those constraints, selecting from available options and affecting probabilities. Neither determines outcomes alone. Both matter.

This view has implications for how we think about personal finance. For individuals, it means taking responsibility for the choices that are within your control while recognizing that some outcomes are not within your control. It means doing what you can without assuming that outcomes entirely reflect what you did. It means neither fatalism (nothing I do matters) nor hubris (everything I have, I earned entirely on my own).

For those who have achieved financial success, it means humility. Success reflects effort and talent, yes, but also circumstances not chosen and luck not controlled. The successful person who recognizes this may feel gratitude rather than only pride, may be generous rather than only satisfied, may support efforts to expand opportunity rather than only defend existing advantages.

For those who struggle, it means neither self-blame nor excuse-making. Struggling against structural headwinds is harder than struggling with tailwinds. This is simply true, and acknowledging it is not weakness. At the same time, effort still matters; the structural headwinds are reasons to push harder, not reasons to stop pushing. Finding the balance between acknowledging barriers and maintaining agency is the practical challenge.

**How Personal Financial Success Relates to Broader Social Conditions**

This book has offered advice about building personal financial security. But personal financial security exists within a broader social context that affects both its possibility and its meaning.

The possibility of personal financial security depends partly on social conditions. The person living in an economy with broadly shared prosperity, functioning institutions, low corruption, and reasonable safety nets has an easier path than the person living in an economy with stagnant wages, captured institutions, and no floor beneath misfortune. The advice "save and invest" presupposes an income from which saving is possible, banks where savings are safe, and markets that function. Where these conditions are absent or impaired, individual effort cannot fully compensate.

This observation is not merely about the developing world. In the United States, different communities face different conditions. The person in a prosperous metropolitan area with a strong labor market has different options than the person in a declining rural area with few employers. The person with access to a good 401(k) plan has different opportunities than the person whose employer offers no retirement benefits. The person who can access credit at reasonable rates is positioned differently than the person who can access only payday lenders. Social conditions affect individual options.

Recognizing this does not mean that personal financial effort is pointless. It means that the results of personal effort depend partly on context. The same effort, the same discipline, the same choices may yield different results depending on where and when they occur. This is simply honest, and pretending otherwise is not.

The meaning of personal financial success is also connected to broader social conditions. Success achieved in a context of reasonable opportunity and fairness has a different quality than success achieved by extracting value from the vulnerable, exploiting monopoly power, or benefiting from corruption. Success achieved while others had roughly similar chances has a different quality than success achieved while others were excluded from opportunity. The meaning of "I earned this" depends on the context in which earning occurred.

This is not to say that success in an unequal society is illegitimate or that the successful should feel guilty. Most people who succeed do so through effort and contribution, not exploitation. But recognizing the social context of success may inform how the successful understand their achievements and their responsibilities.

The relationship between personal success and social conditions runs in the other direction too. Individual financial behaviors, aggregated, create social conditions. If everyone pursues maximum individual advantage with no concern for collective effects, the result may be a society in which the pursuit of advantage becomes harder for everyone. If the wealthy extract value and protect their advantages, opportunity for others narrows. If financial institutions are allowed to prey on the vulnerable, the vulnerable become poorer and the costs show up elsewhere in the system. Individual choices have collective consequences.

This is not an argument for individual self-sacrifice or for ignoring one's own financial wellbeing. But it suggests that how we pursue financial success—not only whether we achieve it—matters for the kind of society we create. The investor who considers not only returns but the effects of investments; the employer who considers not only labor costs but worker welfare; the consumer who considers not only price but supply chain ethics; the citizen who considers not only tax burden but public needs—these choices, multiplied across millions of people, shape the context in which everyone pursues financial life.

### The Tension in Transmitting Advantage

The previous chapter discussed legacy—what we leave to our children and how. This chapter's analysis creates a tension worth acknowledging.

If starting points matter so much—if the advantages transmitted from parents to children explain much of the persistence of inequality—then what should we think about transmitting advantages to our own children? Most parents want to help their children succeed. They want to provide good education, financial support, connections, and the security that comes from knowing help is available. This is natural and, in most framings, admirable.

But these same transmissions perpetuate inequality. The parent who pays for private school, funds the unpaid internship, provides the down payment, and makes the introduction is doing for their child what the parent without resources cannot do for theirs. In aggregate, these transmissions ensure that the children of the privileged start ahead of the children of the non-privileged. The very actions that seem like good parenting are also the mechanisms of stratification.

There may be no resolution to this tension. The solution is not for privileged parents to neglect their children—that would harm those children without obviously helping others. The solution is not to feel guilty about providing advantages—guilt without action is useless, and action that harms your children to help abstract others is hard to defend.

But naming the tension may inform how we think about these transmissions. Perhaps it suggests giving children enough to thrive but not so much that they have no need to develop their own capabilities. Perhaps it suggests transmitting wisdom and values more than wealth, since wisdom compounds while wealth can dissipate. Perhaps it suggests combining private transmission with public support for others—recognizing that we help our own children and also support conditions that help other people's children. Perhaps it suggests humility about the success of our children when they benefit from advantages we provided.

Each family will navigate this differently based on their values and circumstances. But pretending the tension does not exist is a failure of honesty.

**What Follows**

If the analysis in this chapter is roughly right, what follows for personal financial conduct?

First, humility about success. Those who have achieved financial security likely did so through some combination of effort, talent, circumstance, and luck. The proportions are impossible to calculate, but recognizing that all four elements are typically present may temper both self-congratulation and judgment of others. The financially successful person might think: I did work for this, and I am proud of that, but I also had advantages I didn't earn, and things could have gone differently.

Second, compassion for those who struggle. Financial struggle may reflect poor choices, but it may also reflect structural barriers, bad luck, or circumstances beyond control. The person who judges the struggling harshly, assuming that their situation reflects only their failures, lacks both accuracy and grace. A more accurate and humane view recognizes the complexity of causes and treats the struggling with the compassion we would want if our luck were different.

Third, gratitude for advantages. Those who had good starting points—stable families, good education, opportunities, safety—received something valuable that was not earned. Acknowledging this need not produce guilt, but it might produce gratitude. And gratitude often motivates generosity.

Fourth, generosity. If financial success is not purely earned, if others face barriers beyond their control, if structural conditions shape outcomes, then some portion of financial success might reasonably be directed toward helping others or improving conditions. This is not about assuaging guilt; it is about recognizing connection and acting on it. The amount and direction of generosity are personal, but the impulse toward generosity follows from a clear-eyed view of how financial success occurs.

Fifth, civic engagement. If social conditions shape individual outcomes, then the conditions themselves are worth attention. Tax policy, educational policy, housing policy, labor policy, health policy —these are not distractions from personal finance but the context that shapes what personal finance can achieve. Engaging as citizens, not merely as consumers and investors, is part of the picture.

Sixth, proportionality in self-blame and self-credit. If outcomes reflect both choices and circumstances, then we should neither blame ourselves entirely for failures nor credit ourselves entirely for successes. This proportionality is psychologically healthy and also more accurate. It allows us to take responsibility without crushing ourselves, to feel pride without arrogance.

Seventh, persistence despite barriers. Recognizing structural barriers is not an argument for giving up. Agency remains real and powerful. Effort still matters. The path may be harder for some than for others, but there is still a path. The person facing headwinds who keeps walking may not reach the destination as quickly as the person with tailwinds, but they will get farther than the person who stops.

**Beyond Personal Finance**

This book has necessarily focused on personal finance—what individuals can do within existing conditions. It has not addressed what collective action might change those conditions. That is a different subject, one addressed in other books by other authors with different expertise.

But it would be odd to write a book about personal finance as if individual choices were the only thing that mattered, as if collective conditions were simply given and immutable. They are not. The conditions we face today were shaped by past collective choices and can be reshaped by future ones. Tax policy, educational investment, healthcare systems, labor law, housing policy, financial regulation—all of these are choices a society makes, and different choices would produce different conditions for individual financial life.

A person can simultaneously pursue their own financial security and participate as a citizen in shaping conditions. These are not alternatives but complements. The person who ignores personal finance, hoping that collective action will solve all problems, will likely struggle. The person who ignores collective conditions, believing that individual action is all that matters, will have a partial understanding.

This book has addressed the personal dimension because that is what a personal finance book can address. But the reader who finishes this book might also take up questions about the collective dimension: What kind of society do I want to live in? What policies would make financial security more accessible to more people? What is my role as citizen, not only as consumer and investor?

These questions go beyond personal finance, but they arise from thinking clearly about personal finance. They are the natural extension of the inquiry.

**Holding Complexity**

The easy positions on inequality are clear and emotionally satisfying. One can say: people get what they deserve, and inequality reflects different contributions. Or one can say: the system is rigged, and outcomes reflect only power and luck. Both positions have the virtue of simplicity and the flaw of being incomplete.

The harder position holds complexity. It says: individual choices matter greatly, and people should take responsibility for the choices they make. And: structural conditions shape what choices are available and what outcomes those choices produce. And: luck plays a larger role than we like to admit. And: even if inequality partly reflects merit, its extremity may be bad for society. And: we should pursue our own financial security while also caring about conditions for others.

This complexity resists bumper stickers. It offers no simple answer to the question of whether the rich deserve their wealth or the poor deserve their poverty. It refuses both the complacency of assuming justice and the cynicism of assuming injustice. It asks for continued thought about difficult questions.

For the reader of this book, the invitation is to hold this complexity while also acting. You must make financial decisions now, in the conditions that exist now, without waiting for perfect understanding or perfect conditions. You can do so while recognizing that your situation is shaped by factors beyond your control, that others face different conditions, that outcomes are not purely earned or unearned, that both structure and agency are real.

This is not comfortable, but it is honest. And honesty, in the long run, serves better than false comfort.

**Coda: What This Means for Reading This Book**

The reader who has made it through this book has encountered advice that assumes certain conditions: enough income to save, access to banking and investment accounts, sufficient stability to plan for the future. Not everyone has these conditions. For those who do not, some of the advice may seem irrelevant or even mocking.

If you are in survival mode—struggling to cover basic expenses, facing crises that overwhelm planning—much of this book's advice must wait. The priority is stability: getting income, managing immediate needs, surviving. Some chapters may help; others may not apply until circumstances change.

If you have the conditions this book assumes—some income, some stability, some ability to plan—then the advice applies, but with the recognition that your conditions are not universal. You are not better than those who lack these conditions; you have different circumstances. This is not cause for guilt but perhaps for gratitude and for generosity.

And for all readers, the recognition that personal finance occurs within social conditions, and that those conditions matter, may inform not only how you pursue your own financial life but how you think about the financial lives of others. The cashier, the driver, the cleaner—they are pursuing financial lives too, often with fewer advantages and harder constraints. They deserve not judgment but recognition, and perhaps the support that makes their paths a little easier.

This chapter has ranged far from the practical advice that fills most of this book. It returns, finally, to practice: do what you can with what you have, while seeing clearly the larger picture in which your actions occur. This is what it means to pursue personal finance with both effectiveness and wisdom.

## SUMMARY

Personal finance advice focuses on individual choices because those are what individuals can control. But individual choices occur within a broader context of economic inequality that shapes what choices are available and what outcomes those choices produce. A complete understanding of personal finance requires acknowledging this context.

The facts of inequality are stark. In the United States, the top one percent of households hold approximately one-third of all wealth, while the bottom half hold about two percent. Income inequality is also pronounced, with the top one percent receiving roughly twenty percent of all income. These disparities have widened since the late 1970s, and social mobility has declined. Inequality varies by race, gender, and geography, with historical injustices creating effects that compound across generations.

Inequality affects not just material resources but psychological conditions. Financial precarity consumes cognitive bandwidth, making good decisions harder precisely when they matter most. It changes the relationship to time and the future, forecloses options, and creates different conditions for decision-making than financial security provides. The discipline required to make good financial choices under scarcity exceeds what is required under abundance.

Advantage transmits across generations through multiple channels beyond direct inheritance: financial knowledge and habits, networks and connections, psychological security, cultural capital, and beliefs about what is possible. These transmissions mean that formal equality of opportunity does not create equal starting positions.

Three main perspectives interpret these facts. One emphasizes markets, merit, and individual responsibility, arguing that inequality reflects different contributions and that ensuring equal opportunity is sufficient. A second emphasizes structures, history, and power, arguing that advantages are often unearned and that formal opportunity is partly illusory when starting points differ so dramatically. A third focuses on the effects of inequality itself, arguing that extreme inequality harms society regardless of how it arose. Each perspective has genuine force, and most thoughtful people hold some combination of them.

The tension between structural barriers and individual agency is real but need not collapse into fatalism or victim-blaming. Structure shapes options and probabilities; agency operates within those constraints. Both matter. For individuals, this means taking responsibility for controllable choices while recognizing that some outcomes are not controllable. For the successful, it means humility and perhaps generosity. For those who struggle, it means neither self-blame nor excuse-making but continued effort despite headwinds.

Personal financial success depends partly on social conditions and also contributes to them. The possibility of building security depends on having income, functioning institutions, and accessible markets. The meaning of success depends on the context in which it was achieved. And individual financial behaviors, aggregated, shape the conditions that everyone faces.

A tension exists between wanting to help one's own children and recognizing that such help perpetuates inequality. This tension may not be resolvable, but acknowledging it may inform how we think about transmitting advantage—perhaps emphasizing wisdom over wealth, combining private transmission with public support, and maintaining humility about children's success.

What follows from this analysis includes humility about success, compassion for those who struggle, gratitude for advantages, generosity, civic engagement, proportionality in self-assessment, and persistence despite barriers. The invitation is to hold complexity—recognizing that individual choices matter greatly while structural conditions shape outcomes—while still acting. For those in survival mode, the priority is stability, and some advice may not yet apply. For those with the conditions this book assumes, the advice applies but with recognition that those conditions are not universal. Personal finance occurs within social conditions that matter, and seeing clearly the larger picture is part of pursuing financial life with both effectiveness and wisdom.

# TWENTY-FIVE
# CAPITALISM, MARKETS, AND THE SYSTEM WE LIVE IN

## Capitalism and Its Critics

A book about personal finance operates within an economic system. That system—broadly, capitalism organized through markets—is not a fact of nature but a human arrangement, one that has evolved over centuries, taken different forms in different places, and attracted sustained criticism alongside sustained defense. To engage thoughtfully with personal finance therefore requires some understanding of the system in which that finance occurs—its strengths, its failures, and the serious arguments on both sides.

This chapter does not argue for or against capitalism. Its aim is more modest and, I hope, more useful: to present the major criticisms and defenses with enough fairness that readers across the political spectrum may recognize their own views represented, even as they encounter views they reject. The goal is thinking rather than conclusion, understanding rather than persuasion.

This matters because how we understand the system shapes how we participate in it. Someone who sees markets primarily as engines of prosperity and freedom will engage differently from someone who sees them primarily as engines of exploitation and alienation.

Someone who sees both may engage with greater nuance than either. And all of us, regardless of our views, must make decisions within the system as it exists, even while some of us work to change it. The previous chapter examined inequality—how advantages and disadvantages compound across generations, how structure and agency interact. This chapter examines the system within which that inequality occurs, asking not just who wins and loses but whether the game itself deserves our allegiance.

**What Capitalism Is**

Capitalism is a term used loosely to describe many arrangements. At its core, it refers to an economic system characterized by private ownership of the means of production, market exchange of goods and services, wage labor, and the accumulation of capital for investment. Decisions about what to produce, how to produce it, and how to distribute goods are made primarily through markets—decentralized exchanges between buyers and sellers—rather than through central planning.

No pure form of capitalism exists in practice. All real economies mix private and public ownership, market and non-market allocation, competition and regulation. The United States, Scandinavia, and China all combine these elements differently, reminding us that the real question is not whether to have capitalism or something else, but what kind of mixed system to have, and under what constraints.

Markets themselves are not unique to capitalism; they have existed in nearly all human societies. What distinguishes capitalism is the extension of market logic into nearly all areas of economic life, including labor, capital, and increasingly domains once outside markets altogether. Capitalism has also taken different forms across time. The capitalism of nineteenth-century Manchester differs from that of mid-twentieth-century America, which differs again from contemporary Silicon Valley. These differences matter. Criticisms that apply to one form may not apply to others, and defenses of one form may not generalize.

**The Case for Markets**

Markets coordinate economic activity through voluntary exchange. Buyers and sellers, each pursuing their own interests, generate information about what people want, what resources exist, and what things cost to produce. This information is transmitted through prices, which serve as signals guiding production and consumption decisions across millions of actors who could never be coordinated by central authority.

Friedrich Hayek emphasized this informational function. The knowledge relevant to economic decisions is dispersed across countless individuals, each knowing their local circumstances, preferences, and opportunities. No central planner could aggregate this knowledge; it exists only in use, only in the decisions people make. Markets aggregate it automatically, through the price mechanism, enabling coordination that would otherwise be impossible.

Markets also enable specialization. When people can trade, they need not produce everything they consume. They can focus on what they do best and exchange for the rest. This division of labor, as Adam Smith recognized, is the foundation of prosperity. The wealth of nations comes not from hoarding gold but from the productive capacity that specialization enables.

Markets reward innovation and efficiency. The entrepreneur who finds a better way to meet consumer needs captures profits; competitors who fail to adapt lose market share. This dynamic process—what Joseph Schumpeter called creative destruction—drives economic progress. It is not comfortable for those displaced, but it generates the improvements in productivity that raise living standards over time.

The moral case for markets rests partly on these outcomes and partly on process. Markets rely on voluntary exchange rather than direct coercion. In an ideal transaction, both parties benefit—or they would not transact. This voluntariness distinguishes market coordination from command systems that require people to do what authorities dictate.

Markets also distribute goods without requiring agreement on values. In a diverse society, people want different things. Markets allow them to pursue their own conceptions of the good life without requiring collective decisions about whose preferences should prevail. This is a form of freedom: the freedom to make your own choices about what to buy, what to sell, and how to live.

**The Case Against Markets**

The moral case against markets, or against their extension into all domains, emphasizes different concerns.

Markets may generate wealth but distribute it unequally. The previous chapter documented this in detail: the vast disparities in income and wealth, the concentration at the top, the stagnation in the middle and bottom. Market outcomes depend on initial endowments —what you start with—and those endowments are not earned. The child born into wealth has market power the child born into poverty lacks. Markets may be efficient at allocating resources given the existing distribution, but that distribution itself reflects history, luck, and power, not just merit.

Voluntariness may be compromised when power or information is radically unequal. The worker who "chooses" to accept a dangerous job at low wages because the alternative is starvation is free only in a formal sense. The consumer who "chooses" a product without understanding its risks has not genuinely consented. The asymmetries of power and information that pervade real markets make many transactions less than fully voluntary.

Market logic may corrupt goods whose value depends on being outside the market. Friendship cannot be purchased; what you purchase is not friendship but its simulacrum. An apology offered for payment is not a genuine apology. Some things—love, honor, civic participation—lose their meaning when made into commodities. The extension of market logic into ever more domains threatens to erode the non-market relationships and institutions that make life meaningful.

Profit may crowd out other values. Organizations focused on maximizing shareholder returns may neglect worker welfare, environmental protection, community impact, and long-term sustainability. When everything is measured by profitability, what cannot be measured is ignored. The market, which is supposed to serve human needs, becomes a master that subordinates all other considerations.

Competition may be brutal for those who lose. Market discipline sounds benign in economic theory. In practice, it means job loss, business failure, community decline. The creative destruction that drives progress also destroys livelihoods and ways of life. Those on the losing side experience not abstract inefficiency but concrete suffering.

**The Consumerism Critique**

One prominent critique targets consumerism—the cultural orientation that makes consumption central to identity and meaning. In consumerist cultures, satisfaction is pursued through acquisition, creating a cycle of desire, purchase, brief satisfaction, and renewed desire. The treadmill keeps moving, but progress is illusory.

Research on wellbeing consistently finds that beyond a certain point, increased consumption does not produce lasting happiness. People adapt quickly to new possessions and circumstances, returning to baseline satisfaction regardless of material gains. This hedonic adaptation means that the pursuit of happiness through consumption is largely futile.

Consumerism also encourages comparison, status competition, and envy. If your worth is measured by what you own, and others own more, you feel inadequate regardless of absolute abundance. This zero-sum competition diverts energy from pursuits that might actually produce satisfaction: relationships, meaningful work, community engagement.

From a moral or spiritual perspective, consumerism inverts older wisdom traditions. Most religions and philosophical schools emphasized mastery of desire rather than its endless stimulation. The good life was found in moderation, contentment, and the cultivation of internal states, not in the accumulation of external goods. Consumerism represents not just an economic arrangement but a theory of human flourishing—one that the wisdom traditions nearly unanimously reject.

Defenders of consumer culture respond that respecting autonomy means respecting people's preferences, including their preference for consumption. If people choose to spend on material goods, who are we to say they are wrong? Not all consumption is frivolous or status-driven; many purchases meet genuine needs and improve lives. And criticizing consumption can slide into romanticizing poverty, ignoring that material deprivation is genuinely bad and that markets have produced real improvements in human welfare.

A thoughtful position neither celebrates nor condemns consumerism outright. It asks which forms of consumption are worthwhile and which are driven by manufactured desire, how to distinguish genuine satisfaction from hedonic treadmill running, and how to cultivate the discernment that makes good choices possible.

For personal finance, this question is immediate. Building wealth usually requires resisting consumerist pressure, not through joyless deprivation but through intentionality about what actually matters. The person who learns to distinguish real desires from manufactured wants has an advantage both in building wealth and in enjoying life.

### The Commodification Critique

A related critique concerns commodification—the extension of market valuation into more areas of life. Time becomes billable. Attention becomes inventory. Care becomes a service. Relationships become networking opportunities. Every aspect of human existence is measured by its market value.

Some commodification is beneficial. Markets in labor provide options unavailable in feudal or familial systems. The worker who can sell labor to the highest bidder has freedoms the serf did not. Money enables a flexibility in exchange that barter cannot achieve. The extension of markets into some domains has liberated as well as constrained.

But some commodification alters the nature of what is commodified. A purchased friendship is not friendship. A paid apology is not an apology. A commercialized holiday loses the meaning that made it worth celebrating. When market logic penetrates intimate relationships, creative work, civic life, and bodily integrity, something is lost that cannot be measured in efficiency terms.

Markets also distribute by willingness and ability to pay. This makes sense for some goods—luxury cars should go to those who value them enough to pay. But for other goods, market distribution seems inappropriate. Should political influence go to the highest bidder? Should kidneys? Should children? Should justice? Most people have intuitions that some things should not be for sale, even if they struggle to articulate why.

Defenders emphasize freedom and efficiency. If consenting adults want to transact, why should we interfere? Markets often allocate resources better than the alternatives—queuing, political allocation, random assignment. The squeamishness about markets may reflect mere prejudice rather than reasoned objection.

The debate is not whether markets should exist but where their boundaries should lie. Drawing those boundaries requires judgment about which goods can be appropriately commodified and which cannot. This judgment is not supplied by economics; it requires moral and political deliberation about the kind of society we want.

For personal finance, commodification appears in everyday choices. Selling your time for money is commodification. Investing in companies is participation in commodification at scale. Using financial instruments to manage risk is engaging with markets that put prices on uncertainty and mortality. Living within capitalism means participating in commodification whether we like it or not. The question is not whether to participate but whether to do so thoughtfully, with awareness of what is gained and lost.

### The Environmental Critique

The environmental critique of capitalism is both empirical and structural. Empirically, capitalist economies have contributed to climate change, biodiversity loss, pollution, and resource depletion. The scale of environmental damage has grown as capitalist production has expanded globally. The atmosphere, oceans, and ecosystems bear the costs of economic activity that is priced as if these costs did not exist.

Structurally, the critique argues that capitalism requires growth, and infinite growth on a finite planet is impossible. The drive to accumulate capital demands expanding production, which demands expanding resource use and waste. Price signals, which markets rely on, do not reflect environmental costs that are externalized—borne by others, by future generations, by the planet itself. The discount rates that make economic sense in financial markets make no sense ecologically, treating the distant future as nearly worthless.

These are serious concerns. Climate change poses threats to financial stability, to the value of assets, to the conditions for human flourishing. A personal finance book cannot ignore risks this large. The reader who builds wealth in a world becoming uninhabitable has achieved something of questionable value.

Defenders note that environmental harm has occurred in non-capitalist systems as well. The Soviet Union's environmental record was dismal. Central planning does not automatically protect the environment. Markets, moreover, can incorporate environmental costs if regulation requires it—carbon taxes, emissions caps, liability rules. What is needed is not the abolition of markets but their proper regulation.

Defenders also note that market economies have produced the technologies and wealth that make environmental protection possible. Rich countries have cleaner air and water than they did a century ago. Innovation drives efficiency improvements that reduce resource use per unit of output. The solution to environmental problems may come from market-driven innovation, not from abandoning markets.

Whether capitalism can be reconciled with environmental sustainability remains an open question. The optimistic view holds that proper regulation, technological innovation, and changing consumer preferences can align capitalism with ecological limits. The pessimistic view holds that the growth imperative is too fundamental to be reformed away, that only systemic change can avert catastrophe.

This book will not resolve this debate. What it can say is that environmental risk is real financial risk. Climate change will affect asset values, economic growth, and the conditions for building wealth. The investor who ignores this is not being prudent; they are being blind. Incorporating environmental considerations into financial planning is not political correctness; it is risk management.

**The Exploitation Critique**

The exploitation critique, with roots in Marxist analysis, holds that capitalism systematically extracts value from workers. In the classical formulation, workers produce more value than they receive in wages; the difference—surplus value—is appropriated by capital owners. This is not aberration but the normal functioning of the system.

Contemporary versions of this critique emphasize power imbalances that enable exploitation. Workers often lack bargaining power, especially in labor markets with high unemployment or weak unions. Employers can dictate terms. The "voluntary" exchange of labor for wages masks coercion by economic necessity.

Global supply chains extend exploitation geographically. The low prices enjoyed by consumers in wealthy countries depend partly on low wages and poor conditions for workers elsewhere. The person who buys a cheap garment is connected to the person who sewed it in conditions that would be illegal domestically.

The gig economy introduces new forms of precarity. Workers classified as independent contractors lack the protections of employment while bearing its risks. Platforms capture value while shifting costs to workers who lack bargaining power.

These critiques identify real harms. Workers are sometimes

mistreated. Supply chains do involve exploitation. Labor market power is often asymmetric. The question is whether these are features of capitalism as such or problems that can be addressed within capitalism through regulation, unions, and social policy.

Defenders argue that voluntary exchange improves the situation of both parties relative to no exchange. The factory worker in a developing country may face poor conditions by Western standards, but the alternative may be worse—subsistence farming or no work at all. Capitalism has raised living standards over time, including for workers. The solution is not to eliminate markets but to ensure that their benefits are broadly shared.

Reform has historically worked. Child labor laws, workplace safety regulations, minimum wages, unions—all have addressed exploitation within capitalist systems. The capitalism of today is less exploitative than the capitalism of a century ago because of these reforms. This suggests that capitalism is not static; it can be shaped by political action.

For individuals, exploitation concerns arise in multiple roles. As workers, we may face exploitative conditions. As investors, we may profit from companies that exploit workers. As consumers, we may benefit from low prices that depend on exploitation elsewhere. Complete moral purity is impossible in a complex economy. But awareness of these connections may inform choices about where to work, what to invest in, and what to buy.

**History's Verdict**

The historical record provides evidence for both critics and defenders of capitalism.

Capitalism has coincided with unprecedented material progress. Life expectancy has doubled. Extreme poverty has declined dramatically. Material abundance that once was unimaginable is now routine. These gains are real and should not be dismissed. Whatever capitalism's flaws, the world it has produced is in many ways better than the world that preceded it.

But capitalism has also coincided with colonialism, slavery, and imperial extraction. Much of the wealth accumulated in capitalist nations derived from exploitation of colonized peoples and enslaved labor. The material progress of some was built on the immiseration of others. The benefits of capitalism have not been distributed justly across the globe or across history.

Capitalism has produced environmental damage at planetary scale. Climate change, biodiversity loss, resource depletion—these threaten to undermine the material gains that capitalism produced. A system that generates short-term prosperity while destroying long-term conditions for flourishing has not obviously succeeded.

Capitalism has shown capacity for reform. The capitalism of the nineteenth century, with its child labor, unsafe factories, and unregulated markets, was transformed by political action into something less brutal. Labor protections, safety standards, environmental regulation, social insurance—these were not automatic products of market forces but achievements of movements that demanded change. This suggests that capitalism is not a fixed system but a malleable one, capable of improvement.

And capitalism has displaced alternatives that themselves had severe problems. The command economies of the twentieth century produced their own forms of oppression, inefficiency, and environmental destruction. The comparison is not between capitalism and utopia but between capitalism and actually existing alternatives. On this comparison, capitalism's record, while mixed, is not clearly inferior.

The honest assessment is that capitalism has produced both tremendous benefits and tremendous harms. Whether the benefits outweigh the harms depends on whose perspective you take, what time horizon you consider, and what alternatives you think are realistic. Reasonable people disagree, and the disagreement reflects genuine complexity, not mere confusion.

**Living Within the System**

This chapter has surveyed debates about capitalism without

resolving them. The resolution, if there is one, lies beyond what a personal finance book can provide. But some conclusions are relevant for how we engage with finance.

First, the system is not given by nature. Capitalism is a human arrangement that has changed over time and varies across places. The specific forms it takes are products of political decisions. Those decisions can be influenced. The reader who thinks some feature of the current system is unjust or destructive can work to change it. This is not naive; it is how the system has always evolved.

Second, acknowledging critique does not require disengagement. One can recognize capitalism's flaws while still participating in markets, saving, investing, and building wealth. The alternative—refusing to engage until the system is perfected—would be both futile and self-harming. We must live in the world as it is while working to make it better. Engaging thoughtfully with finance is consistent with critical awareness of the system in which finance occurs.

Third, how we engage matters. Within the constraints of capitalism, choices remain. What to buy, what to invest in, how to treat workers, what to support politically—these choices are not unlimited, but they are real. The investor who considers environmental and social factors alongside returns; the consumer who considers supply chain ethics alongside price; the employer who considers worker welfare alongside labor costs; the citizen who considers justice alongside self-interest—these choices, multiplied across millions of people, shape what capitalism becomes.

Fourth, reflexive positions are inadequate. Reflexive celebration of capitalism ignores real harms and real criticisms. Reflexive condemnation ignores real benefits and real complexity. Thinking clearly requires holding both the goods and the bads in view, without collapsing into either cheerleading or denunciation. This is uncomfortable but honest.

Fifth, uncertainty is appropriate. We do not know whether capitalism can be reformed to address its most serious problems—inequality, environmental destruction, exploitation. We do not know whether large-scale alternatives would perform better or worse on the dimensions we care about. We do not know what the system will look like in fifty years or what our grandchildren will think of our choices. This uncertainty does not paralyze; it chastens, reminding us that our judgments are provisional and our understanding limited.

Capitalism is not a god to be worshiped or a demon to be exorcised. It is a human system, like democracy or language, capable of producing both flourishing and harm depending on how it is structured and practiced. The task is not to celebrate or condemn it but to live within it with clarity, responsibility, and a willingness to improve it where possible.

Personal finance unfolds within this larger context. Understanding that context does not dictate your choices, but it may deepen how you make them. The next chapter turns to another dimension of context: the technological transformation that is reshaping the economy in which all financial decisions occur, raising new questions about work, value, and human purpose.

## SUMMARY

Personal finance operates within an economic system—capitalism—that is not a fact of nature but a human arrangement. Understanding the serious arguments for and against this system helps us engage with finance more thoughtfully.

Capitalism refers to an economic system characterized by private ownership, market exchange, wage labor, and capital accumulation. No pure form exists; all real economies mix market and non-market elements. The question is not whether to have capitalism but what kind of mixed system to have.

The case for markets emphasizes their ability to coordinate dispersed information, enable specialization, reward innovation, and rely on voluntary exchange rather than coercion. Markets generate prosperity and allow diverse people to pursue different conceptions of the good life without requiring collective decisions about values.

The case against markets emphasizes unequal distribution of gains, compromised voluntariness when power is asymmetric, corruption of goods that should remain outside markets, crowding out of non-monetary values, and brutality toward those who lose in competition.

The consumerism critique argues that making consumption central to identity leads to futile pursuit of satisfaction through acquisition, hedonic adaptation, status competition, and inversion of wisdom traditions that emphasized mastery of desire. Defenders argue for respecting consumer preferences and note real improvements in material welfare.

The commodification critique worries about extending market logic into domains where it corrupts what is valued—friendship, civic participation, bodily integrity. The question is where market boundaries should lie, requiring moral and political judgment beyond economics.

The environmental critique notes that capitalist growth creates ecological damage that markets do not price, and that infinite growth on a finite planet is impossible. Defenders note that environmental harm occurred in non-capitalist systems too and that regulation and innovation can align markets with sustainability. Whether capitalism can be reconciled with ecological limits remains open.

The exploitation critique argues that capitalism extracts value from workers through power imbalances. Defenders argue that voluntary exchange improves options and that reform has historically addressed exploitation within capitalist systems.

History provides evidence for both sides: unprecedented material progress alongside colonialism, slavery, and environmental destruction; capacity for reform alongside persistent harms. The honest assessment is mixed.

Living within the system means recognizing it is not given by nature and can be changed; acknowledging critique while still engaging; attending to how we engage through choices about consumption, investment, and citizenship; avoiding reflexive celebration or condemnation; and accepting appropriate uncertainty about what we do not know.

Capitalism is a human system capable of producing both flourishing and harm. The task is to live within it with clarity, responsibility, and willingness to improve it where possible.

# TWENTY-SIX
# THE INTELLIGENCE REVOLUTION
## AI, AUTOMATION, AND THE FUTURE OF WEALTH

Three months ago, I took my hands off the steering wheel and did not put them back.

I drive a Tesla Model S. I bought my first in 2013, not long after investing in the company—an investment rooted in my belief that electric vehicles would dominate transportation and that Tesla had the vision to lead. Over the years, I watched the technology improve incrementally: better range, faster charging, smoother acceleration. But nothing prepared me for what happened when Autopilot became truly hands-free.

At first, I used it cautiously. Short stretches on familiar highways. My hands hovering inches from the wheel, ready to intervene. I watched the screen display what the car perceived—other vehicles, lane markings, pedestrians—and waited for a mistake that would justify my skepticism. The mistake did not come. Days turned to weeks. My hands drifted further from the wheel. My attention relaxed into something closer to ordinary awareness.

A physicist friend had been skeptical of Tesla's approach. The company relies entirely on cameras and computational processing—no lidar, no radar in current versions, just visual information interpreted by artificial intelligence. He believed this was hubris. Human vision works because we have brains evolved over millions of years to process visual information. Replicating that computationally seemed insufficient for life-and-death decisions.

Last month, he rode with me from Somerset to Mullica Hill, New Jersey—ninety minutes of hands-free driving through traffic, construction zones, and merging highways. When we arrived, he sat quietly. "I did not think computation alone could do this," he said. "I was wrong."

Technology is transforming life as we go on with our lives. That sentence sounds banal until you experience it viscerally—until you are hurtling down a highway at seventy miles per hour, your hands in your lap, your safety entrusted to software that did not exist a few years ago. Then you begin to understand that we are living through a transformation as significant as any in human history.

**What Is Actually Happening**

To understand what artificial intelligence means for your wealth and your life, you must first understand what it actually is.

Artificial intelligence, in its current form, is not conscious. It does not think, feel, or want anything. It is pattern recognition at a scale and speed impossible for human minds. When the Tesla navigates traffic, it is not "seeing" the road as you see it. It is processing millions of pixels, comparing them to patterns learned from billions of miles of driving data, and predicting what will happen next with sufficient accuracy to act appropriately. The magic is not understanding. The magic is prediction without understanding.

Large language models work the same way. They do not comprehend language as you comprehend it. They predict, with remarkable accuracy, what word should come next given all the words that came before. This prediction emerges from training on essentially all the text humanity has produced. The result is a system that can write, reason, and analyze in ways that appear intelligent because intelligence, in many practical contexts, is simply accurate prediction.

This distinction matters for understanding both the power and the limitations of current AI. These systems can perform tasks that once required human intelligence without possessing anything resembling human consciousness. They can be spectacularly right and bizarrely wrong, often in the same conversation. They are tools of extraordinary capability that require human judgment to wield effectively.

But capability is increasing rapidly. What seemed impossible five years ago is routine today. The trajectory matters more than any snapshot.

**The Three Waves**

I think about AI's economic impact in three overlapping waves.

The first wave, already well underway, is augmentation. AI makes existing workers more productive. The programmer who once wrote fifty lines of code per day now writes two hundred with AI assistance. The lawyer who spent hours researching precedents now has AI surface relevant cases in minutes. The analyst who manually processed data now deploys AI to find patterns across datasets too large for human review. Human judgment remains essential, but human effort is leveraged dramatically.

The second wave, beginning now, is automation of cognitive tasks. Some jobs that once required human intelligence can be performed entirely by AI. Customer service, data entry, basic legal research, routine financial analysis—these roles are not being augmented but replaced. The human is not made more productive; the human is no longer needed for that particular task. This wave creates enormous productivity gains but distributes them unevenly.

The third wave, still emerging, is physical automation through robotics. My Tesla's Autopilot is an early example: a machine performing physical tasks with AI-driven perception and decision-making. Warehouse robots, surgical systems, agricultural machines, construction equipment, and humanoid robots—these extend AI's reach from the digital realm into physical space. When this wave matures, the economic implications dwarf what we have seen so far.

These waves overlap and interact. A warehouse that combines AI logistics optimization with robotic picking and autonomous delivery vehicles has transformed not one task but an entire system. The full impact emerges from the combination, not from any single technology.

**Productivity and Distribution**

Every previous technological revolution increased human productivity and caused enormous short-term disruption. Farmers displaced by tractors, craftsmen displaced by factories, clerks displaced by computers—these transitions were painful for those affected even as they created broader prosperity over time.

Will AI follow the same pattern? This is the crucial question, and honest analysis requires acknowledging uncertainty.

The optimistic case holds that AI increases productivity dramatically, competition drives prices down, goods and services become more abundant, and the wealth created is distributed through wages, returns, and transfers, raising living standards broadly. This is the pattern of previous technological revolutions, and there is no obvious reason it should not continue.

The pessimistic case holds that AI increases productivity but gains accrue primarily to capital owners—those who own the AI systems, the data they train on, the platforms that deploy them. Labor's share of output falls further, continuing the trend documented in the inequality chapter. Displaced workers cannot find new jobs because AI learns faster than they can retrain. Inequality widens to destabilizing levels.

The realistic case lies somewhere between, and likely varies by context. Some workers will be devastated; others will thrive. Some industries will transform entirely; others will integrate AI gradually. Some regions and demographic groups will benefit; others will be left behind. The aggregate outcome may be positive—more total wealth created—but distribution will determine whether it feels like progress or catastrophe to any particular person.

Here the analysis of the inequality chapter becomes relevant. That chapter documented that since the late 1970s, productivity gains have not been broadly shared. Wages for workers without college degrees have stagnated while returns to capital and highly-skilled labor have grown. If the last technological revolution—computerization, globalization—did not distribute gains broadly, why should we expect AI to be different?

The honest answer is that we do not know. AI might distribute gains broadly because it augments workers across skill levels, not just those with advanced education. Or it might concentrate gains even more because it substitutes for human labor more completely than previous technologies. Or it might create entirely new categories of work that we cannot currently imagine, as previous revolutions did. The uncertainty is genuine.

What we can say is that distribution is not automatic. It depends on policy choices, institutional arrangements, bargaining power, and collective decisions that are within human control. The capitalism chapter noted that reforms—labor protections, safety standards, environmental regulations—were not automatic but were fought for. The same will be true for ensuring AI's benefits are broadly shared. Technology does not determine distribution; humans do.

Your task, as an individual navigating this transformation, is to position yourself to benefit where possible while remaining clear-eyed about what you can and cannot control. And the inequality chapter's analysis applies here: your ability to position yourself depends partly on advantages you may or may not have—education, connections, financial margin, geographic location. Recognizing this is not fatalism; it is realism about how structure and agency interact.

### Human Capital in an AI World

Throughout this book, I have focused on financial capital—savings, investments, assets that generate returns. But for most people, especially earlier in life, human capital is more valuable: your skills, knowledge, credentials, and ability to earn income. AI changes the human capital calculus profoundly.

Some skills become less valuable. If AI can perform a task faster and cheaper, the market price for human performance of that task falls toward zero. This is already happening for routine cognitive work: data entry, basic analysis, simple writing, straightforward customer interactions. Tasks that required human intelligence but were repetitive and rule-governed are being automated.

Other skills become more valuable. The ability to work effectively with AI—to prompt it well, evaluate its outputs critically, integrate its capabilities into complex workflows—is increasingly precious. This is not merely technical skill; it is judgment about when AI is trustworthy and when it is not, creativity in applying AI to new problems, and discernment about what AI cannot do.

The ability to do what AI cannot do becomes more valuable as AI does more. Building genuine relationships, exercising judgment in ambiguous situations, creating truly novel ideas, providing human presence and empathy—these remain distinctively human. The work that requires being human, not just performing tasks a human once performed, may be the most durable.

The highest value may accrue to those who understand both the technology and a specific domain deeply. A lawyer who understands AI can deploy it for research while applying human judgment to strategy and client relationships. A physician can use AI for diagnosis while providing the care patients need from another human being. A manager can use AI for analysis while providing the leadership that humans require from other humans. Domain expertise plus AI fluency is a powerful combination.

Think about your own human capital in this light. What skills do you have that AI will augment, making you more productive? What skills do you have that AI cannot replicate, that depend on your being human? What skills might you need to develop as AI capabilities expand? These questions merit serious reflection, because human capital investments made now will compound—or depreciate—over coming decades.

But also think about this through the lens of the inequality chapter. The person who can invest in developing AI fluency—taking courses, experimenting with tools, building expertise—is positioned differently than the person working multiple jobs with no time for learning. The person in a knowledge-economy job where AI augments their work is positioned differently than the person in a job AI simply eliminates. The advice to develop AI fluency is good advice, but it is easier to follow for some than for others. Recognizing this is simply honest.

**The Investment Thesis**

If AI transforms the economy as I expect, where should you invest?

The most direct exposure is to companies building AI infrastructure: the semiconductors powering computation, the cloud platforms hosting AI services, the companies developing foundational models. This infrastructure layer captures value regardless of which specific applications succeed, just as picks and shovels captured value during gold rushes regardless of which miners struck gold.

NVIDIA has dominated AI chips; its stock has reflected that dominance. But dominance in technology is rarely permanent. I invested in NVIDIA years ago, when I noticed that academic researchers overwhelmingly used their GPUs because the CUDA software ecosystem made development dramatically easier. That ecosystem moat, invisible in financial statements, proved decisive—but the moat could erode if competitors develop compelling alternatives. Microsoft, Google, Amazon, and others provide essential cloud infrastructure and are developing their own AI capabilities. This infrastructure layer is where much of AI's value may be captured.

The next layer is companies deploying AI effectively to improve their businesses. Tesla uses AI to differentiate its products and reduce costs—the Autopilot system that prompted this chapter's opening is an example. Any company applying AI to achieve lower costs, better products, or new capabilities has an advantage over competitors that do not.

A third layer is companies whose products become more valuable as AI proliferates. Cybersecurity firms protecting against AI-enabled threats. Energy companies powering data centers. Education and training companies helping workers adapt. These are derivative beneficiaries whose fortunes depend on AI's success without requiring that they develop AI themselves.

Finally, consider broad market exposure. If AI increases productivity economy-wide, corporate profits should rise in aggregate. An index fund provides exposure to this rising tide without requiring you to pick which specific companies will win. This is the most conservative approach and may capture most of AI's economic gains.

I own positions across all four layers. This diversification acknowledges my uncertainty about precisely how AI's value will be distributed while ensuring I participate in the transformation however it unfolds. But I want to be clear about something: I am talking my own book here. I own Tesla stock. I own NVIDIA stock. I have benefited from positions I am describing. This does not make my analysis wrong, but you should weigh it knowing that I have financial interest in the views I am expressing.

**Evaluating AI Capabilities**

Saying you should invest in companies with strong AI capabilities is easy. Identifying which companies actually have strong capabilities is harder. Here is how I think about evaluation.

The first question is whether AI is core to the business or peripheral. Some companies build AI as their primary product. Others deploy AI to improve existing operations. Still others merely mention AI in earnings calls while doing little of substance. The first two categories merit attention; the third is noise. When a company announces an "AI initiative" without specific details about implementation, investment, and measurable outcomes, skepticism is warranted.

For companies where AI is the product, I evaluate technical leadership. Who are their researchers? Are they publishing influential work? What is their compute infrastructure? Do they have proprietary data advantages? Technical leadership in AI requires world-class talent, massive computational resources, and access to data that others cannot easily obtain.

The CUDA observation I mentioned earlier illustrates how to identify durable advantages. NVIDIA's hardware was not dramatically superior to competitors, but their software ecosystem created switching costs that made their platform sticky. Engineers trained on CUDA stayed with NVIDIA even when alternatives emerged. This is the kind of moat—invisible in financial statements, visible in how practitioners actually work—that creates durable value.

For companies deploying AI operationally, the questions differ. How deeply is AI integrated into core processes? What measurable improvements has it produced? Is deployment creating compounding advantages, where more usage generates more data that improves the system further?

Tesla exemplifies this flywheel effect. Every Tesla on the road feeds data back to improve Autopilot. More vehicles mean more data. More data mean better AI. Better AI means more customers. This creates a compounding advantage that competitors without comparable fleet size cannot easily replicate. Whether this advantage will prove decisive remains uncertain—other approaches to autonomous driving may succeed—but the structure of the advantage is clear.

Contrast this with a traditional automaker that announces an "AI initiative" and partners with a technology company. The partnership may produce useful products, but creates no proprietary advantage. When the partnership ends or competitors sign similar deals, the advantage disappears. This is AI as marketing, not AI as moat.

I look carefully at talent flows and capital allocation. Companies serious about AI invest heavily in talent, compute, and data infrastructure. Where are top AI researchers choosing to work? Where are they leaving? Companies hemorrhaging AI talent are often in trouble regardless of public messaging. Companies attracting talent are investing in the future.

Data advantages deserve particular attention. AI systems are only as good as their training data. Companies with proprietary access to unique, large-scale datasets have advantages difficult to replicate. Google has search data. Meta has social graph data. Tesla has driving data from billions of miles. A company without distinctive data access is training on the same public information as everyone else—which may be fine for some applications but limits potential for differentiation.

Finally, I assess management's genuine understanding versus performative enthusiasm. When executives discuss AI, do they demonstrate real comprehension of the technology, its capabilities, and its limitations? Or do they parrot consultant talking points without substance? Do they acknowledge what AI cannot do, or do they promise magic? Do their actions match their words?

I recall an earnings call where a retail CEO announced they were "going all in on AI." The stock rose. But reading carefully, I noticed the CEO could not answer basic implementation questions. The "AI initiative" had no budget, no timeline, no measurable goals. I did not invest. A year later, the initiative had produced nothing.

Contrast this with executives who demonstrate genuine understanding—who can explain not just what AI will do but how it works and why their particular approach might succeed. Whether you agree with their strategies or not, authenticity is visible and meaningful. This is not sufficient for investment success, but its absence is a warning sign.

**The Limitations of AI**

Enthusiasm must be tempered by clear understanding of limitations. AI will not do everything, and pretending otherwise leads to bad investments and bad decisions.

The first limitation is brittleness in novel situations. AI systems excel within their training distribution—the range of situations represented in the data they learned from. Outside that distribution, they can fail dramatically and without warning. A self-driving car trained on California highways may struggle with unusual conditions it has never encountered. I experienced this during early Autopilot days—the system performed beautifully on well-marked highways but became confused at a construction site where temporary lane markings contradicted permanent ones. I had to take control. The system was not generally intelligent; it was narrowly capable within specific parameters.

The second limitation is the absence of genuine understanding. Current AI systems manipulate symbols and patterns without comprehending their meaning as humans do. This manifests as confident incorrectness—stating falsehoods with the same fluency as truths. A large language model can produce plausible-sounding nonsense because it is predicting words, not understanding concepts. Never trust AI output on matters of fact without independent verification. The appearance of intelligence is not intelligence.

The third limitation is embedded bias. AI systems learn from human-generated data, which reflects human biases. A hiring algorithm trained on historical decisions may perpetuate past discrimination, even without explicit discriminatory rules, because the patterns in past data reflect past biases. An AI trained on text from the internet absorbs whatever biases that text contains. These biases hide in statistical patterns rather than explicit rules, making them difficult to identify and correct.

The fourth limitation is opacity. Many powerful AI techniques produce results through processes that resist interpretation. The model works, but we cannot fully explain why it produces particular outputs. This creates problems in contexts requiring accountability. When an AI denies someone a loan, or recommends a medical treatment, or influences a legal decision, the inability to explain why undermines trust and due process.

The fifth limitation is potential for catastrophic misuse. AI can generate convincing disinformation, automate cyberattacks, create synthetic media indistinguishable from reality, enable surveillance at scale, and potentially develop autonomous weapons. These risks are already manifesting. The same capabilities that create value can create harm.

Understanding these limitations does not diminish AI's significance. It contextualizes it. Investing wisely requires understanding both the transformation and the constraints. Companies that deploy

AI thoughtfully, with awareness of limitations and appropriate safeguards, are better bets than companies that promise what AI cannot deliver.

**The Debate About AI's Future**

This chapter has described my view of AI's trajectory. But I should acknowledge that thoughtful people disagree, and the uncertainty is genuine.

AI optimists—and I am closer to this camp—see current capabilities as just the beginning. They expect continued rapid improvement, broader deployment, and transformative economic impact. They point to the pace of progress: capabilities that seemed decades away arrived in years. They see AI following the pattern of previous transformative technologies, creating short-term disruption but long-term prosperity.

AI skeptics see current capabilities as impressive but limited. They note that progress has come from scaling existing techniques, not fundamental breakthroughs, and that scaling may hit limits. They point to persistent failure modes—hallucination, brittleness, opacity—as evidence that something fundamental is missing. They warn against extrapolating from recent progress to assume continued rapid improvement.

AI pessimists worry that AI will succeed too well. They fear economic disruption so rapid that adaptation is impossible, concentration of power in the hands of those who control AI systems, loss of human agency and meaning as machines do more, and potentially existential risks if advanced AI systems pursue goals misaligned with human values.

Each of these perspectives has adherents who are intelligent, informed, and arguing in good faith. I do not think the skeptics are foolish, even though I expect them to be largely wrong. I do not think the pessimists are hysterical, even though I am more optimistic about navigating the risks. The honest position is uncertainty: AI might follow the optimistic trajectory, or progress might stall, or the risks might prove greater than the benefits. We are making decisions under genuine uncertainty about the future.

This uncertainty has implications for investment. Do not bet everything on AI following the optimistic trajectory. Diversify. Maintain positions that would do well if AI disappoints. But also do not ignore AI because the future is uncertain. The expected value of positioning for AI transformation is high even if the probability of transformation is not one hundred percent.

**Bias and the Machines**

Throughout this book, I have emphasized how cognitive biases undermine investment decisions. AI offers a partial remedy. A well-designed system does not panic when markets fall or become euphoric when they rise. It processes information systematically, without emotional interference. It is perfectly consistent, producing the same output for the same input every time.

This is why robo-advisors have gained traction. They construct portfolios based on goals and risk tolerance, rebalance automatically, and ignore the noise that causes human advisors—and human investors—to make ill-timed changes. The behavioral biases that sabotage human decision-making do not affect algorithms.

But AI systems have their own limitations. They are trained on historical data that may not predict future conditions. They can be overfit to past patterns in ways that fail when conditions change. They cannot exercise judgment in genuinely novel situations because they have no genuine understanding, only pattern recognition. And they inherit whatever biases existed in their training data.

My approach is to use AI as complement to human judgment, not replacement. I consult AI tools for analysis, pattern recognition, and information processing. I use automated systems for routine execution and rebalancing. But I reserve major decisions—overall strategy, significant position changes, responses to novel situations—for human consideration, informed but not dictated by AI analysis.

Kahneman spent his final years thinking about the combination of human and algorithmic judgment. He studied what he called "noise"—the unwanted variability in human decisions. Two loan officers evaluating the same application often reach different conclusions, not because they have different information but because human judgment is inconsistent. Algorithms are perfectly consistent; they produce the same output for the same input every time.

Kahneman's conclusion was not that algorithms should replace humans or that humans should ignore algorithms, but that the combination outperforms either alone. Algorithms provide consistency and freedom from emotional bias. Humans provide judgment in novel situations and correction when algorithms fail. The best decisions come from human-algorithm collaboration.

I apply this framework to my own investing. AI can identify patterns I would miss and prevent me from making emotion-driven errors. But I can recognize when conditions have changed in ways that make historical patterns unreliable, and I can exercise judgment that AI cannot replicate. Neither alone is optimal; the combination is better than either.

**Robotics and Physical AI**

My Tesla experience illustrates something important: AI is moving from the digital realm into the physical world.

For years, AI was confined to screens—analyzing data, generating text, classifying images. Valuable, but limited to the digital. Robotics extends AI into physical reality, enabling machines to perceive, decide, and act in three-dimensional space with the same flexibility and judgment that previously required humans.

The implications are staggering. Manufacturing could be transformed by general-purpose robots that adapt to new tasks through learning rather than reprogramming. Logistics could be automated almost entirely—from warehouse picking to delivery. Agriculture, construction, mining—industries that have resisted automation because they require handling variability and unpredictability—could be transformed by robots that perceive their environments and respond appropriately.

Tesla's Optimus humanoid robot represents one vision of this future. A robot that can perform any physical task a human can perform, learning through the same AI techniques that power self-driving cars, would transform the economics of physical labor. Whether Tesla or competitors achieve this vision, and on what timeline, remains uncertain. But the direction is clear. Physical work, like cognitive work, will increasingly be performed or augmented by machines.

This connects to the discussion of human capital. If machines can perform physical tasks with human-like capability, what remains for human workers? The answer may be the tasks that require being human—caring for other humans, creative work that people value because humans created it, judgment in situations where people want human judgment, relationships and community that machines cannot provide. The economics of production change; the economics of being human may change less.

**The Meaning of Work**

A chapter on AI and economics would be incomplete without addressing a deeper question: what happens to human meaning if work becomes optional?

For most of history, work was survival. You worked to eat, to shelter yourself, to stay alive. The notion of work as fulfilling, as a source of identity and purpose, is relatively recent and relatively privileged. But for many people in developed economies, work provides more than income. It provides structure to time, social connection, a sense of contribution, an answer to the question of what you do with your days on earth.

AI threatens this source of meaning even as it promises material abundance. If machines can do everything humans can do, but better and cheaper, what is left for us?

Mises, the economist, understood that economics is ultimately about human action and human purpose. In Human Action, he argued that purposeful behavior is the defining characteristic of human existence. We choose, plan, and act to transform circumstances according to our values. Work is not merely a means to consumption but an expression of human agency—the way we make our mark on the world.

Mises worried about the "anticapitalistic mentality"—the tendency to resent the market despite its benefits. But he might have worried more about a world where the market no longer needs human participants. If AI produces everything humans want, the price mechanism still functions, but humans become spectators rather than actors. What then becomes of the purposeful action Mises considered essential to flourishing?

This is, as Nietzsche understood, a question about meaning and nihilism.

Nietzsche famously proclaimed that "God is dead"—not as theological assertion but as cultural diagnosis. The religious frameworks that once provided meaning were losing their grip on modern consciousness. His concern was psychological: without a transcendent source of meaning, humans would face a crisis of purpose. His proposed solution was the creation of new values, the embrace of life-affirmation, the cultivation of the human who creates meaning through will and action rather than receiving it from tradition.

The AI revolution poses a Nietzschean challenge. If work has been our secular religion—the source of identity and purpose that replaced traditional faith—then the obsolescence of work is another death of God. We are left to create meaning from nothing, or to despair.

Kahneman's research offers a relevant insight. In his distinction between the experiencing self and the remembering self, he showed that what makes us happy in the moment differs from what makes us satisfied in retrospect. The experiencing self enjoys leisure and comfort. The remembering self values accomplishment, narrative coherence, meaning. Humans who optimize only for the experiencing self often report less life satisfaction than those who endure difficulty in pursuit of meaningful goals.

If AI provides abundance without effort, it satisfies the experiencing self magnificently. Food, entertainment, comfort—all available without labor. But it may starve the remembering self, which needs struggle, accomplishment, and narrative to construct a life worth having lived.

What is the answer? I see several possibilities, none certain.

First, humans may always value what other humans create, not because it is superior but because it is human. A handmade table may be worse by measurable criteria than one produced by robot. But knowing a human shaped it connects us to another consciousness in a way machine production cannot. Markets for human-made goods may persist, supported by those who value the human element.

Second, humans may find meaning in what remains distinctively human: relationships, community, care for one another. Machines may produce goods, but humans will still raise children, tend the elderly, comfort the grieving, build friendships, create communities. These activities may become more central to identity as productive work becomes less so.

Third, humans may embrace play, exploration, and creativity as ends in themselves. Freed from necessity, we might become a civilization of artists, athletes, scholars, and adventurers—pursuing excellence for its own sake rather than for survival. The purpose that work provided might be replaced by purposes chosen rather than imposed.

Fourth, and darker: many humans may not adapt successfully. They will lose meaning without finding new sources. They will succumb to what Nietzsche called passive nihilism—filling the void with empty pleasures that satisfy momentarily but compound into despair. The opioid crisis, the epidemic of loneliness, the rise of deaths of despair—these may be early signs of what happens when purpose disappears.

I do not know which possibility will predominate, or in what mixture. What I know is that the question matters enormously, and thinking about it now is wiser than waiting until the crisis is upon us. If you are young, the world you retire into may be radically different from the world you entered. Preparing for that world means more than building financial capital. It means building sources of meaning that do not depend on work for income.

**Practical Implications**

For your investments, maintain broad market exposure while tilting toward AI beneficiaries. But do not abandon diversification in pursuit of a single thesis, however compelling. The future is uncertain, and even a correct thesis can be expressed through specific investments that fail for idiosyncratic reasons.

When evaluating specific investments, apply the framework I described: distinguish AI as core product from AI as operational deployment from AI as marketing, assess technical leadership and talent flows, evaluate data advantages and flywheel effects, judge management's genuine understanding. These evaluations will not guarantee success, but they distinguish informed conviction from speculation.

Remain aware of limitations. Companies deploying AI in high-stakes situations without appropriate safeguards face catastrophic risks from failure. Companies building on brittle technical foundations may fail when conditions shift. Companies whose advantages derive from temporary factors may see those advantages erode.

For your career, develop AI fluency regardless of your field. Learn to use AI tools effectively—not just as novelty but as integral part of how you work. Understand what AI can and cannot do. Position yourself to be augmented rather than replaced. Domain expertise combined with AI fluency is increasingly valuable; domain expertise without AI fluency is increasingly vulnerable.

For your financial planning, consider that returns on capital may rise relative to returns on labor, continuing and perhaps accelerating the trend documented in the inequality chapter. This strengthens the case for saving and investing aggressively, particularly early in life when compounding has longest to work. The person who owns capital in an AI-transformed economy may be better positioned than the person who depends entirely on labor income.

For your mindset, cultivate adaptability. The specific predictions in this chapter may prove wrong in details even if right in direction. What will not prove wrong is that change is accelerating and flexibility is valuable. The ability to learn new skills, adapt to new circumstances, and remain functional amid uncertainty may be more valuable than any specific expertise.

And begin thinking now about meaning. If work becomes optional for you—through investment success, through AI-driven abundance, through any path—what will you do with your freedom? What will structure your days? What will connect you to others? What will make your life worth having lived? These questions may seem premature, but they are not. The answers require cultivation, and cultivation requires time.

**Hands Off the Wheel**

I began this chapter with my hands off the steering wheel, trusting software to navigate a two-ton vehicle at highway speed. That image captures something about our collective situation.

We are all passengers now, in a sense. The technological forces reshaping our economy are not within any individual's control. We did not choose to live through an AI revolution any more than our great-grandparents chose to live through the industrial revolution. The forces are larger than us.

But we are not merely passengers. We make choices—about how to position ourselves, how to invest, how to develop skills, how to think about meaning. We participate as citizens in shaping the rules under which AI develops and deploys. We influence, if only marginally, the collective choices that determine how AI's benefits and harms are distributed. The previous chapters argued that structure and agency both matter; that insight applies here too.

My Tesla investment was an early bet on a specific vision of the future. That bet has been rewarded, though its ultimate outcome remains uncertain. More importantly, making that bet forced me to think carefully about technological change—to distinguish hype from substance, to consider multiple scenarios, to position myself for a future I could see approaching but not fully predict.

I encourage you to make similar bets, sized appropriately to your circumstances and conviction. Not because any particular investment is guaranteed to succeed, but because the process of thinking seriously about the future—really thinking, with money at stake—is itself valuable. It forces clarity. It demands honesty about what you believe and why. It connects abstract analysis to concrete action.

The future is arriving faster than we expected. The economy you will navigate in coming decades will differ dramatically from the economy of today. Your hands may not be on the wheel much longer, metaphorically speaking—AI may do more of what you currently do for income.

But you still choose where to sit in the vehicle. You still choose how to prepare for the journey. You still choose what to do with the time and freedom that AI might provide. Make those choices thoughtfully, with eyes open to both the opportunities and the risks, and with the wisdom that comes from seeing clearly how structure, agency, and luck all shape what becomes of us.

Invest accordingly. Live accordingly. The transformation is underway.

## SUMMARY

Artificial intelligence is transforming the economy in ways that will affect every financial decision you make. Understanding what AI actually is—pattern recognition and prediction at scale, not consciousness or understanding—helps clarify both its capabilities and its limitations.

AI's economic impact unfolds in three overlapping waves. The first wave, augmentation, makes existing workers more productive by leveraging AI tools. The second wave, cognitive automation, replaces some human jobs entirely with AI systems. The third wave, physical automation through robotics, extends AI capabilities into the physical world.

The crucial question is how AI's economic gains will be

distributed. Historical patterns suggest productivity gains do not automatically benefit workers broadly; since the late 1970s, gains have accrued primarily to capital owners and highly skilled labor. Whether AI follows this pattern or distributes gains more broadly depends on policy choices, institutional arrangements, and collective decisions—not on the technology itself.

Human capital implications are significant. Skills that AI can replicate become less valuable; skills that complement AI or remain distinctively human become more valuable. Domain expertise combined with AI fluency is particularly valuable. But the ability to develop AI fluency depends on advantages that are unequally distributed.

Investment exposure to AI transformation can come through infrastructure companies, companies deploying AI effectively, derivative beneficiaries, or broad market exposure. Evaluating AI capabilities requires distinguishing genuine technical leadership from marketing, assessing data advantages and flywheel effects, and judging management's authentic understanding.

AI has significant limitations: brittleness outside training distributions, absence of genuine understanding, embedded bias, opacity, and potential for misuse. Understanding these limitations is essential for both investment evaluation and appropriate deployment.

Thoughtful people disagree about AI's trajectory. Optimists expect continued rapid progress and transformative impact. Skeptics expect progress to slow as current techniques hit limits. Pessimists worry about economic disruption, power concentration, and existential risks. Genuine uncertainty about which view is correct argues for diversification rather than all-in bets.

AI can help overcome human cognitive biases by providing consistent, emotion-free analysis. But AI has its own limitations and biases. The best approach combines human judgment with AI capabilities rather than relying entirely on either.

The meaning of work may be challenged if AI makes human labor optional. Purpose, identity, and fulfillment that work provides may need to come from other sources: human relationships, creative pursuits, community, or deliberately chosen challenges. Thinking about meaning now is wiser than waiting until work is no longer available.

Practical implications include maintaining diversified investment exposure while tilting toward AI beneficiaries, developing AI fluency regardless of field, recognizing that returns to capital may rise relative to returns to labor, cultivating adaptability, and beginning to think seriously about sources of meaning beyond work.

The transformation is underway. Positioning yourself to benefit requires clear thinking about both opportunities and risks, informed by awareness of how structural conditions shape what is possible for different people. Invest accordingly. Live accordingly.

# TWENTY-SEVEN
# A FINAL SYNTHESIS: WEALTH, MIND, AND MEANING

## What Is All This For?

We have traveled a long way together—from the mechanics of budgeting and saving, through investing and insurance, into the psychology of financial behavior, the ethics of wealth and inequality, and the contested terrain of economic systems. We have examined cryptographic assets that challenge traditional conceptions of money and artificial intelligence that may reshape the very nature of work. Now we arrive at the question that should have been first but could only be understood last: what is all of this for?

Personal finance is instrumental. Money is not the point; money is a means. But a means to what? Without an answer—even an imperfect one—the techniques remain hollow: efficient methods for achieving we know not what. The person who optimizes their finances without knowing why is like a traveler who perfects navigation without choosing a destination.

This question has always mattered, but recent chapters give it new urgency. If artificial intelligence transforms work as profoundly as some anticipate—if machines can perform most tasks humans now perform, if abundance arrives without widespread human effort—

then the question of what money is for becomes the question of what life is for. And if new forms of money emerge that operate outside traditional institutions, as cryptocurrency advocates envision, then we must also ask what money itself should be—not merely how to accumulate it, but what role it ought to play in human coordination and flourishing.

The meaning problem, once confined to the wealthy or retired, may soon confront everyone. For most of human history, necessity answered the question for us. You worked because you would starve otherwise. You saved because winter was coming. You invested because your children needed a future. But what happens when necessity recedes? What happens when the struggle for survival that gave structure and purpose to human life becomes optional?

These questions cannot be deferred to some distant future. The future is arriving faster than we expected.

### The Architecture of Economic Life

At the most basic level, economic activity exists for survival. But once survival is secured, its purposes multiply: comfort, security, freedom from constant urgency, the material foundation for education, health, creativity, rest, and relationship. Economic activity also connects us, coordinates our efforts across time and distance, and allows specialization that no individual life could achieve alone. In this sense, markets and money are not merely technical tools; they are deeply social instruments.

Here, Mises helps us see clearly. Markets are not moral arbiters or engines of justice; they are information systems. They coordinate dispersed knowledge, translate preferences into prices, and allow human cooperation on a vast scale. When they function well, they expand possibility. When they are distorted—by monopoly, coercion, corruption, or extreme concentration of power—they mislead rather than inform. Respecting markets without worshiping them means understanding both their power and their limits.

The cryptocurrency movement, at its philosophical best, extends this insight. Bitcoin and its successors represent an attempt to create coordination mechanisms that function without requiring trust in central institutions. Whether this attempt succeeds matters less than what it reveals: a widespread intuition that existing monetary systems may not serve everyone's interests equally, that the power to create and control money is the power to shape economic life, and that alternative architectures deserve exploration. The critique embedded in cryptocurrency—that money should be a neutral medium rather than a policy instrument—carries weight even if particular implementations disappoint.

But neither traditional markets nor cryptographic alternatives protect us from ourselves. Knowing how money works does not guarantee that we will use it wisely. This is where Kahneman's lessons quietly underwrite nearly everything in this book. We are not rational optimizers. We are anxious, biased, loss-averse creatures, prone to overconfidence in good times and panic in bad ones. We confuse recent experience with lasting truth. We chase excitement and avoid pain, even when doing so reliably harms us.

The cryptocurrency markets have provided vivid demonstration of these tendencies. The manias of 2017 and 2021, the spectacular collapses, the conviction that "this time is different"—these episodes illustrate Kahneman's framework with painful clarity. But traditional markets provide the same lessons to anyone paying attention. Financial mistakes are rarely failures of intelligence; they are failures of judgment under pressure.

Understanding this does not make us immune. It makes humility possible. It suggests why automation, simplicity, and restraint matter; why boredom is often a feature rather than a flaw of good investing; and why designing your financial life to protect you from your own worst instincts is not weakness but wisdom.

### The Danger of Hollowness

Still, even a well-designed financial life can go wrong at a deeper level. You can do everything "right" and still feel hollow. You can accumulate security and still feel restless, resentful, or trapped in comparison. This is where Nietzsche enters—not as a financial advisor, but as a psychologist of value. He reminds us that the greatest danger is not losing money but losing oneself: allowing frustration, envy, and comparison to harden into resentment, allowing the pursuit of wealth to become a substitute for the creation of meaning.

The technological transformations we have discussed sharpen this danger. Artificial intelligence may deliver abundance, but abundance without purpose is not flourishing—it is drift. Cryptocurrency may deliver financial sovereignty, but sovereignty over resources you do not know how to use is empty freedom. Both technologies solve problems of scarcity and control. Neither solves the problem of meaning.

Money can amplify who you already are. It can widen your field of action. But it cannot tell you what your life is for. If you do not supply that meaning, money will happily occupy the vacuum—and it will do so poorly. The person scrolling through investment apps at midnight, checking balances that need no checking, monitoring markets that require no monitoring, knows this truth even if they cannot articulate it. The restlessness is diagnostic. Something is missing that money cannot provide.

Seen together, these perspectives converge on a single insight: financial wisdom is not just technical competence. It is self-knowledge, systems awareness, and value clarity held together.

### The Practice of Enough

This brings us back to the idea of enough. The goal is not maximum money but sufficient money—enough to support the life you regard as worth living. What counts as enough varies by circumstance, responsibility, temperament, and desire. But without some felt sense of where "enough" lies, you can spend decades chasing a finish line that keeps moving.

Knowing your number is not only a spreadsheet exercise; it is an existential one. It requires asking what you actually want your days to contain, what relationships you want to sustain, what contributions you want to make, what experiences you want to have before your time runs out. These questions resist quantification, but they inform every genuinely important financial decision.

The coming decades may test our collective understanding of enough more severely than any previous era. If AI generates unprecedented productivity, if material abundance becomes genuinely achievable for billions rather than millions, the old answers—rooted in scarcity, necessity, and survival—may no longer suffice. We will need new answers, or rather, we will need to rediscover old answers that have been obscured by centuries of struggle against material want.

The Stoics knew that tranquility comes from wanting what is appropriate to want. The Epicureans knew that most pleasures have diminishing returns. The religious traditions warned that wealth is spiritually dangerous precisely because it makes means so easy to mistake for ends. These insights are not obsolete; they may be more relevant than ever. The discipline of enough is the discipline of knowing when to stop—and that discipline becomes essential precisely when external constraints no longer force us to stop.

### The Transformation of Work

Work, too, finds its place here. Whether experienced as job, career, or calling, work occupies an enormous share of human life. It can provide identity, structure, connection, mastery, and purpose—or drain all of them. The point is not to romanticize work, nor to reduce it to mere necessity, but to see clearly what role it plays for you, and to let your financial decisions support that role rather than undermine it.

But what happens when work becomes optional? Not optional in the sense of financial independence achieved through decades of saving—that path remains available to the disciplined and fortunate—but optional in the sense that machines perform most tasks more capably than humans can? This is the question the AI chapter posed, and it has no easy answer.

One response is to identify what machines cannot do and double down on those capacities. Machines cannot love. They cannot be present in the way a human can be present. They cannot bear witness to another's suffering with genuine empathy. They cannot create meaning—they can only process and recombine the meanings humans have created. These capacities may become more valuable precisely as technical capacities become abundant.

Another response is to decouple identity from occupation. The question "what do you do?" need not be answered with reference to employment. You might do many things: raise children, tend gardens, create art, serve communities, explore ideas, maintain friendships, care for aging parents. These activities have always constituted life; they have merely been overshadowed by the economic activity that made them possible. If economic necessity recedes, they may step forward.

Financial planning in this context becomes less about maximizing wealth and more about creating optionality. The investor who maintains adequate savings, avoids excessive debt, and develops sources of meaning beyond employment is prepared for multiple futures. The investor who has staked everything—financially and psychologically—on a single career trajectory is exposed to risks that no insurance can cover.

**The Ethics of Consumption**

Consumption follows the same logic. Spending that aligns with values satisfies more deeply than spending driven by anxiety, status, or manufactured desire. Experiences often nourish more than objects; generosity often nourishes more than self-indulgence. These are not commandments but observations. The discipline is attentiveness: noticing what actually sustains you over time, and letting your money become a servant of that knowledge rather than an engine of distraction.

We live surrounded by sophisticated efforts to manufacture desire. Advertising exists to create dissatisfaction; its entire purpose is to make you want what you did not previously want. Social media amplifies comparison, showing you curated highlights of others' lives against which your own ordinary existence seems inadequate. The cryptocurrency manias demonstrated how easily FOMO—fear of missing out—can override judgment, leading people to invest in assets they do not understand based on the apparent success of strangers online.

Resistance requires intentionality. It requires asking, before each significant purchase, whether this expenditure moves you toward or away from the life you actually want. It requires distinguishing between needs, wants, and manufactured desires. It requires recognizing that much of what is sold as necessity is actually status competition, and that status competition is a game with no winner—because the goalposts move with every advance.

For those who accumulate significant wealth, the question of purpose sharpens further. When you have more than enough, what is the surplus for? Enjoyment, security, inheritance, giving, building, contributing—most lives combine these. What matters is not moral purity but intentionality. Wealth that drifts tends to serve ego and inertia. Wealth that is chosen tends to serve something larger.

**The Convergence**

So what can we finally say?

Personal finance is personal, but it is not private. It is embedded in families, communities, systems, and histories. It is instrumental, not ultimate. It is a practice, not a one-time achievement. And it is possible—not perfect, not painless, but possible—to engage money in a way that supports rather than corrodes a good life.

The transformations discussed in this book—artificial intelligence reshaping labor markets, cryptocurrency challenging monetary assumptions—do not invalidate this conclusion. They intensify it. As the external landscape shifts, the internal questions become more important, not less. What do you want? What is enough? What makes a life meaningful? No technology can answer these questions for you, though technology may force you to confront them sooner than you expected.

The principles endure: spend less than you earn, invest the difference wisely, protect against catastrophe, know when you have enough, cultivate meaning beyond accumulation. These principles worked in agricultural economies, industrial economies, and information economies. They will work in whatever economy emerges from the current transformation—because they are not really about economies at all. They are about human beings navigating material existence with limited time and unlimited desires.

A book cannot decide for you. But perhaps it can leave you better equipped to decide well.

# EPILOGUE

## Coda: What Money Cannot Buy

As we close, it is worth remembering what money cannot buy.

Money cannot buy time. It can buy flexibility in how time is spent—freedom from commutes, from labor you find deadening, from the constant calculation of whether you can afford an hour of rest. But it cannot add hours to the day, and the time spent acquiring money is time not spent elsewhere. Every financial decision is also a time decision, and time is the one currency that cannot be earned, saved, or invested. It can only be spent.

Money cannot buy love. It can purchase attention and performance, but not genuine care for who you are beneath your utility and status. The wealthy learn this truth uncomfortably, surrounded by people whose affection is conditional on continued wealth. The lesson is not that money corrupts love—though it can—but that love operates on a different logic entirely, one that money cannot access.

Money cannot buy health—not fully. It can buy excellent care and advantageous conditions: the best doctors, the safest neighborhoods, the freshest food, the time for exercise and rest. These advantages are real and significant; they translate into years of life and quality of life. But money cannot buy invulnerability. The body fails eventually regardless of the resources devoted to its maintenance. Health, in the end, is borrowed time, and no amount of money extends the loan indefinitely.

Money cannot buy meaning. It can buy space—freedom from desperation, room to breathe, the absence of constant financial anxiety. This space is valuable; it creates the conditions in which meaning can be pursued. But meaning itself must be created through purpose, relationship, and contribution. It cannot be purchased, downloaded, or delivered.

This truth may soon be tested at scale. If artificial intelligence delivers the abundance its advocates promise, billions of people may discover what the wealthy have always known: that freedom from necessity is not the same as freedom to flourish. The space that money buys must be filled with something, and that something cannot be purchased. The coming decades may be humanity's first encounter with a meaning crisis not of scarcity but of surplus. We may learn, collectively, what individuals have always had to learn alone: that more is not better past a certain point, and that the good life requires cultivation, not merely acquisition.

Money cannot buy wisdom. It can buy education—access to teachers, books, experiences, and time for reflection. But wisdom is not information; it is the understanding of what is worth pursuing and when enough is enough. This understanding comes through living, through failure and recovery, through attention to what actually sustains you over time. It cannot be accelerated by expenditure or guaranteed by credentials. Some of the wisest people have very little money. Some of the wealthiest have very little wisdom. The correlation is weaker than we might hope.

Money cannot buy trust. The cryptographic systems discussed earlier in this book attempt to create trustless transactions—exchanges that do not require faith in counterparties or institutions. This is a genuine innovation with genuine applications. But it solves only the narrow problem of transactional trust. The deeper forms of trust—the trust between friends, between partners, between parents and children, between citizens and communities—cannot be cryptographically secured. They must be earned through consistency, vulnerability, and time. No blockchain can substitute for the slow accumulation of demonstrated reliability.

Money cannot buy presence. It can buy experiences, but not the capacity to be fully present within them. The distracted wealthy person on an expensive vacation, checking markets and messages, gains less than the attentive person walking through an ordinary afternoon with nowhere else to be. Presence is a skill, perhaps the foundational skill, and it is trained through practice rather than purchased through expenditure.

These limits are not failures of money. They are its proper boundaries. They remind us where technique ends and life begins. They mark the territory that no financial strategy can reach, the questions that no investment thesis can answer, the needs that no portfolio can satisfy.

**An Invitation**

So this book ends not with a strategy, but with an invitation.

Not an invitation to master money—though the skills of financial competence are worth having. Not an invitation to disdain money—though the recognition of its limits is essential. Not an invitation to transcend money—we remain embodied beings with material needs, and pretending otherwise is delusion rather than wisdom.

An invitation, rather, to hold money in its proper place. To use it consciously. To remember, in every financial decision, that you are not merely managing a portfolio but conducting a life.

The technologies transforming our world—artificial intelligence, cryptographic systems, whatever comes next—will change the landscape of wealth. They may change how we earn, how we invest, how we transact. They may change what work means and what money means. But they will not change the fundamental questions: What do you want from your brief time here? What kind of person do you want to become? What obligations do you have to others? What is enough?

These questions predated money and will outlast whatever forms money takes. They are the questions of philosophy and religion, of poetry and friendship, of quiet moments when the noise subsides and you face yourself honestly. Financial literacy helps you navigate material existence. But these questions navigate you.

May your relationship with money be what it should be: useful, thoughtful, and subordinate to the life it exists to serve. May your finances be ordered well enough that you can forget them more often —and attend to what matters most. May you have the wisdom to know when you have enough, and the courage to stop striving when striving no longer serves you.

And may you find, in the end, that you spent your money well because you spent your life well—that the wealth you accumulated was less important than the person you became, and that the portfolio you built mattered less than the relationships you tended, the contributions you made, the moments of genuine presence you achieved.

The money will not remember you.

# APPENDIX

## RECOMMENDED READING

**Foundations of Personal Finance & Investing**

• **The Bogleheads' Guide to Investing** — Taylor Larimore et al.

A clear, disciplined introduction to long-term, low-cost investing grounded in evidence rather than speculation.

• **A Random Walk Down Wall Street** — Burton Malkiel

A classic explanation of market efficiency, asset allocation, and why simplicity often outperforms complexity.

• **The Little Book of Common Sense Investing** — John C. Bogle

A concise argument for index investing and the power of compounding over time.

• **Rethinking Investing** — Charles D. Ellis

A sober, experience-based reflection on how markets actually work for real investors. Ellis argues persuasively that for most people, investment success comes less from brilliance than from avoiding mistakes, minimizing costs, and maintaining discipline over long periods. This book complements earlier investing classics by emphasizing humility, patience, and structural advantage.

- **Get Rich Carefully** — Jim Cramer

Cramer's most mature and restrained work, written after decades inside the markets. Unlike his earlier, more exuberant writing, this book emphasizes risk management, diversification, long-term thinking, and respect for uncertainty. Readers should understand it not as a trading manual, but as a window into how an experienced market participant thinks about risk, opportunity, and temperament.

---

**Meaning, Values, and the Good Life**

- **Man's Search for Meaning** — Viktor Frankl

A profound meditation on meaning, suffering, and responsibility —highly relevant to any discussion of money as means rather than end.

- **The Soul of Money** — Lynne Twist

Explores the ethical and spiritual dimensions of wealth, generosity, and stewardship.

- **Meditations** — Marcus Aurelius

Stoic reflections on control, sufficiency, and inner freedom—antidotes to financial anxiety and excess.

---

**Philosophical & Cultural Context**

- **Human Action** — Ludwig von Mises

A demanding but influential work on markets, choice, and economic coordination.

- **The Protestant Ethic and the Spirit of Capitalism** — Max Weber

A classic exploration of the cultural and moral roots of modern economic life.

---

## Examples of Common Financial Institutions and Tools

The institutions listed below are provided **solely as examples** of widely used categories of financial services. Inclusion does not imply endorsement, and alternatives may be equally or more suitable depending on individual circumstances.

### High-Yield Savings Accounts

These accounts are typically FDIC-insured (up to statutory limits) and offer higher interest rates than traditional savings accounts, though rates fluctuate.

- American Express Personal Savings
- Ally Bank
- Marcus by Goldman Sachs
- Capital One 360

---

### Brokerage Firms (Self-Directed Investing)

These firms allow individuals to invest in stocks, bonds, mutual funds, ETFs, and other instruments.

- Vanguard
- Fidelity Investments
- Charles Schwab
- E*TRADE

---

### Retirement Accounts and Custodians

Many of the above brokerages also serve as custodians for:

- Individual Retirement Accounts (IRAs)
- Roth IRAs
- SEP IRAs
- Employer-sponsored plans (401(k), 403(b), etc.)

The appropriate choice depends on employment status, income, tax considerations, and long-term goals.

# INDEX OF ACTIONABLE TERMS

# ABOUT THE AUTHOR

**Ravinder Bhalla, MD** is a practicing physician who has spent decades observing the intersection of financial stress and human health. His own investment journey—from long-term positions in companies like Amazon and Google to a humbling foray into options trading during the pandemic—taught him that financial wisdom requires integrating economic understanding, psychological self-awareness, and clarity about what money is ultimately for. Dr. Bhalla synthesizes insights from economics, psychology, and philosophy to address the complete picture of financial life that traditional guides neglect. He lives and practices in the United States.

## ALSO BY RAVINDER BHALLA

WISDOM IN PSYCHIATRY: UNDERSTANDING BEGINS HEALING

NIETZSCHE A GUIDED TOUR: A Path Through His Works

Made in the USA
Monee, IL
04 November 2026

67386756R00262